This book offers the first history of philosophical dialogue during the British Enlightenment. It explains why important philosophers – Shaftesbury, Mandeville, Berkeley and Hume – and innumerable minor translators, imitators, and critics wrote in and about dialogue during the eighteenth century; and why, after Hume, philosophical dialogue either falls out of use or undergoes radical transformation. It describes the extended, heavily coded, and often belligerent debate about the nature and proper management of dialogue; and it shows how the writing of philosophical fictions relates to the rise of the novel and the emergence of philosophical aesthetics. Novelists such as Fielding, Sterne, Johnson, and Austen are placed in a philosophical context, and philosophers of the empiricist tradition in the context of British literary history.

CAMBRIDGE STUDIES IN EIGHTEENTH-CENTURY
ENGLISH LITERATURE AND THOUGHT 31

Philosophical dialogue in the British Enlightenment

The frontispiece to Shaftesbury's *An Inquiry concerning Virtue, or Merit*, designed by Shaftesbury in Naples in 1711, engraved by Simon Gribelin for the second edition of *Characteristicks* (1714). The design was one of a series of emblem works that Shaftesbury commissioned shortly before his death. The Janus-faced figure, situated above a chess-board and below a chameleon, torn between ancient idealism and modern materialism, presides over the following history of dialogue in the British Enlightenment. (Reprinted with the permission of the Harvard College Library.)

Philosophical dialogue in the British Enlightenment
Theology, aesthetics, and the novel

MICHAEL PRINCE

Boston University

CAMBRIDGE
UNIVERSITY PRESS

Published by the Press Syndicate of the University of Cambridge
The Pitt Building, Trumpington Street, Cambridge CB2 IRP
40 West 20th Street, New York, NY 10011–4211, USA
10 Stamford Road, Oakleigh, Melbourne 3166, Australia

First published 1996

Printed in Great Britain at the University Press, Cambridge

A catalogue record for this book is available from the British Library

Library of Congress cataloguing in publication data
Prince, Michael
Philosophical dialogue in the British Enlightenment: theology, aesthetics,
and the novel / by Michael Prince.
p.   cm. – (Cambridge studies in eighteenth-century English literature and thought: 31)
Includes bibliographical references and index.
ISBN 0 521 55062 9 (hardback)
1. English fiction – 18th century – History and criticism.
2. Great Britain – Intellectual life – 18th century.
3. Philosophy, British – 18th century.   4. Aesthetics, British – 18th century.
5. Enlightenment – Great Britain.   6. Philosophy in literature.
I. Title.   II. Series.
PR858.P45P751996
823'.509384 – dc20   95-42217   CIP

ISBN 0 521 55062 9 hardback

for my parents, David and Reva, who taught me to consider both sides of the question, without losing faith

Mayhaps there is more meant, than is said in it, quoth my father. –
Learned men, brother Toby, don't write dialogues
upon long noses for nothing. –

Laurence Sterne, *Tristram Shandy*

Contents

xi

Acknowledgments

Since many of my intellectual debts are also personal, let me thank first my family – my parents, David and Reva, to whom this book is dedicated, and my sister Erica and brother Paul. You have accompanied me on this long and loving development; I thank you for enriching my life.

Ralph Cohen proposed the questions that first made the following pages possible. The work began as a dissertation under his direction, and afterward, because the questions were good ones, became a book. I thank him and Libby for their guidance and friendship through the years.

The challenge of studying eighteenth-century works began for me at Stanford University with Ian Watt and his course on the novel. The need to rethink literary history through an inquiry into *poesis* began for me also at Stanford with Wesley Trimpi. I thank both teachers for asking me to consider why literature changes, and what remains the same.

A kind spirit brought me to the University of Virginia at a time when Irvin Ehrenpreis was still alive. The paper I wrote in the spring of 1984 for his graduate seminar on Austen and Scott became an idea for a dissertation, and evolved later into chapter 9 of this work. There, too, I met Martin Battestin, who read and corrected each chapter with a keen eye. I am grateful also to Robert Leventhal for his friendship and encouragement, and to Lyell Asher, Benjamin Bennett, James Berger, Mary Collins, Regina Marz, Barbara Nolan, Richard Rorty, and Walter Sokel for enlivening my days in Virginia. Then and since David Radcliffe read the chapters and offered useful criticism.

At Boston University I have again been fortunate to encounter unusual teachers and supportive colleagues. Christopher Ricks unsettled old complacencies and opened new prospects on the eighteenth century; I thank him for the constant reminder of wit. Roger Shattuck, with Nora a friend of many years, held my prose accountable to a high standard of clarity and integrity. Other members of the community here – Julia Brown, Charles Griswold, Jon Klancher, Charles Rzepka, and John Riely – kindly read portions of the manuscript and offered useful advice. I thank Gerald Fitzgerald, John Paul Riquelme, William Vance, and Lyle Borg-Graham for their support through the years.

I am especially grateful to John Richetti, whose explorations of the boundary between philosophy and literature provided a context for this study. He brought this book to the Cambridge *Eighteenth-Century Series*. Douglas Patey and Michael Seidel read the manuscript for Cambridge: I thank both for recognizing the truth of Walter's surmise that learned men don't write dialogues upon long noses for nothing.

The American Council of Learned Societies and the Boston University Humanities Foundation provided fellowships that allowed me to complete the manuscript. Thanks also to the editors of *Eighteenth-Century Studies* and *Modern Language Quarterly* for permission to reprint portions of chapter 5 ("Hume and the end of religious dialogue") and 6 ("The eighteenth-century beauty contest"), which appeared first in their journals. I have benefited from the assistance of the librarians and curators at the Houghton and Widener libraries at Harvard Univeristy, the Library of Congress, Alderman Library at the University of Virginia, the Green Library at Stanford University, the Mugar Memorial Library at Boston University, and the Folger Shakespeare Library. A generous subvention from the Provost of Boston University, Jon Westling, allowed this book to be published in its present form.

Finally, I wish to thank Abigail Gillman, my wife, friend, collaborator, and mother of Jacob, who has made this work in part her own.

Introduction: dialogue and Enlightenment

This book presents a history of philosophical dialogue in the British Enlightenment and an account of the British Enlightenment by means of a history of philosophical dialogue. As such, two questions arise at the outset: first, why is philosophical dialogue relevant to an understanding of the Enlightenment; second, why does genre provide a basis for historiography?[1] Although the methodological question would seem to take precedent, I shall not begin with a theoretical defense of a genre-based literary history. The issues involved are too complex to be treated in the abstract and will therefore be addressed at points throughout this book, especially in chapter 1, where I discuss the way genre distinctions functioned during the early eighteenth century as a means of classifying readers, stipulating preferred values, and instituting normative modes of interpretation; in chapter 8, where I describe attempts to restrict the composition of philosophical dialogue through a "poetics" of the genre; and in the epilogue, where I explain why I have written a generic history of dialogue and dialectic rather than a dialectical history of genre and Enlightenment.

An answer to the second question, why philosophical dialogue is relevant to the British Enlightenment, must also be the work of the following chapters. Nevertheless, because I shall be referring to the "failure" of philosophical dialogue and the project it represented during the Enlightenment, it is necessary to preface a few remarks about the history of the form prior to this period.

The problem dialogue poses for Enlightenment philosophy and theology is implicit in a profound ambivalence situated at the origin of dialogue in Greek philosophy, an ambivalence that becomes untenable once Christian Neoplatonism encounters the secularizing tendencies of Modernity. Origins are usually located in etymologies or in myths; therefore, I shall offer two genetic accounts, in order to argue that both present the same dilemma, a problem Enlightenment philosophers feel they must solve, and cannot.

Dialogue's etymological ambivalence derives more from confusion about its prefix than its root. The prefix *di*, understandably but erroneously

---

[1] A third question, *whether* the term Enlightenment is adequate to the British eighteenth century, will be taken up at the end of this introduction and throughout this book.

extracted from *dia*, implied for some the division of the *logos* into two. "The tendency is to confine it [dialogue] to two persons, perhaps through associating dia with di," remarks *The Oxford English Dictionary*. The important point about this reduction of many to two is not that the number of speakers is restricted, but that the division of the *logos* is always in principle reversible, from many to two, from two to one. Indeed, it might be more accurate to say that the *logos*, conceived as absolute unity, permits itself to be divided for the sake of human comprehension, with the proviso that division remain all the time a propaedeutic to the recovery of a coherent whole. Thus, one definition of dialogue became a discourse between two speakers leading to a synthesis of viewpoints – not mere eristic, but the purposeful discovery of truth.[2] With this reduction of *dia* to *di*, dialogue became synonymous with a remarkably useful concept called dialectic. Richard McKeon, summarizing the equation, writes, "The method of dialogue is dialectic in the sense that two or more speakers or two or more positions are brought into relations in which it becomes apparent that each position is incomplete and inconclusive unless assimilated to a higher truth."[3]

If not fanciful, this definition at least involved a selective blindness to the actual prefix, which is *dia*. *Dia* means passage, transition, movement, with no limitation upon the number of voices sharing in the *logos*. The important point here is that emphasis shifts from the *logos* to the activity it enjoins among thinking subjects, finally irreducible one to the other. Thus, another definition of dialogue simply referred to any verbal interaction among two or more voices, leading to no necessary resolution. Again, Richard McKeon captures this other conception of the genre: "Dialogue is statement and counterstatement, based on ordinary ways of life and ordinary uses of language, with no possible appeal to a reality beyond opposed opinions except through opinions about reality. Truth is perceived in perspective, and perspectives can be compared, but there is no overarching inclusive perspective."[4]

Maurice Blanchot describes the same split conception of dialogue through the recitation of an originary myth. For him dialogue's ambivalence derives from an essential opposition between human being and being God. Blanchot writes, "I think of what Apollo affirms when, through the mouth of the poet,

---

[2] See Plato, *Republic*, bk. 5. 454a. Socrates (to Glaucon): "Many appear to me to fall into it [the art of contradiction] even against their wills...They pursue purely verbal opposition, practicing eristic, not dialectic on one another." The one who engages in dialectic thus "attempts through discourse of reason and apart from all perceptions of sense to find his way to the very essence of each thing and does not desist till he apprehends by thought itself the nature of the good in itself" (*Republic*, bk. 7. 532a-b). *The Collected Dialogues of Plato, Including the Letters*, eds. Edith Hamilton and Huntington Cairns, Bollingen Series LXXI (Princeton: Princeton University Press, 1985). All subsequent references to modern translations of Plato refer to this edition.

[3] Richard McKeon, "Dialogue and Controversy in Philosophy," in *The Interpretation of Dialogue*, ed. Tullio Maranhão (Chicago and London: The University of Chicago Press, 1990), p. 28.

[4] *Ibid.*, p. 35.

Bacchylides, he says to Admetus: *'You are a mere mortal; therefore your mind must harbor two thoughts at once.'* In other words a multiplicity of speech in a simultaneity of language."[5] For Blanchot, being's division from absolute unity produces two divergent interpretations of dialogue. The first acknowledges duplicity as the fallen state of mere mortals, while aspiring, through dialogue, to regain the unitary condition of Godhead; the second revels in the liberating *difference* between the divine monologue and a human polyphony, emphasizing, exaggerating an irreducible plurality of voices. In the first case, Admetus remains enclosed in the circle of the God, fascinated with unity; in the second, Admetus leaves that circle to seek out what Blanchot calls a truly plural speech, "to receive the other as other, and the foreign as foreign."[6]

Whether one locates dialogue's ambivalence in its etymology or in an imaginary scene of genesis, the split conception has influenced the entire history of the genre. Plato seems to have understood dialogue in both senses. As Gadamer and Bakhtin both observe, the early (aporetic) Platonic dialogues and the Seventh Letter differ from later Platonic texts setting forth the theory of knowledge or ideal form.[7] We have, in the first case, dialogue as a basis for potentially interminable inquiry, search, and questioning, and, in the second, dialogue as a means of ascending from error (appearance, division) to truth (reality, synthesis). This latter sense of dialogue is, according to Gadamer, hardened into the dialectical method codified by Aristotle and subsumed within Christian Neoplatonism.

Plato's divided response to dialogue corresponds with the plurality of meanings he assigned to dialectic. Charles Griswold describes "three senses of 'dialectic' in Plato. The first can be traced to *'dialegesthai,'* i.e. to dialogue, the asking and answering of questions ... The second sense of dialectic ... is not critical, skeptical, or zetetic, but is rather the exposition of the dialectic of thought purified of its human and rhetorical context. [It] allows us to speak of 'Plato's system' – a positive but incompletely developed teaching essentially independent of the cumbersome dialogue form ... [And] the third sense of dialectic ... is the 'method of division and collection' of classes evidently described in the *Phaedrus* on analogy with the butcher's art."[8] In other words, the concept of dialectic repeats the etymological and existential ambivalence

---

[5] Maurice Blanchot, *The Infinite Conversation*, trans. Susan Hanson (Minneapolis: The University of Minnesota Press, 1993), p. 80.

[6] *Ibid.*, p. 82.

[7] For Bakhtin's discussion of the early versus late Socratic dialogues, see especially *Problems of Dostoevsky's Poetics*, ed. and trans. Caryl Emerson (Minneapolis: University of Minnesota Press, 1984), pp. 109–112. And for Gadamer's discussion of transformations in the concept of dialectic from the early Socrates to late Plato to Aristotle, see *Dialogue and Dialectic: Eight Hermeneutical Studies on Plato*, trans. P. Christopher Smith (New Haven and London: Yale University Press, 1980), especially chapters 5 and 6. See also Gilbert Ryle, *Plato's Progress* (Cambridge: Cambridge University Press, 1966), especially chapter 4.

[8] Charles Griswold, "Reflections on 'Dialectic' in Plato and Hegel," *International Philosophical Quarterly* 22 (1982) 115–116.

associated with the word dialogue, especially if one allows that Griswold's
third definition (division and classification) might be considered a subset of
the second (synthesis) within a dialectical theory of knowledge.

The same division occurs throughout the long history of critical
commentary on dialogue. In the *Poetics* Aristotle cannot decide what to do
with philosophical dialogue, so he places Socratic Conversations in a
nameless class of texts with the mimes of Sophron and Xenarchus, thus
lumping together the Socratic Conversations he would have known from his
teacher's polished performances and the parodic, extemporaneous invectives
of the mimic performers.[9] Kojève will find in Platonic dialogue a rudimentary
expression of Hegel's stronger dialectical thought: "the dialectical method
was consciously and systematically used first by Socrates-Plato. But in fact it is
as old as philosophy itself. For the dialectical method is nothing but the way
of dialogue–that is, of discussion."[10] Yet Bakhtin, anxious to free dialogue
from any totalizing system, arrives at just the opposite conclusion, celebrating
the antic Socrates and disparaging the equation between dialogue and
transcendental dialectic: "Dialogue and dialectics. Take a dialogue and
remove the voices ... remove the intonations ... carve out abstract concepts
and judgments from living words and responses, cram everything into one
abstract consciousness – and that's how you get dialectics."[11]

The opposition between these two conceptions might be likened to the
difference between comedy and tragedy. In comedy initial divisions among
characters often reach a happy reconciliation, usually a marriage of some
sort. In tragedy, divisions threaten never to be healed. If dialogue embodies
transcendental dialectic, then its structure can be called comedic. If, however,
dialogue enacts the possibility of impasse, then it resembles tragedy.[12]
Throughout the history of philosophical dialogue, the tendency in both
composition and commentary has been to emphasize one of these definitions
at the expense of the other. Nietzsche, for instance, in *The Birth of Tragedy*,

[9] The relevant passage appears in *Poetics* ii, p. 2316 (1447a 28–30). "There is further an art which
imitates by language alone, and one which imitates by metres, either one or a plurality of metres.
These forms of imitation are still nameless today. We have no common name for a mime of
Sophron or Xenarchus and a Socratic Conversation." Aristotle, *The Complete Works of Aristotle*, ed.
Jonathan Barnes, 2 vols. (Princeton: Princeton University Press, 1984), ii, p. 2316. For a fuller
discussion of the place of dialogue in Aristotle's *Poetics*, see chapter 8 of this study. For discussions of
this issue with regard to Renaissance dialogue, see K. J. Wilson, *Incomplete Fictions: the Formation of
English Renaissance Dialogue* (Washington, DC: The Catholic University of America Press, 1985); and
Jon Snyder, *Writing the Scene of Speaking: Theories of Dialogue in the Late Italian Renaissance* (Stanford:
Stanford University Press, 1989).
[10] Alexandre Kojève, *Introduction to the Reading of Hegel*, ed. Allan Bloom, trans. James H. Nichols, Jr.
(Ithaca and London: Cornell University Press, 1980), p. 179.
[11] Mikhail Bakhtin, *Problems of Dostoevsky's Poetics*, p. xxxii. The passage is taken from the editor's
introduction.
[12] Although over-simplified, the distinction between the synthetic potential of comedy and the divisive
threat of tragedy is commonplace in the history of criticism, just as it is in Nietzsche's *The Birth of
Tragedy*.

defines philosophical dialogue as wholly comedic. In this genre "poetry played the same subordinate role with regard to dialectic philosophy as that same philosophy was to play for many centuries with regard to theology."[13] In other words, dialogue provides a thin representational veneer for transcendental dialectic; and since, for Nietzsche, Socratic dialogue transforms the titanic oppositions at war in tragedy into a domesticated intellectual drama, philosophical dialogue infects and destroys classical tragedy:

Socrates, the dialectical hero of the Platonic drama, shows a close affinity to the Euripidean hero, who is compelled to justify his actions by proof, and for that reason is often in danger of forfeiting our tragic compassion. For who among us can close his eyes to the optimistic element in the nature of dialectics, which sees a triumph in every syllogism and can breathe only in an atmosphere of cool, conscious clarity? Once that optimistic element had entered tragedy, it overgrew its Dionysiac regions and brought about their annihilation and, finally, the leap into genteel domestic drama.[14]

Nietzsche's strength as a writer is such that the question, "is this an accurate statement about the history of dialogue?" seems beside the point. Yet the view of dialogue as inherently optimistic fails to account for the ambivalence situated at its etymological heart; nor does it explain why anti-metaphysical skeptics like Bernard Mandeville, David Hume, and Allan Ramsay will attack Christian Neoplatonism by writing philosophical dialogues. While it is entirely true that within the Christian Neoplatonic tradition, "poetry played the same subordinate role with regard to dialectic philosophy as that same philosophy was to play for many centuries with regard to theology," a tragic shadow, the other interpretation of dialogue, accompanies this tradition, never entirely repressed.

From the beginning of the Christian era until the middle of the eighteenth century, dialectic became one of the dominant methods of argument for Christian theology.[15] Opposition to dialectic (for example, as a mere tool of the sophists, or as a banal school exercise) no doubt arose, but there was little doubt that dialectic, correctly conceived and executed, provided a method for bridging reason and revelation. Thomas Stanley, summarizing the

[13] Nietzsche, *The Birth of Tragedy*, in *The Birth of Tragedy and the Genealogy of Morals*, trans. Francis Golffing (Garden City, New York: Doubleday Anchor, 1956), p. 88.
[14] *Ibid.*, p. 88.
[15] Comments Richard McKeon, "Dialectic became the method of Christian theology and philosophy until the translation of Aristotle in the thirteenth century suggested the possibility of two methods and two ways; dialectic was also opposed during the Middle Ages because it is a purely verbal art and because it applies reason to matters that transcend reason" ("Dialogue and Controversy in Philosophy," pp. 29–30). I would argue that dialectic remains central to Christian theology through the middle of the eighteenth century: it is a necessary operation for any rational Christianity based upon analogy or induction from known sensory phenomena to an unknown supersensible domain. It therefore underlies the conceptual movement of physico-theology, the dominant theological position attempting to reconcile science and faith after the development of the Royal Society (1660) and before Hume's critique of analogy.

tradition of Platonic dialectic in his *History of Philosophy* (1st edn., 1655–1662), calls dialectic "a Science, but, neither Mathematick, nor Opinion, because it is more perspicuous than sensible things; nor a Science, because 'tis more obscure than first Intelligibles."[16] Situated between opinion and certainty, sense data and first intelligibles, ethics and geometry, dialectic was thought to provide the means of ascent from the human to divine realm. Such was its comedic potential. Dialogue added to the logic of ascent the fiction of bodies assenting.

In metaphysical dialogues of the Christian Neoplatonic tradition – works such as Augustine's *Soliloquies*, Boethius' *The Consolation of Philosophy*, Petrarch's *Secretum*, Firenzuola's *Dialogue on the Beauty of Women*, and Berkeley's *Three Dialogues between Hylas and Philonous* – the skeptical interpretation of dialogue is both incorporated and overcome: the teleological plot driven by transcendental dialectic carries us from thought's potentially tragic division from the good, its immersion in an endless and aimless dialogue, to its final marriage with divine wisdom. But how did this overcoming of skepticism take place? The more probing the dialogue, the more fundamental its encounter with a skeptical "other," the less implicit the *modus* of transition (the plot, dialectic) could remain. I shall discuss two moments in this complex history as a way of leading into the problem dialogue poses for philosophy and theology during the Enlightenment.

Augustine's *Soliloquies* begins in the following way:

While I was turning over in my mind [*volventi mihi*] many and various matters, and searching zealously through many days for my very own self and my good, and what evil should be avoided; suddenly something spoke to me, whether it was I myself, or something external, or something internal, I do not know; for that is what I am struggling most to understand.[17]

Suddenly, private meditation gives way to dialogue, and even though Augustine cannot be sure about the origin of the second voice, he appears confident that it will lead him beyond *volventi mihi* to *scire*. Yet this visitor, which Augustine calls Ratio, begins to pose difficult questions. It first asks how Augustine intends to proceed from one matter to another (*fac te invenisse aliquid; cui commendabis, ut pergas ad alia?*). Augustine responds that he will secure his dialogue against slips of memory by writing it down. But his response only shows that Augustine has failed to grasp the more vital methodological question bound up in the phrase *cui commendabis, ut pergas ad alia?* Ratio restates the question:

---

[16] Thomas Stanley, *The History of Philosophy: Containing the Lives, Opinions, Actions and Discourses of the Philosophers of Every Sect*, 3rd edn. (London: W. Battersby, 1701), p. 183. A second edition appeared in 1687 and a fourth in 1743.

[17] Augustine, *The Soliloquies of Saint Augustine*, trans. Thomas F. Gilligan (New York: Cosmopolitan Science and Art Service, 1943), p. 3.

A: I desire to know God and the soul.
R: Nothing more?
A: Absolutely nothing.
R: Begin therefore to search. But first explain how, if God is demonstrated to you, you will be able to say that it is sufficient [*si demonstretur Deus, possis dicere, Sat est*].
A: I do not know how He would have to be demonstrated to me so that I could say it is sufficient [*ut dicam, Sat est*], for I do not think I know anything as I want to know God.

Here is an extreme self-consciousness about the problem of method, threatening to transform the comedic progress of dialogue, *pergas ad alia*, back into a tragic *volventi mihi*. The tension resides in the ambivalent sense of the word "how" (*quomodo*). It doubles as a reference to method (*nescio quomodo mihi demonstrari* ...) and as a statement of comparison (*non scire aliquid sic, quomodo scire Deum desidero*). What troubles Augustine is the dependence of the first sense of *quomodo* upon the second; for if method relies on comparison, always relating a deduction to known premises, then God, arrived at in this way, must be colored by and reduced to the familiar – must, in other words, be fundamentally *intrinsicus* rather than *extrinsicus*. If God, conversely, is entirely other, then Augustine can have no idea when or how to say *Sat est*.

Much as Augustine would like to align dialogue with the logical stages of transcendental dialectic, an element of doubt remains. Reason does not so much solve the problem as shift attention from epistemology to psycho-pathology: "How do you, who do not yet know God, know that you know nothing like God?" (*Qui nondum Deum nosti, unde nosti nihil te nosse Deo simile?*). Because Augustine begins, like most intellectual voyagers in this tradition, a sick and partially blinded pilgrim, he cannot really say that he knows nothing like God, only that he has forgotten or suffered separation from what he already knows. The rudimentary fiction – an embodiment of the Platonic doctrine of *anamnesis* (recollection) – saves dialogue from any excessive encounter with skepticism. The young man is sick with something, but if he attaches himself to the one true image and holds it in place, guiding his faltering steps, he will reach his end. His sickness is a form of forgetting; dialogue is his medicine; and the dialectical discovery of a truth already known confirms the cure, the ability to say *Sat est*.

Poetic elements play a subordinate role in metaphysical dialogue, as Nietzsche observed, because they are called upon mainly to supplement a comedic ascent always in danger of circling back on itself and becoming tragic. They draw our attention away from the question Augustine cannot answer, representing dialectical reason as a capacity the pilgrim shares with the being of God, if only he could free himself of his mortal disease. The fiction must be partial, however, because the more fully the pilgrim's disease – his doubts, his fascination with the things of this world and alienation from the beyond – gains representation, the more arduous and doubtful his recovery becomes.[18]

Boethius' *The Consolation of Philosophy*, which one commentator describes as the dramatic completion of Augustine's *Soliloquies*, arrives at a similar point of crisis, and reaches again for fiction as a means of staving off impasse.[19] Unlike Augustine, Boethius is more certain about the nature of the second voice. She is Philosophy, a remarkable woman. She has her feet on the ground but her head in the clouds. And so the remorseful, half-blind pilgrim will need to travel up her, allegorically speaking, from toe to crown, body to intellect.

Although the student rarely objects to any of the cures Philosophy offers, he does interrupt on one notable occasion. In book III, Philosophy attempts to prove that evil does not exist, first by having her disciple agree that nothing is impossible for the Almighty, and then by arguing that since God can do no evil, evil must be nothing, since God can do anything. Bothered by the syllogism, Boethius responds, "You are playing with me ... by weaving a labyrinthine argument from which I cannot escape. You seem to begin where you ended and to end where you began. Are you perhaps making a marvelous circle of the divine simplicity? ... You proved all this without outside assumptions and used only internal proofs which draw their force from one another."[20] Philosophy calls her answer "the most important point of all":

It is the nature of the divine essence, neither to pass to things outside itself nor to take any external thing to itself ... You ought not to be surprised that I have sought no outside proofs, but have used only those within the scope of our subject, since you learned, on Plato's authority, that the language we use ought to be related to the subject of discourse.[21]

Philosophy's response begs the question as fully as Augustine's "How do you, who do not know God, know that you know nothing like God?" Philosophy makes a virtue of necessity by claiming that a God whose essence is circular and autonomous must be grasped through a method also circular and self-contained.

---

[18] For a discussion of dialogue as a mode of "partial fiction" see K. J. Wilson, *Incomplete Fictions*; and Evlyn Gould, *Virtual Theater from Diderot to Mallarmé* (Baltimore: The Johns Hopkins University Press, 1989).

[19] On the relation between Boethius and Augustine, see Edmund T. Silk, "Boethius's *Consolatio philosophiae* as a Sequel to Augustine's *Dialogues* and *Soliloquia*," *Harvard Theological Review* 32 (1939), 19–39. Silk's summary of the *Consolation* demonstrates how completely the plot of dialogue could be equated with the stages of transcendental dialectic: "there is a gradual but steady movement and unswerving progress towards the goal. As the work begins, it is true, the *nebulae tristitiae* hang just as low as often at Cassiciacum, but Philosophia emerges from the cloud, majestically performs her function as healer, exactly charts the course of the journey, and completes it. The promise held out to Licentius and Romanianus is triumphantly fulfilled" (35).

[20] Boethius, *The Consolation of Philosophy*, trans. Richard Green (Indianapolis: The Library of Liberal Arts, 1962), p. 72.

[21] *Ibid.*, p. 73.

Whether the explanation satisfies the pilgrim we do not learn. No reply follows. Instead, the prose dialogue breaks off, giving way to a proem recounting the myth of Orpheus and Eurydice. Orpheus, in his grief over his wife's death, threatens the very order of the universe. His music makes the Furies weep. "Tantalus, long maddened by his thirst, ignores the waters he might now drink." By some miracle Orpheus has employed human instruments to touch the divine. Even mythic figures are subservient to his song. We know the rest. Orpheus descends to the underworld, where he is granted Eurydice again, on the sole condition that leaving he not look back. He does, she is snatched away, and Orpheus is left staring into the abyss. Boethius supplies the moral: "This fable applies to all of you who seek to raise your minds to sovereign day. For whoever is conquered and turns his eyes to the pit of hell, looking into the inferno, loses all the excellence he has gained."[22]

When the dialogue and proem are juxtaposed, it becomes clear what "hell" is. Hell, the inferno, is dialectic, the method that has brought one to a point of revelation. To question that method, as the student does in the prose section, is to risk losing everything the method has produced. Philosophy, when asked to provide a ground for her own method, produces myth. Naturally, we are not meant to take this recourse as a fault. On the contrary, myth establishes a marvelous isomorphism between human reason and divine revelation, while issuing a warning against any further doubts. Dialectic is not a self-driven, tautological engine; it is presided over by an absolute sanction, whose authority can only be represented figuratively. As in Augustine, fictional elements supplement dialectical reason where it is most threatened, but always remain subordinate.

As the preceding examples show, more was at stake in the viability of philosophical dialogue than the truth of any specific doctrine. By fusing dramatic encounter with the logic of transcendental dialectic, metaphysical dialogue made the transition from reason to revelation, tragic division to comedic unity, seem a realizable fact of human experience. Yet these examples also foretell the fate of dialogue and dialectic under the skeptical, secularizing conditions endemic to Modernity. When the student questions the tautological appeal of dialectical syllogism, Philosophy must produce the authority in light of which a natural give-and-take of opinions on both sides of the question transforms itself into a truth. Myth silences doubt; but its very appearance within philosophical dialogue also brings into question the value that a given writer, or age, or religion has chosen to place beyond doubt.

In other words, under the pressure of a secularizing reason, metaphysical dialogue begins to thematize its own juridical structure: two or more parties exchange ideas, but their dialogue is not aimless; it is presided over by a

[22] *Ibid.*, p. 74.

transcendental authority – here, myth, elsewhere *logos*, God, Reason itself – assuring the transition from division to synthesis, doubt to determination. This authority, the transcendent third or *criterium veritatis*, both permitted human agents to reason their way towards divinity and was in turn confirmed by the success of their deliberations. Once thematized in this way, however, the third term begins to lose its transcendental aura: myth appears less like an emblem of divine revelation and more like a crude warning to the fledgling philosopher not to trespass on sacred ground.[23]

The problem philosophical dialogue poses for the Enlightenment follows directly from these observations. What happens during an increasingly skeptical age, an age of methodological self-consciousness, of hell-gazing, when dialogue and dialectic begin to lose the transcendental reference point whose stability had assured the transition from tragic division to comedic unity? In 1644 Hezekiah Woodward expressed the problem with particular poignancy. Having written "A Dialogue Arguing that Arch-Bishops, Bishops, Curates, Neuters, Are to be Cut Off by the Law of God" (1644), the polemicist paused in his Preface to the work, alert to the objection that his dialogue might be taken to be nothing more than another *volventi mihi*, a form of intellectual onanism:

It is a Dialogue: and therein I dispute and argue the case with myselfe; and so wise I am, I will put no other arguments to my selfe, but what I can tell myselfe how to answer: and so I must needs overcome, as the Boy must winne the game, that plays with himselfe.

Changing garb from controversialist to judge, he responds,

I say againe, and as in the ears of GOD; that I have, by His good hand on me, *thoroughly* considered the present Controversie, and have desired to take-in, as my understanding did supply, what I thought could be suggested for the maintaining of the fore-mentioned [contrary positions]; That I might cast-out all scruples, and cleare the minds of the ignorant."[24]

Here again the circle is closed, this time not with a myth but with a direct appeal to the authority whose violent antagonism towards the writer's enemies the dialogue is about to prove. This was playing trump with a vengeance, but the extremity and tenuousness of the appeal would not have

---

[23] Strains within the history of Christian Neoplatonic dialogue are already evident in the Renaissance, as several historians have noted. Virginia Cox finds that "In contrast with the programmatically 'disordered' dialogue of Castiglione's era, the dialogue of the late sixteenth century shows an increasing preoccupation with system, method, and order." *The Renaissance Dialogue: Literary Dialogue in its Social and Political Contexts, Castiglione to Galileo* (Cambridge: Cambridge University Press, 1992), p. 99. And Walter Ong has described the decline of humanist dialogue under the weight of Ramus' revision of scholastic dialectic. *Ramus: Method, and the Decay of Dialogue: From the Art of Discourse to the Art of Reason* (Cambridge, MA: Harvard University Press, 1958). See also Snyder, *Writing the Scene of Speaking.*
[24] Woodward, "A Dialogue Arguing that Arch-Bishops ... Are to be Cut Off by the Law of God" (London: T.P. and M.S., 1644), sig. A3 verso.

been necessary if all sides in "the present Controversie" were not similarly adducing God's good hand to smash recreant opinions. Dialogue, in other words, has become a mere trope, an empty gesture towards disinterested inquiry.

The view that dialogue rarely if ever staged a fundamental opposition of contested viewpoints was commonplace during the factious period after the English Civil War and through the middle of the eighteenth century. Mandeville only had to observe the spate of polemical dialogues written during the years of most intense social unrest to conclude that "when partial Men have a mind to demolish an Adversary, and Triumph over him with little Expense, it has long been a frequent Practice to attack him with Dialogues, in which the Champion, who is to lose the Battel, appears at the very beginning of the Engagement, to be the Victim, that is to be sacrificed, and seldom makes a better Figure, than Cocks on Shrove-Tuesday, that receive Blows, but return none, and are visibly set up on purpose to be knock'd down."[25]

As Mandeville observes, dialogue became a particularly potent weapon in theological and political polemics. Not only could it be used by religious skeptics and political radicals to deprive sovereign authority of its divine credentials, but it could also be used by orthodox theologians and political conservatives to illustrate the danger of tolerating dissenting opinions in matters temporal and spiritual. Thus, the Tory polemicist Roger L'Estrange constructs a dialogue in 1670 between a Conformist (L'Estrange's hero) and a Non-conformist. Written in response to debates about the Act of Uniformity and the Exclusion Act, *Toleration Discuss'd* uses the threat of a radically inclusive (democratic) dialogue to convince even the Non-conformist that some degree of conforming opinion is essential to the state. Time and again the Conformist drives discussion to the question the author of 1644 could not answer without falling into tautology. "What if the Dissenters should call that Sound Doctrine, which the Church defines Heresie? What if the Subject shall Account ... That Liberty Consciencious, Which the Governour esteems Unlawful? who shall over-rule?"[26] Who shall over-rule? What shall be the *criterium vertitatis* in a political and religious dialogue whose topic has become the status of authority itself? The Non-conformist can only respond, "[There remains] the Word of God to repair to, in what concerns Sound Faith; and the Light of Nature for our Guide, in the Duties of the Good Life" (p. 20). But the Conformist, unwilling to grant subjects any autonomy to decide the nature and extent of allegiance owed to sovereign authority, responds, "This is to make that which was the Ground of the first Controversie, the Umpire of the Second. For what is the Origin of All our Grand Disagreements, but

[25] Bernard Mandeville, *Fable of the Bees: Or, Private Vices, Publick Benefits*, ed. F. B. Kaye, 2 vols. (Oxford: Clarendon Press, 1924), II, pp. 7–8.
[26] Sir Roger L'Estrange, *Toleration Discuss'd; in Two Dialogues* (London: printed by E. C. and A. C. for Henry Broma, 1670), p. 17. Subsequent references are given by page number in my text.

(as St. Augustine has it) *Bonae Scripturae male intellectae;* Good Scriptures ill understood? ... Because the Multitude cannot agree upon a Rule, there shall be None at all. Pursue this Argument, and there shall be No Law, No Religion, No Scripture, No Truth, left in the World" (pp. 20–22).

L'Estrange uses dialogue to rule out dialogue. Those continuing the tradition of Christian Neoplatonism will need to do the opposite. In either case political, religious, and philosophical debates are not just being conducted *within* dialogue; they are being waged in terms of an extended, heavily coded, often belligerent struggle to define nature and proper management of dialogue as a genre. Dialogue became a focal point for debates about how social, political, and religious differences should be adjudicated. In *Leviathan* (1651), for instance, Hobbes describes reason itself in terms of a juridical dialogue between contending parties, presided over by an arbitrating authority:

> when there is a controversy in an account, the parties must by their own accord, set up for right Reason, the Reason of some Arbitrator, or Judge, to whose sentence they will both stand, or their controversie must either come to blowes, or be undecided, for want of right Reason constituted by Nature; so is it also in all debates of what kind soever: And when men think themselves wiser than all others, clamor and demand right Reason for judge; yet seek no more, but that things should be determined, by no other mens reason but their own, it is as intolerable in the society of men, as it is in play after trump is turned, to use for trump on every occasion, that suite whereof they have most in their hand.[27]

Obviously, the success of this mode of rational adjudication depends upon the authority of the third figure and the willingness of the disputing parties to subordinate their interests to the Judge's final edict. But in the course of the short passage reason slides precipitously from an authority "constituted by nature" to a purely conventional reference point, chanced upon like a suit made trump in a game of cards. It would seem we must refer our differences to this judge not because he possesses some infallible knowledge of "right reason constituted by nature," but because, pragmatically speaking, the game of controversy we have agreed to play requires us to agree also about a standard of judgment else we come to blows. In this case, however, could reason ever preside over a theological controversy whose primary question (in an increasingly secular age) concerned the existence and attributes of a divine Arbitrator?

In that the transition from tragic division to comedic unity depended upon a transcendental reference point not itself subject to dispute, one might assume that dialogue would cease to be a dominant form of theological and philosophical exposition in the age of Hobbes, Locke, and Hume. Just the opposite occurs: between 1650 and 1750 dialogue became a central mode of

---

[27] Thomas Hobbes, *Leviathan*, ed. C. B. Macpherson (Hamondsworth: Penguin, 1968), pp. 111–112.

philosophical writing. Dryden, Shaftesbury, Mandeville, Berkeley, and Hume all composed important works in dialogue form, as did innumerable minor figures; and dialogue became the object of extensive critical reflection.[28]

Many factors influence the production of dialogues during the Enlightenment. In this book, I concentrate upon the role of philosophical dialogue in mediating – or failing to mediate – fundamental conceptual and discursive tensions of Modernity. During a time when inductive method was being extended to all fields of inquiry (including theology), when political authorities were being forced to transfer their right to govern from a divine to a contracted sanction, when moral philosophers and educators were attempting to disseminate Enlightenment to an expanding, increasingly heterogeneous and skeptical reading public – during a time, in short, when cultural and intellectual changes threatened to exceed the mediating capacity of any transcendental, dialectical scheme, philosophical dialogue became a source of intense preoccupation *both* because of its power to revalidate the imperiled dialectic, *and* because of its capacity to destroy the last vestiges of Platonic metaphysics. The split conception of dialogue and dialectic, always implicit within the history of this genre, becomes a source of open conflict during the eighteenth century, as comedic and tragic interpretations compete for dominance.

The writing of dialogue took place in many venues: periodicals, letters, essays, reviews, criticism, travel accounts, satire, farce, drama, novels, conduct manuals, party polemics, ballads, verse epistles, catechisms, school primers all were written in dialogue form. I make no effort to catalogue the number and type of independent dialogues, especially since this work has already been done.[29] I am interested here in the dominant role dialogue played in eighteenth-century moral philosophy. The task moral philosophers

---

[28] On the sheer number of minor dialogues written between 1650 and 1750 see B. V. Crawford, "The Prose Dialogue of the Commonwealth and Restoration," *PMLA* 34 (1919) 601–609; and Eugene Purpus, "The 'Plain, Easy, and Familiar Way': The Dialogue in English Literature, 1660–1725," *ELH* 17 (1950) 47–58. Crawford's article includes a graph tying the greatest proliferation of prose dialogues to years of most intense social unrest. See also Elizabeth Merrill, *The Dialogue in English Literature*, Yale Studies in English, vol. XLII (New York: Holt and Company, 1911); Kevin Cope, ed., *Compendious Conversations: the Method of Dialogue in the Early Enlightenment* (Franfurt-on-Main: Peter Lang, 1992). The most extensive study of philosophical dialogue from the classical age to the eighteenth century remains Rudolph Hirzel's *Der Dialog: ein Literarhistorischer Versuch*, 2 vols. [1895]; rprt. (Hildesheim: Georg Olms Verlagsbuchhandlung, 1963).

[29] Purpus' dissertation, "The Dialogue in English Literature, 1660–1725," (Ph.D. diss., UCLA, 1943), though unpublished, offers an informative survey of the different occasions eighteenth-century authors found for composing dialogues (for instance, in philosophy, in periodical essays, as a mode of education, in dialogues of the dead). Because primarily encyclopedic, Purpus' treatment fails to advance a more general thesis as to why, for a relatively short period of time, the dialogue became such a significant form, especially among major authors. His most frequent explanation is that dialogue offered an "easy and familiar" means of conveying otherwise difficult material to a heterogeneous group of readers. For the various contexts in which dialogues were written in eighteenth-century France, see D. J. Adams, *Bibliographie d'ouvrages français en forme de dialogue, 1700–1750*, Studies on Voltaire and the Eighteenth Century 293 (Oxford: Voltaire Foundation, 1992).

set for dialogue did not have to do primarily with ease of communication, inculcating manners, or even selling books. Dialogue did nothing less than replicate the fundamental problems of modern philosophy in fictional form. It represented the stages of analytical method – division, analysis, synthesis, and composition – in philosophical fictions. Dialogue portrayed a mind capable of enacting division, of breaking wholes (received truths) down into disparate parts, yet capable also of recovering coherence through the free use of reason. Dialogue dramatized one being made two, and two being made again one. Whatever the topic of debate, the "turn" in dialogue from divided opinion to consensus offered a concrete analogue for the difficult "turn" in Cartesian method from division to synthesis. The progress of scientific understanding and the progress of method each hinged upon a moment when the skeptical division of entities or concepts into smaller and smaller units (data), reached its natural conclusion, and the constructive work of forming conclusions could begin. At the turn in his own description of method, Descartes can only advise the scientist to treat "as though ordered, materials which were not necessarily so."[30] Dialogues of the period transform the weak "as though" into a strong fiction; for this reason, it is in terms of dialogue, an ancient genre put to modern use, that many of the period's most urgent debates in epistemology, theology, ethics, politics, and literary criticism occur.

In Part 1, I describe the role of dialogue in fostering and challenging a philosophical theology during the Enlightenment. Philosophical dialogue was thought to dramatize the claim of a broad range of philosophical Christians and divines of the High and Low Church that the free and impartial exercise of reason was compatible with being a sound Christian.[31] It was virtually a truism during the Enlightenment that conflicting opinions (especially in theological controversy) should be tried at the bar of unbiased reason. In the "Letter to the Sacred Faculty of Theology at the Sorbonne" introducing his *Meditations*, Descartes writes that "faith is a gift of God, and the very God that gives us the faith to believe other things can also give us the faith to believe that he exists." But then, in the characteristic turn that marks the rational Christian's concern with method and style, Descartes acknowledges that to a reader who is "without faith" this argument will sound like what "the logicians call circular reasoning."[32] The anticipation of a skeptical reader who must yet be convinced of his unhappiness leads the rational Christian to

[30] René Descartes, *Discourse on Method and Mediations*, trans. Laurence J. Lafleur (Indianapolis: Bobbs-Merrill Co., Inc., 1960), p. 15.
[31] Here and throughout this study, I emphasize those dialogues written more or less in imitation of classical models (predominantly Plato and Cicero) and thought to contain a genuinely skeptical element. Catechistical dialogues abounded during the period but were mocked by writers of serious philosophical dialogue as being wholly unlike their own works. To what extent philosophical dialogues really were skeptical is a constant point of interest in the following chapters.
[32] Descartes, *Discourse on Method and Meditations*, pp. 61–62.

reject deductive, a priori modes of argument and to seek out forms that move gradually, inductively from part to whole, critical reason to faith.

Dialogue provided one means of literalizing the trial that all sides declared themselves ready to undergo. "It is certainly the duty of every rational creature," argued the dissenting cleric Philip Doddridge, "to bring his religion to the strictest test, and to retain or reject the faith in which he was educated, as he finds it capable or incapable of rational defense." So too Francis Atterbury, leader of the Jacobite element of the High Church, held that the Church of England "desires nothing more than to be tried at the bar of unbiased reason, and to be concluded by its sentence."[33] Within religious dialogue, as within a providentially ordered cosmos, an initial appearance of randomness and heterogeneity would give way to a final point of unity and order: dialogue would express a theodicy of the social realm through the staging of rational consensus, just as natural religion offered a theodicy of the phenomenal world through the subordination of chance to design. Dialogue thus permitted moral philosophers to make allowance for the increasing autonomy of individual subjects and an increasing diversity within the social order while still portraying an inevitable consolidation of viewpoints, characters, and interests under a providential scheme.

Throughout this book, I discuss the breakdown of formal, intellectual, and sociological conditions that favored the writing of religious dialogues during the eighteenth century. The metaphysical interpretation of dialogue inherited from Christian Neoplatonism comes under attack from two directions. Within moral philosophy itself, the assumed compatibility of dialogic inquiry and theological commitment began to seem dubious. The theoretical basis for this change can be discerned in Henry Dodwell's *Christianity not Founded on Argument* (1742): "Whereas, were religion indeed a rational institution, a man might surely well dispute it without a crime ... A free and amicable correspondence might well be admitted, and the wildest opponent received upon an equal foot with his most orthodox and approved antagonist. All other methods of proceeding bespeak plainly the question already determined beyond all possibility of controversy. And so indeed it is."[34] Dodwell sees that if the primary tenets of Christianity are in fact susceptible to reasoned demonstration, a radically inclusive dialogue would be the most pious form of religious writing. The point leads to a formal Manichaeism: either one composes dialogue *in extremis*, or one abandons the pretense of reasoned dispute and adopts a form suitable to a subject that has been "already determined beyond all possibility of controversy." Dodwell views "religious dialogue" as an oxymoron.

[33] Both passages are quoted in Roland N. Stromberg, *Religious Liberalism in Eighteenth-Century England* (Oxford: Oxford University Press, 1954), p. 9.

[34] Quoted in E. Graham Waring, ed., *Deism and Natural Religion, a Source Book* (New York: Ungar, 1967), p. 223.

Throughout the eighteenth century the metaphysical interpretation of dialogue favored by Shaftesbury, Berkeley, and the mid-century Platonists came under attack from skeptics such as Mandeville, Hume, and Allan Ramsay. Recognizing the integral connection between argument and art in their opponent's dialogues, these skeptics sought to redefine dialogue as a genre that destroyed the vestiges of Christian Neoplatonism. In their dialogues the motives and desires of bodies always color the transcendental aspirations of minds; no divine arbitrator reconciles differences of opinion; theology and the conduct of human agents are driven apart.

In addition to the "high" critique of religious dialogue occurring within moral philosophy, one finds metaphysical dialogues degraded from "below," as it were. For during the Enlightenment, dialogue was one of a number of genres that developed in conjunction with what Habermas has called an emerging public sphere.[35] Often set in coffee-houses, public walks, salons, stage coaches, and the like, dialogue was one of the genres that represented the public exchange of ideas taking place among subjects who were (at least in theory) free and equal. During these years, authors of dialogue transmit substantive knowledge such as the principles of astronomy, physics, and botany through the easy and familiar form of prose dialogue in order to educate female readers and an emerging middle class. They transcribe actual debates and submit them to periodicals. They invite their readers to propose objections, which they promise to include in subsequent editions. And they continue the tradition of representing norms for conduct through dialogues exemplifying the art of conversation.[36] Dialogue allowed philosophers to reach a new reading public made up of common readers whose taste for strong fictions and distaste for dry, pedantic treatises was assumed.[37]

Responding to the changing demography of audience, writers believed (at first) that they could include a broader range of interests, opinions, and social types within the framework of a genre that *conventionally* (as an embodiment of metaphysical dialectic) subordinated the many to the one. Nevertheless, the attempt to ameliorate opposition through its partial representation instigates

---

[35] Jürgen Habermas, *The Structural Transformation of the Public Sphere: an Inquiry into a Category of Bourgeois Society*, trans. Thomas Burger, (Cambridge, MA: MIT Press, 1989), especially chapters 4–5.

[36] On dialogue and the art of conversation, see Jack Prostko, "Instructive and Delightful Talk: Conversation and Eighteenth-Century English Literature," (Ph.D. diss., Stanford University, 1985) and "Natural Conversation Set in View: Shaftesbury and Moral Speech," *Eighteenth-Century Studies* 23 (1989) 42–61.

[37] By 1762 Spens, the first English translator of Plato's *Republic*, expressed a commonplace when he observed that "In our age ... the taste for pleasure is so prevalent, and the prejudice so great against every thing that has the appearance of philosophy, [that] a writer is likely to be but ill received, who shall venture to entertain the public, with a treatise on morals, delivered in a dry didactic manner; which hath derived no aids from dress or ornament; in order to succeed, he must call in assistance from proper incidents, and characters; from striking images, and allegories, and the like." *The Republic of Plato: with a preliminary discourse concerning the philosophy of the ancients* (Glasgow: R. and A. Foulis, 1763), p. xv.

a dynamic of its own: the very same cultural conditions that promote the writing of philosophical dialogue threaten the viability of that genre as a means of reconciling differences. In a dialogue from the factious year 1710, *Both Sides Pleas'd; or a dialogue between a Sacheverelite Parson and an Hoadlean Gentleman,* the anonymous author responds to the trial of Henry Sacheverell (which had already caused rioting in London) by staging a dialogue in a London coffee-house.[38] The main adversaries are a Hoadlean Gentleman and a Sacheverelite Parson, but the subtitle reads, "many Gentlemen and Tradesmen (of each Party) present; and all at liberty to ask Questions, in order to a Reconciliation." When tradesmen actually intervene in the dispute (which is, after all, about passive obedience), the dialogue implodes. The Hoadlean Gentleman pleads for "MODERATION," at which point a Sacheverelite Butcher calls him, "a Low-Church Man, to the last Degree, and the greatest Enemy to the Church and Queen."[39] And when the Sacheverelite Parson says he would not oppose a king to save his own wife from becoming the king's concubine, a Hoadlean Shoemaker calls the parson "a Pimp to your own Wife." As the dialogue disintegrates, the Hoadlean Waterman explains, "Pray, Master, don't be angry with the Company for making some pleasant Remarks upon your more serious Discourses; for this is some Refreshment to us working Men, after twelve hours hard Labor, and with my Head all day in the Rain (p. 20)." The minor dialogue concentrates into twenty pages a process of generic decline that occurs gradually in the high philosophical dialogue over the course of the eighteenth century.

Looking back in 1776 upon the entire body of works that make up this history, Richard Hurd concluded,

there was something ... in the character of the writer imitated [Plato], of a very ticklish and dangerous nature; and of which our tribe of imitators were not sufficiently aware. A very exact critic of antiquity hath told us what it was. It lay in Plato's bringing the tumour of poetic composition into discourses of philosophy ... And though the experiment, for the most part, succeeded not amiss (as what contradiction is there that superior genius cannot reconcile?) yet it sometimes failed even in his hands.[40]

---

[38] *Both Sides Pleas'd* was written in what G. S. Rousseau has called "the heyday of the coffee house and neighborhood academy," when rising literacy and greater economic autonomy "increased the demand – a veritable hunger – for knowledge among adults." "Science Books and their Readers in the Eighteenth Century," in *Books and their Readers in Eighteenth-Century England,* ed. Isabel Rivers (Leicester: Leicester University Press, 1982), p. 208. Habermas calls the coffee-house one of the new institutions of the bourgeois public sphere and links these institutions to the development of new literary genres (such as the periodical essay) that replicate the public, open, and dialogic nature of these associations. Here, according to Habermas, one found "a kind of social intercourse that, far from presupposing the equality of status, disregarded status altogether" (*The Structural Transformation of the Public Sphere,* p. 36).

[39] "Both Sides Pleas'd: or, a Dialogue between a Sacheverelite Parson, and An Hoadlean Gentleman" (London: S. Popping, 1710), p. 6.

[40] Richard Hurd, *Epistolae ad Pisones, et Augustum: With an English Commentary and Notes ... by the Reverend Mr. Hurd,* 5th edn., 3 vols. (London: Printed by W. Bowyer and J. Nichols for T. Cadell and J. Woodyear, 1776), I, p. 252.

The fiction that had been counted upon to create a bridge between one sense of dialectic and another has proven toxic to the very body of philosophy. Dialectic and rhetoric, after a long and difficult marriage, are ready for divorce. What could have occasioned such a harsh assessment? One of my purposes is to account for Hurd's diagnosis by tracing the gradual dismantling of textual and philosophical assumptions that had promoted the writing of philosophical dialogue during the first half of the eighteenth century.

The metaphor of a deadly tumour is inadequate to the case, however, because the patient does not die, but is instead transformed. The more general project of reconciling science and divinity, material diversity and a providential scheme, was too important to be allowed to give up the ghost just because a favored embodiment of that project took ill. Throughout this book, and especially in chapters 7, 8, and 9, I argue that philosophical aesthetics and the novel, emerging simultaneously by the middle of the eighteenth century, can be seen as divergent responses to the failed project of philosophical dialogue.

Proponents of a metaphysical interpretation of dialogue who recognized the difficulty of grounding consensus in reason looked to aesthetic experience as a new means of guaranteeing uniformity of response among diverse characters. Although describing an increasingly private and subjective aspect of human experience, early exponents of the science of taste continued to favor the form of dialogue because it allowed them to "prove" the objective universality of aesthetic response. Between 1730 and 1770 there occurred a revival of interest in Platonic dialogues on beauty. These were translated and imitated in English dialogues on beauty, taste, understanding, decency, refinement, and the like. The works of the Platonic Revival form a previously unexamined bridge between rational models of consensus and the more fully developed idealist aesthetics of Kant's *Critique of Judgment*. They suggest that aesthetics continues and transforms the failed project of Christian Neoplatonism in general and metaphysical dialogue in particular.

Theorists of the novel have had a notoriously difficult time accounting for the emergence of prose fiction in writers as different as Defoe, Fielding, Sterne, and Burney. Yet within the contemporary discussion of the nature and viability of dialogue, we find an important (and previously overlooked) basis for understanding the general move towards prose fiction even among writers who differ in their philosophy, politics, and religion. Ironically, *both* the metaphysical *and* anti-metaphysical interpretations of dialogue share in the call for fictions of characterized intellectual debate. Both discuss the role of character, plot, setting, and author. And both describe the kind of reception they anticipate from a reading public that has grown larger and more diverse. This is not to say that writers of dialogue *want* to be novelists; rather, within the history of dialogue one finds an often reluctant drift from

metaphysical dialogue to philosophical novel.[41] Proponents of metaphysical
dialogue begin to stress elements of plot, setting, and character once
confidence in a disembodied criterion of arbitration (reason, logic, common
sense) declines. Writers of anti-metaphysical dialogue (particularly Mandeville
and Hume) stress character and circumstance all along in order to show why
the contingencies of human desire and self-interest frustrate any move to a
forced consensus.[42] As the appeal to transpersonal criteria of judgment
becomes less confident within dialogues, writers turn to the "evidence"
supplied by the responses of characters to specific circumstances. The
declining status of philosophical dialogue thus provides a basis for understanding the elevation of prose fiction as a dominant mode of moral
philosophy.

Throughout these introductory remarks, I have been avoiding another
question suggested by my title. Is it even accurate to use the term
"Enlightenment" to refer to the literary and intellectual history of eighteenth-century Britain? The expectation that "Enlightenment" stands for a
radical, skeptical movement, relatively pure in its opposition to established
authority, whether political or religious, has resulted in the claim that
"Enlightenment" fails to characterize conditions in "Augustan" or "Neoclassical" Britain. As a consequence, a purer Enlightenment has been
located elsewhere. The idealization has resulted in the assumption that the
pure values of a Continental Enlightenment appear to undergo a dialectical
reversal whereby they are transformed, by an inner fatalism, into their very
antitheses. Enlightenment is therefore held responsible for the worst excesses
of instrumental reason in the twentieth century.

But what if there never was a pure Enlightenment? What if the example of

[41] Throughout this book I have resisted the impulse to relate dialogue to more popular forms of prose
fiction through a shared "dialogism" (heteroglossia, carnivalized proliferation of discourses).
Indeed, I have operated from very different assumptions: during the eighteenth century the relation
between philosophical dialogue and the novel might better be seen in terms of conscious
antagonism. For many writers the purpose of dialogue was not to celebrate but to restrict
heterogeneity, through dialogue's special embodiment of a dialectical mechanism that transforms
the social miscellany into a beautiful and ordered whole. For the purpose of understanding a
process of transformation whereby the novel becomes dominant, competing interpretations of the
same (high, philosophical) genre have struck me as more important than a shared dialogism, which,
after all, has little to do with the existence of a work as a dialogue or novel, since dialogism (we are
now told) is present in every text and indeed in every relation. Dialogism, writes Michael Holquist,
"is an attempt to frame a theory of knowledge for an age when relativity dominates. . . when *non-
coincidence* of one kind or another – of sign to its referent, of the subject to itself – raises troubling
new questions about the very existence of mind . . . The non-identity of mind and world is the
conceptual rock on which dialogism is founded."*Dialogism: Bakhtin and his World* (London and New
York: Routledge, 1990), p. 17. The problem is not just that absolute relativity and "conceptual
rock" make strange bedfellows. The tendency to universalize a state of contingency leads also to the
transformation of a concrete genre into a metaphor, dialogism, which is further abstracted into the
"differential relation between a center and all that is not the center" (p. 18).
[42] For the notion of "coerced speech" as it relates to dialogue, see Aaron Fogel, *Coercion to Speak:
Conrad's Poetics of Dialogue* (Cambridge, MA: Harvard University Press, 1985).

philosophical dialogue is entirely representative of a period marked by divergent political, religious, and discursive strains – Enlightenment and counter-Enlightenment, moderns and ancients, non-Christian and Christian? Might not the concept of reversal then appear an optical illusion? A matter of squinting away complexity for a time in order to declare a set of values pure, and then opening one's eyes to their contamination, blamed, erroneously, on those values themselves? The question, therefore, is not whether intellectual and literary developments in seventeenth- and eighteenth-century Britain fulfill the definition of a pure Enlightenment; rather it is whether the mixed character of the British Enlightenment might not actually be representative of the Enlightenment as a whole.

A history of dialogue provides the basis for a more general account of the Enlightenment only if one abandons the assumption that genres embody transhistorical ideals or theoretical essences. While writers in the past constantly refer to their chosen rhetorical weapons as if they were grounded in a natural correspondence between language and truth, the case of philosophical dialogue is representative of most every genre that assumes a position of cultural dominance. Genres become sites of competing interpretations because what is at stake in the definition of form is the power to establish normative frameworks for understanding complex phenomena. Comedic and tragic conceptions of philosophical dialogue, implicitly at odds since Plato, come into open conflict during the first half of the eighteenth century. At issue in this opposition was the status of dialectic itself, its efficacy in reconciling sensory and intellectual realms, the empirical sciences and liberal Protestant theology. Consequently, a generic history of dialogue and dialectic cannot be premised upon an overriding dialectical scheme. On the contrary, the history of philosophical dialogue in the British Enlightenment entails a critique of dialectical historiography. I return to this point in the epilogue.

PART I

Strains of Enlightenment

For after all the Objections that I have heard against such a free Way of urging Theistic Arguments in Dialogue, I still think it is more like to do good among Infidels, than a methodical Discourse, ranged into Chapter and Section ... For those that are tainted with these Opinions ... every Thing which is designed for their Use must be attempered to their Palates, to make it go down with them.

William Nichols, *A Conference with a Theist* (1723)

Shaftesbury's characteristic genres: concepts of criticism in the early eighteenth century

The problem of definition

At the beginning of the eighteenth century, philosophical dialogue holds a liminal position between one hierarchy of genres premised upon formal unity and metaphysical certitude and another hierarchy of kinds engendering formal variety and the loss of any higher (metaphysical) locus of truth. Dryden captured this liminal quality when he defended his own dialogue, the *Essay of Dramatic Poesy* (1668), in these terms: it "was Sceptical according to that way of reasoning which was used by Socrates, Plato, and the Academiques of old, which Tully and the best of the Ancients followed, and which is imitated by the modest Inquisitions of the Royal Society."[1] Suspended between old and new conceptions of textual order – skeptical without overturning the wisdom of the ancients, pious without ignoring the methodologies of the new science – dialogue was an unstable form, a genre near its end, according to Shaftesbury, during the very years when it was also counted most alive. To begin by defining dialogue or recounting Platonic or Ciceronian models, therefore, is immediately to miss the point: the meaning of dialogue during the eighteenth century needs to be approached through an understanding of the way genre distinctions functioned as a religious and political vocabulary.[2] Rival critical schemes for the evaluation of works

---

[1] *A Defense of an Essay of Dramatic Poesy*, in John Dryden, *The Works of John Dryden*, ed. H.T. Swedenberg, Jr. 20 vols. (Berkeley: University of California Press, 1966), ix, p. 15.

[2] In this regard the "literarhistorischer Versuch" attempted here differs from that informing Hirzel's monumental *Der Dialog* (1895). Hirzel narrates the history of what he takes to be the "king of genres" ("Der Konig der Gattungen"), emphasizing those works in which an ideal balance between form and content is achieved: "In the complete or perfect dialogue ... the conversation is raised to a special life in which scenery is only decoration, and then in such a situation dialogue becomes a closed being (a distinct form in and of itself apart from drama and conversation) ... So now we can say that the dialogue is the climax of conversation in literature, and the conversations which we have in literature before we have dialogue are only a preliminary step towards the development which has its zenith in dialogue" (*Der Dialog*, i, pp. 8–9). The idealization of one definition of dialogue allows Hirzel to dispense with variations, and so with the historicity of genre. Instances of dialogue that depart from the norm, such as Lucian's satirical dialogues of the dead or medieval morality plays, fail to express "the essential being of the form purely. Not the Lucianic dialogues because they belong to an epoch of decline when the dialogical was mixed with the dramatical, and not the oldest Christian plays because they are embryonic" (p. 9). The present study rejects notions

generated competing conceptions even of individual forms, and dialogue, perhaps more than any other genre, was subject to radically different interpretations. Linked at times to so-called "open" forms such as the miscellany, familiar essay, letter, and encyclopedia, philosophical dialogue was just as often grouped with heroic drama, allegory, prosopopoeia, and the scholastic treatise. The battle between ancients and moderns was fought not only in St. James' Library but also on the conceptual and discursive field marked out by this ancient modern genre.

Statements about genre from Aristotle's *Poetics* to our own discussion of soap opera, rap, and MTV have always entailed more than a fetish for taxonomic order and hierarchy. Artists and critics use distinctions among genres to target specific audiences, to influence the reception of a work, and to assert political and theological values bound up in the affirmation or rejection of discursive conventions. Genres provide an especially important point of concentration because they mark the meeting place of three crucial elements in the field of literary production and reception: the intention of an author, an imagined reception, and the range of rhetorical options available at the time. When writers themselves talk about genre, they are therefore reflecting upon the historical conditions that shape the production and evaluation of works.

It is important to begin with this point, because the decision to limit this study to writings identified at the time as dialogues might otherwise seem arbitrary. It could be argued, for instance, that *most* eighteenth-century writers, especially writers of moral philosophy, think and write in terms of dialogue. Whether because pedagogical training in the arts of dialectic and rhetorical disputation accustomed writers to dialogical displays, or because a generation of writers following the Civil War and Restoration found their allegiances torn between rival theological and political claims, or because, as Donald Davie asserts, conversation and candor were defining values of the age, what might be called "dialogic" elements characterize *most* textual production from the late seventeenth through the middle of the eighteenth century.

What is Dryden's great poem, *Religio Laici*, after all, if not a poetical dialogue among rival theological positions – Catholic, Calvinist, and Deist. Even the structure of the poem, with its survey of opinions, objections raised and answered, and final verdict, could be described as a religious dialogue embedded in a didactic verse epistle (which Dryden also calls a treatise). And

---

of formal essence or completion. Instead, it views literary history in terms of the competing interpretations and uses assigned to a form considered both ancient and modern, secular and Christian, systematic and haphazard. Even those who defend an ideal of philosophical dialogue during this period, like those who defend many precedent ideals, so alter form in actual presentation that the "imitation" of dialogue becomes an activity wherein philosophical and literary invention occurs.

this poem is by no means atypical. *Paradise Lost* has been called a philosophical dialogue.[3] Pope's *Essay on Man* is no less a philosophical dialogue, if one is willing to extend the definition of dialogue to cover any work in which a debate occurs among competing voices. In this case, however, a history of eighteenth-century dialogue would need to include georgic poems, verse epistles, pastoral dialogues, most instances of prose satire, many sermons, most essays, treatises, all drama, and, of course, the novel.

My argument in this chapter is that genre constitutes a meaningful unit of textual and historical analysis because eighteenth-century writers themselves used differentiations among kinds to carry out practical ends. A critic such as Shaftesbury, who habitually frames his moral and political philosophy in terms of a discussion of genre, becomes important neither because of a coherent philosophical output (lacking in his case), nor because of polished literary productions (also missing), but because he manages to capture a vibrant yet invidious climate of uncertainty through a criticism focused upon the language of forms. Shaftesbury's evaluation of genres is so pervasive, and his political, philosophical, and theological beliefs so mixed, that the result is a split conception of criticism generating rival schemes for the evaluation of forms. Torn in two, a Janus-faced being, Shaftesbury captures the period's most profound contradictions and anticipates its most characteristic developments in moral philosophy.

Divided interests

We can, if we wish, boil Shaftesbury down to his ideological simple. We can claim with Terry Eagleton that Shaftesbury is "a central architect of the new political hegemony" or with Robert Markley that in "Shaftesbury's writings, the 'self-consuming artifacts' of epistemological questioning give way to the reification of moral values – virtue, truth, and even aesthetic beauty – as idealized, ahistorical absolutes."[4] Understandably this kind of historicism will take little interest in distinctions among genres. For Lawrence Klein a term like "politeness" functions as a "guiding metaphor," a value operative in many different genres, and everywhere asserting the same ideology – Whig apologia. Shaftesbury made politeness "the focus of his entire endeavor in moral and cultural criticism," concludes Klein.[5] It was through this master

[3] On *Paradise Lost* as philosophical dialogue, see Stanley E. Fish, *Surprised by Sin* (New York: St. Martin's Press, 1967), p. 49; and Elaine B. Safer, "The Use of Contraries: Milton's Adaptation of Dialectic in *Paradise Lost*," *Ariel* 12 (April, 1981) 55–69.
[4] Terry Eagleton, *The Ideology of the Aesthetic* (Oxford: Basil Blackwell, 1990), p. 36; Robert Markley, "Style as Philosophical Structure: the Contexts of Shaftesbury's *Characteristicks*," in *The Philosopher as Writer: the Eighteenth Century*, ed. Robert Linsberg (Selinsgrove: Susquehanna University Press, 1987), p. 143.
[5] "Berkeley, Shaftesbury, and the Meaning of Politeness," *Studies in Eighteenth-Century Culture* 16 (1986) 59. Klein does grant that in Berkeley's dialogue *Alciphron*, two concepts of politeness are set in

trope that Shaftesbury "reformulated commerce on a high cultural plane and secured virtue to it."[6] "Shaftesbury was the ideologist for a culture that would be philosophical and gentlemanly, moral and conversable – in a word, polite."[7] Klein does not acknowledge that in Shaftesbury's *The Moralists*, the values he associates with politeness are enunciated by only one of two main figures, Theocles, and that the other character, Philocles, the radical skeptic, mocks the very idea of an ahistorical absolute and suggests that Theocles' love of beauty and refinement may have something to do with his ownership of a substantial landed estate. Nor does he recognize that Shaftesbury's early readers, among them Mary Astell, considered the notorious defense of wit and ridicule the opposite of polite.[8]

The critical methodology of recent historicism is different in tone, though not at all in kind, from an older tradition of intellectual history (*Geistesgeschichte*) that saw Shaftesbury as a precursor of Romanticism and the Kantian aesthetic. Cassirer explains in his "Preface" to *The Philosophy of the Enlightenment* that the Enlightenment had to be "approached in its characteristic depth rather than in its breadth, and to be presented in the light of the unity of its conceptual origin and of its underlying principle rather than of the totality of its historical manifestations and results ... The tensions and solutions, the doubts and decisions, the skepticism and unshakable conviction of this philosophy must be seen and interpreted from one central position if its real historical meaning is to be made clear."[9] From such a position it is possible to reduce the surface complexity of Shaftesbury's writings to the main philosophical idea he contributes to the sequence leading to Kant (disinterested aesthetic reflection), just as today that one central position reveals politeness as the synthesizing concept.

The methodologies of both the new historicism and *Geistesgeschichte* solve the problem that bothered so many of Shaftesbury's early readers, namely the confusion and internal inconsistency of his political, philosophical, religious, and literary commitments. These accounts simplify the difficult position of the Country Whig at the beginning of the eighteenth century. For Caroline Robbins, the Old Whigs or Commonwealthmen (among whom she

---

opposition. But he seems unwilling to discuss the question of how a single guiding metaphor, whose meaning is being contested, becomes the emblem of a set ideology.

[6] Klein, "The Third Earl of Shaftesbury and the Progress of Politeness," *Eighteenth-Century Studies* 18 (1984–85) 214.

[7] Klein, *Shaftesbury and the Culture of Politeness: Moral Discourse and Cultural Politics in Early Eighteenth-Century England* (Cambridge: Cambridge University Press, 1994), p. 119.

[8] Upon the appearance of Shaftesbury's *Letter concerning Enthusiasm*, Mary Astell asked, "Is it then *Good Manners* to behave our selves towards GOD and Religion, which is His Law, in a way that wou'd cost us our Lives did we dare to shew such Manners towards our Sovereign, and the Laws of our Country?" *Bart'lemy Fair or an Enquiry after Wit* (London: R. Wilkin, 1709), pp. 34–35. My thanks to Colin Harris and Kirk Melnikoff for alerting me to this passage.

[9] Enst Cassirer, *The Philosophy of the Enlightenment*, trans. Fritz C. A. Koelln and James P. Pettegrove (Boston: Beacon Press, 1955), p. v.

numbers Shaftesbury) are defined by contradiction: "the Commonwealthmen could be regarded as the conservators of the older order; they must also be seen as spiritual heirs and ancestors of revolutionaries everywhere."[10] In contrast to the New Whigs associated with city interests and aligned eventually with Walpole, these Commonwealthmen agitated for more extensive social reforms (such as the Treason Bill guaranteeing legal representation even for those charged with treason, a bill Shaftesbury actively endorsed); they supported a federalist system, attacked ministerial prerogatives, urged religious toleration, sought a wider franchise, and were sympathetic to the American colonies. At the same time, Robbins describes Shaftesbury as "truly monarchical in his principles" (p. 129).

Klein's more recent account of Shaftesbury's politics enriches without fundamentally altering this view of Shaftesbury as a Country or Old Whig whose allegiances become increasingly complex and tortured. On Klein's account Shaftesbury's early affiliation with the Country Whigs and Commonwealthmen gave way to a more wholesale defense of the dominant Whig regime. By the time Shaftesbury compiled *Characteristics* (1711), according to Klein, "his project in cultural ideology was very different from that of the Country ideology"; yet, Klein adds, "Shaftesbury did remain loyal throughout his life to certain elements of the Country program."[11] Klein's account of Shaftesbury's shifting political allegiances is detailed and convincing, but why should it be the case that a writer whose politics are so mixed becomes the architect of a single, monolithic cultural ideology? When Klein turns from politics to art, his sensitivity to mixed commitments evaporates: Shaftesbury articulates a single cultural ideology, a single view of criticism, a single notion of "discursivity," and a single scheme of moral development.[12]

I do not think it is possible to assess either Shaftesbury's ideology or his relevance to the history of ideas without addressing his divided interests. In this respect, I favor Laura Brown's decision to abandon the expectation that authors can be reduced to a monolithic ideology or evaluated according to modern standards of correctness and consistency. In an essay on Swift, Brown seeks to explain the fact that the poet and satirist was "an explicit misogynist and also an explicit anti-colonialist." The seeming contradiction makes Swift "a test case for political criticism and a proving ground for the nature of the 'politics' of such a criticism."[13] One is uncertain whether to expose another canonical misogynist or to praise "an early ally in the struggle against colonialism."[14] But why did political criticism ever get to the

---

[10] Caroline Robbins, *The Eighteenth-Century Commonwealthman*, (Cambridge, MA: Harvard University Press, 1959), p. 5.

[11] Klein, *Shaftesbury and the Culture of Politeness*, pp. 132–135.

[12] *Ibid.*, see especially chapter 10, "The culture of liberty."

[13] Laura Brown, "Reading Race and Gender: Jonathan Swift," *Eighteenth-Century Studies* 23 (1989) 425.

[14] *Ibid.*, p. 426.

point where this kind of complexity comes as a surprise? Are we not, as members of different "classes" (whether of institution, race, gender, discipline, or economic level), simultaneously involved in various structures of power, articulations of authority, constructions of identity? And do we not, as political beings, find ourselves as often standing for what is right and true as having to explain away (to ourselves at least) embarrassing inconsistencies in our commitments and failures to commit? William Empson's remarks are pertinent here: "Life involves maintaining oneself between contradictions that can't be solved by analysis ... it may be that the human mind can recognize actually incommensurable values, and that the chief human value is to stand up between them."[15]

In turning to Shaftesbury, therefore, I return to a question A. O. Aldridge posed in 1945. At that time Aldridge remarked upon "the one glaring example of inconsistency in Shaftesbury, [namely] his recurrent stress on the necessity of classical unity in a work as spasmodic as the *Characteristics*." Why, Aldridge asked, "did he go blithely ahead disregarding his own standards?"[16] The inconsistency is glaring, but not Shaftesbury's disregard: he is aware of generating two contradictory sets of critical standards, one based upon the comic ridicule and the other based upon classical unity and decorum, one promoting social and political transformation in light of Enlightenment ideals, the other seeking to limit the intrusion of novel interests into the prevailing structures of order. Thus, rather than assume a privileged perspective from which Shaftesbury's contradictions appear unified, I shall describe a range of critical principles informing Shaftesbury's discussion of genre. Shaftesbury uses distinctions among genres to address political and religious schism, a rapidly expanding audience for print, and the separation of philosophical works from problems of everyday experience. But having established the link between social and artistic structures, and having endorsed forms that promote Enlightenment values (freedom of thought, skepticism, pluralism, educational emancipation), Shaftesbury finds himself defending textual practices that run counter to the standards Aldridge calls more truly his own. Like the female in the frontispiece to his *An Inquiry concerning Virtue, or Merit*, Shaftesbury is a split figure, torn between emancipation and control, transformation and stasis, the Cumean Sibyl dispersing fragments and a just Prometheus forging wholes. Eventually, he will personify his inner antagonisms through the characters of Philocles, the radical skeptic, and Theocles, the rhapsodic defender of ancient order, hoping to reconcile these most representative divisions within a philosophical dialogue, *The Moralists*.

---

[15] Quoted in Christopher Ricks, *The Force of Poetry* (Oxford: Oxford University Press, 1987), pp. 183–184.
[16] A. O. Aldridge, "Lord Shaftesbury's Literary Theories," *Philological Quarterly* 24 (1945) 49, 53.

Genre as political and religious vocabulary

Eighteenth-century readers were alert to the arguments Shaftesbury carried out through a discussion of genres, just as they were alarmed by the inconsistencies in his *Characteristics*. In *Bart'lemy Fair, or an Enquiry after Wit* (1709), Mary Astell derides Shaftesbury for his defense of mixed, comic forms:

> I shou'd now fall into a Method, define Wit, describe it by infallible Characters ... But let it be remember'd, that it is the very Essence of Wit to be out of Rule, and above all Measure ... Besides, Method is a Restraint, not to be suffer'd by Free Writers in a *Free Nation*. So Free that not anything is sacred enough to be Privileg'd; not our Laws, nor our Religion, not our Sovereign, nor our GOD.[17]

Wits like Shaftesbury are no more concerned with methodical treatment than they are with the laws of the nation, the sanctity of established religion, the authority of the king or queen, or even the being of God. Indeed, *only* someone who sought to depose state, sovereign, and God would dare discompose so freely. Astell identifies Shaftesbury as a foe of the High Church, a republican, an anarchic defender of the regicide and Commonwealth, and a libertine. Other readers, including John Brown, viewed Shaftesbury's non-systematic exposition as part of a political position. "It has been the Fate of Lord Shaftesbury's *Characteristics*, beyond that of most other Books, to be idolized by one party, and detested by another."[18] Brown, writing in 1751, urges his readers to remember that "At the Period when our Author wrote [persecution] not only revived but was heightened by a terrible Accession of Bitterness and Rancour." Although his main purpose is to attack Shaftesbury, Brown acknowledges that the unsystematic, haphazard organization of *Characteristics* entailed a political position, a defense of "Truth and Liberty" against those who would "deprive others of the common Privilege [freedom of expression] which they had so nobly exercized themselves."[19]

In Shaftesbury's own defense of the *Letter concerning Enthusiasm*, the connections between genre and systems of social and political power are made quite explicit. The discussion of the *Letter* in *Miscellaneous Reflections* moves immediately to a defense of the epistolary form. Shaftesbury takes aim at one attack in particular, that of a critic he identifies as French Catholic, who complained that "*Ses pensees ne semblent occuper dans son Ouvrage que la place que le hazard leur a donneé*" – in his work his thoughts seem not to occupy any order other than what chance has given them (III, p. 18).[20] For Shaftesbury, the

---

[17] Astell, *Bart'lemy Fair*, pp. 18–19; Astell accused Shaftesbury of "the saving of Men's Sense, by the Damning of their Souls!" (p. 23).

[18] John Brown, *Essays on the Characteristics of the Earl of Shaftesbury* (London: C. Davis, 1751: rprt. Hildesheim and New York: Georg Olms Verlag, 1969), pp. 1–2.

[19] *Ibid.*, p. 3.

[20] Shaftesbury, *Characteristicks of Men, Manners, Opinions, Times*, 3 vols., 6th edn. corrected (London: James Purser, 1737). All citations from *Characteristicks* refer to this edition and will be given by volume and page number in my text.

Catholic's insistence on order betrays a fundamental failure of his critical method. He insists that "they who wou'd neither observe this [that the *Letter* was addressed to a great man] nor apprehend the Letter it-self to be *real*, were insufficient Criticks, and unqualify'd to judg of the Turn or Humour of a Piece which they never consider'd in a proper light" (III, p. 19). Inadequate criticism fails to read the work in its proper light, that is, according to the conventions governing the genre to which it belongs. Shaftesbury argues that the writing of an actual letter frees him from the received organizational precepts of the treatise. As if to underline the fact that this insistence upon order is a particularly Catholic failing, Shaftesbury cites the response of a French Protestant critic to the same work. This critic observes that "*l'Auteur ne s'y est pas proposé un certain plan pour traiter sa matiere methodiquement; parceque c'est une Lettre, et non un Traité*" (III, p. 20, n. 1) – the author does not propose a specific plan for the methodical treatment of his subject because it is a letter and not a treatise.

Why this insistence? Why attack an obscure, specifically Catholic critic for his insensitivity to literary form when more formidable critics closer to home were lambasting the concept of ridicule itself? Further, why delay comment on the crucial question raised by the *Letter*, the value of ridicule as a test of truth, in favor of a seemingly peripheral discussion of genre? In *The Figure of Theater*, David Marshall argues that Shaftesbury's insistence on calling his text a letter derives from a wish to deny "the public character of the book and remove the author from the stage of the world."[21] He continues: "Shaftesbury formulates this rhetorical strategy precisely *because* his text will appear before the eyes of the world. This is a prospect that Shaftesbury will not admit ... the *Letter* provides a formula which by definition keeps readers in their place: outside the text's address." Marshall's assessment captures Shaftesbury's ambivalent feelings about publication, his participation in what Alvin Kernan has called "an old courtly order of letters, in its last neoclassical mode, in England in the first half of the eighteenth century."[22] But Marshall simplifies the problem by ignoring the political basis of Shaftesbury's frequent recourse to genre criticism.

The significance of distinctions among genres begins for Shaftesbury with the view that texts are types of social institutions and thus share the problems of other political structures. The Fifth Miscellany of *Miscellaneous Reflections* begins with this observation:

Of all the artificial Relations form'd between Mankind, the most capricious and variable is that of *Author* and *Reader*. And tho ... every *Author in Form*, is, in respect of the particular matter he explains, superior in Understanding to his *Reader*, [yet no] Author

[21] Marshall, *The Figure of Theater: Shaftesbury, Defoe, Adam Smith, and George Eliot* (New York: Columbia University Press, 1986), p. 25.
[22] Kernan, *Printing Technology, Letters, and Samuel Johnson* (Princeton: Princeton University Press, 1987), pp. 8–9.

should assume the upper hand, or pretend to withdraw himself from that necessary Subjection to foreign Judgment and Criticism, which must determine the Place of Honour on the Reader's side.   (III, pp. 227–228)

Texts, like "all relations," imply a system of hierarchy and power. To some extent, of course, it is the writer's prerogative to assume and enhance his or her authority: the author takes the active part and is superior in understanding. But this superiority extends only to the particular matter under discussion. The problem is that writing generalizes the advantage, setting the activity of textual production above that of reception, quite apart from the particular matter in question. In addition to indicting "the commercial relations between professional authors and the reading public,"[23] Shaftesbury likens writers to sovereigns who must be held accountable for the way they exercise authority over the public.

In this view of literary works as systems of hierarchy and concealment, Shaftesbury seems close to critics influenced by Nietzsche and Foucault, who argue that all texts conceal their ideological commitments and are coercive of readers. He differs fundamentally, however, in attempting to distinguish among different constitutions of power created by different kinds of writing. Just as some social institutions (constitutional monarchy, liberal Protestantism) seemed to Shaftesbury more equitable than others (absolute monarchy, Roman Catholicism), so certain textual institutions, or genres, go further than others in promoting "that necessary subjection to foreign Judgment and Criticism." The observation that both democracies and monarchies are essentially systems of power would make as little sense to Shaftesbury as would the claim that a skeptical dialogue and a writ of execution are the same.

As Shaftesbury's emphasis upon a "necessary subjection to foreign Judgment or Criticism" indicates, the defense of the reader and of formally inclusive genres such as the letter, dialogue, and miscellany derives from a more general concept of criticism. As I shall argue, however, the priority of criticism eventually leads the radical side of Shaftesbury to defend genres whose cultural implications are anathema to the lord aesthete. Shaftesbury's attack on the treatise, on received forms of discursive rule in general, is shaped by concern over factional unrest in England at the turn of the century. The terms with which Shaftesbury characterizes this climate make it clear why criticism becomes so important. Consider, for instance, the sardonic comment with which Shaftesbury, writing in the persona of a "secular GENTLEMAN," closes *Characteristics*:

in the midst of this irreconcilable Debate concerning heavenly *Authoritys* and *Powers*, we shou'd be as confident of the Veracity of *some one*, as of the Imposter and Cheat of

---

[23] Marshall, *The Figure of Theatre*, p. 26.

all the other Pretenders: and that, believing firmly there is still *A real* COMMISSION at
the bottom, we shou'd endure the misery of these Conflicts, and engage on one side
or the other, as we happen to have our Birth or Education; till by *Fire* and *Sword*,
Execution, Massacre, and a kind of *Depopulation* of this Earth, it be determin'd amongst
us, "Which is the *true* COMMISSION, *exclusive* of all others, and superior to the rest."

(III, p. 343)

Rather than take the multiplicity of claims to the "true commission" as
evidence for the non-existence of any single hot line to the absolute, the mad
projectors radicalize their views and entrench themselves within forms that
enforce their differences from others, forms amenable to hints of divine
intervention and of the possibly violent consequences of disagreement.

For Shaftesbury no difference in doctrinal position was as significant as the
general sameness of rhetoric marking "these conflicts." Thus, criticism
develops within a violent political climate in order to reveal the rhetorical
redundancy of seemingly distinct doctrines. The birth of criticism out of
faction is portrayed explicitly at the beginning of *The Moralists*. After both
Theocles and Philocles agree that there exists a certain harmony between
atheism and zeal, Theocles is asked to explain. Philocles says, "Here then
began his Criticism of Authors, which grew by degrees into a continu'd
Discourse" (II, p. 258). The introduction of criticism into the dialogue occurs
at the point where Theocles must explain why seemingly opposite *ideas* are
fundamentally the same. The scene is indicative of the general movement of
Shaftesbury's defense of criticism: discussion of extreme positions (atheism,
religious zeal) is displaced onto the more tractable plane of a "criticism of
authors" where stylistic comparisons (such as that between the treatise and
the feigned letter) take the place of direct polemics.

The terms of Shaftesbury's defense of criticism raise an obvious problem.
It is one thing to argue, as Shaftesbury does, that factional disputes need to
be addressed through rhetorical analysis and that criticism can point out the
error of magisterial styles. But it is something else altogether to aver, as
Shaftesbury often seems to, that criticism is important because no belief is
ever so true that it should command uncritical acceptance. Mary Astell was
quite right, in other words, to suspect that Shaftesbury's defense of criticism
moves in the direction of philosophical relativism, political anarchy, and
religious heterodoxy. It is fine for Shaftesbury to burlesque the sacred pens
and divine styles of obvious phonies, but his method of critique, a principled
defense of criticism and the need to test truth-claims against the caustic of
ridicule, does not distinguish – or threatens not to distinguish – between true
prophecy (for example, Scriptures) and the babblings of French prophets.

This problem of critical relativism becomes clearest in the last sections of
Miscellaneous Reflections, where Shaftesbury takes up the issue of religious
writing directly. We have already seen that the "capricious" and "arbitrary"
relation between writer and reader calls for works that question the bases of

their own authority. In *Miscellaneous Reflections* Shaftesbury adds the more disturbing view that language itself, as a system of invented signs, involves the writer in "the Mechanick rules of *human arbitrary* Composition," in a language formed by *"human Arbitration"* and thus always enmeshed within contingent desires and interests (III, p. 229). It is the very arbitrariness of language, its difference from a script "deliver'd down from Heaven," that makes critical interpretation less something appended to a completed text and more something already involved in the creation and use of language. The claim that some inspired texts escape the contamination of a mundane, human origin and thus stand beyond criticism, Shaftesbury calls "plainly . . . no other than mere ENTHUSIASM' (III, p. 231).

To say the least, such a view is not exactly conducive to reading in the spirit of prophecy. If criticism reminds the reader of the contingent character of language, prophetic discourse seeks the opposite – a forgetfulness of linguistic form in the full apprehension of spiritual meaning. Expressed in these terms, the implication of Shaftesbury's defense of criticism is a complete desanctification of sacred Scripture. After all, the content of the Bible, however conveyed to its scribes, was no doubt communicated and passed down through human languages. Shaftesbury is not comfortable with this implication and grows evasive (though not evasive enough to avoid giving a "hint" to one of Berkeley's atheists in the dialogue *Alciphron*).[24] He seems to make an exception for instances "where *the supreme Powers* have given their Sanction to any *Religious Record*, or pious *Writ*," in which case it becomes "immoral and profane in any one, to deny absolutely or dispute the *sacred Authority* of the least Line or Syllable contain'd in it." Then he adds:

But should *the Record*, instead of being *single*, *short*, and *uniform*, appear to be *multifarious*, *voluminous*, and of *the most difficult Interpretation*, it wou'd be somewhat hard, if not wholly impracticable in the Magistrate, to suffer this Record to be *universally current*, and at the same time prevent its being *variously apprehended* and *descanted on* by the several *differing Genius's* and *contrary Judgments* of Mankind.   (III, p. 231)

And what record regarding religious tradition is not "multifarious"? According to this concession, the long history of Church debate and the Bible

---

[24] In making Shaftesbury one of the favored authors of the atheists in his own dialogue, *Alciphron, or the Minute Philosopher* (1732), Berkeley drew attention to just this problem. In the Sixth Dialogue, the milder of the two atheists, Alciphron, argues with the theists, Crito and Euphranor, over the value of transmitted texts as a basis for divine faith. Crito claims that "things once committed to writing are secure from slips of memory," and thus provide a certain basis for faith. Alciphron replies that the parishioner "believes in his parson and not in God," that the reader of the Bible has faith in the "printers, editor, and transcriber, none of which can with any pretence be called divine." Alciphron then indicates the source of his argument: "I had the hint from Cratylus; it is a shaft out of his quiver, and believe me, a keen one" (III, pp. 223–224). The shaft, of course, belongs to Shaftesbury. Unless otherwise noted all citations of Berkeley refer to *The Works of George Berkeley, Bishop of Cloyne*, eds. A. A. Luce and T. E. Jessop, 9 vols. (London: Thomas Nelson and Sons Ltd., 1949).

itself (which Shaftesbury describes as a miscellany) become the best
refutations of what Church debate and the Bible had hoped to accomplish!
Shaftesbury's sudden, pre-critical respect for the decrees of supreme powers
sounds somewhat disingenuous. Granted, the assertion that criticism must
remain active even within the realm of religious discussion is mainly meant
as an attack on Catholicism, which scruples "to annex the Supreme
Authority and Sacred Character of Infallibility to SCRIPTURE it-self" (III,
p. 235); however, given the critical principles Shaftesbury articulates above,
it is difficult to see why criticism should confine itself to an attack on the
sacred truths of Catholicism – why, that is, any religion, including the
Protestant, should find itself exempt from a proto-Nietzschean (though it is
actually neo-Hobbesian) reduction of transcendent values to mundane
interests.

When, for instance, Shaftesbury defends himself against the objection that
his plea for toleration opens the door to irreligion and political anarchy, he
explains

had he [his antagonist] happen'd to be in a Nation where he was no *Conformist*, nor
had any Hope or Expectation of attaining the Precedency for his *own* Manner of
Worship, he wou'd have found nothing preposterous in this our Doctrine of *Indulgence*
... The Mystery therefore of this Animosity or rising Indignation of my devout and
zealous *Reader* is only this; "That being *devoted* to the Interest of A PARTY already in
possession or expectation of the temporal Advantages annex'd to a particular Belief;
he fails not, as a zealous *Party-Man*, to look with jealousy on every unconformable
Opinion, and is sure to justify those *Means* which he thinks proper to prevent its
growth."
(III, pp. 110–111)

Was this an argument likely to calm the outrage of devout readers like Mary
Astell or to impress people with the author's polite manners? Shaftesbury
merely explains that the beliefs the reader took for truth are motivated by
material self-interests and might have been different at another time or in
another country. Here the purpose of criticism, much like that of cultural
materialism today, is to annex supposedly transhistorical values to mundane,
temporal interests. Although the critique may have been aimed at the zealous
party-men of all sides, it is difficult to see why its scope should be limited only
to extreme beliefs. Would it not be possible to insist that the values of
moderation and tolerance were themselves annexed to the expectation of
temporal advantage? Such is the charge of a butcher sympathetic to Dr.
Sacheverell in the dialogue "Both Sides Pleas'd" (1710): "a moderate man I
take to be a great Lover of the Dissenters, and of a Common-Wealth, and,
therefore, an Enemy of both Church and Queen."[25] The point here is not so
much whether or not belief in religious toleration is truer or more selfless

---

[25] "Both Sides Pleas'd", p. 6.

than its opposite; rather, it is whether the concept of criticism deployed to defend that position does not undermine settled beliefs of all sorts by reducing them to expressions of self-interest. Shaftesbury no doubt thought that his views about toleration were not similarly annexed; but how he was to escape the grasp of his own relativism becomes a difficult problem.

The radical aesthete: between miscellany and plastic arts

The reader who is familiar with Shaftesbury's writings and their reception may at this point register a complaint of the following sort: while it is certainly true that many passages of *Characteristics* suggest the radical understanding of criticism outlined above, I have unfairly exaggerated their significance to the exclusion of numerous statements that counteract them and for which Shaftesbury has come to be best known. The doctrines of an innate moral sense, of an aesthetic standard of moral judgment, and of the enthusiastic apprehension of providential design in nature, for instance, are central to most of Shaftesbury's writings and imply a philosophical faith that seems contrary to the implications I have drawn from Shaftesbury's defense of criticism.[26] Further, I have made no allowance for the trajectory of Shaftesbury's development, which, according to his most recent biographer, moves away from the skeptical deism of the *Letter* and towards the rhapsodic faith found late in *The Moralists* and throughout his late essays on the fine arts.[27] This faith was of the sort that could find, even in a tract on manure, an "inexpressible Satisfaction in these sorts of Speculations; that with their help in this Country-Retirement I can converse more intimately with Nature; view the greatness of her Design and Execution, & in the Simplicity and Uniformity of her Operations descry that Sovereign Hand that guides & governs all, with infinite Wisdom and Bounty."[28] My antagonist would seem justified in pointing out that belief in a "sovereign hand that guides and governs all" was hardly a notion to which Shaftesbury always applied the caustic of ridicule. Finally, it must also be observed that Shaftesbury's mockery of a transparent language "delivered from heaven" is contradicted by numerous passages throughout his writings. "No *Poet*," he tells Somers in the *Letter*, "can do anything great in his own way, without the Imagination or

---

[26] For the relation of Shaftesbury to moral sense philosophy, see William Alderman, "Shaftesbury and the Doctrine of the Moral Sense in the Eighteenth Century," *PMLA* 46 (1931) 1087–1095; for Shaftesbury and the equation of beauty and truth, see the following: John Andrew Bernstein, "Shaftesbury's Identification of the Good with the Beautiful," *Eighteenth-Century Studies* 10 (1977): 304–325; Ernst Tuveson, "The Importance of Shaftesbury," *ELH* 20 (1953) 267–299. And for Shaftesbury's relation to the design argument and enthusiasm, see Stanley Grean, *Shaftesbury's Philosophy of Religion and Ethics: a Study in Enthusiasm* (Ohio: Ohio University Press, 1967).

[27] See Robert Voitle, *The Third Earl of Shaftesbury, 1671–1713* (Baton Rouge: Louisiana University Press, 1984), pp. 348ff.

[28] Quoted *ibid.*, p. 266.

Supposition of a *Divine Presence* ... So that *Inspiration* may be justly call'd *Divine* ENTHUSIASM: For the Word it-self signifies *Divine Presence*" (I, pp. 51, 53). Nothing would seem further from Shaftesbury's thoughts here than the annexation of divine presence to private need. Where in the preceding analysis of Shaftesbury's suspicion of texts have I allowed for the values he held to be beyond suspicion?

The aim of this chapter is not, however, to interpret Shaftesbury's central contribution to the history of philosophy or aesthetics or to establish his responsibility for a hegemonic order – procedures whose main drawback, as Quentin Skinner has argued, is anachronism.[29] Rather, I am arguing that Shaftesbury is most representative because he generates two contradictory schemes for the evaluation of literary genres. It is altogether true that Shaftesbury judges artistic productions according to standards drawn from his beloved ancients – standards that value unity, scope, and the just subordination of part to whole. "If he [the artist] has not the least Idea of PERFECTION to give him Aim," Shaftesbury writes in *Advice to an Author*, "he will be found very defective and mean in his Performance" (I, p. 332). Surely this idea is not to be drawn by attending to the reader or immediate circumstances. The writer's accommodation to an expanding, increasingly heterogeneous reading public threatens the notion of a perfect performance, whose model, after all, must be found elsewhere. "Tho his Intention be to please the World, he must nevertheless be, in a manner, *above* it; and fix his Eye upon that consummate *Grace*, that Beauty of *Nature*, and that Perfection of *Numbers*, which the rest of Mankind, feeling only by the Effect, whilst ignorant of the Cause, term the *je-ne-sçay-quoy* [*sic*]" (I, p. 332). The artist who departs from eternal standards of taste, proportion, and symmetry composes an illegitimate piece, a bastardized composite, an immoral work.

Yet, as I argue above, the skeptical side of Shaftesbury generates different grounds for the evaluation of texts. The priority Shaftesbury assigns to criticism, ridicule, toleration, and a more egalitarian pedagogy leads also to a defense of mixed and low genres. The doctrine of ridicule, for instance, accompanies a defense of satiric, parodic, and comic genres: "the only Manner left," he writes, "in which Criticism can have its just Force amongst us, is the *antient* COMICK; of which kind were the first *Roman* Miscellany or

---

[29] See Quentin Skinner, "Meaning and Understanding in the History of Ideas," *History and Theory* 7 (1969) 3–53. Skinner criticizes Cassirer's view that "Shaftesbury's treatment of the theodicy problem is notable because it 'in a certain sense anticipated Kant'" (11). But his attack is less against any single historian and more against historiographical methods that trade in one way or another upon the notion of an "anticipation," that is, upon an anachronistic reading of the past in terms of a future conceived as the goal towards which the past was all along striving. I believe this critique is as applicable to Cassirer as it is to Eagleton. Whether we view Shaftesbury as an anticipation of Kantian aesthetics or as the progenitor of the bourgeois social order, historical narration becomes an easier matter, removed from a detailed engagement with the complexities, the contradictions, the multi-valencies of texts. The genre-based history offered here attempts to resist this reductiveness.

Satirick Pieces" (I, p. 258). Here he elevates the miscellany and satire; elsewhere Shaftesbury defends burlesque and the parodic novel. These forms are valued for their active agency in the world. They effect change through parody of outmoded values, through a more easy and familiar dissemination of cultural knowledge, and through a textual model of inclusiveness that replicates and encourages new patterns of social transformation.[30] The exemplary artist in this case is not the virtuoso who has set himself "in a manner" above the world. He is instead the "counter-pedagogue" who, if necessary, *violates* order and proportion for the sake of criticizing false values. "Had I been a *Spanish* CERVANTES, and with success equal to that comick Author, had destroy'd the reigning Taste of *Gothick* or *Moorish* CHIVALRY, I cou'd afterwards contentedly have seen my *Burlesque*-Work it-self despis'd and set aside; when it had wrought its intended effect, and destroy'd those *Giants* and *Monsters* of the Brain, against which it was originally design'd" (III, 253). Shaftesbury likens himself to Cervantes in order to explain why his own writings ("these my Miscellaneous Works") are so mixed, why the champion of classical unity is himself a "*mere* comick Humourist" and compositor of "*Prose-Satir.*"

Two senses of criticism, therefore, filter through Shaftesbury's writings. On the one hand, criticism is roughly synonymous with skepticism or secular reason: it challenges ensconced authority, whether in texts or in social institutions. On the other hand, criticism entails the derivation of rules for poetic composition and moral order from the most approved performances of the ancients. While it is true that "criticism" was routinely understood to have had more than one definition at this time, the tension between two different operations – one idealizing and the other materializing, one based upon abstracting to generalities and the other based upon dividing into parts, one providing the basis for a philosophical faith, and the other serving a secular historicism – permeates all of Shaftesbury's writings.[31] The odd

---

[30] These genres correspond with the forms Habermas discusses in his analysis of the "social structures of the public sphere" in *The Structural Transformation of the Public Sphere*. Such forms of cultural mediation, together with the public institutions with which they were associated, – the coffee-house, salon, and *Tischgesellschaft* – promoted "an equality and association among persons of unequal social status." Habermas continues, "there was scarce a great writer of the eighteenth century who would not have first submitted his essential ideas for discussion in such discourse, in lectures before the academies and in salons. The salon held the monopoly of first publication: a new work, even a musical one, had to legitimate itself first in this forum" (Habermas, *The Structural Transformation of the Public Sphere* p. 34.)

[31] James Harris, Shaftesbury's nephew and disciple, defined no fewer than four senses of criticism alive in his day. He lists these in order of descending importance:
   (1) philosophical criticism, establishing the "general Rules of Art, either for judgment or for writing, confirmed by the example not of one Author, but of many";
   (2) historical criticism, describing contingent features of "Languages, Customs, Manners, Laws, Governments, and Religions" altering over time;
   (3) authoritative criticism, supplying the best texts through scholarship, collation, and editing;

agglomeration of arguments and artistic elements in *Characteristics* should be understood in these terms, not, I would claim, as the articulation of a single master metaphor (for example, "politeness") or as the expression of a nascent ideology, but as a scene of contestation where the period's most representative (if antagonistic) values are brought into proximity.

Once again, Shaftesbury's early readers were alert to just this feature of his *Characteristics*, and it impressed them not with the author's politeness, but with his confusion and evasiveness. John Brown accused Shaftesbury of "frequently affecting a mixture of solemn praise and low Buffoonry; not only in the same Tract, but in the same Paragraph." And he continues:

We have seen the noble Writer assuming the Character of a professed Dogmatist, the Reasoner in Form ... [but] concerning Revealed Religion and Christianity, we shall find him chiefly affecting the *miscellaneous* Capacity; the Way of Chat, Raillery, Innuendo, or Story-telling: In a word, that very Species of the present modish Composition, which he so contemptuously ridicules [he also treats] as the Man in the Fable did his Pears; unconscious he should be ever afterwards reduced to diet on them himself."[32]

Brown plays Shaftesbury at his own game by taking issue with his treatment of a genre, knowing that political and religious values are bound up in the affirmation and rejection of literary forms. He focuses upon the miscellany because it is here that the split in Shaftesbury's identity and in his political philosophy becomes most evident.

In that Shaftesbury frequently asserts his "Privilege as a MISCELLA-NEOUS or ESSAY-*Writer*" (III, p. 132), one would think his praise of the miscellany would be unmixed. It begins this way: "Peace be with the Soul of that charitable and courteous Author who ... introduc'd the ingenious way of MISCELLANEOUS Writing!" (III, p. 1). Miscellany has "increased the harvest of wit"; it has undermined the severe and rigid conditions prescribed by the treatise; it has enlarged the spiritual freedom of mankind; it has enabled the learned to convey their knowledge to "the rude *Taste* of unpolish'd Mankind" (III, p. 3). Miscellany, like satire and parody, is valued for its active agency in the world. Its formal inclusiveness captures the

---

(4) and conjectural criticism (which Harris also calls "critical Quackery"), mending the lacunae in old manuscripts with speculative additions.

Harris wrote that Shaftesbury offered the last preeminent instance of the first and most important kind of criticism, ancient and philosophical. I am arguing that Shaftesbury also offers one of the first preeminent instances of the second kind of criticism, modern and historical. For Harris philosophical criticism represents the first and highest activity of the critic. The contamination of classical texts through historical transmission necessitates the appearance of other kinds of critics, but these must never usurp the first position. That is why Harris does not dignify with a category yet a fifth and lowest class of critics that has appeared in his own day, "an adventurous race (those I mean who scribble for pay upon every kind of subject)." Harris, *Upon the Rise and Progress of Criticism* [1752]; rprt. (New York: Garland Publications Inc., 1971), pp. 5–16.

[32] John Brown, *Essays on the Characteristics*, pp. 244–245, 242.

undirected energy of a society increasingly mobile, mixed, and impervious to received structures of subordination.

Yet, as Brown suggests, Shaftesbury also laments the loss of Neoclassical standards and mocks "that very Species of the present modish Composition." When narrating the origin of miscellany at the beginning of *Miscellaneous Reflections*, the patrician lord reasserts himself:

The primitive Authors perhaps being few in number, and highly respected for their Art, fell under the weight of *Envy*. Being sensible of their Misfortune in this respect, and being excited, as 'tis probable, by the Example of some popular Genius; they quitted their regular Schemes and accurate Forms of Workmanship, in favour of those *Wits* who cou'd not possibly be receiv'd as AUTHORS upon such difficult Terms ... And nothing cou'd better serve this popular purpose, than the way of MISCELLANY, or *common* ESSAY; in which the most confus'd Head, if fraught with a little Invention and provided with *Common-place-Book* Learning, might exert it-self to as much advantage, as the most orderly and well-settled Judgment.

(III, pp. 3–4)

Miscellany is now being judged by a different standard. Writers of miscellany now appear to violate nature's own order.

So which is it? Are we to believe Shaftesbury when he writes that essay writers or miscellanarians "may plead as their peculiar Advantage, That they follow the *Variety* of NATURE" (III, p. 95); or should we credit his claim that writers of miscellany, like "certain *Grotesque*-Painters ... keep as far from Nature as possible?" (III, p. 6) Shaftesbury's indecision about the status of miscellany is understandable: to the extent that he continued his analogy between political institutions and artistic forms, the defense of miscellany was tantamount to a leveling openness to social differences, something the patrician lord was hardly prepared to accept; to the extent that he called miscellany an accurate imitation of nature, he abandoned the Augustan view that nature, when imitated most faithfully, revealed general properties over particulars, coherence rather than disorder.

The larger eighteenth-century context for this split conception of criticism is a fissure within the rhetorical tradition itself, brought into the open early in the period through the spread of literacy, the accessibility of all kinds of printed material, and the empowerment of a middle class not privy to a classical education. Students trained within the rhetorical tradition had always been told to accommodate their speeches to the anticipated character of their audiences. This skill was part of rhetoric's traditional concern for both disposition and invention – the accommodation of oratory to the changing characteristics of different audiences. As Gregory Clark has asserted, the rhetorical tradition was never concerned merely with the manipulation of discourse to compel the assent of audiences. It was as much a practice of discursive adjustment through a kind of contract between speaker and audience, as it was an art of verbal manipulation. On this view, Aristotle's definition of rhetoric as "the faculty of observing in any given case the available means of persuasion" requires rhetoric to include, to some extent, a sociology of audience.[33] Clark goes so far as to argue that the principle of accommodation asks the rhetor to "function as but one voice in a pluralistic process of collaborative exchange through which a community of equals discover and validate what they can collectively consider true."[34] In this respect, traditional rhetoric could be said to promote democracy and pluralism.[35]

But rhetorical accommodation held an increasingly strained relation with another imperative of a sound rhetorical performance – namely, coherence. An equally prominent part of traditional rhetoric *minimized* differences within audiences in order to stress the universal patterns of response a rhetor could be confident of triggering through crafted speech and imitation of received models. How else could the rhetor's practice provide the basis for marketable handbooks and courses, unless one assumed predictable responses of audiences to teachable strategies? Even (and especially) when literate audiences became more diverse, it was not in the interest of rhetorical guides to foster an overly precise sociology of audience, for that might well put them out of business.[36] By the beginning of the eighteenth century the conflict between accommodation and coherence issued in works such as *Characteristics*, in which continuity with earlier canons of order, asserted only on the level of thematic content, was not supported by literary performance.

John Brown was alert to just this predicament. He calls Shaftesbury a defender of "the present modish Composition," though he knows that Shaftesbury despised the novel in literate culture. However much Shaftesbury may have defended the miscellaneous air when dodging charges of explicit

---

[33] Aristotle, *The Complete Works of Aristotle*, ii, p. 2155 (*Rhetoric* 2, 1355b 27–28).

[34] Gregory Clark, *Dialogue, Dialectic, and Conversation: a Social Perspective on the Function of Writing* (Carbondale and Edwardsville: Southern Illinois University Press, 1990), p. 21.

[35] On the democratic potential of traditional rhetoric, George A. Kennedy observes, "the creation of rhetorical handbooks and the claims of sophists to teach rhetoric made the art vulnerable to criticism. Bold claims about the role of the orator and the power of speech replaced tacit assumptions about aristocratic leaders, and rhetoric could now be learned by anyone interested. Intimately involved with democracy, it awakened the hostility of oligarchs." *Classical Rhetoric and Its Christian and Secular Tradition from Ancient to Modern Times* (Chapel Hill: The University of North Carolina Press, 1980), p. 41.

[36] A striking example of the conflict within rhetorical theory between accommodation and coherence can be found in George Campbell's *Philosophy of Rhetoric* of 1776. Campbell devotes twenty-four pages to "the Consideration which the Speaker ought to have of the Hearers as Men in General," but when he turns to "the consideration which the Speaker ought to have of the Hearers as Men in Particular," he writes only one page. The idealized conception of a uniform audience allows Campbell to describe how persuasive oratory appeals to common psychological habits, shared passions, and uniform tastes. But when he comes to specifics, there's nothing to say except that "the characters of audiences may be infinitely diversified," but that a "person of discernment" will know how to meet the challenge. George Campbell, *The Philosophy of Rhetoric*, ed. Lloyd Bitzer (Carbondale and Edwardsville: Southern Illinois University Press, 1963), pp. 71–95, 95–96.

atheism or deism, he had no doubt what the effect would be if writers really
did heed the needs of common readers:

Our modern Authors are turn'd and model'd (as themselves confess) by the publick
Relish and current Humour of the Times. They regulate themselves by the irregular
Fancy of the World; and frankly own they are preposterous and absurd, in order to
accommodate themselves to the Genius of the Age. In our Days *the Audience* makes *the
Poet*; and *the Bookseller the Author*: with what Profit to *the Publick*, or what Prospect of
lasting Fame and Honour to *the Writer*, let any one who has Judgment imagine ...
Nor have we any [author], whom by mutual Consent we make to be our *Standard*. We
read *Epicks* and *Dramaticks* as we do *Satires* and *Lampoons*. For we must of necessity
know what *Wit* as well as what *Scandal* is stirring.   (I, pp. 264–265)

Having advised the writer to consider the requirements of the reader,
Shaftesbury now finds himself attacking a literary marketplace based upon
that very principle: writers in the first decade of the eighteenth century now
make "an exact Calculation in the way of Trade [and] feed us thus from
hand to mouth; resolving not to over-stock the Market, or be at pains of
more Correctness or Wit than is absolutely necessary to carry on the
Traffick" (I, p. 265). The result, in Shaftesbury's words, is literature that is
trivial, brutish, indulgent, scurrilous, prostituting, fulsome, abandoned,
sterile, degraded, deformed. Having offered a philosophical defense of low,
parodic, popular genres, Shaftesbury now disparages these as signs of
degraded taste.

One reason for the violence of the attack is that Shaftesbury felt his own
writings slipping away from the canons of classical simplicity he so much
admired. He was, after all, the author of one of the most miscellaneous
collections of philosophical, literary, political, ethical, and historical observations written during the period. And, speaking of himself in *Miscellaneous
Reflections*, he has to admit that "as high as our Author in his *critical* Capacity,
wou'd pretend to carry the refined Manner and accurate SIMPLICITY of
the Ancients; he dares not, in his own Model and principal Performance,
attempt to unite his Philosophy in one solid and uniform Body, nor carry on
his Argument in *one* continu'd Chain or Thred" (III, pp. 286–287). He dares
not, presumably, because no one outside his elite circle would choose to
read it. "The Way of Form and METHOD," Shaftesbury observes, "the
didactic or *preceptive* Manner ... has so little force towards winning our
Attention, that it is apter to tire us than the Metre of an old Ballad" (I, p.
258). When, in other words, Shaftesbury puts into effect his "adjustment"
between writer and reader, accommodating his own texts to the modern
reader – literate but uneducated, easily seduced by powerful images, bored
by preceptively administered knowledge – he ends up writing a book that
resembles the thing he despises. In all of the positive attempts to define the
"rise" of the novel, have we perhaps overlooked a body of writers who

become reluctant theorists of the novel? I return to this question at the end of the next chapter.

Shaftesbury's dilemma has been described by J. Paul Hunter with reference to the entire field of literary production early in the eighteenth century. "Mixing and additiveness," he explains, "characterized available materials, [produced] a larger generic uncertainty and anxiety about textual direction, [and] gave even the most ambitious and formal texts a seeming randomness and lack of governing certainty."[37] Such are the preconditions of the novel; these were not, however, conditions acceptable to Lord Shaftesbury. Once he has drawn political analogies between genres and institutions, equating mixed genres with a desirable solution to political absolutism, Shaftesbury must decide to what extent he really intends to promote legitimate "mixing" in both a formal and political sense. Similarly, once he has established theological analogies between magisterial modes and schismatic debate, prescribing comic forms as a cure for textual absolutism, Shaftesbury must decide how forms mixed on principle might still convey the assertion of ultimate (providential) coherence. Having defended the role of the reader and having advocated a range of dialogic and comic genres, Shaftesbury must respond to an increasing diversity of value and randomness of artistic structure within literate culture. Unlike Pope and Swift, who are able to demonize these forces of change through metaphors of war and madness, dullness and chaos, the enemy Shaftesbury faces, a hydra of his own creation, cannot be so easily scotched.

To some extent, Shaftesbury solves this problem through outright retraction. Although he seems to defend freedom of speech and toleration of difference in his assertion that all received ideas should be subject to the test of ridicule, Shaftesbury adds later that the freedom he had in mind was limited to "Liberty in private Conversation, and under prudent Management ... the liberty of *the Club*, and of that sort of Freedom which is taken amongst *Gentlemen* and *Friends*, who know one another perfectly well. And that 'tis natural for me to defend Liberty with this restriction, you may infer from the very Notion I have of Liberty it-self" (I, p. 75). Shaftesbury's restriction bears out Habermas' observation that the promulgation of Enlightenment "had a dialectical character. Reason, which through public use of the rational faculty was to be realized in the rational communication of a public consisting of [equal] human beings, itself needed to be protected from becoming public because it was a threat to any and all relations of domination."[38] From open discussion to closed club, from miscellaneous inclusion to the decorous conversation of gentlemen, the tendencies of Shaftesbury's critical side must constantly be checked by seemingly opposite claims. He must conclude that

---

[37] J. Paul Hunter, *Before Novels: the Cultural Contexts of Eighteenth-Century English Fiction* (New York and London: W. W. Norton & Co., 1990), p. 86.

[38] Habermas, *The Structural Transformation of the Public Sphere*, p. 35.

"what is contrary to good Breeding, is in this respect as contrary to Liberty" (I, p. 76). And while it might be possible to take this recourse to politeness as Shaftesbury's final solution, one would have to forget that he also rejects "the invidious Distinctions of *Bastardy* and *Legitimacy*, [which] being at length remov'd; the natural and lawful Issue of the Brain comes with like Advantage into the World: And *Wit* (*mere* W I T) is well receiv'd; without examination of *the Kind*, or Censure of *the Form*" (III, p. 2).

Unwilling to bank on a philosophically suspect concept of politeness, Shaftesbury attempted to heal his split identity in two ways, both decisive for the subsequent philosophical and literary history of the eighteenth century. The first, which I shall discuss in the remainder of this chapter, is the development of the distinctive vocabulary of philosophical aesthetics (four decades before Baumgarten). The second, which I shall discuss in the following chapter, is the renovation of philosophical dialogue as a means of both representing and reconciling his divided allegiances, a development in philosophical writing that provided one blueprint for the emerging novel.

Plastics; or the emergence of philosophical aesthetics

Shaftesbury's struggle between inclusive and exclusive standards repeats on the level of literary form what for Milton had been the problem of theodicy. The epic poet's attempt to justify the ways of God to man by asserting eternal providence becomes for Shaftesbury an effort to reconcile material multiplicity within a vision of formal unity. Mixed genres such as the miscellany are not incidental to this project. They are the test cases of a *formal theodicy*. The attempt to infer a transcendental cause of order from an inclusive survey of nature must find a way to describe even the most heteronomous forms in terms of design, accommodation in terms of coherence.

The distinctive arguments of philosophical aesthetics take shape in three stages in Shaftesbury's late writings. First, Shaftesbury turns his attention away from wide-ranging analyses of social and political conditions, literary history, pedagogy, and ethics. He focuses instead on the analysis of what he calls plastic forms, specifically, painting and sculpture. Having traveled to Italy in 1711 to seek relief from tuberculosis, Shaftesbury commissioned a painter to complete a heroic tablature according to the philosopher's own specifications (as given in his treatise *A Notion of the Historical Draught or Tablature of the Judgment of Hercules*). Shaftesbury then developed philosophical analyses of this and other works depicting moral and heroic subjects.

Shaftesbury's definition of a heroic tablature indicates why painting and sculpture become the models for philosophical reflection. The tablature is "a *Single Piece*, comprehended in one *View*, and form'd according to *one single* Intelligence, Meaning, or Design; which constitutes a *real* W H O L E, by a mutual and necessary Relation of its Parts, the same as of the Members in a natural Body" (III, p. 348).[39] In contrast to the polyvocal text he endorsed earlier, the advantage of the tablature is its unity of design and singularity of intention. Plastic forms supply ahead of time the subordination of part to whole characteristic not only of beautiful art but of the well-ordered being and the healthy body politic. Knowledge of order in these emblems (what Shaftesbury calls "second characters") can then be taken analogically for the efficacy of an ordering principle in the human and divine domains (what Shaftesbury calls "first characters").

In the second phase Shaftesbury relocates the Neoclassical appeal to order, unity, coherence, simplicity, and decorum within the internal formal organization of plastic art. Shaftesbury develops the principle of internal purposiveness, which will later become so important to Kant. This principle of internal order operates to hold variety in check, or to render variety a perverse departure from nature. Within an aesthetic reading of literature, even the mixed breed of satire now obeys an inherent principle of coherence. In notes to *Plastics, Or the Original Progress and Power of Designatory Art* (1712), Shaftesbury writes,

had not the creatrix or sovereign plastic nature set the boundaries, the caprice (i.e. wantonness and bestiality) of corrupt man would long since have gone beyond the worst painters ... as well beyond the worst poets in composing new complicated forms of satire, etc. with which the breed would have run out and been lost. But now even within the inward, several species (within the genus) as in dogs and fowls, which breed with one another, a natural propensity for like joining with like; so that the breed when mixed or blended, in time and after several consequent generations displays and opens itself, and the orders return to their first natural secretions, purity and simplicity of form.   (pp. 121–122)

In retreat from his earlier skeptical philosophy, his principle of ridicule that had rendered any single concept of order more and more elusive, Shaftesbury relocates coherence now in the ability of plastic forms to bring historical process, the passions, material divisions, into the frame of a single, static representation. A theory promoting textual mixture has been replaced by a theory arguing the inevitable purity of texts under the aegis of a "creatrix or sovereign plastic nature." Satire itself has gone from being a means of correction, inevitably mixed and potentially ephemeral, to an exemplification of an abiding aesthetic order.

While the Neoclassical appeal to unity invokes a standard existing outside

---

[39] Beginning in 1714, two of Shaftesbury's late essays on the fine arts were appended to editions of *Characteristicks*. These appear in the second edition as "Treatise VII. viz. A Notion of the Historical Draught or Tablature of the Judgment of Hercules" and "A Letter concerning the Art, or Science of Design." All of the late writings on art were not grouped together until 1914, when Benjamin Rand compiled *Second Characters, or the Language of Forms* (Cambridge: Cambridge University Press, 1914). Whenever possible I cite from the 1737 (sixth, corrected) edition. Other references to *Second Characters* are given by page number in my text and refer to the Rand edition.

the text (nature, ideal beauty, the absolute), the logic of this passage points to a cause of order existing wholly within the formal organization of plastic art. As an ancient, Shaftesbury reminds us that "Even the SATIRICK, or MISCELLANEOUS *Manner* of the polite Ancients, requir'd as much *Order* as the most regular Pieces. But the *Art* was to destroy every such Token or Appearance, give an *extemporary Air* to what was writ, and make the *Effect* of Art to be felt, without discovering the *Artifice*" (III, pp. 21–22). Yet as a modern struggling to perpetuate ancient values, Shaftesbury cannot situate the source of order in a transcendental criterion or in a whimsical appeal to the "something I know not what." A far more pervasive principle of order is necessary because Shaftesbury comes to the aesthetic not as a cultural ideologue but as a moral philosopher seeking to ground ethics in an enduring principle of commonality. Something must hold miscellaneous forms like satire together, something abiding within form itself, providing the principle of order from within. Not good breeding, though this might be one of its after-effects, but an environmental necessity, the plastic nature of all things (internal formal purposiveness), organizes the aesthetic whole.

Finally, the concept of formal purposiveness provides a basis for the turn from aesthetics back to ethics. If ridicule casts suspicion upon all external authorities, if the individual subject is advised never to surrender "his *Taste*, or *Judgment*, to an *Author* of ever so great a Name, or venerable Antiquity," then here, nevertheless, is a standard that cannot be questioned. The sovereign has become "plastic," causing the growth and coherence of form from within, obeying virtually biological principles of genesis and order. Form, in and of itself, asserts a coherence of parts. Even though forms differ from other forms, as a human being differs from a tree, the *principle* of coherence remains the same in each. The similarity justifies Shaftesbury in asserting an analogy between what he calls second characters (external form, art works) and first characters (human identity, ethics, divinity). The self participates in this natural order and receives its cue from the same principle of internal formal coherence. The relationship is wholly reciprocal: just as the self embodies the aesthetic principle of dialectical cohesion, so all of nature, an emblem of the beautiful, resembles a self writ large. Charles Taylor describes this position as an inward turn in the history of the subject, "the internalization, or we might say the 'subjectivization,' of a teleological ethic of nature [and] the transformation of an ethic of order, harmony, and equilibrium into an ethic of benevolence."[40]

Although the discussion of literary genres is central to the enterprise of *Characteristicks*, one immediate effect of Shaftesbury's turn to the incipient vocabulary of philosophical aesthetics is to negate the significance of genre distinctions. An aesthetic philosophy premised upon concepts of inner formal

[40] Taylor, *Sources of the Self: the Making of Modern Identity* (Cambridge, MA: Harvard University Press, 1989), p. 255.

purposiveness or sovereign plastic nature renders genre superfluous, since it is something more general than genre that leads all forms to exemplify the Same. Concepts of beauty, of design, of formal autonomy, of the sublime (and the taste to discern these) replace generic distinctions as the dominant means of establishing the value of texts, texts increasingly cordoned off from what Kant will call mere concepts (instrumental concerns in the realm of history, politics, ethics). Shaftesbury's aesthetic turn subsumes the modern appeal to accommodation within the ancient assertion of beauty. Even the most inclusive texts, even the social system itself with all its ugliness and rank inequality, may be said to confirm the synthetic power of beauty, if viewed with the proper aesthetic detachment.

Throughout the late essays, Shaftesbury takes pains to allude to parallel passages in *Characteristics*; nevertheless, he also betrays, on occasion, a recognition that the turn to philosophical aesthetics constitutes a retraction of, and atonement for, the statements of the radical miscellanarian. In fragmentary notes to *Plastics*, he writes, "Also this concerning excursions, deviations, diverting tales, episodes, miscellany, occasional reflections (partly as Lucullus said, for my own sake). I have always thought strange that authors should be found (and readers to support them) who could purpose, write, and couch their fragments and spare thoughts, as if pity the world should lose the least. With respect to self, (apologizing for it). Thus reconciliation of plastics, etc." (pp. 121–122). The frequent references back to *Characteristics* obscure the extent to which the later works shift emphasis from the restless, amorphous miscellany to the static (though fruitful) moment of the heroic painting. What Shaftesbury apologizes for is the fact that his defense of criticism, ridicule, and ironic, self-questioning genres, his commitment to a more egalitarian pedagogy and the dissemination of Enlightenment knowledge all helped erode the very cultural standards that his late recourse to philosophical aesthetics was intended to shore up.

Between the early radicalism of the *Letter concerning Enthusiasm* and Shaftesbury's late essays on the judgment of the fine arts stands his decision to compose a philosophical dialogue between a skeptic and an aesthetic theist. This dialogue, *The Moralists*, attempts a different kind of reconciliation between the emancipatory and exclusionary sides of the radical aesthete, one more relevant to the development of the novel than to the history of aesthetics. Divided in his own allegiances, Shaftesbury turned to a genre itself divided, a form akin to both the miscellany and heroic drama. The only problem Shaftesbury faced in adopting philosophical dialogue was his sense that the genre was dead to his age. This dilemma – the need for and impossibility of dialogue at the beginning of the eighteenth century – is the subject of the following chapter.

2

Shaftesbury's *The Moralists*: a dialogue upon dialogue

In the previous chapter I described the system of values according to which Shaftesbury ranks literary genres. It became clear, however, that two distinct concepts of criticism generate opposing standards for the evaluation of texts. The same genre, for instance, the miscellany, might be viewed as admirable or debased, depending upon whether the radical aesthete were promoting the values of Enlightenment or defending the ideals of Neoclassicism. Shaftesbury was aware of this problem, and, through the turn to philosophical aesthetics, developed a new vocabulary for moral philosophy, one that discounted the political and religious differences at stake in his earlier criticism of genres.

In the last years of his life, Shaftesbury apologized for "excursions, deviations, diverting tales, episodes, miscellany" and sought to shift attention to what he then held to have been paramount all along, "the grandeur of parts in perspective" and "the higher and nobler species of humanity." He did not apologize for his dialogue; yet, one does find, late in *Miscellaneous Reflections*, this description of *The Moralists*:

'Tis not only at the bottom, as *Systematical, Didactic*, and *Preceptive* as that other Piece of formal Structure [*An Inquiry Concerning Virtue, or Merit*]; but it assumes withal another Garb and fashionable turn of Wit. It conceals what is *Scholastical* under the appearance of a polite Work. It aspires to *Dialogue*, and carrys with it not only those Poetic Features of the Pieces antiently called MIMES; but it attempts to unite the several Personages and Characters in ONE *Action*, or *Story*, within a determinate Compass of Time, regularly divided and drawn into different and proportion'd Scenes; and this too, with a variety of STILE; the *Simple, Comic, Rhetorical*, and even *Poetick* or *Sublime*; such as is the aptest to run into Enthusiasm and Extravagance.

(III, p. 285)

Despite its novel admixtures, Shaftesbury's dialogue is formal and systematic. Its seeming miscellaneousness amounts only to a polite concealment of "what is scholastical." Shaftesbury redescribes his dialogue, as Horace and Boileau evaluate classical drama, in terms of its spatial and temporal unity, decorum, and the subordination of parts to whole. The dialogue, despite its assimilation of a "variety of styles," is simply a systematic treatise cast in more fashionable garb.

Yet in a footnote to the same passage, Shaftesbury finds he has more explaining to do; for the description contradicts, or appears to contradict, his own advertisement of the work on its title-page. There Shaftesbury called *The Moralists* "a Philosophical Rhapsody" and "a Recital of certain Conversations on Natural and Moral Subjects." Such designations imply, as Shaftesbury admits in the footnote, that *The Moralists* "were merely of that *Essay* or mix'd kind of Works, which come abroad with an affected Air of Negligence and Irregularity" (III, pp. 285–286). Obviously anxious to stave off the charge of "irregularity," Shaftesbury, characteristically, assigns the original claim about *The Moralists* to the voice of a third person, "our author," and then corrects his error:

But whatever our Author may have affected in his Title-Page, 'twas so little his Intention to write after that Model of incoherent Workmanship, that it appears to be sorely against his Will if this *Dialogue-Piece* of his has not the just Character, and correct Form of those antient *Poems* described. He would gladly have constituted O N E single *Action* and *Time*, suitable to the just Simplicity of those Dramatick Works. And this, one wou'd think, was easy enough for him to have done. He needed only to have brought his first Speakers into Action, and sav'd the *Narrative* or *Recitative* part of P H I L O C L E S to P A L E M O N, by producing them as speaking Personages upon his stage. The Scene all along might have been the *Park* . . . By this means the *Temporal* as well as *Local* Unity of the Piece had been preserv'd. Nor had our author been necessitated to commit that *Anachronism*, of making the first part, *in order*, to be the last *in time*.   (III, p. 286n)

Clearly, Shaftesbury is trying to have things both ways, patching up, through critical commentary and footnotes, a work he originally advertised as a rhapsody. (*The Oxford English Dictionary* indicates that during the seventeenth and eighteenth centuries "rhapsody" could mean "a literary work consisting of miscellaneous or disconnected pieces; a written composition having no fixed form or plan.") The references to unity and simplicity make sense if we read the philosophical dialogue as a heroic drama. But how are dramatic conventions relevant to a work of intellectual prose setting philosophical and religious positions in opposition through long speeches, narrative descriptions, lyrical effusions, and epistolary exchange?

The very need to append these critical reflections to *The Moralists* suggests Shaftesbury's nervousness about his dialogue's ability to achieve a convincing sense of closure. The work seems to require a second-order guide to correct interpretation. Although Shaftesbury's references to a "polite concealment" might lead us to think that generic complexity amounts to little more than window dressing, the work actually experiments with combinations of genres in order to avoid philosophical indeterminacy. Calling the work a heroic drama distracts attention from the failure of the characters to achieve a convincing theological resolution through rational debate.

The Moralists is not a heroic drama. It is actually a letter written by Philocles to Palemon, which recounts an earlier dialogue between the two during which the main dialogue between Philocles and Theocles was first repeated. The main dialogue contains extended passages of lyrical rhapsody, a sermon, sharp Socratic exchanges, natural description, and descriptions of character. Shaftesbury acknowledges the difference between a dialogue recounted in a letter and a directly staged drama when he writes, "Nor had our author been necessitated to commit that *Anachronism*, of making the first part, *in order*, to be the last *in time*"; for the effect of recounting a dialogue in a letter *is* to invert temporal sequence, upsetting the temporal succession assumed by the heroic plot. Even if Shaftesbury claims he could have written *The Moralists* as a heroic drama, the fact is, he didn't. Something "necessitated" him to complicate the work's generic structure. Why, then, does *The Moralists* assume such a complicated structure? And how does the combination of genres influence our interpretation of the work?

Two interpretations of dialogue

The most important point to make about *The Moralists* at the outset is that it is a dialogue about the nature of dialogue at the beginning of the eighteenth century. The two main characters, Philocles the skeptic and Theocles the rhapsodic theist, are in large measure defined by their different conceptions of the nature and ends of philosophical dialogue. Theocles and Philocles share what might be called a sociological justification of dialogue. Both acknowledge that in "Times of less Strictness in Matters of Religion, and Places less subject to Authority" (II, p. 265), received didactic modes such as the deductive treatise are inappropriate. Under such conditions, magisterial pronouncements must be avoided since they further polarize an already factious nation. Moreover, the figure of the atheist can no longer be ignored or simply referred to the magistrate. He must be reasoned with, and since, with the habitual non-believer "what was never *question'd*, was never *prov'd*" (II, p. 265), the writer must avoid the tendency to assume from the start the very points most in contest. Both characters advocate dialogue because of its fairer, inductive movement; both recognize that as the audience for moral philosophy expands, philosophers must accommodate their discourse to the pedagogical needs of the multitude.

While the two main characters share these views, they differ completely in their understanding of the aims and limitations of inductive method. Theocles' defense of induction is linked to a hypothesis about the fundamental orderliness of nature. Referring to the author of *An Inquiry Concerning Virtue, or Merit* (Shaftesbury), Theocles explains, "We begin surely at the wrong end, when we wou'd prove MERIT, *by Favour*, and ORDER *by a Deity*. – This our Friend seeks to redress. For being, in respect of VIRTUE, what you lately call'd *a Realist*; he endeavors to shew, 'That It is really something *in it-self*, and in the nature of Things'" (II, p. 267). Theocles wants to invert the usual

deductive strategy of proving order by the prior assumption of an ordering
Deity. Instead, he holds that a realistic survey of natural effects, an "accurate
Judgment in *the Particulars* of Natural Beings and Operations" (II, p. 282),
inevitably leads to an apprehension "of the Structure of Things *in general* and
the Order and Frame of NATURE" (II, pp. 282–283). Theocles' willingness to
engage in inductive reasoning is based upon his faith that something "in the
nature of things" guides a free examination of viewpoints to a stable
conclusion. Like the Cambridge Platonists and the virtuosi of the early Royal
Society, he holds that a "Providence must be prov'd from what we see of
Order in things present. We must contend for Order" (II, p. 277). For
Theocles, philosophical dialogue stages the design argument in social terms.
It transfers the analogical correspondence between parts and wholes,
phenomena and noumena, into a model for the way social contradictions –
the competing assertions of interested individuals – might be resolved
through rational debate. One divides in order to unite, locates differences in
order to achieve synthesis.

According to this comedic interpretation there exists no contradiction
between lyrical rhapsody, the mode for which Theocles is best known, and
philosophical dialogue; for rhapsody represents the culmination of a process of
dialectical inquiry, a point at which apparent antagonisms synthesize in ecstatic
recognition of an unmoved mover. That is why Theocles' enthusiastic diction
is shot through with references to formal logic, and why his rational
demonstrations frequently conclude with enthusiastic flights of imagination.
Theocles speaks of his argument as being "evidently demonstrable" (II,
p. 288), and, after a particularly impassioned flight, demands of Philocles "tell
me, then ... how you can refuse the name of Demonstration to the remaining
Arguments, which establish the Government of a Perfect Mind" (II, p. 363).

Philocles differs completely in not viewing dialogue as a means of
discovering any certain truth. "You know my Sceptick Principles," he tells
Theocles, "I determine neither way" (II, pp. 353–354). Philocles describes
dialogue as an activity that "goes on no establish'd Hypothesis, nor presents
us with any flattering Scheme, talks only of Probabilitys, Suspence of
Judgment, Inquiry, Search, and Caution not to be impos'd upon or deceiv'd
... [Nor is he one] who exalted *Reason* above *Faith*, or insisted much on what
the Dogmatical Men call *Demonstration*" (II, pp. 191, 207). When Theocles asks
Philocles to accede to his proof that disorder is only illusory, Philocles
responds, "Your solutions ... of the *ill Appearances* are not perfect enough to
pass for Demonstration. And whatever seems vitious or imperfect in the
Creation puts a stop to further Conclusions, till the thing be solv'd" (II,
p. 302). Yet according to his own definition, Philocles seems unlikely to
acknowledge the truth of any argument beyond mere probability. Quite
possibly, "further conclusions" are preempted by Philocles' very understanding of the kind of discourse in which he is engaged.

Philocles links his own conception of dialogue to the skepticism of the Academy, but other characters, including Theocles, refer to Philocles as "a true Proselyte to Pyrrhonism" (II, p. 351). The difference is important, for while a dialogue modeled on Cicero's might still offer probabilistic grounds of agreement between skeptic and rhapsodist, the Pyrrhonist holds himself aloof from any determination.[1] Dialogue brings only more dialogue, but it does not result in any binding conclusion, least of all in a rhapsodic apprehension of unity. Unlike Theocles and the Cambridge Platonists, Philocles does not justify induction with the faith that it tops out in stable deductions.

A dialogue structured along these lines, as a confrontation between two senses of dialogue, seems an odd way of staging what R. L. Brett calls "the conversion of Philocles (the sceptic) to theism by Theocles (the philosopher)."[2] Indeed, Philocles' response to the claims of the rhapsodist anticipates the most damaging attacks that will be leveled against Shaftesbury himself during the rest of the century. Philocles sees (as will Hume) that Theocles' natural religion, like all versions of physico-theology, depends upon an analogy between order in nature and an ordering cause in heaven. And it is here, at the analogical hinge, that Philocles ventures his most destructive criticism.

On one occasion Theocles takes up the problem of multiplicity and unity with regard to the individual being. He argues that even someone who experiences a sudden change of belief remains "the self-same," and thus there must exist "a strange Simplicity" in identity (II, p. 351). Just as the single being evinces a subordination of diverse voices to self-identity, so the entire social system and the universe itself "share this simple Principle, by which they are really *One*." Turning to the skeptic, Theocles asks how, given the force of this reasoning, "we can be so unnatural as to disown Divine Nature, our common Parent, and refuse to recognize the *Universal* and *Sovereign* GENIUS?" Philocles replies,

SOVEREIGNS ... require no *Notice* to be taken of 'em, when they pass *incognito*, nor any *Homage* where they appear not *in due Form*. We may even have reason to presume they should be displeas'd with us for being too officious in endeavouring to discover them, when they keep themselves either wholly invisible, or in very dark disguise ... I find no warrant for our being such earnest Recognisers of a controverted Title.

(II, pp. 352–353)

For Theocles it is crucial that the inductive survey of particulars be presided

---

[1] Douglas Patey summarizes the difference between these positions in the following way: "Whereas Pyrrhonism, essentially a practical doctrine, denied that any truth may be known and advocated a thoroughgoing suspension of judgment in all matters, the Academics ... developed a doctrine of probability and methods of argument for justifying assent based on probabilities." *Probability and Literary Form: Philosophic Theory and Literary Practice in the Augustan Age* (Cambridge: Cambridge University Press, 1984), p. 15.

[2] Brett, *The Third Earl of Shaftesbury: a Study in Eighteenth-Century Literary Theory* (London: Hutchinson's University Library, 1951), p. 63.

over by a power that is not itself an analogy for something else. In his analogical cosmography, the Sovereign is that unmoved Mover, who energizes and brings to a stand the upward flight from natural effects to primal cause. Yet the Pyrrhonist subverts this transcendental movement: "sovereign" for him becomes only another sign for a further, material signification, in this case the Old Pretender, James II's son James Edward, then hiding "incognito" in France. Philocles likens the appeal to a distant but powerful sovereign to support for the banished Jacobite succession. He suggests that a disguised political sovereign might have his own reasons for encouraging belief in a distant but potent religious sovereign.[3] Philocles' ridicule politicizes the vocabulary of design.

On another occasion, Theocles conducts Philocles up the ladder of lesser forms, from the "entrails" and plains and aqueous reaches of the earth, past the sun, towards the "luminous Matter so wide diffus'd, the *invisible ethereal Substance*," which supplies even the sun, and "kindles a soft, invisible, and vital Flame in the Breasts of living Creatures," but which, "once broken, the acquited Being takes its course unrul'd. It runs impetuous through the fatal Breach, and breaking into visible and fierce *Flames* passes triumphant o'er the yielding Forms, converting all into it-self ... " (II, pp. 379–380). Here Philocles interrupts the rhapsodist. Theocles thanks him: "I was growing too warm," he says, "in these high Flights I might possibly have gone near to burn my Wings" (II, pp. 380–381). Philocles answers:

Indeed ... you might expect the Fate of ICARUS for your high-soaring. But this, indeed, is not what I feared. For you were got above Danger; and with that devouring Element on your side, had master'd not only the *Sun* himself, but every thing which stood in your way. I was afraid it might, in the issue, run to what they tell us of a *universal Conflagration*; in which I knew not how it might go, possibly, with our GENIUS. (II, p. 381)

Once again, Philocles annexes the rhapsodist's rhetoric to suspect temporal interests. The very passages for which Shaftesbury will become best known (the purple passages of ecstatic encomium to nature) have been mocked ahead of time as a language rife with metaphors of high-flying, domination, mastery, consumption, even apocalypse.

The criticism becomes even more telling when we remember that the two speakers stand before a vast prospect on Theocles' property. The vantage the rhapsodist claims in imaginative terms is matched by the very real advantage

---

[3] The connection between Tory politics and the defense of a distant sovereign is explicit in Berkeley's *Passive Obedience* (1712). Here, as John Richetti puts it, Berkeley "argues for the inviolable loyalty owed to the king by urging his audience to shift their perspective, from 'the too near view of the little present interests of ourselves, our friends, our country' to the more detached view of 'ourselves [as] distant spectators of all that is transacted and contained' " in the world. *Philosophical Writing: Locke, Berkeley, Hume* (Cambridge, MA: Harvard University Press, 1983), p. 176.

he enjoys as the owner of a substantial landed estate.[4] In Philocles' hands, Pyrrhonian skepticism politicizes the logic of analogy: the vista necessary to translate accidental signs into a coherent order must be sufficiently elevated, sufficiently detached, so as to blur or altogether omit the nasty particulars. With unrecognized irony, Philocles praises his friend for passing over the most familiar part of the globe in his flight through exotic climes, avoiding "that *politic* Face of Affairs, which wou'd too much disturb us in our *Philosophical* Flights" (II, p. 392) – affairs, one hears Mandeville adding, such as the hopeless lives of chimney sweeps and prostitutes, figures who cannot be reconciled with the optimistic vision of a social system modeled on the beautiful work of art.[5] Elsewhere, Philocles ridicules the notion that from the "Misery and Ill of *Man* there was undoubtedly some GOOD arising," and he asks Palemon "whether it must not be a very strong Philosophical Faith, which shou'd persuade one that those dismal Parts you set to view were only the necessary Shades of a fine Piece, to be reckon'd among the Beautys of the Creation" (II, p. 204).[6]

However effective these criticisms of Theocles' providential assertion may be, they are countered at points in the dialogue when, in turn, the skeptic's posture of principled debunking is linked to a limited set of motives. Theocles recognizes that concepts of beauty and harmony are always open to attack, especially by those not attuned to higher forms of delight. "Imagine then," he says to Philocles, "if being taken with the Beauty of the Ocean, which you see yonder at a distance, it shou'd come into your head to seek how to command it; and like some mighty Admiral, ride Master of the Sea" (II, p. 396). Philocles admits that this hunger to own the prospect would be absurd. But a moment later Theocles asks his friend to apply the same lesson to "some other *Forms* of a fair kind among us" (II, p. 398). "I FEAR'D ... where this wou'd end," replies Philocles, for he cannot adopt the appropriate detachment from those who "the more they are view'd, the further they are from satisfying by mere View" (II, p. 398). Theocles, speaking for the radical turned aesthete, begins the century-long process of divesting aesthetic

---

[4] See Raymond Williams, *The Country and the City* (New York: Oxford University Press, 1973), especially "Pleasing Prospects."

[5] I take up Mandeville's attack on Shaftesbury in chapter 7.

[6] In light of Philocles' attack upon Theocles it is surely necessary to modify the claim of Cassirer and others that Shaftesbury's single great contribution to intellectual history is the doctrine of disinterested aesthetic contemplation. Cassirer holds that Shaftesbury's contemplation "is free of all desire for possession and of any act of direct seizure of the object [and involves] a pleasure not motivated by any interest" (*The Philosophy of the Enlightenment*, p. 153). While Theocles articulates such a view, Philocles attacks it with criticisms as damaging as anything Mandeville or Berkeley would venture. The kind of narrative Cassirer constructs based on a sequence of leading figures articulating large ideas leading to Kant cannot account for the oppositional voices present within a text like *The Moralists*. Intellectual history and, more recently, cultural studies continue to identify the split figure with only one of his voices, thereby backreading the lyrical necessity of a unified consciousness onto a period and author that still saw the mind as capable of sustaining a dramatic interplay of diverse voices.

contemplation of merely instrumental concerns. He implies that the skeptic's refusal to accept the equation between ideal beauty and truth may only bespeak a mind incapable of ridding itself of sensualism: the libertine, Theocles hints, is naturally prone to interpret "aesthetic contemplation" as a lascivious glance with a bad conscience.

Other characters second this attack upon Philocles. After hearing Philocles ventriloquize a series of opposed philosophical positions, Palemon asks coldly "Whether with that fine SCEPTICISM [Philocles] made no more distinction between Sincerity and Insincerity in *Actions*, than [he] did between Truth and Falsehood, Right and Wrong, in Arguments?" (II, p. 208). Philocles then admits to having been influenced by "some fashionable Conversations of the World [which expressed] the worst sort of *Scepticism*, such as spar'd nothing; but overthrew all Principles, *Moral* and *Divine*" (II, p. 208). The old gentleman at the dinner party goes even further, complaining that " 'he was sorry to find ... [Philocles'] Principle of Liberty extended in fine to a Liberty from all Principles' (so he express'd himself), 'and none,' he thought, 'besides a Libertine in Principle could approve of such a Picture of Virtue, as only an *Atheist* could have the impudence to make' " (II, pp. 254–255).

Impasse, non-interruption, silence

Although *The Moralists* has generally been read as the narrative of a skeptic's conversion to theism, Theocles' insistence upon the demonstrative force of his own arguments and the compatibility of dialogue and rhapsody, and Philocles' tendency to annex his beautiful music to mundane temporal interests, taken together, do not bode well for the development of *The Moralists* towards an easy conversion of one position to the other. Indeed, one reading of *The Moralists*, a reading Philocles might well favor, locates its conclusion not in a unity of viewpoints, but in tragic impasse, a resounding silence between the main characters.

This moment arises late in the discussion, as Theocles propels himself on one of his many rhapsodies through "ALL Nature's Wonders," past the "neighboring Planets," beyond the "PRODIGIOUS ORB! Bright Source of vital Heat," and even up to the "*Sovereign* and *Sole Mover*, by whose high Art the rolling Spheres are govern'd" (II, pp. 371–372). In mid-flight, however, Theocles interrupts himself. The narrator, Philocles, explains this interruption in a letter to his friend Palemon:

Here again he broke off, looking on me as if he expected I shou'd speak; which when he found plainly I wou'd not, but continued still in a posture of musing Thought: Why, PHILOCLES! (said he with an Air of Wonder) What can this mean, that you shou'd suffer me thus to run on without the least Interruption? Have you at once given over your scrupulous Philosophy, to let me range thus at pleasure thro these aerial Spaces and imaginary Regions where my capricious Fancy or easy Faith has led me? I wou'd have you to consider better, and know, my PHILOCLES, that I had never trusted my-self with you in this *Vein* of *Enthusiasm*, had I not rely'd on you to govern it a little better.   (II, p. 374)

The skeptic has fallen silent before the song of the rhapsodist. One might argue that such silence indicates his complete acceptance of Theocles' position. John Richetti notes, for instance, that "Silence is an admission of defeat within the challenges that constitute dialogue and keep it moving."[7] Theocles does not hear silence in this way. He feels threatened by the skeptic's failure to interrupt, sensing not victory but bemused indifference.

Theocles' position depends upon a meaningful intersection between dialogue and rhapsody. His enthusiasm differs from that which Shaftesbury attacked in the *Letter concerning Enthusiasm* because it has been won through a careful contemplation of nature. It is the hymn of praise to providence following the scientist's discovery of order. Philocles' silence threatens this intersection, implying that the music of rhapsody and the rigors of rational analysis finally occupy distinct domains. No doubt, Philocles enjoys rhapsody; he frequently encourages Theocles to grow yet more sublime ("let me advise you in my own behalf, that since you have kindled me, you do not by delaying give me time to cool again" [II, p. 361]). But he appreciates rhapsody the way a gourmand loves his sauces, as a delectable embellishment void of substance. The effect of the sublime flight lasts only as long as the sound and carries no binding intellectual force.

For Philocles, a lyric meditation whose productive condition precludes interruption is finally incommensurable with a dialogue that depends upon interruption. And this is precisely the way Theocles understands Philocles' silence. Theocles elsewhere reacts angrily to his friend's blandishments – "I Wou'd have you know ... I scorn to take advantage of a warm Fit and be beholden to Temper or Imagination for gaining me your Assent" (II, p. 107). For Theocles, rational dialogue and lyric rhapsody are simply two means of arriving at the same truth. He rejects the suggestion that rational dialogue *needs* a fictional supplement to gain its transcendental end. His aim is to reveal to Philocles "some deep view of *Nature* and the *Sovereign* GENIUS" either "in my poetick Extasys, or by any other Efforts" (II, pp. 399–400). Philocles, however, does not view different modes as transparent to the same meaning, and when he falls silent, Theocles hears just this charge. In this respect, silence marks a point of crisis within the text, an intersection of genres (skeptical dialogue and lyric rhapsody) and attitudes towards knowledge (a posteriori induction and a priori deduction) that resists any simple reconciliation through a synthesis of characters.

It has become fashionable of late to argue, on theoretical grounds, that an

---

[7] Richetti, *Philosophical Writing: Locke, Berkeley, Hume*, p. 159.

impartial philosophical dialogue (or any impartial use of reason) never occurs, that all dialogues are polemical. In an essay on *The Moralists* aptly titled "The Philosophical Dialogue and the Forcing of Truth," Daniel Brewer claims, for instance, that the "conversations related in most philosophical dialogues end in unity between their fictional characters. This unity is supported by a fiction and is emblematic of a powerful philosophical ruse, all the more necessary because of what is at stake. The end of philosophical dialogue is to eliminate, subjugate or at least postpone difference."[8] Every dialogue, according to Brewer, is a disguised monologue, a rhetorical ploy concealing its ideological designs upon the reader through mock encounter with "difference."[9]

In "The Impossibility of Philosophical Dialogue," David Roochnik raises logical (rather than rhetorical and political) doubts about the possibility of a truly skeptical dialogue. He holds that a philosophical dialogue staging an opposition between essentially contested categories (or what he calls fundamental issues) can never take place. The reason for this claim is disarmingly simple:

A philosophical dialogue is about fundamental issues ... Fundamental issues are precisely what constitute the common ground needed for the controversial conversation to take place. Therefore, if there is a disagreement about fundamental issues there can be no common ground. The conclusion is that philosophical dialogue is impossible. If there is a philosophical disagreement about FI's [fundamental issues], and there certainly can be, the result is not *dialegestai* but *polemos*, polemical speech, or silence.[10]

Because prior decision about "fundamental issues" (for example, rules of argument, means of arbitration) constitutes the permitting premise of a philosophical dialogue, a dialogue cannot simultaneously take place and interrogate its conceptual bases. The very existence of a dialogue consequently proves it is not about fundamental issues. I would agree with Roochnik's own appraisal of this position: "there is, I concede, a kind of logical triviality to my argument."[11] But tautology notwithstanding, one should note that *The Moralists* fulfills Roochnik's requirements for a dialogue about fundamental issues. The work stages a confrontation between charac-

[8] Brewer, "The Philosophical Dialogue and the Forcing of Truth," *Modern Language Notes* 98 (1983) 1245.

[9] Brewer's reading derives from assumptions about textuality inherited from Nietzsche and Foucault, predominantly the view that authority (the author) never allows itself to become an object of effective criticism. In *Daybreak: Thoughts on the Prejudices of Morality*, Nietzsche opines, as long as "the world has existed no authority has yet been willing to allow itself to become the object of criticism." Friedrich Nietzsche, *Daybreak: Thoughts on the Prejudices of Morality*, trans. R. J. Hollingdale (Cambridge: Cambridge University Press, 1982), p. 2.

[10] David Roochnik, "The Impossibility of Philosophical Dialogue," *Philosophy and Rhetoric* 19 (1986) 149.

[11] *Ibid.*, 154

ters who disagree about the nature of philosophical dialogue, its rules, its limits, and the means by which it achieves (or resists achieving) coherence and closure. Here we find no either/or between dialogue and silence, but a dialogue that represents silence as one of its possible outcomes.[12]

To accuse *The Moralists* of concealing its dogmatism through a mere display of impartial questioning or to fabricate a theoretical refutation of the possibility of a fundamental dialogue is to fail to recognize just what is at stake in the confrontation between Theocles and Philocles. The cultural implications of their impasse are everywhere borne out in the subsequent philosophical, religious, and political history of the eighteenth century. The proponent of rational theology (Theocles) and the proponent of secular, analytical reason (Philocles); the owner of a substantial landed estate, voicing High Church if not Jacobite sentiments (Theocles) and the visitor from the bustling city, whose theological convictions are uncertain (Philocles); the proto-mystic or evangelical Christian and the proto-atheist or secular scientist stand before each other, and the result, it would seem, is non-intersection. A recourse to enthusiastic rhetoric, deeply suspect in the decades following the Civil War, seems the only means of recovering faith from scientific skepticism; yet it is a recourse to which the skeptic himself assigns no validity.

Why, then, has Shaftesbury structured *The Moralists* as a dialogue between two characters who agree about the need for dialogue but who disagree entirely about whether dialogue provides a method of theological inquiry? In the previous chapter I described a split in Shaftesbury's conception of criticism. Now it appears evident that Shaftesbury reformulates that division within a genre divided in a similar way. Theocles understands dialogue as the embodiment of a teleological movement from division to unity. His interpretation of dialogue is "Platonic" in this oddly modern sense: for him Platonic (metaphysical) dialogue confirms the efficacy of an escape route (transcendental dialectic) from a theory of knowledge (Locke's) threatening to

[12] It is always possible to argue, in hindsight, that a dialogue between fundamentally contested categories has excluded an opposition, an otherness, that now seems even more significant. Women, the working poor, anarchists, radical atheists, and tradesmen do not participate in *The Moralists*, and so it would seem that its oppositions are unified by the attempt to exclude unthinkable challenges to the norm of gentlemanly converse about metaphysical topics. Indeed, this kind of challenge will be used by subsequent writers of dialogue, who attack the preceding text by including more and by showing how such inclusiveness damages what is earlier taken to be the necessary conclusion of impartial debate (a favorite trick of Mandeville, who brings both women and the working poor into his dialogic attack on Shaftesbury in *Fable of the Bees, Part II*). Nevertheless, within critical practices devoted to disclosing the workings of power and ideology in the past, the dismissal of dialogue generates self-contradiction. If writers always reproduce the same, even when they pretend to represent difference, then radical critique can claim no other status for itself than an exemplification of bad faith or paradox. The specification of ideology assumes a fundamental distinction between repetition of hegemonic interest and resistance to hegemony in the name of some other preferred value, however much undisclosed. But such a difference must be ruled out for the same reason that one denies the possibility of a skeptical dialogue between essentially contested categories. I discuss this issue more fully in the epilogue.

bar all access to the realm of the supersensible. A similar logical operation permits the Neoclassical critic to derive ideal (eternal) norms of a genre from the most approved performances of the ancients. Philocles understands dialogue as a means of *resisting* metaphysical induction, a resistance *also* traditionally described in terms of dialectic, only here a skeptical dialectic derived from the pre-Platonic Socrates, Zeno, and Pyrrho. A similar resistance leads the skeptical critic to subvert the transcendental appeal, annexing it to material interests. Thus, the two interpretations of dialogue, one metaphysical and the other skeptical, are matched by two interpretations of dialectic, one Platonic and the other Pyrrhonian. And these competing views of dialogue and dialectic provide the philosophical correlatives of Shaftesbury's divided commitments as a critic.

An early eighteenth-century reader would have found both interpretations of dialectic represented side by side without a sense of their antagonism in Thomas Stanley's popular *The History of Philosophy*.[13] In a section devoted to "Dialectick" in Platonic philosophy, Stanley observes that "the Judgment arises from the *Sense*, yet the judgment of Truth is not in the Senses."[14] Though summarizing an ancient predicament, the statement also captures a paradox that troubled philosophical Christians of the early Royal Society: if knowledge comes from sense, where does the criterion for judging the reports of sense come from? Surely not sense. There must be some higher mediating term capable of effecting the *translatio* from sense to the judgment of truth.

While Boethius appealed to myth to solve this difficulty, in the modern period a Neoplatonic or transcendental conception of dialectic itself supplies this third figure: dialectic negotiates the transition from the slow and obtuse workings of sense to the simple, uniform, and certain realm of ideas. Dialectic is "a Science," writes Stanley, "but, neither Mathematick, nor Opinion, because it is more perspicuous than sensible things; nor a Science, because 'tis more obscure than first Intelligibles."[15] A science that is not a science, both perspicuous and obscure, dialectic has taken on the entire burden of establishing a correspondence between the domains of sense and intellect, part and whole, phenomena and noumena. What Foucault calls the "semantic web of resemblance," a rich constellation of social, intellectual, and textual practices operative through the middle of the seventeenth century and premised upon a sacred correspondence of microcosm and macrocosm, has been funneled by the end of the seventeenth century into an attempt to preserve a single quasi-empirical, quasi-intuitive operation.

In that the validity of dialectic as a logical operation seems tied to the status of rational induction, one wonders why the fate of dialectic is so often tied to that of dialogue (and vice versa). Stanley's definition of the one

---

[13] Stanley's *The History of Philosophy* appeared between 1655 and 1662. A third edition appeared in 1701 and a fourth in 1743.
[14] *Ibid.*, p. 162.   [15] *Ibid.*, p. 183.

immediately entails mention of the other: "Dialogue is composed of questions and answers Philosophical ... Political, aptly expressing the Characters of those persons that are the speakers in an elegant Stile; Dialectick is the Art of Discourse, whereby we confirm or confute any thing by Questions and Answers of the Disputants."[16] Conjoined in this way, dialectic provides the intellectual movement (the plot) for an otherwise aimless exchange of question and answer; and dialogue provides an otherwise homeless entity (dialectic belonging neither to sense nor to intellect) with a grounding in experience. Dialectic therefore bridges the rhetorical world of human desire and the logical world of pure reason: "Dialectick is the Art of Discourse," writes Stanley, "whereby we confirm or confute any thing by Questions and Answers of the Disputants."

Yet dialectic is one of those primary words whose force is antithetical. In Stanley's *The History of Philosophy*, a late seventeenth-century reader would also have found this statement under the heading "Dialectick" in a section detailing Sextus Empiricus' account of Pyrrhonism:

Induction ... may easily be overthrown; for, that by it they [dogmatists] would prove an Universal from Particulars, either they must do it, as having examined all Particulars, or only some. If only some, the Induction will not be valid, it being possible, that some of the omitted Particulars may be found contrary to the Universal Proposition. If they would examine all, they attempt Impossibles, for Particulars are infinite and undeterminate. Thus it happens, that Induction cannot subsist either way.[17]

Hume will add little more. A skeptical dialectic subverts induction, the logical basis of transcendental dialectic. "Realism," which Theocles called upon to verify natural religion, now presents the eye with an "infinite and undeterminate" number of particulars, the scattered atoms of chance curiously hurl'd beyond the framework of design.

Shaftesbury was well versed in the Pyrrhonian commonplaces. Although Theocles prides himself on having constructed a rational proof of the Deity, without assistance from miracles, faith, or biblical authority, Philocles constantly turns Pyrrho against Plato, overthrowing transcendental induction:

You go (if I may say so) upon *Fact*, and wou'd prove that things *actually are* in such a state and condition, which if they really *were*, there wou'd indeed be no dispute left. Your UNION is your main Support. Yet how is it you prove this? ... So far are you from *demonstrating* any thing, that if this uniting Scheme be the chief Argument for Deity (as you tacitly allow) you seem rather to have demonstrated, "That the Case itself is incapable of Demonstration." For, "How, say you, can a narrow Mind see *All Things?*" – And yet if, in reality, It sees not All, It had as good seen *Nothing.*"

(II, pp. 297–298)

For the most part, Shaftesbury's *Characteristics* shares in an older rhetorical

---

[16] *Ibid.*, p. 174.   [17] *Ibid.*, p. 505.

practice, common to Montaigne and Stanley, of compiling contradictory positions without fear that one's book will stand *refuted* because of inconsistencies. Yet this latter-day humanist also belongs to a newer age, an age of method, rigor, and system, when the value of one's ideas would be tested according to their internal consistency, their ability to produce knowledge.[18] Shaftesbury realizes that if inductive method is to have any place in theology, as Thomas Sprat, Theocles, and most of liberal Protestant theology hope, a transition will need to be effected from skeptical to transcendental dialectic. Yet, at the same time, Shaftesbury has constructed *The Moralists* as an opposition between two characters who differ, fundamentally, on questions of method (epistemology): the philosophical theist believes in an arbitrating power, standing above and beyond the fray, directing the progress of divided particulars to rational order; the Pyrrhonian skeptic, in the course of negating induction, denies also the authority of any such arbitrator, any criterion for establishing a hierarchy of parts ascending to the whole.

Dialogue as heroic drama

The Moralists is situated historically at the precarious divide between these rhetorical/humanist and systematic approaches to the representation of knowledge. Philosophical dialogue, in this context, is not so much a classical genre Shaftesbury chooses to imitate as a problematic representative of both ancient and modern worlds. One reads optimistic statements written during these years about the ideal role dialogue plays in bridging ancient and modern learning. Spens, the first English translator of Plato's *Republic*, holds that "the present seems to be no improper season for making an attempt of this kind; as, in some, a laudable taste for the ancients is still to be discovered, and in others, there appears a generous disposition towards the revival of knowledge, and the love of letters."[19] But Shaftesbury, who experiences the rift between ancients and moderns as a fundamental division in his own critical practices, finds this reconciliation through dialogue a far more difficult matter. Bridging ancients and moderns requires, in addition to the composition of a dialogue, an elaborate, even tortured, supplemental commentary telling readers how dialogues should be composed and (more to the point) interpreted.

We have already seen in the opening pages of this chapter, Shaftesbury's after-the-fact attempt to redefine his miscellaneous dialogue as a heroic

---

[18] For a discussion of the transformation from a humanist, rhetorical model of textual organization (as in Montaigne) to a modern, scientific model (as in Descartes), see Stephen Toulmin, *Cosmopolis: the Hidden Agenda of Modernity* (Chicago: University of Chicago Press, 1990), especially chapters 1–3.

[19] Plato, *The Republic of Plato: with a Preliminary Discourse Concerning the Philosophy of the Ancients*, trans. H. Spens (Glasgow: R. and A. Foulis, 1763), p. vi.

drama whose plot provides a polite concealment of a scholastic, metaphysical treatise defending natural religion. Linking dialogue to heroic drama provides one way to distract the reader from Philocles' unanswerable Pyrrhonism. Other conventions of drama, especially the existence of a clear-cut hero who triumphs in the end, free Shaftesbury (or so he suggests) from the charge that he has written a heretical work.

"'Twill be alleged," Shaftesbury admits, "That shou'd a DIALOGUE be wrought up to the Exactness of these Rules [of impartial inquiry], it ought to be condemn'd as the worse Piece, for affording the *Infidel* or *Sceptick* such good Quarter, and giving him the full Advantage of his Argument and Wit" (III, p. 294). But this need not be the case: "Gentlemen! Be not so cautious of furnishing your *Representative* SCEPTICK with too good *Arguments*, or too shreud a Turn of *Wit* or *Humour* ... Allow your Adversary his full Reason, his Ingenuity, Sense, and Art. Trust to the *chief Character* or HERO *of your Piece*. Make him as dazzling *bright* as you are able. He will undoubtedly overcome the utmost Force of his Opponent, and dispel the Darkness or Cloud, which the Adversary may unluckily have rais'd" (III, pp. 294–295). Solving the threat of skepticism in this way transfers the burden of proof from theological argument to literary talent. The theological hero will not only match the skeptic reason for reason, but will also be a more appealing character. Should the skeptic triumph, should the writer appear of the devil's party, the fault must be with the author, and not the thesis: If "your *chief Character* cannot afterwards prove a match for him, or shine with a superiour Brightness; Whose Fault is it? The Subject's? This, I hope, you will never allow. Whose, therefore, besides *your own*?" (III, p. 295).

Despite the complacency of these observations, Shaftesbury was acutely aware that philosophical dialogue may have become an impossible genre. The writer of dialogue imitates the exchanges of a lively conversation. Dialogue to this extent is a form of accurate imitation. But the genre also portrays a utopian world in which good always triumphs over evil, theological conviction over skeptical suspension. Dialogue to this extent is a form of imitation closer to allegory than to comic drama or the new romance. Like Boethius' appeal to myth, the decorum of heroic drama distracts the reader from the possibility that a dialogue between skeptic and theist might well end in impasse. The hero, by being heroic, makes an inarguable case for the victory of transcendental over Pyrrhonian dialectic. His fate controls the plot. A skeptical hero is a contradiction in terms.

Nevertheless, the two senses of imitation are not so easily reconciled. Shaftesbury is therefore eager to define dialogue as a special kind of mirror, one which takes in an indiscriminate array of characters, ideas, and circumstances, but gives back the utopian image. Here again the generic parallel with heroic drama proves useful. In *Advice to an Author* Shaftesbury observes:

The Philosophical HERO of these Poems ... was in himself *a perfect Character* ...
However, it was so order'd, that notwithstanding the oddness or mysteriousness of the
principal Character, the under-parts or *second Characters* shew'd Human Nature more
distinctly and to the Life. We might here, therefore, as in a *Looking-Glass*, discover ourselves, and see our minutest Features nicely delineated, and suited to our own
Apprehension and Cognizance ... And, what was of singular note in these *magical
Glasses*; it wou'd happen, that by constant and long inspection, the Partys accustom'd
to the Practice wou'd acquire a peculiar *speculative Habit*; so as virtually to carry about
with 'em a sort of Pocket-Mirrour, always ready, and in use.   (I, pp. 194–195)

In the process of describing dialogue as a mimetic genre, Shaftesbury subtly
shifts the scene where dialogue takes place from society to the stage to the
theater of the mind. Dialogue becomes a dramatic method for self-inspection.
The external drama between hero and under-characters both provokes and is
provoked by an inner struggle to unite an identity similarly divided between a
higher (or better) self and lower drives and interests. Itself reflecting two faces,
the ideal and the real, the hero and the reader's stand-in, the pocket mirror
would provide the individual with a constant standard or guide, a way of
gauging the distance between character as it stands, fallen and faulty, and
character as it might become, through imitation of the hero. Dialogue would
provide not just a reflection of reality, but a transfiguring mirror, taking in
error and giving back truth. Dialogue therefore synthesizes the two views of
representation implicit in Shaftesbury's split conception of criticism: it turns
the mirror on nature, offering accurate imitations of reality (and is in this
respect like a history or miscellany), but only in order to turn the mirror on
the self, offering a resolution of two voices into one (and is in this respect like
a heroic drama or allegory).

   At the same time, one should remember that Shaftesbury has found it
necessary to internalize the mirror, relocating the public drama in a private
soliloquy. The cerebral theater finesses the difficulty posed by two divergent
conceptions of mimesis. One allows to the "pocket mirror" what one might
deny to any more accurate imitation of public nature. However improbable
the notion may be, that dialogue provides *both* an accurate imitation of actual
conversation *and* the story of a philosophical knight slaying all comers, the
critical case Shaftesbury makes for his magical glass will influence all
discussions of representation during the next seventy years of the eighteenth
century. To fulfill the Horatian edict in a time of rampant vice and
licentiousness (as it was sometimes called), or a time of rapid social change (as
it was also sometimes called) required writers to theorize kinds of writing that
satisfied the test of probability without losing the old appeal beyond. The
special kind of mimesis Shaftesbury postulates becomes attractive to moral
philosophers and theologians of the early eighteenth century (even those who
did not write dialogues) because it allows them to identify the plot of
transcendental dialectic with a realizable *fact* of human experience. The

controversial claim about dialectic's ability to mediate sensual and intellectual realms becomes the all-but-hidden backing of a magical mirror that takes in an accurate representation of mixed phenomena but gives back an orderly and moral design.

The reading I am offering here is based in large part upon the criticisms Shaftesbury received from his first readers. One of the most trenchant objections Shaftesbury faced came from George Berkeley in the Fifth Dialogue of *Alciphron*. There Shaftesbury's antagonistic ideas about imitation provide the basis for a parody of *Characteristicks*. In the dialogue, Alciphron, the gentler of two atheists (a Mandeville stand-in being the other), rises to the defense of "the most consummate critic this age has produced," by which he means Shaftesbury (III, pp. 198–199). After hearing lavish praise of his style and thought, one of the other characters asks Alciphron to read an example of Shaftesbury's prose to instance what he means by mirror-writing or inner colloquy. Here is the way Berkeley represents Alciphron's recitation of the lines:

> Here the
> Fantastic tribe itself seems scandalized.
> A civil war begins: the major part
> Of the capricious dames do range themselves
> On reason's side,
> And declare against the languid Siren.
> Ambition blushes at the offered sweet.
> Conceit and vanity take superior airs.
> Ev'n Luxury herself, in her polite
> And elegant humour, reproves th' apostate
> Sister,
> And marks her as an alien to true pleasure.   (III, pp. 198–199)

The passage continues for some time before Euphranor interrupts, "What! will you never have done with your poetry? Another time may serve: but why should we break off our conference to read a play?" (III, p. 200).

Berkeley's attack is both witty and fundamental. Why break off a conference to read a play? And which is philosophical dialogue? Berkeley suggests that the magical mirror does not in fact reconcile two degrees (if they are not kinds) of mimesis. He imagines a different kind of dialogue in which greater "realism" is preserved, even while he sustains the Christian part with a braver act of reason depending less upon allegorical elements. The result (as we shall see) was a work one reader called likelier to make than to break atheists, a work whose realistic repetition of the most alluring atheistic manifestos provides the fascinated reader with great entertainment and very little teaching, apart from some thin-spun metaphysics hardly up to the apologetic task. Berkeley played a dangerous game when he parodied Shaftesbury's inner colloquy on grounds of its insufficient realism as a philosophical dialogue.

Shaftesbury did not need Berkeley to alert him to the incredulity that
would attend any modern representation of classical dialogue. Despite being
the most articulate defender of philosophical dialogue during the eighteenth
century, he also saw most clearly that dialogue was a dead or dying genre.
Dialogue, as we have noted, was a magical mirror, a successor to allegory,
taking in error and reflecting back the better image. Yet, as a species of
imitation, dialogue was also linked to comic drama, polite conversation,
everyday forms of social exchange. According to Shaftesbury, writers of
dialogue must be answerable to the more mundane sense of imitation.
"Where Personages are exhibited, and natural Conversation set in view; if
Characters are neither tolerably preserv'd, nor *Manners*, with any just Similitude
describ'd; there remains nothing but what is too gross and monstrous for
Criticism or *Examination*" (III, pp. 293–294). Because mimetic, dialogue must
represent particularized scenes and characters. The reader must be able to
gauge "the bottom" from which characters speak, "what Kind or Species of
understanding they possess ... For an Artist who draws naturally, 'tis not
enough to shew us merely Faces which may be called *Men's*: Every Face must
be a certain *Man's*" (I, pp. 201–202).

Shaftesbury believed that the ancients when they met together routinely
engaged in the kind of dialogues represented by Plato and Cicero, so that
the magical mirror producing truth also offered an accurate imitation of
reality.[20] But he realized that the more closely dialogue imitated known
patterns of social converse at the beginning of the eighteenth century (even
when restricted to polite circles), the further dialogue removed itself from
anything like its classical seriousness. He therefore admits to being "put to
hard shift to contrive how or with what probability he might introduce
Men of any Note or Fashion, reasoning expressly and purposely, without
play or trifling, for two or three hours together on mere PHILOSOPHY
and MORALS. He finds these Subjects (as he confesses) so wide of
common Conversation, and by long Custom, so appropriated to the
School, the University-Chair, or Pulpit, that he thinks it hardly safe or
practicable to treat of them elsewhere, or in a different Tone" (III,
pp. 286–287).

Although one often finds discussion of philosophical dialogue linked to "the
art of conversation," here the relation between the two seems antithetical.[21]
The conventions of classical dialogue impose requirements of intellectual
focus and rigor that depart, according to Shaftesbury, from the norms of
fashionable conversation. Rather than reconciling the split conception of

---

[20] James Burnet, Lord Monboddo concurs: "The stile [of Xenophon's dialogues] is exactly the stile of
Attic conversation, which I hold to be as perfect of the kind as their historical, oratorical, or poetic
stile." *Of the Origin and Progress of Language*, 2nd edn., 6 vols. (Edinburgh: J. Balfour and London:
T. Cadell, 1774), v, pp. 319–320.
[21] See Jack Prostko, "Natural Conversation Set in View: Shaftesbury and Moral Speech," 42–61.

mimesis, philosophical dialogue, as a now impossible genre, shatters the transfiguring mirror. Shaftesbury declares the genre dead:

This is the plain *Dilemma* against that ancient manner of Writing, which we can neither well imitate, nor translate ... If we avoid Ceremony, we are unnatural: if we use it, and appear as we naturally are, as we salute, and meet, and treat one another, we hate the Sight. – What's this but *hating our own Faces?* ... What remains for him [the writer of dialogue] but to throw away the Pencil? – No more designing after the Life: no more *Mirour-Writing*, or personal Representation of any kind whatever.

THUS *Dialogue* is at an end. The Antients could see their own Faces, but we can't. (1, pp. 204–205)

However answerable classical dialogue may seem as a mode of modern philosophical and religious inquiry, as a literary genre it has become moribund. Writing half a century later, Ebenezer Macfait will repeat this observation in his *Remarks on the Life and Writings of Plato* (1760): "One great beauty of ancient dialogue was its being a picture of real life; but modern manners, as has been observed by Lord Shaftesbury, cannot be seriously intermingled with a philosophical discourse. Modern dialogue must therefore be unavoidably defective in the life and action, the painting and the scenery."[22] Even defenders of philosophical dialogue call it "defective" drama.

Like the skeptic's version of dialectic, a more mundane mirroring of reality (modern manners) defeats philosophy's higher (transcendental) aims. To the extent dialogue offered an accurate account of "men and manners," it threatened to become merely a vehicle for aimless conversation and theological uncertainty; to the extent it continued to uphold its classical function as a vehicle of sustained inquiry into a limited topic, it threatened to falsify the habits of the characters represented. To be didactic, it had to violate mimesis; to be mimetic it apparently had to abandon overt didacticism. This is the dilemma that leads Maurice Roelens, in an important discussion of the seventeenth- and eighteenth-century French dialogue, to declare the genre "impossible":

a double conflict lets itself be glimpsed in the theoretical field of philosophical dialogue, a conflict between the value that one will call the "literary" within philosophical dialogue, which concerns representation, and on the other hand, the exact and immediate conceptual interest [the lesson] of the work. [This is a] conflict poorly surmounted, badly resolved, or most often eluded in the innumerable works of ideas in the form of the dialogues of the seventeenth and eighteenth centuries.[23]

---

[22] Ebenezer Macfait, *Remarks on the Life and Writings of Plato. With Answers to the Principal Objections Against Him; and a General Review of His Dialogues* (Edinburgh: A. Kincaid and J. Bells, 1760), p. 88.

[23] Maurice M. Roelens, "Le Dialogue Philosophique, Genre Impossible? L'Opinion des Siècles Classiques," *Cahiers de l'Association Internationale des Etudes Françaises* 24 (1972) 49. For the tension between content and style in dialogue, see also Albert William Levi, "Philosophy as Literature: the Dialogue," *Philosophy and Rhetoric* 9 (1976) 1–20. Notes Levi, "Too much personal idiosyncracy would obscure the generality of philosophical response. Too little would make the drama into a contest of bloodless abstractions" (10).

"The exact and immediate conceptual interest" in *The Moralists* and most metaphysical dialogues of this period is that of confirming the teleological movement of transcendental dialectic, the subordination of part to whole, character to ideal, opinion to truth. The "literary" conflicts with this interest because representation is being linked increasingly to a concept of mimesis based upon a probable imitation of observed reality, wherein material is not always so obedient. Dialogues begin to be viewed either as weak philosophy (because not rigorous, systematic, and economical enough) or bad literature (because still too conceptual to be entertaining as prose fiction).

Dialogue into letter: Shaftesbury as theorist of the novel

We are now in a position to return to the questions with which this chapter began: why does *The Moralists* assume such a complicated structure, and how does the combination of genres influence our interpretation of the work? It becomes clear that Shaftesbury complicates the structure of *The Moralists* in order to make classical dialogue more credible to modern readers. The most important addition in this respect is the letter frame, into which the primary dialogue has been placed. Instead of a staged performance taking place in the present, dialogue is now the object of a character's memory. A dialogue narrated retrospectively strains credulity somewhat less than a work presented as a virtual stage drama. More importantly, the letter frame permits narrative interruptions, commentary, and changes of setting. These additions adjust for the forced formality of the philosophical exchange. Shaftesbury now links *The Moralists* not to dramatic *performances* but to the narrative possibilities that accrue to drama once it is written down to be printed and sold:

almost every other Leaf [contains] Descriptions or Illustrations of the Action, not in the *Poem* it-self, or in the Mouth of the Actors; but by the Poet, in his own Person; as appears to help out the Defect of the Text, by a Kind of marginal Note, or Comment, which renders these Pieces of a *mix'd* kind between *narrative* and *dramatick* ... 'Tis out of the same Regard to Ease, both in respect of Writer and Reader, that we see long Characters and Descriptions at the Head of most Dramatick Pieces, to inform us of the Relations, Kindred, Interests and Designs of the *Dramatis Personae*.
                                                                    (III, p. 289)

Readers who find nothing unusual about printed dramas containing lengthy narrative additions should have no difficulty lending credence to a philosophical dialogue embedded in a letter, where abstract, metaphysical discussion has been broken up by a dinner party, rhapsodic hymns to nature, and the story of Palemon's turn from the attractions of the park to the love of wisdom.

But just as the parallel with heroic drama implied one framework for interpretation, so this second parallel with the letter and mixed narrative provides different cues for interpreting the work. The most important effect of the letter frame is to invert temporal sequence. Because Philocles repeats the dialogue with Theocles in a letter, everything occurring at the beginning of the work actually follows the decisive dialogue with Theocles. Shaftesbury refers to this fact when he writes of "that *Anachronism*, of making the first part, *in order* to be the last *in time*." Although Shaftesbury appears to apologize for this violation of strict temporal unity, the temporal inversion has important implications. One realizes that the passages at the beginning, where Philocles expresses the greatest reservation about Theocles' ideas, actually follow his supposed conversion. "O ... that it had been my fortune to have met you the other day, just at my Return out of the Country," Philocles tells Palemon, "from *a Friend* whose Conversation had in one day or two made such an Impression on me, that I should have suited you to a Miracle. You wou'd have thought indeed that I had been cur'd of my *Scepticism* and Levity" (II, p. 217). Obviously, some falling away from sanctity has occurred in the meantime, and when Palemon wishes that "those good and serious Impressions of your *Friend* had without interruption lasted with you till this Moment," Philocles responds that he would still be capable of resurrecting that elevated mood, "were I not afraid. Afraid! said you. For whose sake, good PHILOCLES, I entreat you? For mine or your own? For both, reply'd I. For tho I was like to be perfectly cured of my Scepticism; 'twas by what I thought worse, downright *Enthusiasm*. You never knew a more agreeable ENTHUSIAST!" (II, p. 218) Even after his "conversion," it would seem, Philocles still views Theocles' rhapsody as a form of dangerous musical enchantment. Indeed, many of Philocles' most skeptical pronouncements occur at the beginning of the work, *after* his supposed conversion.

If one agrees to read *The Moralists* as a heroic drama, the plot of the philosophical dialogue does seem to enact the conversion of Philocles to Theocles' position. Philocles admits as much in the latter stages of the dialogue. "Your *Genius*, the *Genius* of the Place, and the GREAT GENIUS have at last prevail'd ... O Theocles! ... You have indeed made good your part of the Condition, and may now claim me as a Proselyte ... all sound Love and Admiration is ENTHUSIASM" (II, pp. 393, 400). In addition, the work appears to be based on other structural patterns of transcendence, moving geographically from city park to country estate to universal prospect, moving thematically from a discussion of "nearer beauties" (Palemon's probable love interest) to the most distant and exalted beauty, moving discursively from polite conversation to dialogue to rhapsody. Yet the temporal structure of the work is not, finally, determined by the pattern of heroic drama but by the odd mixture of dialogue and letter. This combination bends the apparently teleological plot into a circular, repetitive pattern. There has been no final conversion of the Pyrrhonist, just as there has been no conclusion of the work, whose end turns out to be its beginning.

This circular structure seeks to overcome the irreducible oppositions between skepticism and faith, dialogue and rhapsody, Pyrrho and Plato, by shifting concern from metaphysics to education. Philocles' purpose in repeating the dialogue is, after all, to help a friend (Palemon), whose turn from the delights of the park to the rarefied atmosphere of philosophy has been too sudden. The repetition of the dialogue, now for the second time, requires the skeptic to abandon his calcified position as a pure debunker and to re-create within a unified narrative his and the theist's best arguments. His pedagogical role forces him to set aside his own dogmatism. In this respect, the dialogue shifts from one in which distinct characters are associated with essentialized philosophical positions (a debate between "schools of thought"), to one in which each character undergoes a mutual modification requiring him to internalize aspects of the other's identity.

This educative process is described quite explicitly just after the point of impasse indicated above. Theocles urges his friend to object freely ("I am resolv'd not to go on till you have promised to pull me by the sleeve when I grow extravagant" [II, p. 375]). Philocles agrees to serve "in the same capacity as that Musician, whom an antient Orator made use of at his Elbow, to strike such moving Notes as rais'd him when he was perceiv'd to sink; and calm'd him again when his impetuous Spirit was transported in too high a Strain" (II, p. 375). Here, Theocles senses his advantage: "how," he asks the skeptic, "if instead of rising in my Transports I should grow flat and tiresome? What Lyre or Instrument wou'd you employ to raise me?" (II, p. 375). If Philocles identifies himself with a posture of pure debunking, how, Theocles wants to know, can he make good on his promise to rhapsodize the rhapsodist, should the need arise? What does the merely therapeutic function of the ironist offer to elevate the spirit of the diminished lover? Philocles avoids the question, responding from the sudden distance of a narrative report to Palemon. "The Danger, I told him, cou'd hardly be supposed to lie on this hand. His Vein was a plentiful one; and his *Enthusiasm* in no likelihood of failing him" (II, p. 375).

Yet the implication is clear: the skeptic, no less than the theist, is locked within a single, calcified view of his own identity. The situation of dialogic exchange, like the situation of letter-writing, however, requires that each participant to some extent abandon his existing conception of self and take on the role of the other. As the teacher of Palemon, Philocles moves away from a simple equation of his identity with a thoroughgoing Pyrrhonism. His repetition of the dialogue with Theocles involves recreating along with the powerful doctrinal views on both sides the perhaps more significant spectacle of two friends reasoning together, a spectacle which includes, not incidentally, the scenario according to which two characters who remain entrenched within their doctrines cease to communicate.

As the work begins, Philocles has forgotten most of the beneficial effects of his discourse with Theocles. His position is not so different from that of Palemon, who has heard the dialogue once and desires a repetition, or for that matter, from that of the reader, who concludes the work only to discover that he has returned to the beginning. Emphasis thus shifts from didactic, metaphysical precept to what might be called a performative experience whereby contradictory modes of interpretation (inscribed by drama and letter) are held simultaneously. Characters become dynamic embodiments of the paradox Shaftesbury elsewhere articulates that "Even the highest *implicit* Faith is in reality no more than a kind of *passive* SCEPTICISM" (III, 73).

The form of dialogue thus permitted Shaftesbury to bring into opposition the two opposing tendencies of his thought and to create a context within which they were, if not synthesized, at least reconciled. This reconciliation occurs primarily on the level of literary form, rather than within the polemics of debate. In all likelihood, we are meant to read *The Moralists* both as a heroic drama leading to the victory of Theocles and as a letter indicating the skeptic's ongoing resistance to any such conversion. The generic structure moves the reader from a metaphysical either/or to an ironic both/and.

My argument is not that Shaftesbury overcame the fetters of his dying genre; it is instead that Shaftesbury works out intractable oppositions in his own schemes of valuation by inventing new kinds of writing, combining older forms into novel assemblages. In the process he provides a theoretical rationale for the practice of many early novelists. In particular, the combination of letter and dialogue in *The Moralists* becomes a model for works of prose fiction setting a digressive encounter with error, opinion, experience, phenomenal diversity within a progressive narrative leading to moral edification. As Eve Tavor has also observed, "What Shaftesbury does is a great deal more rudimentary than what Richardson achieved in *Clarissa*, but Shaftesbury may be said to have formulated the generic principles Richardson was to develop, and to have provided a pointer as to how classical dialogue might be adapted to the eighteenth century."[24] Tavor's insight is far-reaching and can be supported through reference to a general habit of generic combination marking many works of prose fiction during the early eighteenth century.

The combination of letter and dialogue was a common strategy, and was, on another occasion, the topic of explicit critical commentary. At the end of Marie Huber's *The World Unmask'd: or the Philosopher the Greatest Cheat* (1736), we find "A Letter to Mr. * * * , Being a Parallel between the LETTERS and the DIALOGUES" in the previous work. The author of this letter is responding to the fact that some readers have expressed a preference for the dialogues over the letters; whereas others have preferred the letters. Rather than judging between these, the author details why both letter and dialogue are

---

[24] Eve Tavor, *Scepticism, Society, and the Eighteenth-Century Novel* (New York: St. Martin's Press, 1987), p. 98.

necessary in a religious work. Huber begins by explaining that the two genres have different ends in view. The narrative character of the letter promotes a more systematic exposition of religious doctrine, a "short sketch of the universal Plan of the Deity, in regard to Mankind."[25] The dialogue, by contrast, seeks to "unveil Man, shew him his false [*sic*], and how little he is disposed to enter into the views of the Deity."[26] The opposition between revelation and nature, the divine and the human, is here redescribed in terms of a difference in the kind of authority possible within different genres. Theodicy, the attempt to reconcile human experience with a divine plan, is asserted formally through the combination of genres: "The Writer of the *Letters* has given us a compendious Description of the ways of God: The Writer of the Dialogue applies himself particularly to an account of the ways of Men." It follows, then, that a justification of the ways of God to man (and man to God), conceived in terms of the problem of reconciling different kinds of textual authority, will find the combination of epistle and dialogue necessary. "These perhaps were the Author's reasons for giving his work so *original* a Form, instead of making it a regular Treatise."[27]

This author, like Shaftesbury, is using genre to control the plot of the work. The plot, in turn, stands for an epistemological claim about our means of access to knowledge of the divine. In an age increasingly suspicious of any claim to direct revelation or transcendental authority (whether in theology or in politics), the plot must meander, knowledge must be indirect, ethical guidelines must be gained through experience; and this indirection is represented by the haphazard structure of the human dialogues. The dialogic element brings the audience into sympathy with a set of fallen characters. They identify with their faults, see themselves in the mirror. But this identification is not allowed to lose its larger aim. The reader is led to his own conversion "by a secret sentiment, without perceiving that he himself is the case. He cannot resist the force of Truth, the proofs of which he finds within himself." In this way, "the Religion which is offered him, has no need of foreign authority for enforcing its reception. He finds the Principles of it engraved on the bottom of his own Heart."[28]

In *The Moralists* the epistemological authority assigned to letter and dialogue is reversed: the letter, because narrated by a skeptic, expresses the more tentative appeal to transcendence; the dialogue, on the other hand, because modeled upon philosophical allegory and heroic drama (for example, Boethius' *The Consolation of Philosophy*) provides the more immediate access to a transcendental dimension. Nevertheless, what is significant for the

---

[25] Marie Huber, *The World Unmask'd: or the Philosopher the Greatest Cheat; in twenty-four dialogues ... To which is added, The State of Souls separated from their Bodies: being an epistolary treatise* (London: A. Millar, 1736), p. 357. The work is a translation of *Le Monde fou préferé au monde sage, en vingt-quatre promenades de trois amis ...* 2 vols. (1731). Subsequent English editions appeared in 1743 and 1786.
[26] *Ibid.*, p. 358.   [27] *Ibid.*, p. 359.   [28] *Ibid.*, pp. 359, 357.

early history of the novel is the way genres that have been assigned different degrees of epistemological authority are being combined. These new combinations ask the reader to interpret in a new way: *The Moralists* should be read not only as a heroic drama but also as a miscellany, even though the hermeneutic codes built into these distinct forms are contradictory. To hold these codes together, to embrace both Theocles and Philocles, Plato and Pyrrho, would be to promote a new mode of reading that really might reconcile ancients and moderns. The ironic both/and preserves both realms – sense and intellect, phenomena and noumena – by *not* forcing a transition from the one to the other. It is created through a combination of generic features that signal *contradictory* modes of interpretation, but which, taken together, move one past the metaphysical impasse between Plato and Pyrrho.

Early prose fictions are philosophical in a similar way: they seek to preserve the logic of transcendental dialectic through the inclusion of textual elements (allegory, typology, romance, gothic supernaturalism) that assume a transcendental mode of interpretation; yet these same works will acknowledge the inadequacy of these genres in isolation by incorporating other elements (formal realism, natural dialogue, heterodox characters and opinions, aimless plots, hobby-horses) that resist any easy sublimation within a transcendental scheme.

In *Pilgrim's Progress* the theological goal of bridging human and divine realms leads Bunyan to combine dialogue and allegory, a mixture novel enough to require an elaborate defense in "The Author's Apology for his Book." Bunyan writes,

> *I find that men (as high as Trees) will write*
> *Dialogue-wise; yet no Man doth them slight*
> *For writing so: Indeed if they abuse*
> *Truth, cursed be they, and the craft they use*
> *To that intent; but yet let Truth be free*
> *To make her Sallies upon Thee, and Me,*
> *Which way it pleases God. For who knows how,*
> *Better than he that taught us first to Plow,*
> *To guide our Mind and Pens for his Design?*
> *And he makes base things usher in Divine.*[29]

Bunyan apologizes specifically for the parts of the book written in dialogue form. He knows there are readers who will fault him for representing such characters as Wordly-Wiseman and Ignorance, who, like the deists after them, believe they can win their way to the celestial city through the light of reason alone. The danger is that the reader, like Christian, will lose his or her way, will be seduced by the human dialogue into human ways, rather than

---

[29] Bunyan, *The Pilgrim's Progress, from this World to That which is to Come*, 2nd edn. (Oxford: Clarendon Press, 1960), p. 6.

ascend to the celestial city. Yet Bunyan takes his example from another
preacher who used parables and common stories and who conversed
familiarly with his flock. He assures his reader that dialogue serves allegory,
and not the reverse. Base things are *all along* ushering in the divine because
something greater than a haphazard exchange of question and answer guides
the pilgrim's thoughts (like his steps) to a higher destination.

The pattern of generic combination is similar in the construction of
Richardson's *Clarissa*. Here the "base" dialogic element is the exchange of
letters, especially during the first half of the book. As Richardson saw, this
epistolary element brought immediacy, psychological complexity, and the
clash of competing interpretations to the work. It also introduced moral
indeterminacy. Because written by many hands about the same events, the
letters introduce a multiplicity of viewpoints with no controlling narrator able
to reassert didactic control. Clarissa, the heroine, may appear willful, proud,
naive, scheming, self-deluded, or saintly, depending upon whose letter we are
reading. Yet a profound "event" transforms this epistolary dialogue into
religious allegory.

That event, of course, is her rape. It will be Clarissa's entire purpose, after
the rape, to prove that this event is not simply one more empirical episode
among others (as Lovelace would like to believe), but a cataclysm whose effect
upon *her* reanimates the connection between body and spirit. But the
transformation of her story after the event calls for a change also in the
dominant genre. As Richardson makes clear in his "Postscript," the mode of
interpretation generated by the letters gives way to a reading informed by
the conventions of Christian tragedy, and, finally, allegory.[30] In this way,
Richardson rescues the novel from potentially aimless dialogue (as Sterne will
not) through a combination much like Bunyan's, a combination theorized by
Shaftesbury in his attempt to revive philosophical dialogue for moral
philosophy.

Shaftesbury's writings suggest the three directions taken within philosophical
theology during the remainder of the period. First, in the impasse between
Plato and Pyrrho, transcendental and skeptical dialectic, Neoclassicism and
Enlightenment, Shaftesbury anticipates a broader secularization of culture
that will eventually be asserted quite directly by Hume. We should remember
that most of the arguments Mandeville and Hume will use against both
rational Christianity and the fledgling discourse of philosophical aesthetics
were already circulating within the skeptical and deistic moments of

---

[30] See the "Postscript" to *Clarissa*. Richardson writes of that "catastrophe ... [that] necessarily follows
the natural progress of the story," and of a "religious plan" that justifies a spectacle of suffering "till
it meets with a completion of its reward" (*Clarissa, or the History of a Young Lady*, ed. Angus Ross
[London: Penguin Books, 1985], p. 1495). This plan derives not from the conventions of the letter,
but from a Christianized conception of tragedy.

Characteristics, particularly in Philocles' attacks against Theocles. Second, in solving the dilemmas raised by his own skeptical inclinations, Shaftesbury generates during the last years of his life (as in the closing speeches of *The Moralists*) the characteristic arguments and conceptual vocabulary of philosophical aesthetics. As we have seen, this recourse to the philosophical analysis of taste constitutes an "apology" for Shaftesbury's earlier defense of mixed, popular forms and the social values annexed to them. Finally, Shaftesbury advised writers to reformulate moral philosophy in fictions of characterized intellectual debate. He advocated a detailed representation of character, the combination of narrative and dramatic elements, the division of works into chapters, the inclusion of natural description and commentary. He sought out a textual ground between the orderliness of classical drama and the randomness of the miscellany, the private meditation of rhapsody and the public exchange of social conversation. Shaftesbury attempted to mediate between a priori and a posteriori epistemological claims by embedding dialogues within the narrative framework of an epistle. His solution to the anticipated death of dialogue thus became a model for other moral philosophers who would attempt to combine serious ethical and theological arguments within popular narrative structures.

3

Berkeley and the paradoxes of empiricism:
A Treatise concerning the Principles of Human Knowledge and Three Dialogues between Hylas and Philonous

Among the other insults comprising John Hervey's *Some Remarks Upon the Minute Philosopher*, published in 1732, the same year as Berkeley's *Alciphron, or the Minute Philosopher*, we find a mean account of Berkeley's development as a writer. His early philosophical productions having failed to attract much attention ("the Ignorant stared and the Learned laughed"), Berkeley will now scratch where he's sure the reading public itches: he will turn novelist. Hervey offers lugubrious praise of Berkeley's command over fictional technique, his landscapes (more accomplished than any of Claude Lorrain's), his "Description of Sportsmen," and so on. Then he suggests where Berkeley's career should lead:

if weary of metaphysical Novels, he should turn his Pen to any of a softer Kind; if from the Luxuriancy of his Imagination, and Love of Variety, he should change the Style of his Romances, from the Philosophic to the Tender, from theological Opinion, to amorous Sentiments, and instead of treating Schoolmen and Free-thinkers, should write of fighting Nymphs and perjur'd Swains; the Sale of his *Minute Philosopher* would be such a Trifle to the Profits of this Production, that for Two Editions of the one, there would be Twenty of the other: Not a Greensickness Girl, nor an idle School-boy, but would have him in their Hand; and so differently would his Readers treat him in a Performance of that sort, that I dare say no body would begin it, that would not read it out.[1]

Despite the venom, Hervey's response at least has the merit of taking into account the trajectory of Berkeley's stylistic – if not intellectual – development. From the early *Principles* through *Three Dialogues between Hylas and Philonous* to *Alciphron, or the Minute Philosopher*, Berkeley's major statements of moral philosophy depend increasingly upon fictional representations to supplement the claims of reason.

Unlike Hervey's inclusive though unflattering view, the academic reception

[1] John Lord Hervey, *Some Remarks On the "Minute Philosopher,"* 2nd edn. (London: J. Robinson, 1752), p. 26.

of Berkeley has tended to divide its attention between the properly philosophical works, such as the *Treatise concerning the Principles of Human Knowledge* and *Three Dialogues between Hylas and Philonous*, and such mixed performances as *Alciphron* and *Siris*, which are variously labeled literature, Christian apology, or even satire.[2] Such divisions have helped secure Berkeley's place within the great triumvirate of English empiricists, but only at the expense of an artificial sense of homogeneity within this tradition. As Gary Shapiro has observed with respect to Hume, "such traditions [as the British empiricist] are hardly as uniform as we had once supposed: we may have to face the possibility that there are multiple histories and traditions where we had thought there was only one."[3]

One way of suggesting the complexity rather than the uniformity of a tradition is to ask what leads its dominant figures to experiment with different forms of exposition. The history of ideas taking us from Descartes to Locke to Berkeley to Hume to Kant will look different when the sequence of ideas is read alongside the contest to control the interpretation of ideas being carried out through generic innovation.[4] One does not need to agree with Hervey that profit was Berkeley's leading motive to see that dependence upon the resources of fiction becomes more prominent as he moves from the *Principles* to *Hylas and Philonous* and finally to *Alciphron*.[5] Because we cannot assume that Berkeley shared the divisions of academic labor we have inherited, it is not adequate to explain such transformations in terms of his decision to suspend philosophical inquiry in order to write religious apology or to leave off metaphysics for a time to write ethics. Better, perhaps, is the opposite assumption – that Berkeley would have resented the description of himself as a metaphysical novelist, and, by the same token, that he would have resisted, to the extent he could, any pressure, whether economic, intellectual, or literary, driving him from philosophy towards romance. Even if overstated, this view should make the direction of Berkeley's philosophical and discursive career all the more noteworthy. Why did a moral philosopher who started out writing empiricist philosophy in the genre of the treatise move to a restatement (by his own

[2] I discuss the reception of Berkeley's *Alciphron* in chapter 4.
[3] Gary Shapiro, "The Man of Letters and the Author of Nature: Hume on Philosophical Discourse," *The Eighteenth Century: Theory and Interpretation* 26 (1985) 134.
[4] For an especially good example of the way an analysis based upon genre counters received period conceptions, see Franco Moretti's discussion of tragedy in *Signs Taken for Wonders*, trans. Susan Fischer, David Forgacs, and David Miller (London: Verso, 1983), especially pp. 48–49.
[5] At the same time, the sales potential of a more lively dialogue should not be discounted: unlike Berkeley's earlier works, *Alciphron* was immediately successful. It went through two more editions in 1732, appeared in a third edition in 1752, was translated into Dutch (1733) and French (1734), and appeared separately in posthumous editions in the years 1757, 1767, 1777, and 1803. For the early reception of *Alciphron*, see David Berman's edition of the First, Third, Fourth, and Seventh Dialogues in *Alciphron in Focus* (London: Routledge, 1993), pp. 1–6; and Harry M. Bracken, *The Early Reception of Berkeley's Immaterialism 1710–1733* (The Hague: Martinus Nijhoff, 1959).

account) of the treatise in a dialogue; and why, nineteen years later, did Berkeley reframe his moral philosophy in a rambling dialogue (*Alciphron*) so different from the preceding work (*Hylas and Philonous*) that one of his early antagonists feigned disbelief that the two works could have been penned by the same man?[6] Answers to these questions lead to larger conclusions about the relation between empiricism and literary form during the eighteenth century.

My claim will be that Berkeley's ongoing confrontation with Lockean empiricism, now radicalized through the immaterialist hypothesis of *esse percipi*, leads him (in the *Principles*) to outright skepticism, to utter solipsism, and to something resembling pantheism, the very conclusions he had sought to avoid. While it is undoubtedly true, as Berkeley claimed, that the easy and familiar form of dialogue in *Hylas and Philonous* allowed him to recast the immaterialist hypothesis in a more accessible way, the fiction of metaphysical dialogue premised upon a transcendental interpretation of dialectic also helped Berkeley avoid these unwanted implications of the earlier treatise. My reading of *Hylas and Philonous* as a more systematic and pious exposition of the *Principles* directs our attention away from the specific doctrinal views aired in the dialogue, which repeat the positions set forth in the *Principles*, and towards the elements of fiction that lend support to the precarious claims of a theological immaterialism.

Yet, as a metaphysical dialogue establishing Christianity on rational foundations, *Hylas and Philonous* must also disclaim the support of fiction. Its inevitability resides in nature, in a dialectical process that might have been purely logical, purely impersonal, but for the need to popularize important philosophical discoveries. Such a reading of Berkeley's first dialogue as a mode of rational demonstration makes the break represented by *Alciphron* all the more striking, for it is a dialogue whose vividness of characterization and impartiality of argument potentially undermines the author's didactic aims, a contradiction that Hervey delights in pointing out. *Alciphron* anticipates by about twenty-five years the issues raised in Hume's essay "Of the Standard of Taste" (1756). It dramatizes the breakdown of consensus about any possible standard for adjudicating differences of opinion. As Berkeley gropes about for a textual solution to this relativity of viewpoints, his philosophical dialogue does indeed begin to resemble a metaphysical novel.

Berkeley himself suggests several reasons why the form of dialogue presented itself as a suitable means of recasting the ideas of his *Principles*. "I thought it requisite," he writes in the "Preface," "to treat more clearly and fully of certain principles laid down in the First [the *Principles*] and to place

---

[6] *A Vindication of the Reverend D——— B———y, from the Scandalous Imputation of being Author of a late Book, intitled, Alciphron, or the Minute Philosopher* (London: A. Millar, 1734). The work has been attributed to William Wishart.

them in a new light. Which is the business of the following *Dialogues*" (II, pp. 167–68). The weak interpretation of this statement would be that "in a new light" means little more than "the same ideas offered in a pedagogically more effective way." We find support for a pedagogical rationale for dialogue within *Hylas and Philonous* itself. Philonous tells Hylas his "attention must be awakened and detained by frequent repetitions of the same thing placed oft in the same, oft in different lights" (II, p. 223).[7] These directions echo several of Locke's ideas about repetition and recursion in the scene of education.[8] According to the weaker thesis, Berkeley's thinking remains fundamentally the same between 1710 and 1713. He has been forced to recognize the difficulty of the earlier text and is resolved to reframe it "in the most easy and familiar manner," namely as a polite, pedagogical conversation.

A stronger thesis, the one I shall argue here, would be that Berkeley found it "requisite" to rewrite the *Principles* as a dialogue because the earlier work had not satisfactorily reconciled the implications of a radicalized empiricism with the demands of Christian orthodoxy. On the title-page of *Hylas and Philonous*, Berkeley indicates that the design of the work "is plainly to demonstrate the reality and perfection of human knowledge, the incorporeal nature of the soul, and the immediate providence of a Deity; in opposition to Sceptics and Atheists" (II, p. 147). This formulation is far stronger than that at the beginning of the *Principles*: "wherein the chief causes of error and difficulty in the Sciences, with the grounds of Scepticism, Atheism, and Irreligion, are inquired into" (II, p. 1). Berkeley does not say that the former inquiry necessitated the latter demonstration; however, as a reading of the *Principles* will make clear, such is precisely the case. Philonous must convince Hylas that the doctrine of immaterialism solves all the difficulties raised by skeptics and Pyrrhonists; just as Berkeley had tried, largely unsuccessfully, to convince the reader of his earlier treatise that however much immaterialism may seem to resemble Pyrrhonian skepticism, it actually affords the soundest refutation of irreligion.

---

[7] Peter Walmsley cites a letter from Percival to Berkeley congratulating him on just this pedagogical effect: "The new method you took by way of dialogue, I am satisfied has made your meaning much easier understood, and was the properest course you could use in such an argument, where prejudice against the novelty of it was sure to raise numberless objections that could not anyway so easy as by dialogue be either made or answered." *The Rhetoric of Berkeley's Philosophy* (Cambridge: Cambridge University Press, 1990), pp. 65–66.

[8] See in particular *Some Thoughts Concerning Education* (Cambridge: Cambridge University Press, 1913). In section 167 Locke argues that the tutor should make instruction attractive through change and variety. In section 195 Locke adds that pedagogical method should move gradually from the known to the unknown. Perhaps even more relevant are Locke's observations about the training of the body. The feet, for instance, should be hardened "by a frequent and familiar Use of cold Water … thereby to prevent the Mischiefs that usually attend taking wet in the Feet" (section 1). Education, whether of mind or body, moves through a repetitive and recursive sequencing of activities. These concepts underlie discussions of dialogue as an "easy and familiar" means of instruction.

Berkeley against the materialists

The thread linking the three works discussed in this and the following chapter is Berkeley's encounter with Pyrrhonism.[9] Berkeley's attitude is not dismissive. It cannot be. For Pyrrhonian arguments, in particular the relativity of sense perception, underlie the genesis of his famous immaterialist position, *esse* is *percipi* or *percipere*, whose express purpose is to refute irreligion. The great aim of reconciling orthodox Christianity with the methodology and findings of the New Science required Berkeley to acknowledge the relativity of perspectives but also to disavow the conclusions that Pyrrhonian skeptics drew from the allowance. He thus advances, as Hume would later observe, an extreme philosophical skepticism, but only in the name of establishing orthodoxy on firmer ground.

Berkeley's early philosophy can be said to advance first a destructive and then a constructive movement. In order to understand the reason for this double movement, it is important to ask why Berkeley became obsessed with disproving the concept of material substance. In 1710 Berkeley found himself positioned in the history of secularization at just the point when all of the attributes previously ascribed to a transcendental dimension (order, wisdom, intelligence, agency) were being relocated within the material realm itself. Not only was the analogical link between natural and supernatural realms in the process of being dissolved, but also the animating principles of natural operations were being attributed to powers internal to nature. Berkeley lumps these tendencies together under the term "materialism." His animus is not against external reality *per se*. Berkeley is always ready to grant the existence of what "the vulgar" call matter – the stone Johnson kicked, thinking to refute Berkeley – but only on condition that one does not take the allowance of objective matter to mean that nature contains its own cause or animating principle.

Berkeley believed that if one allowed any of God's animating work to be delegated to even the smallest part of nature, soon, *all* of God's handiwork would be attributed to a mundane mechanistic force. Hume would take just this step in "Of the Idea of Necessary Connection": "it argues more wisdom to contrive at first the fabric of the world with such perfect foresight that of itself, and by its proper operation, it may serve all the purposes of Providence than if the great Creator were obliged every moment to adjust its parts and animate by his breath all the wheels of that stupendous machine."[10] Hume's affected piety notwithstanding, the most

---

[9] My understanding of Berkeley is indebted to the lucid account of the centrality of Pyrrhonism to Berkeley's thought in Richard H. Popkin's, *The High Road to Pyrrhonism*, eds. Richard A. Watson and James E. Force (San Diego: Austin Hill Press, 1980), pp. 277–369.

[10] Hume, "Of the Idea of Necessary Connection," in *An Inquiry concerning Human Understanding*, ed. Charles W. Hendel (Indianapolis: The Bobbs-Merrill Co. Inc., 1955), pp. 81–82.

perfect expression of wisdom so conceived would be divinity's complete delegation of power to the quotidian. One would then identify the principle of causal agency (to the extent nature exhibited coherence) with some material substrate, which was its own cause and the cause of other natural effects. Berkeley calls the belief in material substance the very "corner-stone" of all skepticism and atheism, which when "once removed, the whole fabric cannot choose but fall to the ground" (II, 92, p. 81).[11]

The odd double movement of Berkelean immaterialism, the baffling skepticism about the existence of anything outside our own ideas, followed by a remarkably smooth transition to belief in the existence of a benevolent and all-powerful Deity, will seem less puzzling if one bears in mind the materialist threat. Berkeley concluded that refuting the materialists required two things: first, that he destroy matter completely, and with it the belief in any active agency belonging to nature distinct from mind; second, that he reanimate existence without locating the principle of agency within nature itself. In this way, his philosophical theology assumes destructive and constructive parts, each associated with a different way of "doing" philosophy.

"The infinite divisibility of matter is now universally allowed": Berkeley's critique of necessary connection

In a move that puzzled even Berkeley's contemporaries, the pious philosopher joined the most radical skeptics of his day in asserting the relativity of perceptions. Berkeley sought to destroy matter, and the best method of doing so had already been proposed by the skeptics, especially those skeptics of a scientific bent, whose new inventions, the telescope and microscope, were exploding the stability of objective forms. What these new lenses demonstrated was that any objective report about matter based on evidence supplied by the senses inevitably failed to account for the relativity of sensate understanding:

the infinite divisibility of matter is now universally allowed, at least by the most approved and considerable philosophers, who on the received principles demonstrate it beyond all exception. Hence, it follows there is an infinite number of parts in each particle of matter which are not perceived by sense. The reason therefore that any particular body seems to be of a finite magnitude, or exhibits only a finite number of parts to sense, is, not because it contains no more, since in itself it contains an infinite number of parts, but because the sense is not acute enough to discern them. In proportion therefore as the sense is rendered more acute, it perceives a greater number of parts in the object ... And at length, after various changes of size and shape, when the sense becomes infinitely acute, the body shall seem infinite. During all which there is no alteration in the body, but only in sense.   (II, 47, p. 60)

---

[11] Citations of the *Principles* refer to the Luce–Jessop edition and are given by volume number, section, and page number.

Berkeley writes of an objective world which, like Gulliver's, offers no inherent and consistent reality apart from the subjective state of the observer; it has become "infinite and shapeless." Now, not only do the secondary qualities of objects (color, smell, texture, and the like) depend upon the psychological state of the observer (as Locke had acknowledged); the primary qualities (shape, extension, weight) themselves also vary as the internal condition and external position of the perceiver changes (an extreme Locke resisted in his view of simple ideas as the solid and shared building blocks of complex ideas). "*Great* and *small, swift* and *slow*, are allowed to exist nowhere without a mind; being entirely relative, and changing as the frame or position of the organs of sense varies" (II, 11, p. 45).

The challenge Berkeley set himself was to grant what he felt could no longer be denied – that it is "impossible that any colour or extension at all, or other sensible quality whatsoever, should exist in an unthinking subject without the mind, or in truth, that there should be any such thing as an outward object" – while reclaiming this argument from skeptics and atheists, who had drawn conclusions from it so damaging to Christianity (II, 15, p. 47).[12] Berkeley's celebrated doctrine of immaterialism is his solution: if the distinction between primary and secondary qualities cannot be upheld, then the existence of objects depends entirely upon their appearance in mind, not upon some realist substratum or matter rendering all perceptions copies of a true original: *esse* is *percipi*, or (allowing for the one doing the perceiving) *percipere*.

Although the argument seems to deprive mechanists of matter, it also required Berkeley to represent a cataclysmic reduction of the external world to a phantasm of subjectivity. Berkeley assumes the Lockean commonplace that all knowledge comes from sense experience. He transforms it from a liberating proposal into a ghastly spectre by dwelling upon the implication that if we follow Locke's empirical way, nature can *only* be said to exist in our mental theater, a flat white screen imprinted with colored splotches, raw feels, pricks and pulls, screams and whispers, or, as Berkeley calls them, ideas. Just when all appears lost, however, Berkeley puts down his pen and walks into the street. To the first person he meets he says these words: "Sir, I side in all things with the mob, and so I request a simple answer to a simple question." "Shoot," his interlocutor replies. "Do you see that stone there, the one that gentleman is about to kick?" "Yes," comes the reply. "Would you say that it exists, and would continue to exist even if you and I and he were not here to perceive it?" Berkeley's interlocutor seems puzzled by the question, but replies, commonsensically, in the affirmative, after which Berkeley thanks him and ascends again to his study.

Berkeley now has his clue for the constructive turn. Strict empiricism

---

[12] See Robert Muehlmann, "The Role of Perceptual Relativity in Berkeley's Philosophy," *Journal of the History of Philosophy* 29 (1991) 397–425.

brings us a world wholly subjective and ideal; yet common sense assures us of an objective world independent of finite minds. Berkeley concluded that a philosophical theology could be established by combining these views. Says Philonous to Hylas at the end of their dialogue: "My endeavours tend only to unite, and place in a clearer light that truth, which was before shared between the vulgar and the philosophers: the former being of the opinion, that *those things they immediately perceive are real things*; and the latter, that *the things immediately perceived are ideas, which exist only in the mind*. Which two notions put together, do in effect, constitute the substance of what I advance" (II, 262, p. 484).

Only a God, Berkeley knew, could make both claims true at the same time. Hence, the conclusion follows: "So long as they [external objects] are not actually perceived by me or do not exist in my mind or that of any other created spirit, they must either have no existence at all, or else subsist in the mind of some eternal spirit" (II, 6, p. 43). And because, as the mob well knows, it would be the greatest absurdity to deny the real existence of external objects, a God is proven by the existence of phenomena pure and simple: "When in broad day-light I open my eyes, it is not in my power to choose whether I shall see or no, or to determine what particular objects shall present themselves to my view; and so likewise as to the hearing and other senses, the ideas imprinted on them [the senses] are not creatures of *my* will. There is therefore some other Will or Spirit that produces them" (II, 29, p. 53). The unmoved Mover has become an unperceived Perceiver, an argument that continues into *Hylas and Philonous*, where Philonous calls it "a direct and immediate demonstration, from a most evident principle, of the *being of a God*" (II, p. 212).

Berkeley thus sought to avoid materialism (atheism) by radicalizing empiricism. It was an odd but decisive tactic, one motivated, one assumes, as much by the confidence that it might really work as by the need to wrest the perspectivalist maneuver away from skeptics. But what sort of theology emerges from the Pyrrhonian gambit? Berkeley proves the existence of a deity through the bare fact of perception ("When in broad daylight I open my eyes ... "). Any and every part of nature, by its mere existence, confirms the being of a Deity or greater Mind. The argument works as well for the part as for the whole; it replaces more traditional versions of physico-theology, based upon concepts of design in nature, with an ecstatic phenomenalism that holds every part of nature, "even the most rude and shapeless," to be a "manifest token" of divinity. Philonous tells Hylas,

Divines and philosophers had proved beyond all controversy, from the beauty and usefulness of the several parts of the creation, that it was the workmanship of God. But that – setting aside all help of astronomy and natural philosophy, all contemplation of the contrivance, order, and adjustment of things, an infinite mind should be necessarily inferred from the bare existence of the *sensible world*, is an advantage to them only who have made this easy reflection: that the sensible world is that which we perceive by our several senses; and that nothing is perceived by the senses besides ideas; and that no idea or archetype of an idea can exist otherwise than in a mind. You may now, without any laborious search into the sciences, without any subtlety of reason, or tedious length of discourse, oppose and baffle the most strenuous advocate of atheism ... the whole system of Atheism, is it not entirely overthrown, by this single reflexion on the repugnancy included in supposing the whole, or any part, even the most rude and shapeless, of the visible world, to exist without a mind?   (II, pp. 212–13)

While Berkeley stops short of denying the validity of the design argument, two difficulties have begun to render it inoperative.[13] First, and less significantly, a God established through design may be available only to a philosophical elite able to follow the stages in a complex rational analogy moving from the investigation of nature here to the assertion of an ordering principle there. More importantly, statements about contrivance, order, design, and the like are incompatible with Berkeley's destructive, Pyrrhonian phase. To have knowledge of contrivance in nature assumes the ability to comprehend necessary connections among parts. Yet Berkeley, in his effort to destroy materialism (through *esse percipi*), denies any possible knowledge of imperceptible causal connections in nature. He constantly and strenuously denies that an idea can cause another idea or that a mind can form an idea of active agency or spirit.

In other words, it was Berkeley, not Hume, who first drew the logical consequence from the Lockean epistemology that causal connections because imperceptible cannot, strictly speaking, be said to exist as objects of knowledge.[14] According to Berkeley, all we perceive are events or effects, more or less frequently conjoined with other events or effects. As Philonous tells Hylas,

when I hear a coach drive along the streets, immediately I perceive only a sound; but from the experience I have had that such a sound is connected with a coach, I am said to hear the coach. It is nevertheless evident that, in truth and strictness, nothing can be *heard* but *sound*; and the coach is not then properly perceived by sense, but suggested from experience.   (II, pp. 204)

[13] For another discussion of Berkeley and design, see Michael Hooker, "Berkeley's Argument from Design," in *Berkeley: Critical and Interpretative Essays*, ed. Colin M. Turbayne (Minneapolis: University of Minnesota Press, 1982), pp. 261–270.

[14] An incipient critique of necessary connection is already evident in Berkeley's *An Essay Towards a New Theory of Vision* (1709): "Not that there is any natural or necessary connexion between the sensation we perceive by the turn of the eyes and greater or lesser distance, but because the mind has by constant experience found the different sensations corresponding to the different dispositions of the eyes to be attended each with a different degree of distance in the object, there has grown an habitual or customary connexion between those two sorts of ideas" (I, p. 174).

We think we perceive a necessary connection between one effect and a determinate cause, but in fact the relation only arises "when, from a frequently perceived connection, the immediate perception of ideas by one sense suggest to the mind others, perhaps belonging to another sense, which are wont to be connected with them" (II, p. 204). Hylas, who hears Philonous speak these words, can only respond, "you are disposed to raillery." Hume, of course, heard more than a jest:

It appears, then, that this idea of necessary connection among events arises from a number of similar instances which occur, of the constant conjunction of these events ... [when] after a repetition of similar instances the mind is carried by habit, upon the appearance of one event, to expect its usual attendent and to believe that it will exist.[15]

Why do we find the pious Berkeley supplying Hume with such ammunition?[16] As we have already seen, Berkeley was determined to strip materialism of its conceptual bases. One of those bases was the claim that nature exhibits intrinsic causal connections. Unfortunately, the same view supported the design argument of physico-theology. In the former case, causality is attributed to nature itself; in the latter, the attribution is to a higher source. Berkeley, no doubt suspicious of the tendency (for example, within deism) for design to begin to sound like mechanism, tries to place theology on a different footing. Nature need no longer be *represented* to the senses in terms of order; its bare *presentation* is evidence enough to affirm God's constant attentiveness in upholding phenomena:

withersoever we direct our view we do at all times and in all places perceive manifest tokens of the divinity: everything we see, hear, feel, or any wise perceive by sense, being a sign or effect of the Power of God.   (II, 148, p. 109)

Statements such as these have invited comparisons to the pantheism of Romantics and even to Islamic mysticism.[17] Although unmindful of the traditional aims of Berkeley's larger theological project, these comparisons

---

[15] Hume, "Of the Idea of Necessary Connection," p. 86.

[16] In a well-known note in his *Inquiry concerning Human Understanding*, Hume wrote of Berkeley, "most of the writings of that very ingenious author form the best lessons of skepticism, which are to be found among the antient or modern philosophers, Bayle not excepted" ("Of the Academical or Skeptical Philosophy," in *An Inquiry concerning Human Understanding*, p. 163, n. 2).

[17] Jessop writes of Berkeley's theology, "the note of wonder in his writings at the wealth and beneficence of the corporeal universe when taken concretely as it is experienced lifts him out of the Age of Newton and makes him a precursor of the Romantic period, as Whitehead ... has noticed." ("Berkeley as Religious Apologist," in *New Studies in Berkeley's Philosophy*, ed. Warren E. Steinkraus [New York: Holt, Rinehart, and Winston, 1966], p. 104). Popkin holds that Berkeley sought to transform "the Pyrrhonian denial of the reality of anything into an affirmation of the entire sensible universe" (*The High Road to Pyrrhonism*, p. 309). For the relation between Berkeley and Islamic mysticism, see Waheed Ali Farooqi, "Berkeley's Ontology and Islamic Mysticism," in *New Studies in Berkeley's Philosophy*, ed. Warren E. Steinkraus (New York: Holt, Rinehart and Winston, Inc., 1966), pp. 123–133.

suggest that the theology emerging from Berkeley's destructive phase, ecstatic phenomenalism, is remarkably thin on Christian content.

We should pause, therefore, to consider just how much Berkeley gives away when he destroys the conceptual basis for physico-theology. The design argument, in various forms, had been the dominant means of reconciling reason and faith within liberal Protestant theology in the early eighteenth century. Design established more than the being of a God; it held creation to be the providential testament of a beneficent Deity. As the phrase "physico-theology" implies, the design argument assumed a correspondence between our experience of order in the natural world and our derivation of behavioral norms for self and society. Just as nature exhibited a spontaneous subordination of chance to design, part to whole, so each human being *should* willingly sublimate private desires to the public good. In addition, by describing all natural effects as expressions of a providential plan, design provided the basis for a theodicy. What appear to be accidents and catastrophes from our limited perspective are but part of a coherent plan, when viewed from the proper perspective.

Physico-theology thus provided both a theology and a theodicy. Yet Berkeley's ecstatic phenomenalism seems to leave us with a theology without theodicy.[18] In his love-hate relationship with Pyrrhonism, Berkeley seems to draw just close enough to perspectival relativism to give away the conceptual underpinnings of the design argument, but not so close that he loses the ability to argue that nature, regardless of its seeming disorder, offers "manifest tokens" of divinity. But what has he thereby recovered beyond the mere assertion of God's existence? Berkeley was clearly aware of the problem. In response to the "manifest tokens" argument, Hylas tells Philonous, "You are not aware ... that, in making God the immediate author of all the motions of Nature, you make him the author of murder, sacrilege, adultery, and the like heinous sins" (II, p. 236).

Berkeley still wanted to write a theodicy. As Jessop remarks, a "mere proof of the *existence* of God was not enough. His interest was in the kind of God, and in the kind of relation He stands in to the corporeal universe and us humans."[19] The question therefore became how the radical empiricist could make room for the pious Christian who also believes

if we attentively consider the constant regularity, order, and concatenation of natural things, the surprising magnificance, beauty and perfection of the larger, and the exquisite contrivance of the smaller parts of the creation, together with the exact harmony and correspondence of the whole ... we shall clearly perceive that they belong to the aforesaid spirit, *who works all in all* and *by whom all things consist.*

(II, 146, p. 108)

---

[18] For a further discussion of Berkeley and theodicy, see Jackson P. Hershbell, "Berkeley and the Problem of Evil," *Journal of the History of Ideas* 31 (1970) 543–554.

[19] Jessop, "Berkeley as Religious Apologist," p. 106.

Whereas elsewhere Berkeley found the relativity of perspectives advantageous to his argument, here he sloughs off that Pyrrhonian maneuver and extends to a single perspective, the comprehensive view of the scientist or natural philosopher, the sanction of truth. Yet even if one grants the priority of this viewpoint, why should the passive ideas derived from enhanced empirical observation suddenly have something to tell us about Spirit?

Spirits and *ideas* are things so wholly different, that when we say *they exist, they are known,* or the like, these words must not be thought to signify anything common to both natures.   (II, 142, p. 106)

A little attention will make it plain to anyone, that to have an idea which shall be like that active principle of motion and change of ideas is absolutely impossible.

(II, 27, p. 52)

Berkeley's own principles would seem to prohibit him from recouping the vocabulary of design. In a telling sequence of question and answer in the *Principles*, Berkeley admits that "it will be asked how, upon our principles, any tolerable account can be given, or any final cause assigned, of an innumerable multitude of bodies and machines, framed with the most exquisite art" (II, 60, p. 67). To which he can make only this response: "there were some difficulties relating to the administration of Providence, and the uses by it assigned to the several parts of nature, which I could not solve by the foregoing Principles" (II, 61, p. 67).

The difficulties associated with Berkeley's destructive mood do not stop here. As the passages cited above indicate, in driving empiricism to its extreme through *esse percipi*, Berkeley seems to have argued himself out of any possible knowledge of other minds or spirits. To exist is to be perceived, or, Berkeley is sometimes careful to add, to perceive. But these two – *percipi* and *percipere* – though they go together in the formulation, cancel each other in the argument: "A human spirit or person is not perceived by sense, as not being an idea; when therefore we see the colour, size, figure, and motions of a man, we perceive only certain sensations or ideas excited in our own minds" (II, 148, pp. 108–109). But if things exist to the extent they are perceived, *how else* should we say another person exists? We may be confident of our own existence to the extent we perceive, but our perceptions of other people only produce in our minds the passive ideas drawn from sensation. Again, "*Spirits* and *ideas* are things so wholly different, that when we say *they exist, they are known,* or the like, these words must not be thought to signify any thing common to both natures" (II, 142, 106).

As before, Berkeley grapples with an extreme consequence of empiricism – utter solipsism – which had been suggested but by no means confronted directly in Locke's *Essay*. As is well known, Locke described the mind before it comes to knowledge as a "white paper, void of all Characters." Because we have no innate ideas, all knowledge derives from sensory experience: "To ask, *at what time a Man has first any Ideas*, is to ask, when he begins to perceive; having *Ideas* and *Perception* being the same thing" (bk. ii, ch. 1, 9, p. 108). This empirical epistemology makes our knowledge of the world entirely dependent upon perception: "For to imprint any thing on the Mind without the Mind's perceiving it, seems to me hardly intelligible" (bk. i, ch. 2, 5, pp. 49–50). What enabled Locke to move forward confidently into a discussion of the way big thoughts are derived from little parcels of percepts? Why didn't this project founder immediately upon the shoal of innumerable blankly slated individuals being inscribed in innumerable ways by the idiosyncracies of private experience? Why wasn't solipsism, in other words, Locke's first concern? Locke sidesteps this problem in several ways. Perhaps the most important, though least noticeable, is the employment of passive phrases to describe the transition from a blank paper or empty cabinet to a mind full of ideas. The page "is imprinted" with sense data; the empty cabinet "is furnished"; ideas "are fitted" to the mind. These phrases finesse the question of how an inevitably random accumulation of sense experience becomes intelligible as knowledge to the mind. The passive structures allow Locke to avoid the suspicion that he too has imported innate ideas into his epistemology: whatever does the fitting and furnishing, whatever transforms random experiences into ordered form, must be a mental apparatus or faculty (what Locke calls reflection) not altogether different from the faculty of perception, yet prior to it. But if all knowledge comes from sense experience, how do we come to have knowledge of what fits or furnishes the mind ahead of time to receive sense experience?

Locke seems most conscious of and nervous about this question when he takes on the distinction between "natural" and "artificial" associations of ideas. Just as the mind can be well or ill fitted, beautifully or recklessly furnished, so "some of our *Ideas* have a natural Correspondence and Connexion one with another ... [while] there is another Connexion of Ideas wholly owing to *Chance* or *Custom*" (bk ii, ch. 33, 5, p. 395). As Hume will later argue (in "Of the Idea of Necessary Connection") and Sterne will later dramatize (in Toby's transformation of a train of ideas into a train of artillery), the distinction between natural and artificial associations does not follow from the empiricist's own premises: only an appeal to an innate principle standing outside experience would provide the criterion necessary to distinguish between associations drawn from experience that are natural and associations drawn from experience that depend upon chance or custom. Deny innate ideas and all we are left with is a standard based upon the probability of repetition, or, in Shandean terms, hobby-horses.

If Locke could side-step this difficulty, it was hardly a problem Berkeley could avoid. The benefit he derives from radicalizing Lockean empiricism comes at the immediate expense of having to acknowledge the radical separation of minds or spirits, one from another.[20] Again, Berkeley's heckler, Hylas, is alert to the problem: "But the same idea which is in my mind, cannot be in yours, or in any other mind. Doth it not therefore follow from your principles, that no two can see the same thing? And is not this highly absurd? (II, p. 247). Just as in the earlier "difficulty in the administration of Providence," this movement towards solipsism threatens to deprive Berkeley of any rationally derived basis for ethics. "We have alternately felt the serious Effects of Superstition and Fanaticism," Berkeley would write in 1736, "and our present impending Danger, is from the setting up of private Judgment, or an inward Light, in Opposition to the humane and divine Laws."[21] And he is no doubt correct, judging from the drift of his own immaterialist hypothesis.

Berkeley's radicalization of Lockean empiricism would seem, therefore, to lead to conclusions anathema to the theologian: pantheism or atheism instead of faith, and solipisism instead a mind capable of knowing other spirits. What I want to stress is that these implications follow directly from Berkeley's decision to better the materialists at their own game. Once he sets the relevant level of philosophical analysis at the unit *idea*, the mental sign derived from untrustworthy sensation, all of the unwanted conclusions follow. Any more complex gradient, any natural or necessary association of ideas (such as "contrivance" or "design") could always be refuted by arguments drawn from Berkeley's own destructive phase: what looks like design through one lens will look like chaos through another.

Berkeley does attempt to address these problems of pantheism and solipsism in his *Principles*. I shall argue, however, that the intractability of these dilemmas led to his decision to recast the argument of immaterialism in the fiction of a philosophical dialogue. Berkeley's attempts in the *Principles* to explain the theological value of *esse percipi* are set forth in somewhat piecemeal fashion. In *Hylas and Philonous*, by contrast, the problem of the turn from Pyrrhonism to orthodoxy and from private perception to public demonstration becomes inseparable from the formal and thematic structure of a skeptical dialogue that ends in a point of agreement between adversaries.

The problem Berkeley faced was how to reconcile two sides of his own identity. Berkeley was a philosopher raised in the school of Locke, himself contributing to advances in several sciences; he was also a pious Christian,

---

[20] Dowling links the spectre of solipsism to more immediate consequences of changes in the economic system: "possessive individualism, the new epistemology brought about by a market system allowing human beings value only as owners of their own labor, their labor as just another commodity in an impersonal world of exchange value, is what the Augustan verse epistle will encounter as the dilemma of solipsism." *The Epistolary Moment: The Poetics of the Eighteenth-Century Verse Epistle* (Princeton: Princeton University Press), p. 16. But Dowling also goes on to claim that solipsism arose "as an unintended consequence of Lockean empiricism" (p. 22). See also A. D. Nuttall, *A Common Sky: Philosophy and the Literary Imagination* (Berkeley and Los Angeles: University of California Press, 1974), especially chapter 1.

[21] George Berkeley, *A Discourse Addressed to Magistrates and Men in Authority Occasioned By the enormous Licence, and Irreligion of the Times*, (Dublin: George Faulkener, 1738), p. 33.

later a bishop of the High Church. The conflict between these was more than temperamental. Doing philosophy in the school of Locke meant applying Cartesian method to the study of mind; it meant dividing wholes into parts and parts into even smaller parts before building these back (if they could be built back) into wholes (if they were indeed the same wholes). Yet philosophical theology, as it had been practiced by the Cambridge Platonists and early apologists for the Royal Society, assumed the existence of a more complex level of analysis. Johnson's Imlac will speak of a "power that thinks; a power impassive and indiscerpible," where the key word is the last, indiscerpible, something incapable of being divided into parts.[22]

The fissures opening within the *Principles* suggest the incommensurability between two different levels of philosophical analysis. In Berkeley's destructive phase, the level is the Berkelean idea derived from Lockean sense. As we have seen, this "unit" is (in theory) infinitely divisible. Yet the Christian who would like to reconstitute the vocabulary of design must *presuppose* a different unit or level of inquiry, such that having an idea of spirit again becomes possible. I stress this point of tension in Berkeley's writings because I think it is here, in the working through of what amounts to a discursive as well as philosophical problem, that Berkeley's inventiveness as a writer of dialogues comes into play. Indeed it is not too much to argue that in response to this problem of the contrary units of analysis, Berkeley changes the dominant model through which he writes philosophy. Breaking with Locke, Berkeley shifts from perception of ideas to interpretation of signs as the dominant model for understanding. With this change dialogue as both concept and form becomes integral to Berkeley's project.

From perception to interpretation: Berkeley and the language of nature

What unites philosopher and Christian in the *Principles*? The philosopher looks through his lenses and sees "an infinite number of parts"; the Christian looks through his and sees a beautiful order. To bridge the two halves required a mode of interpreting signs that saw arbitrariness in terms of coherence. Berkeley found this principle in the metaphor of language itself. What if, he suggests, nature appears to us as a language, a system of arbitrary yet internally coherent signs, organized according to a grammar of natural laws? Philosopher and Christian might then be united by their common activity as readers or interpreters. It will no longer be apprehension of phenomena pure and simple that confirms the Deity, but a miraculous interpretative power that somehow suits us ahead of time, through a kind of foresight, to have notions (though not ideas) of active agency or spirit.

---

[22] Samuel Johnson, *The Yale Edition of the Works of Samuel Johnson*, ed. Gwin J. Kolb, 16 vols. (New Haven and London: Yale University Press, 1990), xvi *Rasselas and Other Tales*, ch. xlviii, p. 173.

Berkeley turns to the language of nature when it becomes clear that he needs a third term, something between passive ideas derived from sense and active agency or spirit, that will permit a transition or bridge from one to the other. In other words, after supplying Hume with the rudiments of the critique of necessary connection, Berkeley supplies Kant with the rudiments of the *Critique of Judgment*. He posits a third domain of philosophical analysis, not mind or idea (phenomena) but the faculty that allows us to "read" nature as if it were a prearticulated language of the Deity, or, as Kant will put it, as if nature were a manifold in unity.

Berkeley begins in the "Introduction" by stressing the philosopher's view of language, its arbitrariness and contingency. His purpose is clear: by attacking Locke's thesis that signs have "only one precise and settled signification" (II, 18, p. 76), Berkeley hopes to challenge the view that "there are certain *abstract determinate ideas*, which constitute the true and only immediate signification of each general name" (II, 18, p. 76).[23] Berkeley calls this error the *source* of the doctrine of abstract ideas. Abstraction is virtually built into language, according to Berkeley, and the only way to resist the tendency to move from general names such as "tree" to the illusion of inherent substance such as "treeness" is to remember that general terms are built up from concrete, particular ideas. Any general name signifies "indifferently a great number of particular ideas." This means, however, that any given noun substantive, like any given object, evokes multiple meanings in the minds of interpreters. Thus, in the *Principles* a negative theory of language emerges that parallels Berkeley's skepticism about our ability to designate the real substance of objects.[24] Multiple viewpoints in the realm of perception and ambiguity in the realm of verbal signs make the concepts of material substance and abstract idea equally incoherent. The best thing for the "advancement of the sciences" would be to avoid the "hindrance" of language altogether. Berkeley promises in the first edition "to make as little use of them [words] as possibly I can," a promise he removed from the third edition.[25]

Nevertheless, the positive metaphor of language as a whole is indispensable to Berkeley. With it he is able to mediate between the apparently incommensurable realms of idea and spirit. As he shifts from the first to the second view of language, the important transformation is from emphasis upon the sign itself to the conditions of its interpretation, from the admittedly arbitrary status of linguistic components to the repetitive and binding patterns of interpretation granted by God through the gift of language. Laws of

[23] For another account of Berkeley's theory of language, see Robert L. Armstrong, "Berkeley's Theory of Signification," *Journal of the History of Ideas* 7 (1969) 163–176.

[24] Herbert Rauter holds that this negative theory of language influences Berkeley's choice of the dialogue form in *Three Dialogues between Hylas and Philonous*. See "'The Veil of Words' Sprachauffassung und Dialogform bei George Berkeley," *Anglia* Band 79 (1962) 378–404.

[25] In *The Works of George Berkeley*, ed. Alexander Campbell Fraser, 4 vols. (Oxford: Clarendon Press, 1901), I, p. 253.

internal coherence mark languages, just as they characterize our experience
of the language God speaks through nature:

> The ideas of Sense ... are not excited at random ... but in a regular train or series –
> the admirable connexion whereof sufficiently testifies to the wisdom and benevolence
> of its Author. Now the set rules or established methods, wherein the mind we depend
> on excites in us the ideas of sense, are called the *Laws of Nature*: and these we learn by
> experience, which teaches us that such and such ideas are attended with such and
> such other ideas, in the ordinary course of things.
> 31. This gives us a sort of foresight, which enables us to regulate our actions for the
> benefit of life.   (II, 30–31, pp. 54–55)

As an empiricist, Berkeley generates arguments that Hume will use to show
that there are no "admirable connections whereof" necessity marks the
relation; but as a Christian Berkeley finds it self-evident that such connections
exist all around us. By shifting the primary unit of analysis from "idea" to
"sign," Berkeley is able to redefine philosophical inquiry on the model of
dependable interpretation rather than reliable perception. If we think of ideas
as signs, that is, as elements in a *language*, then it seems obvious that signs are
part of a grammar; and grammars, though made up of signs, are themselves
irreducible since they organize the meaning of units otherwise mute (or
infinitely iterable) in themselves. Instead of being pure perceivers, we are
primarily readers of complex signs, predisposed to interpret arbitrary marks
as a coherent language. Berkeley concludes, "And it is the searching after,
and endeavouring to understand this Language (if I may so call it) of the
Author of Nature, that ought to be the employment of the natural
philosopher; and not the pretending to explain things by *corporeal* causes,
which doctrine seems to have too much estranged the minds of men from
that Active Principle, that supreme and wise Spirit 'in whom we live, move,
and have our being.' "[26]

With the shift from perception to interpretation a new cluster of
philosophical terms gains centrality in Berkeley's lexicon. The key term in the
passage above is the word "foresight." The concept of foresight belongs
neither to idea nor to spirit. We gain foresight through experience; yet
foresight frames experience, assuring the natural (correct) association of ideas.
Here the passive phrases in Locke's *Essay* – the mind is fitted, is furnished, is
imprinted – are transformed into the more subtle (though perhaps no more
explanatory) principle of an inborn faculty of judgment. Having cornered
himself in mind, Berkeley seeks out a mediating term that will reanimate
external phenomena. Once the disparate signs of nature become part of a
grammar, our knowledge of any phenomenon depends upon some advance

---

[26] I have quoted the Fraser edition here because it preserves the phrase "Language of the Author of
Nature," found in the first edition. Berkeley changed the phrase to read "these signs instituted by
the Author of Nature" (II, 66, pp. 69–70).

conception of the way languages work, the way parts build up meanings greater than the sum of their arbitrary marks. This prior conception cannot be derived from perception, even though it controls our reading of phenomena. Berkeley therefore establishes a non-sensory basis for the coherence and reliability of sense impressions.

Here Cassirer thought he detected Berkeley in a contradiction. According to *esse percipi* one would have to argue that foresight, to the extent it exists, is perceived. Yet foresight frames perception. "The means of establishing relations are not themselves sensory. Berkeley's fundamental thesis now seems to be reduced to an absurdity; the equation of being (*esse*) and being perceived (*percipi*) seems to have vanished. In the midst of the phenomena which are immediately perceived by our senses, and which we cannot avoid, something has been discovered which lies beyond all the limits of perception."[27]

Perhaps this solution (from the year 1710) sounded too Kantian. Cassirer is unfair to Berkeley because he neglects to mention that Berkeley *wants* foresight to contradict *esse percipi*. According to *esse percipi*, nature should appear to us a chaos of disconnected atoms. The fact that the "ideas of Sense [are excited] ... in a regular train or series" requires the epistemologist to identify the origin of knowledge with a source other than perception. Just as Kant will argue that certain kinds of perceptions (of beauty and sublimity) *should not* occur unless we possessed a special faculty whose predilection it is to interpret the manifold as if it were a unity, so Berkeley had already advanced the term "foresight" to explain just such a "lucky chance favoring our design," a special faculty of judgment. His "fundamental thesis," like Kant's, is that a "concept of subjective purposiveness in nature in its forms according to empirical laws is not a concept of the object, but only a principle of the judgment for furnishing itself with concepts amid the variety of nature."[28] Kant cannot place order in the object because he too accepts as a philosophical given Berkeley's critique (later Hume's) of necessary connection, the mind's inability to pass from disconnected phenomena (ideas) to noumena (active agency, or spirit). Foresight furnishes the mind with concepts in advance of percepts; Kant's judgment does the same.

In the context of early eighteenth-century theology, the metaphor of the language of nature allows Berkeley to preserve the vocabulary of design without relying upon an analogical link between the ideas of sense and the realm of spirit. Philosopher and Christian, joined now by the activity of textual interpretation they share, endeavor "towards Omniscience" by tracing the "analogies, harmonies, and agreements ... discovered in the works of nature" (II, 105, p. 87). The analogy granted here is between the arbitrary yet consistent patterns observable in nature and the arbitrary yet consistent

---

[27] Ernst Cassirer, *The Philosophy of the Enlightenment*, p. 111.
[28] Kant, *Critique of Judgment*, trans. J. H. Bernard (New York: Hafner Press, 1951), "Introduction," p. 30.

patterns of God's language: "the steady consistent methods of nature may not unfitly be styled the Language of its Author, whereby He discovers His attributes to our view ... Those men who frame general rules from the phenomena, and afterwards derive the phenomena from those rules, seem to consider signs rather than causes. A man may well understand natural signs without knowing their analogy, or being able to say by what rule a thing is so and so" (II, 108, pp. 88–89).[29] Notice how careful Berkeley is not to reintroduce any concept of necessary connection among phenomena. Still wary of the materialists, he establishes necessary connections neither in phenomena themselves (which are signs rather than causes) nor in a vertical relation between effect and cause (which also assumes unperceived necessary connections), but in the horizontal relations among signs in a language.[30] Notice also how contorted the phrasing becomes when Berkeley has to name the kind of thing the mind does when it apprehends order ("may not unfitly be styled" "may well understand," "without being able to say"). He wants to but cannot say that we have an *idea* of spirit. But he has long since used up that word for a meaning almost opposite. Along with "foresight," then, Berkeley needs a new term to name our ability to apprehend active agency or spirit through interpretation. "I have a notion of spirit," says Philonous, "though I have not, strictly speaking, an idea of it" (II, p. 233).

"Notion," like "foresight," mediates between the idea/spirit opposition; it provides a term close enough to "perception" not to upset the thesis of *esse percipi*, yet different enough to escape the implication that we can never have any idea of active relations, since these are not perceivable by sense. Having a notion of spirit, Berkeley now has a response to those who charge that *esse percipi* leads to solipsism. What we perceive of others is little different from the arbitrary, physical marks in a book. Yet when we go to work as interpreters of these marks, our reading, like Newton's of nature, arrives at conclusions greater than the sum of arbitrary signs:

God is known as certainly and immediately as any other mind or spirit whatsoever, distinct from ourselves ... For it is evident that in affecting other persons, the will of man hath no other object, than barely the motion of the limbs of his body; but that such a motion should be attended by, or excite any idea in the mind of another, depends wholly on the will of the Creator. He alone it is who, *upholding all things by the word of His power*, maintains that intercourse between spirits whereby they are able to perceive the existence of each other. And yet this pure and clear light which enlightens every one, is itself invisible.   (II, 147, p. 108)

---

[29] Berkeley dropped the sentence equating nature and "the Language of its Author" from the second edition. For the wording of the first edition, see *Berkeley's Complete Works*, ed. Alexander Campbell Fraser, 4 vols. (Oxford: Oxford University Press, 1901), I, 108, p. 317.

[30] At this point and throughout the remainder of this chapter, I shall be answering Anthony Flew's question, "was Berkeley a precursor to Wittgenstein?" in the affirmative. See "Was Berkeley a Precursor to Wittgenstein?" in *Hume and the Enlightenment: Essays Presented to Ernest Campbell Mossner*, ed. William B. Todd (Edinburgh: Edinburgh University Press, 1974), pp. 153–163.

In this escape from solipsism, we see the same pattern of argument as in Berkeley's previous escape from materialism: a radicalized empiricism would seem to leave us with nothing but bare phenomenal signs, producing only passive ideas in the mind; if common sense informs us, however, that we are conversing with a spirit like our own, then it becomes clear that God intervenes at every moment to transform the passive ideas of sense into evident spirit. Readings would be impossible, dialogues with others could not take place, unless God *constantly interceded* in the space between signs and signs, subjects and subjects, rendering intelligibility possible. God the unperceived Perceiver has become God the Conversationalist, the transformer of private signs into public discourse.[31]

In this way, an implicit theory of dialogue enters Berkeley's *Principles*. As the model for philosophy shifts from perception to interpretation, the *place* where understanding occurs changes accordingly – from the mind thinking itself thinking to the mind reading nature "as if" it were the *prearticulated* language of another mind. Knowledge takes shape between minds rather than within mind – a transition from a subject-centered epistemology to a hermeneutic model of intersubjective understanding.[32]

In attempting to understand the philosophical basis for a literary shift in genre, I have been focusing attention upon the two competing "units" of analysis that exist within the negative and positive moments of Berkeley's early thought. These divergent units are not peculiar to Berkeley; they are

[31] In his editorial notes to Berkeley's *Works*, Fraser describes this argument as the "*rationale* of Berkeley's rejection of Panegoism or Solipsism." Although he questions whether the argument is "consistent with [Berkeley's] conception of the reality of the material world [since it might be objected that] ... ideal realism dissolves our faith in the existence of other persons," Fraser finally grants the persuasiveness of the claim: "Solipsism is not a necessary result of the fact that no one but myself can be percipient of my sensuous experience." But this is only because God is "the indispensable presupposition of trustworthy experience." *Works*, I, p. 339, n. 3; I, p. 341, n. 1.

[32] In *Eighteenth-Century Hermeneutics: Philosophy of Interpretation in England from Locke to Burke* (New Haven: Yale University Press, 1993), Joel C. Weinsheimer describes a general series of conditions that attended the development of "philosophy of interpretation" in England. Although Weinsheimer does not discuss Berkeley, I would argue that many of these conditions are met within Berkeley's last-ditch attempt to reconcile experimental method with Christian theology. A "turn" from epistemology to hermeneutics occurs, according to Weinsheimer, when "the problems of interpretation" begin to trouble philosophers (p. ix), when "the understanding of understanding itself" becomes an issue (p. xi), when interpretation of Scripture precedes faith in its authority (p. 49), when "reading for truth" (that is, reading allegorically) has been problematized (pp. 51–52); a "full blown hermeneutics" develops, Weinsheimer continues, when "self-reflection" has been displaced by "understanding others" as "the exclusive method of human science" (p. 106); when foundationalism gives way to interpretation (p. 107); when a "comprehensive science of man" develops (pp. 110–111); when knowledge is understood to exist between rational and feeling subjects, rather than within the isolated mind. The generality of these conditions make it difficult to identify a single moment when modern hermeneutics develops in response to specific historical and intellectual challenges. For a recent inquiry into the historicity of eighteenth-century hermeneutics, see Robert Leventhal, *The Disciplines of Interpretation: Lessing, Herder, Schlegel and Hermeneutics in Germany, 1750–1800* (Berlin: Walter de Gruyter, 1994), a work that places the emergence of modern hermeneutics between 1770 and 1800 in the German States.

characteristic of an early modern condition in which the empirical underpinnings of the New Science, at first held to be compatible with liberal
Protestant theology through "design" in nature, begin to produce results
inimical to physico-theology. Hume, Locke's most advanced student,
welcomed this development. But Shaftesbury and Berkeley, no less
responsive to Locke (who was Shaftesbury's early tutor), had to find a way to
rescue philosophy from the encroachment of what they took to be a hyper-
"minuteness". They were not prepared to let natural and moral philosophy
go their separate ways: philosophical speculation should still subserve
theology, or, at least, a metaphysically grounded ethics. But philosophy's
modern minuteness had to do with the primary decision to equate knowledge
and perception. If concepts were in theory reducible to ever smaller
antecedents, and if a method were popularized (as in Locke's *Essay*) that
showed people how to divide large and seemingly irreducible ideas down
into their relative, material components, then modern philosophy would
seem to have entered upon a course where it would inevitably have less and
less to say about what human beings should value and how they should
behave.

Thus, philosophers of this period involved themselves as much in a debate
about ideas as in an attempt to control the framework through which nature
would be interpreted. And it is here, again, that "genre" provides a means of
foregrounding important issues in eighteenth-century thought. The eighteenth-century preoccupation with genre has to do not so much with a self-
conscious Neoclassicism as with a condition of deepest skepticism regarding
the categories or frameworks through which nature was to be studied. At the
zero-point of eighteenth-century empiricism, Berkeley's *esse percipi*, where
every category or "necessary connection" of unlike entities appears to be a
fiction (habit of mind), the moral philosopher had to recognize that there
exist more complex units of philosophical analysis (for example, whole
languages, notions, foresight), which, though divisible in theory, are yet
necessary to explain our common sense understanding of human experience.
The truth of one unit over another cannot be proven; the principle of
adequation is different in each case; and it is for this reason that the shift from
one framework of inquiry to another brings with it changes in vocabulary, in
rhetoric, in methodology. These changes entail an alteration in "genre."[33]

Shaftesbury and Berkeley share in the attempt to redefine the relevant unit
of philosophical analysis. The change was as much conceptual as rhetorical
and brought with it new requirements for philosophical writing, along with

---

[33] Changing the framework of interpretation might be likened to what Thomas Kuhn has called a
"paradigm shift," with the difference that the alteration occurs gradually, is seldom announced as a
"revolution" in thinking, and actually seeks to preserve continuity with some imagined past, not
disrupt it. "Genre" provides a more historically responsive means of describing such changes than
the notion of a change in paradigms.

new limits as to what should and should not be investigated. Berkeley avoids "minuteness" by redescribing perception as a kind of reading:

As in reading other books, a wise man will choose to fix his thoughts on the sense and apply it to use, rather than lay them out in grammatical remarks on the language; so in perusing the volume of Nature, it seems beneath the dignity of the mind to affect an exactness in reducing each particular phenomenon to general rules, or showing how it follows from them. We should propose to ourselves nobler views, such as to recreate and exalt the mind, with a prospect of the beauty, order, extent, and variety of natural things: hence, by proper inferences, to enlarge our notions of the grandeur, wisdom, and beneficence of the Creation.   (II, 109, p. 89)

The distinction between "grammatical remarks" and "nobler views" signals a change in the level or unit of philosophical analysis. Begin with the premise of the infinite divisibility of matter and philosophy fractures into specialized sub-disciplines – psychology, physiology, linguistics, grammatology. Berkeley seeks to preserve the connection between philosophy and Christian theology. For this reason he must contradict his earlier view that any part is infinitely divisible. While the mock-Pyrrhonist holds that "the same thing bears a different denomination of number as the mind views it with different respects [so that] the same extension is one or three or thirty-six, according as the mind considers it with reference to a yard, a foot, or an inch" (II, 12, p. 46), the theologian finds a way to limit division: "men ... slide into a belief that the small particular line described on paper contains in itself parts innumerable. There is no such thing as the ten-thousandth part of an inch" (II, 127, p. 100). Strictly speaking, these positions are incommensurable: an inch cannot be infinitely divisible without having a ten-thousandth part. The transition from one unit to the other is not marked by rational justification but by a change in rhetoric. The hortative mood ("we should propose nobler views") invokes the aura of civic humanism, shaming us into a recognition that minute philosophy does not breed noble action.

Shaftesbury also opposed the positivistic direction philosophy seemed to be taking. In one of his most direct attacks on Locke, Shaftesbury wrote in *Advice to an Author*:

What signifies it how I come by my *Ideas*, or how *compound* 'em; which are *simple* and which *complex*? If I have a right Idea of *Life*, now when perhaps I think slightly of it, and resolve with my-self, "That it may easily be laid down on any honourable occasion of Service to my Friends, or Country"; teach me how I may preserve this Idea ... If this be the Subject of the *Philosophical Art*; I readily apply to it, and embrace the Study. If there be nothing of this in the Case; I have no occasion for this sort of Learning; and am no more desirous of knowing how I form or compound those *Ideas* which are mark'd by Words, than I am of knowing how, and by what Motions of my Tongue or Palat, I form those *articulate Sounds*, which I can full as well pronounce, without any such Science or Speculation.   (I, pp. 302–303)

Once again, the distinction between "a right idea of life" and "Motions of my Tongue or Palat" indicates a fundamental choice about the level of philosophical analysis. Locke might have responded that the method of dividing big ideas into small parts provided a good start in learning how to form a "right Idea of *Life*." Shaftesbury himself, in his more skeptical mood, was often of that opinion. But the issue here is a perceived disjunction between experimental method and any theological or metaphysical ground for ethics. What is it that creates a willingness to sacrifice one's life for an idea or a person or a plot of land? Philosophy, Shaftesbury fears, is passing beyond such questions, or renaming them as topics in politics, psychopathology, anthropology, linguistics.

Berkeley and Shaftesbury reach a decision *vis-à-vis* Locke not unlike the decision Bakhtin reaches in response to Saussurean lingusitics and Searle reaches against Derridean grammatology.[34] In each case either the genre or a concept of dialogue is invoked as a means of redefining the terms of inquiry. When Bakhtin says that the utterance is the salient unit of analysis, not the sign, when Searle says that communication is the essence of language, not infinite iterability, they are setting dialogue or a concept of dialogue in opposition to a rival discourse whose conclusions follow just as fully from a prior decision to investigate nature or language in a different way. The interesting thing about Berkeley's recourse to dialogue is that he still believes that philosophy meant following out the implications of Lockean empiricism. Both units are present in Berkeley's thought, and dialogue becomes a means of drawing these together and inferring a path from the one to the other, part to whole. "Natural religion," "rational Christianity," and "philosophical dialogue" expressed the same hope – or, looked at another way, the same oxymoron.

The skeptic's progress; or, dialogue as demonstration

Seduction into the maze of particulars and extrication from that maze constitute the defining moments of the kind of philosophical theology common to Descartes' *Meditations* and Berkeley's *Hylas and Philonous*. The *Meditations* had provided Descartes with a form of intellectual drama. The

---

[34] In the essay "On the Problem of Speech Genres," Bakhtin cites a passage from a recent academy grammar that breaks language down from sentences to words to syllables. Bakhtin responds: "The terminological imprecision and confusion in this methodologically central point of linguistic thinking result from ignoring the *real unit* of speech communication: the utterance. For speech can exist in reality only in the form of concrete utterances of individual speaking people, speech subjects." Bakhtin, "On the Problem of Speech Genres," in *Speech Genres and Other Late Essays*, trans. Vern W. McGee, eds. Caryl Emerson and Michael Holquist (Austin: University of Texas Press, 1986, pp. 70–71. Conceiving of Derridean deconstruction as an attack upon his teacher, Austin, Searle directs speech-act theory against the view that signs are infinitely iterable. See "Reiterating the Differences: a Response to Derrida," *Glyph* I (Baltimore and London: Johns Hopkins University Press, 1977), pp. 198–208.

autobiographical narrative recounts a sequence of ideas, with the meditator
falling into a nearly hopeless skepticism, only to be snatched from the jaws
of despair by the lucky recollection of a word for the supersensible –
perfection – and the undoubted logic of causality. This drama gains its turn,
its discovery, at the point where mind (*cogito*) finds itself either absolutely cut
off from the sensory world whose existence it has just denied or suddenly
saved by the interposition of a necessary third, a God who bridges mind
and phenomena, permitting scientific knowledge. The case for Descartes'
metaphysics is repeated every time one rereads his text, as one repeats the
plot of seduction, fall, and recovery. This is to say that one's suspicion about
the logical validity of the meditator's late recourse to an outmoded
ontological proof is assuaged by evidence from a different register, the
pleasing fiction of an intellectual pilgrim saved from despair by a sudden
recollection.

What for Descartes is a conscious process of radical doubt is for Berkeley
the simple allowance of perspectivalism. No less than before, however, this
allowance leaves the philosopher with an intransitive consciousness, a *percipio
sum* no less self-reflexive than Descartes' *cogito sum*. The implications of
Pyrrhonian skepticism I enumerated above – atheism or pantheism and
solipsism – await the intransitive mind, the mind cut off from direct objects,
trapped in an external labyrinth that mirrors, lightly, the dark internal maze.
Berkeley could not have felt that his *Principles* constituted an adequate
response to these dilemmas. Not only did his first readers mock the work and
insist upon misunderstanding it, but the division of the text into one hundred
and fifty-six sections follows only the most general structure of hypothesis,
objections, and implications, often positing crucial objections in the sections
covering implications and clarifying the hypothesis only after responding to
objections.[35] While the *Principles* can be said to theorize the pattern of
seduction, fall, and recovery, this plot does not contribute significantly to the
conscious organization of the *Principles*.

The important changes in *Hylas and Philonous* are not primarily doctrinal.
On the level of argument, *Hylas and Philonous* advances little that had not been
propounded in one place or another in the *Principles*. Berkeley is not being
ironic when he calls the work a restatement of the immaterialist hypothesis,
and this aim makes Philonous his spokesman.[36] My concern here is not,

[35] Fraser groups the *Principles* under three main parts: (1) the Rationale of the Principles (sections 1–
33); (2) Objections to the Principles answered (sections 34–84); and (3) Consequences and
applications of the Principles (sections 85–156). Yet Berkeley introduces in the last sections
objections which he had not entertained previously (such as the problem of theodicy). In these
sections, he also develops his theory of the divine language of nature, which is central to the
rationale of the *Principles*.

[36] K. M. Wheeler argues against the claim that most of *Hylas and Philonous* simply restates the *Principles*.
"The reader [of *Hylas and Philonous*] should abandon the notion that Philonous is the mouthpiece of
Berkeley's philosophy." "Berkeley's Ironic Method in the *Three Dialogues*," *Philosophy and Literature* 4

therefore, with the repetition of the sequence of arguments leading to and
following from *esse percipi*; it is instead with the way Berkeley manipulates the
resources of fiction latent within the dialogue to solve the difficulties he
addressed in piecemeal fashion in the earlier work.

The dialogue begins with Berkeley's description of its intellectual plot:

> it may, perhaps, seem an uneasy reflexion to some, that when they have taken the
> circuit through so many refined and unvulgar notions, they should at last come to
> think like other men: yet, methinks, this return to the simple dictates of Nature, after
> having wandered through the wild mazes of philosophy, is not unpleasant. It is like
> coming home from a long voyage: a man reflects with pleasure on the many
> difficulties and perplexities he has passed through, sets his heart at ease, and enjoys
> himself with more satisfaction for the future.   (II, p. 168)

Such is the itinerary Hylas will follow. The metaphor of a voyage is
appropriate because the philosophical voyager of the early eighteenth
century chooses to cast himself adrift in the Pyrrhonian sea. He cannot be
assured of a safe homecoming, and this makes the eventual return all the
more pleasurable.

In addition to dividing the positive and negative moments of his philosophy
into different legs of a round-trip, Berkeley cast these moods in the personae
of two characters, Hylas, who stands for belief in incorporeal substance or
matter, and Philonous, spokesman for Berkeley's immaterialism. Hylas is no
mere stooge. He stands for, among other things, the quite understandable
response the *Principles* met from early readers who concluded that *esse percipi*
meant a denial of the material world. Berkeley places what he took to be the
false reception of the *Principles* in the voice of Hylas, who either mocks the
absurdity of *esse percipi*, or, accepting the dictum, declares himself enmeshed
in the most hopeless skepticism. It is the second response, the fall into despair,
that corresponds with the moment of reversal in Berkeley's empirical
theology. Why regret the loss of matter, Philonous will ask, if it can be more
than made up for by a God affirmed by each and every phenomenon in itself,
manifest tokens of divinity?

It was a difficult turn, and Berkeley no doubt hoped to keep the
consequences of *not* making that turn in his reader's mind. Thus, Hylas,
having cast himself upon the uncertain seas of modern thought, becomes
increasingly despondent as the discussion continues. At the end of the first
dialogue, he can only respond, "I am at present so amazed to see myself
ensnared, and as it were imprisoned in the labyrinthes you have drawn me
into." By the beginning of the third his fall is complete. "All our opinions are
alike vain and uncertain. What we approve to-day, we condemn tomorrow.

(1980) 18. Wheeler holds that Berkeley used dialogue as a means of "exposing the weaknesses of two
extreme positions [materialism and subjective idealism] and suggesting his own posture of a
transcendent third" (18). For a response to Wheeler, see Richard T. Lambert, "The Literal Intent
of Berkeley's *Dialogues*," *Philosophy and Literature* 6 (1982), 165–171.

We keep a stir about knowledge, and spend our lives in the pursuit of it, when, alas! we know nothing all the while: nor do I think it possible for us ever to know anything in this life. Our faculties are too narrow and too few. Nature certainly never intended us for speculation" (II, p. 27).[37]

The constant irony of Hylas' fall into despair is that it comes as a result of his accepting the first stage of Philonous' immaterialism. If *esse* is *percipi*, all understanding is subjective; we never meet things in their real essence or people in their essential spirit. Berkeley therefore plays a dangerous game, keeping the conclusions not to be drawn from *esse percipi* constantly before the reader. The tactic has obvious dramatic effect. We read on to discover what will become of Hylas. The plot gives fictional vivacity to Berkeley's prosaic instructions to his reader: "A treatise of this nature [*Hylas and Philonous*] would require to be once read over coherently, in order to comprehend its design, the proofs, solution of difficulties, and the connexion and disposition of its parts. If it be thought to deserve a second reading; this, I imagine, will make the entire scheme very plain: especially if recourse be had to an Essay I wrote, some years since, upon vision, and the Treatise concerning the *Principles of Human Knowledge*. Wherein divers notions advanced in these Dialogues, are farther pursued, or placed in different lights, and other points handled, which naturally tend to confirm and illustrate them" (II, "The Preface," p. 169).

The conjunction of characters serves a further purpose. As Hylas himself suggests, Philonous' proof of the existence of a Deity through the bare fact of perception (what I previously called Berkeley's ecstatic phenomenalism) may only restate the common wisdom, that God exists in all things. But Berkeley did not want his reader to draw this conclusion so directly: it might be mistaken, as the deists were mistaking it, for the claim the mechanists made when they ascribed causal agency to matter. Berkeley wants a circuitous route to the popular wisdom; thus, Hylas, with all of his false statements about matter, needs to be present all along in order to remind us why Berkeley's Pyrrhonian gambit had been necessary.

Other aspects of the fiction help Berkeley refute the unwanted implications of his own theory. As has been seen, *esse percipi* might easily lead to doubts about the "reality" of the external world. But dialogue, with its quasi-mimetic setting, offers the philosophers a constant external reference point, one which Philonous invokes on several occasions. "Hark," he exclaims at the end of the first dialogue, "is not this the college bell?" To which Hylas responds, "It rings for prayers" (II, p. 207). "Look!" Philonous urges at the beginning of the second day, "are not the fields covered with a delightful verdure," a rhapsodic description that continues for a rather unphilosophical page and a half before ending with the not unexpected, "What treatment,

---

[37] Peter Walmsley has observed that the first part of *Hylas and Philonous* recounts Hylas' entrapment in the mazes of existential uncertainty. *The Rhetoric of Berkeley's Philosophy*, pp. 95, 99.

then, do those philosophers deserve who would deprive these noble and delightful scenes of all reality?" (II, pp. 210–211).

Behind the appeal to a shared external nature (which somehow bypasses *esse percipi*) is common sense. Here too, the exchange of positions in dialogue allows the characters to appeal to a force guiding debate and moving them towards agreement. Although a shared or common sense is precisely what one seems to lose when existence is made dependent upon fleeting and changeable sensation, both characters routinely appeal to common sense to resolve their differences.

HYLAS. Were our dispute to be determined by the most voices, I am confident you
     would give up the point without gathering the votes.
PHIL. I wish both our opinions were fairly stated and submitted to the judgment of
     men who had plain common sense, without the prejudices of a learned
     education.   (II, p. 237)

The great joke (one might almost call it an Irish Bull) about Berkeley's appeal to common sense is that nothing could be less commonsensical than the doctrine that the external world exists first and last in our minds. The humor of the situation, which Beckett would condense into a single phrase in *Murphy* – "the idealists tar" – shows through in Philonous' last great appeal to common sense late in the work:

that the least particle of a body contains innumerable extended parts [this and the like novelties] are the strange notions which rock the genuine uncorrupted judgment of all mankind ... And it is against these and the like innovations I endeavor to vindicate Common Sense. It is true that in doing this I may, perhaps, be obliged to use some ambages and ways of speech not common.   (II, p. 244)

In a single breath Berkeley credits himself with speaking for the common uncorrupted judgment of mankind and with speaking in *ambages*, a word whose definition, drawn from both the Latin *ambāges* and the medieval French *ambages*, might mean anything from a circumlocution to a false figure of speech to an outright lie.[38] Berkeley forgets to add that his own immaterialist hypothesis begins with the Pyrrhonian assumption that the least particle contains innumerable parts. Ambages are not just ornamental in Berkeley's philosophy.

Whatever indirection the dialogue may pretend, Hylas is brought inexorably to confess his complete devotion to immaterialism. "I agree to all you have now said and must own that nothing can incline me to embrace your opinion more than the advantages I see it attended with ... I own myself entirely satisfied for the present in all respects ... I am content to give up the notion of an unthinking substance exterior to the mind" (II, 259, p. 61).[39]

---

[38] The *Oxford English Dictionary* defines "ambages" as "roundabout or indirect modes of speech" or
     even "deceit, equivocation, dark or obscure language."
[39] I shall not repeat the stages by which Hylas is brought to this admission. The decisive arguments

Having taken the circuit of "unvulgar" philosophical abstrusities, Hylas is brought back to the fold of common humanity. The plot thus results in a marriage of minds. For this reason the dialogue has been called "comedic."[40] But despite the happy resolution, it is important to remember just how close *esse percipi* comes to ending tragically. Immaterialism does tend towards solipsism; it does separate mind from phenomena; it does divorce human beings from the knowledge of spirit. Berkeley thought that he had identified the corner-stone of eighteenth-century atheism: by reducing all the various sects of free thinkers to their shared belief in material substance, he thought he could construct a metaphysical refutation, focused exclusively on that single point. Yet this metaphysical retort, immaterialism and the theological demonstration following from it, was for many readers as problematic as atheism itself. Not *esse percipi* but the image of successful dialogue finally carries Berkeley's theological demonstration. For the dialogue proves that the language God speaks to people through the laws of nature also controls the interaction of people with each other, through the laws of reason. Even if metaphysical argument has not succeeded in reducing all the wretched sects to a simple presupposition, and then refuting it, dialogue has shown how a similar process of dialectical reduction operates to transform competing viewpoints, the labyrinth of perspectivalism, into a marriage of minds. Dialogue, then, reconciles skepticism and orthodoxy. Its design, or at least the design of the genre as Berkeley conceived it, establishes the validity of a philosophical Christianity. Berkeley writes in the "Preface,"

by shewing that such parts of revelation as lie within the reach of human inquiry are most agreeable to right reason, [*Hylas and Philonous*] would dispose all prudent, unprejudiced persons to a modest and wary treatment of those sacred mysteries which are above the comprehension of our faculties.   (II, pp. 168–169)

are taken almost verbatim from the *Principles*, except that the haphazard order of rationale, objections, and implications in the earlier work is replaced by a development over the course of three days, beginning with the establishment of *esse percipi*, moving to the major objections Hylas can muster, and ending finally with an account of the benefits of the new theory.

[40] Donald Davie refers to the work as "the drama of a slow mind with a quick one," and as a "chastening comedy." "Berkeley and the Style of Dialogue," in *The English Mind: Studies in the English Moralists Presented to Basil Wiley*, eds. Hugh Sykes Davies and George Watson (Cambridge: Cambridge University Press, 1964), p. 9. Peter Walmsley writes, "the comic movement of Philonous' abandonment of Hylas is thus the herald of a larger comedy in *Three Dialogues*. Its movement from doubt to confidence is accompanied by a thematic transition from purely epistemological to spiritual concerns. All Berkeley's major writings share something of the fully-developed comic narrative of *Three Dialogues*" (*The Rhetoric of Berkeley's Philosophy*, p. 98). In a similar regard, Martin Battestin has argued that the philosophical and aesthetic assumptions of the Augustan Age are essentially comedic: "the cosmic system they assume and celebrate is ultimately benign—comic in the profoundest sense. It is a universe not only full and various, but regular, created by a just and benevolent Deity whose genial Providence governs all contingencies, comprehends every catastrophe, from the bursting of the world to the fall of a sparrow." *The Providence of Wit: Aspects of Form in Augustan Literature and the Arts* (Oxford: Clarendon Press, 1974), p. 141.

Dialogue reveals a point of intersection between "the reach of human inquiry" and "parts of revelation." This is the more important marriage in *Hylas and Philonous*, a union performed not so much for the happy couple as for the method whose ability to unite them is thereby reaffirmed.

Both *esse percipi* and immaterialism, then, are means to a larger end. That is why the dialogue does not end with Hylas' concession but continues to spell out the methodological principles that add inevitability to the sequence of question and answer producing truth. "I own myself entirely satisfied for the present in all respects," says Hylas, who then asks to be innoculated against the skeptical virus. "What security can I have that I shall still continue the same full assent to your opinion, and that no unthought-of objection or difficulty will occur hereafter?" (II, p. 259). Philonous responds with a rudimentary logic manual:

> But to arm you against all future objections, do but consider that which bears equally hard on two contradictory opinions, can be proof against neither ... You should likewise take heed not to argue on a *petitio principii* ... But above all things, you should be aware of imposing on yourself by that vile sophism which is called *ignoratio elenchi* ... Think on these points; let them be attentively considered and still kept in view. Otherwise you will not comprehend the state of the question; without which your objections will always be wide of the mark.   (II, pp. 259–60)

One assumes that if Hylas had not committed certain logical blunders along the way, the marriage of minds might have occurred sooner. Indeed, it is difficult to see why the dialogue would have been necessary at all. Had Hylas not committed the error of *petitio principii*, for instance, he would not have argued for the real existence of an unknown substratum of objects, which is the cause of our ideas about the same; for this begs the question about the real existence of that external substratum. Similarly, if Hylas had not fallen into the sophism of *ignoratio elenchi*, he would never have mistaken the question by thinking that Philonous' rejection of matter was the same as a rejection of what the "vulgar" call the "real" (material) world. So by not falling into logical errors, Hylas would have agreed with the basic tenets of immaterialism from the start. In this respect the apparently inductive dialogue doubles as a deductive treatise.[41] Although Philonous invites Hylas to hit "the mark," that is, to venture the best possible objections and thus, presumably, to lengthen the discussion, he also chastises the student for not arriving at the mark, the point of demonstration, sooner. Logic establishes, as Donald Davie observes, "rules which the mind, however unwillingly, must observe ... Disputation observes a discipline, an order that the shifty mind continually seeks to evade.

---

[41] Walmsley argues that in "the *Three Dialogues* the rules of logic order the debate, and dialogue educates the reader, not just in immaterialism, but in the method of demonstration so influential in the composition of the *Principles*" (*The Rhetoric of Berkeley's Philosophy*, p. 76). While accurately summarizing Philonous' intent, this reading of the rhetoric of Berkeley's philosophy fails to consider the strains involved when reason legitimates itself through reason (logic).

To admit the discipline and bring one's own mind into line – this is one respect of candour."[42] Dialogue becomes something of a conduct manual for reason.

Yet, even after the lecture on logic, Hylas reiterates the fundamental objection that will occur to any reader of the *Principles*: how has Berkeley managed the turn from the skeptical premises of Pyrrhonism to the conclusions of orthodox Christianity? Logic, it would seem, does not explain enough: "You set out upon the same principles that Academics, Cartesians, and the like sects usually do," Hylas tells Philonous, "and for a long time it looked as if you were advancing their philosophical *scepticism*, but in the end your conclusions are directly opposite to theirs" (II, p. 262). Philonous' response, the famous metaphor of the fountain, ends the dialogue:

> You see, Hylas, the water of yonder fountain, how it is forced upwards, in a round column, to a certain height; at which it breaks, and falls back into the basin from whence it rose: its ascent as well as descent, proceeding from the same uniform law or principle of *gravitation*. Just so, the same Principles which, at first view, lead to scepticism, pursued to a certain point, bring men back to common sense.
>
> (II, pp. 262–263)

The image stands for the conceptual movement of Berkeley's *Principles* and for the literary structure of *Hylas and Philonous*. Skepticism, the destructive movement of *esse percipi*, drives the philosopher upward and outward into a potentially debilitating uncertainty. By the same token, skeptical dialogue opens inquiry to all the prejudices of materialism and heterodoxy. But something in the order of things commands a turn from scattering particles and erroneous opinion to a coherent and intelligible whole. The fountain is Berkeley's aesthetic image for interpretation; it condenses the language of nature into a single beautiful emblem that embodies the highest degree of atomic dispersal compatible with design.

Taken together, the two explanations – the logic manual and the fountain – naturalize logic and rationalize nature. One might have suspected that the teacher figure, who controls the debate, has also taken it upon himself to define the rules of argumentation. Now, however, we learn that these rules are as much a matter of debate as gravity. One might also have thought, with Shaftesbury's Philocles, that a skeptical dialogue lacks predictability, moving randomly, playfully, according to the chance associations of the speakers.

---

[42] Davie, "Berkeley and the Style of Dialogue," p. 96. For Davie, *Hylas and Philonous* is the best dialogue written during the eighteenth century, precisely because its display of vigorous opposition does not come at the expense of a determinate conclusion. He calls the balance between conflict and order the ideal of "candour." Few written dialogues, he argues, attain this ideal. Dryden's *Essay of Dramatic Poesy* is ordered by the extreme politeness of the characters, but the work lacks a vigorous exchange of strong opinion. The conversation of characters in other eighteenth-century dialogues, such as *Alciphron*, is vigorous, even heated, but these lack order, and therefore conclusiveness. Only in *Hylas and Philonous*, Davie holds, do we find a synthesis. Thus, Davie calls *Hylas and Philonous* "implicitly a treatise in ethics, an exemplification of the virtue of candour" (p. 97).

Now, however, it becomes clear that something in the nature of things –
belonging neither to phenomena nor to noumena but bridging both – guides
discourse through the "wild mazes" to consensus. Late in the *Principles*
Berkeley had developed the argument that the meaningful converse of two
people offered evidence of God's intercession in the world, since, according
to *esse percipi*, communication between spirits should be impossible. Within the
dialogue this late recourse becomes an overriding structural principle. That
which promotes intersubjective understanding and that which drives the
dialectical movement through division to unity become identical. To witness
the one on the level of dramatic exchange is to be assured of the other on the
level of theological belief. Hylas' conversion to the immaterialist position is
therefore meant to double for the response of Berkeley's ideal reader, and the
terms of Berkeley's assurance to the reader in the "Preface" ("methinks, this
return to the simple dictates of nature, after having wandered through the
wild mazes of philosophy, is not unpleasant ... ") are thus repeated in
Philonous' assurances at the end: "My endeavors tend only to unite and place
in a clearer light that truth, which was before shared between the vulgar and
the philosophers" (II, p. 262).

Berkeley's *Hylas and Philonous* is the last great philosophical dialogue belonging
to the Christian, Neoplatonic tradition. Its Platonism has little to do, finally,
with a technique of *elenchus* shared with the master.[43] Berkeley is a profound
Neoplatonist, profound because his encounter with that which would
frustrate the dialectical move up the chain of being from matter to spirit –
namely, modern concepts of mechanism and materialism – animates a final,
valiant attempt to save Christian Neoplatonism from the combined threats of
Modernity. Appropriately, the dialogue ends with an emblem for itself, the
fountain of dialectic. The fountain operates here in the same way as did the
myth of Orpheus and Eurydice in Boethius' *The Consolation of Philosophy*: it
announces a natural limit, a boundary, policed not by an arbitrary, coercive
authority, but by reason itself, attuned to higher laws.
    To be sure, the discovery of limit, however philosophically derived, carries
political force. It establishes the religious magistrate's epistemological
authority to govern opinion in society. The austere, static quality of the
emblem testifies to the existence of a fixed point of certainty, where the
upward and outward striving force of individuals finds itself restrained,
returned, by a principle internal to itself. Play is always possible; a certain

---

[43] Walmsley describes *Hylas and Philonous* as an imitation of Plato largely because both Berkeley and
Plato use the technique of *elenchus* in dialogic disputation. Although Walmsley acknowledges that
elenchus alone is a rather thin basis for drawing a parallel with Plato, he doubts that Berkeley's
Platonism is any more substantial: "Despite the Neoplatonic overtones of *Siris*, Berkeley's early
insistence on the reality and value of the sense-data sets him at odds with Plato. Perhaps the only
unquestionable legacy is the style of dialogue known as 'elenchus'" (p. 69).

degree of skepticism is to be tolerated; but when conduct departs from that fixed point of order, when nature's own limit is transgressed, then the magistrate stands within his right enforcing the law.

In a later work, Berkeley explains why he most often subordinates direct discussion of political institutions and policies to theology and moral philosophy: "it is useless to worry about the outward Form, the Constitution, and Structure of a State; while the Majority are ever governed by their inward Ways of thinking, which at Times will break out and shew themselves paramount to all Laws and Institutions whatsoever ... The Spirit which prevails against the Church and Religion, proceeds from an Opposition rather to the Laws of the Land, than to the Gospel."[44] Although Berkeley places theology above discussion of laws and institutions, he does so only because he believes the position he stakes out within theology must be understood, simultaneously, in political terms. Enemies of the Church are, more concretely, enemies of the State; and both kinds of opposition are joined where they become most visible, when they "break out" from an inward way of thinking into the full light of disobedient conduct. For Berkeley metaphysical speculation represented the head attempting to control its wayward members: "Religion is the Centre which unites, and the cement which connects the several Parts or Members of the political Body."[45] Even though the tendency of recent scholarship is to reverse these polarities – as William Dowling does when he argues that Humean skepticism presents us with "merely the symptom of an underlying crisis, the abstract or philosophical formulation of a dilemma elsewhere being played out in existential terms" [i.e. in the material, economic realm] – it is misleading to argue that moral philosophers of this period were avoiding politics, or were pursuing abstract speculation for its own sake.[46]

For eighteenth-century readers the correlation of theological, political, and even economic positions was a given, and it was far from clear which was the symptom and which the disease, which the abstraction and which the concrete, existential agent. Thomas Hayter, writing in 1732, worries that "the tenets of a private club" of skeptics and atheists "may soon grow to be the national Topicks of Conversation ... the secret Springs by which irreligion has gain'd so much ground among us." And he continues: "the exact

---

[44] Berkeley, *A Discourse Addressed to Magistrates*, p. 20.

[45] *Ibid.*, p. 20.

[46] *The Epistolary Moment*, p. 16. For the claim that philosophical dialogues of this period were engrossed in idle, apolitical speculation, see Timothy Dykstal, "Conversation and Political Controversy," in *Compendious Conversations: the Method of Dialogue in the Early Enlightenment*, ed. Kevin L. Cope. (Frankfurt-on-Main: Peter Lang, 1992). Dykstal holds that for the "most eminent practitioners of dialogue [the form] is not a means to resolve differences of opinion, but a realm of discourse in which difference is not so destructive, where it can exist without the interests of individual discussants getting in the way. Dialogue is, in other words, purely 'philosophical,' not political ... Dryden, Shaftesbury, and Hume want not to 'use' philosophy at all. They pursue it for its own sake, or for the sake of disinterested speculation" (p. 311).

Congruity which their [skeptics' and atheists'] Books have with the Appetites and Passions of the Generality of Mankind, circulates them thro' the Kingdom with a wonderful Swiftness, and makes them greedily read by the Libertine, as instructive Lessons, how to be profligate upon Principle."[47] Berkeley shared this concern. He wrote philosophical dialogues both to represent the threat and to establish a truer principle that would circulate through the kingdom with equal swiftness.

One of the main arguments of the first part of this book has been that the popularity of philosophical dialogue parallels the dominance of rational Christianity, extending through the first quarter of the eighteenth century. In this history, Berkeley's *Hylas and Philonous* presents us with the most accomplished and confident example of a metaphysical dialogue placed at the service of rational Christianity. But within the eighteenth-century debate about the viability of dialogue, one also finds the optimistic link between dialogue and transcendental dialectic challenged by philosophers who themselves wrote dialogues. Berkeley's *Hylas and Philonous* represents the culmination of the Christian, Neoplatonic interpretation of dialogue. As I suggest in the following two chapters, Berkeley's own *Alciphron, or the Minute Philosopher* (1732) already threatens this ideal, and Hume's *Dialogues concerning Natural Religion* (1751, 1779) marks its undoing.

[47] Hayter, *A Short View of Some of the General Arts of Controversy Made Use of by the Advocates of Infidelity* (London: S. Buckley, 1732), p. 10.

4

Berkeley's *Alciphron*, or the
Christian Cicero

Atheism and Theism are now got from the Court to the Exchange, they
begin to talk them in Shops and Stalls, and the Cavils of Spinosa and
Hobbs are grown common, even to the very Rabble.

William Nichols, A Conference with a Theist (1723)[1]

Crito. "The new theories, which our acute moderns have endeavoured
to substitute in place of religion, have had their full course in the present
age, and produced their effect on the minds and manners of men. That
men are men is a sure maxim: but it is as sure that Englishmen are not
the same men they were."

George Berkeley, Alciphron (1732)

Trading Plato for Cicero

The single-mindedness with which Berkeley explicates the immaterialist
hypothesis in both his *Principles* and *Hylas and Philonous* is directly attributable
to the conviction that all varieties of heterodoxy could finally be boiled down
to a single shared concept, namely the pernicious abstraction, "material
substance" (or unthinking matter). "How great a friend *material substance* has
been to atheists in all ages were needless to relate," Berkeley writes. "All their
monstrous systems have so visible and necessary a dependence on it that,
when this cornerstone is once removed, the whole fabric cannot choose but
fall to the ground, insomuch that it is no longer worth while to bestow a
particular consideration on the absurdities of every wretched sect of
atheists."[2] Yet by 1732, it would seem Berkeley no longer credited his
philosophically convenient reduction of all the wretched sects to a single
wrong doctrine. Instead, he shares the view of William Nichols: whether or
not atheism and theism have a single, tractable source, their tributaries have
spread into the very shops and stalls, where the haphazard mixture of

---

[1] William Nichols, *A Conference with a Theist: containing an Answer to all the most usual Objections of the Infidels
Against the Christian Religion*, 3rd edn., 2 vols. (London: J. Holland and J. Bowyer, 1723), p. v.
[2] *Works*, II, 92, p. 81. Subsequent references will be given by volume, section (where appropriate), and
page number in my text.

unbaked and half-baked notions renders the immaterialist "solution" a quaint species of optimism.[3]

Berkeley's moral philosophy will thus have to abandon the systematic defense of *esse percipi* and the pious consequences following from it: the varieties of irreligion will need to be tracked, the positions aired and answered, even if the answers are not themselves internally consistent. Philosophy will have to descend, if not to the streets, then at least to a gentleman's farm in Rhode Island, where an expanded cast of characters, two atheists and two Christians, run through the catalogue of apostacies for a full week. The purpose of *Alciphron*, as Berkeley puts it in the "Advertisement," is "to consider the free-thinker in the various lights of atheist, libertine, scorner, critic, metaphysician, fatalist, and sceptic" (III, p. 23).

Unlike the fine architectonics of Berkeley's first dialogue, *Hylas and Philonous*, whose closing emblem of the fountain offers mute but glorious evidence of a natural language God shares with man, evidence that simultaneously ratifies the conceptual movement of dialogue itself, passing from suspension of belief to resolution – unlike this most austerely Platonic of eighteenth-century dialogues, *Alciphron* is a mess. Contemporary readers were alert to the difference. The author of *A Vindication of the Reverend D—B——y, from the Scandalous Imputation of being Author of a late Book, intitled, Alciphron, or the Minute Philosopher* (1734), whose main purpose is to defend Shaftesbury against Berkeley's scornful attack in the Fifth Dialogue, insists that Berkeley could not possibly have written *Alciphron*: "One might have observed from the beautiful Dialogues he wrote long ago, (another Sort than this spurious Collection) that he was well acquainted with *Plato* ... But what Man, who had but *tasted* of these Fountains, could have been capable of attempting to paulm [*Alciphron*] upon us ... " (p. 24).[4] Certainly not Berkeley: "And the more I read on, and considered the Matter, I was the more confirmed in this Perswasion; and convinced it was impossible that D. B——y should be the author of this strange Rhapsody of Dialogues" (p. 15).

Alciphron, then, departs from the model of Berkeley's first, "beautiful" dialogue. In terms of the critical categories current during the early eighteenth century, the change amounted to a shift from the Platonic to the Ciceronian manner. In *A Conference with a Theist*, Nichols defends Ciceronian dialogue in these terms:

These Considerations have put me upon Writing the following Dialogues, and have encouraged me to consider the chief of their Arguments, which they [infidels] are wont to make use of in their Discourse, or which have been published of late in

---

[3] Berkeley's Crito complains that English youth now pick up all their improvement "Where our grave ancestors would never have looked for it – in a drawing room, a coffee-house, a chocolate-house, at the tavern, or groom-porter's. In these and the like fashionable places of resort, it is the custom for polite persons to speak freely on all subjects, religious, moral, or political" (II, p. 50).

[4] Subsequent citations of this work are given by page number in my text.

Atheistical Writings: To the End that well and religious Men, whose Leisure or Education will not let them search so narrowly into these Disputes, may from this Treatise be furnished with sufficient Answers to such Infidel Arguments. I have not indeed brought in such frequent Interlocutions as are requisite for a just Dialogue, like those of Plato and Lucian; for that would have taken up a great deal more Paper to little Purpose, only to please a few curious Criticks; and at last the Argument would be but the more obscured by it. And on the other side I have avoided the dry Method of scholastick Objection and Solution; where the Objection is posed without any Manner of Life, only in order to be refuted ... I have therefore made use of the middle Way, in clothing the Objections in such a Dress, as two men that had a Mind to convince one another, can be supposed to use. And this is the Pattern which the best of Writers, Cicero, in his philosophical Tracts, has set for us; whose very Faults I should never be ashamed to imitate. (pp. viii–ix).

Like Berkeley, Nichols finds it necessary to air "the chief of their arguments," whether drawn directly from texts or overheard in spoken discourse, and to provide answers for each. What makes such a work specifically Ciceronian is not only the staging of a conference, an encyclopedic survey of omnifarious opinion, but also a decision the writer makes *vis-à-vis* the degree of fictional representation.[5] Clearly, the philosophical dimension of learned argument must still take precedent. The characters "have a mind to convince one another," which is to say, the doctrines they articulate supersede dramatic elements. At the same time, however, the moral philosopher has been drawn to this more inclusive interpretation of dialogue because of a sociological observation about the effect of strong representations on common readers. He wishes to reclaim such readers through a probable fiction that retains some degree of liveliness and mimetic detail. The eighteenth-century imitator of Cicero thus seeks out a middle way between the excessively poetic (representational, *mimetic*) dialogues of Plato and Lucian and the excessively pedantic exercises of scholastic disputation.

If the "new theories" are now "got" from court to exchange to market; if, in addition, modern infidels have developed a taste for strong representations; then the moral philosopher will need to take a chance: against the entertaining sallies of all the wretched sects, he will have to pit his own form of entertainment, a dialogue whose free airing of the most dangerous opinions, like multifarious serpents offering bushels of apples in manifold gardens, would raise the reader's uncertainty to a higher pitch, before showing the way out of trouble. "For after all the Objections that I have

[5] The view of Cicero as encyclopedist of Greek philosophy was a commonplace. Henry Dodwell observed in 1702, "he has preserved Memoirs of the Sects which took most with the Romans, the Platonists, the Stoicks, and the Epicureans ... The greatest part of [Cicero's] Philosophical Works is only a Translation of the Sense of others." Cicero, *Tully's Five Books De Finibus; or Concerning the Last Object of Desire and Aversion ... With an Apology for the Philosophical Writings of Cicero, in a Letter to the Translator, by Henry Dodwell* (London: J. Tonson and R. Gibson, 1702). The pages are unnumbered at this point in the text.

heard against such a free Way of urging Theistic Arguments in Dialogue,"
writes Nichols, "I still think it is more like to do good among Infidels, than a
methodical Discourse, ranged into Chapter and Section ... For those that are
tainted with these Opinions ... every Thing which is designed for their Use
must be attempered to their Palates, to make it go down with them"
(pp. vi–vii). The philosophical elements of the dialogue should still predominate, but this imperative brought the writer's sociology (his "attempering" of
discourse to fit the imagined condition of common readers) into open conflict
with his theology. The Horatian ideal of balancing entertainment and
instruction was placed at special risk in dialogues whose topic of instruction
was a defense of Christianity, but whose entertainment value involved a
representation of aggressively heterodox opinions.

By adopting a lively, fictional imitation, the moral philosopher risked
tainting the very positions he sought to defend. Form is not an innocuous
coating for content. The time-honored metaphor of the sugar-coated pill
understates the reciprocal influence of the one upon the other. For early
readers of *Alciphron*, as for eighteenth-century commentators on Cicero, the
sweetness that made the pill go down might also make it come back up again
in an unsightly form (some would call it "the novel"). *Alciphron*'s first readers
expressed shock at the vividness with which heterodox opinions and
incendiary characters were represented. The author of *A Vindication* questions
"How strangely are all Sorts of Free-Thinkers jumbled together? And how
unfairly are the several Schemes and Arguments his Defenders of Religion
and Christianity (if we'll believe him) have to answer, represented? As a
Balance to this: How weakly is the Side the Author espouses, defended?"
(pp. 18–19). John Hervey lodges the same complaint: though sent up as "a
pair of most consummate Coxcombs," the atheists, Alciphron and Lysicles,
deviate into "so much Sense, and so much Nonsense; so much Reason, and
so much Absurdity; so much Learning, and so much Ignorance; so much Wit
and so much Folly" that the reader cannot finally extricate him or herself
from the labyrinth of opinion:

By this manner of proceeding therefore, he has stated *Scepticism*, and the strongest
Objections to our excellent Religion, in so clear a Light, that they are ...
comprehensible to every common Reader; whilst all the Answers to those Objections,
are so abstruse, so thin-spun, so wire-drawn, and so sublimated ... that they are ...
no more calculated for universal Commerce and Apprehension, than the Confusion
of Languages at the Tower of Babel.[6]

Eighteenth-century translators of Ciceronian dialogue were themselves met
with the same charge. "I OWN, however," writes Abbé d'Olivet in his
Thoughts of Cicero, "that Cicero's system of morals ... wants ... to be
sometimes corrected, and at other times supported, by the morality of the

---

[6] Hervey, *Some Remarks On the Minute Philosopher*, p. 13.

gospel ... To form a Christian, then, it will be necessary to supplement often, and much, to Cicero's ethics."[7] Nichols, while defending the Ciceronian style, acknowledges "those Tragical Exclamations that some honest People have made concerning my urging the Infidels arguments, [namely] that I help vitious Men to Arguments against Religion" (pp. vi–vii, xi).

Berkeley was aware that vivid portraits of atheists might get him into trouble. But he was quite clear as to his intentions. In developing characters who were not simply mouthpieces of set philosophical positions (as in Hylas for Matter and Philonous for Mind), Berkeley was portraying a process whereby high-level philosophical discourse became popularized. The characters select out those improbable (though all too probable) combinations of method, diatribe, corrosive wit, rigorous reasoning, and rhetorical flourish, forming identities that are, in effect, sites of intertextuality. "The ambiguous character is, it seems, the sure way to fame and esteem in the learned world, as it stands constituted at present," complains Crito (III, p. 320). And what has *esse percipi* to do with this? Berkeley's great concern in 1732 is to expose all of the false and tattered shreds of argument that go into making up a debased modern identity.

Mandeville did not understand, or chose not to express his understanding of this point when he attacked Berkeley for false representation immediately upon the appearance of *Alciphron*. "As you have no where declared in Words at length ... that you never read the *Fable of the Bees*, it is possible I might be ask'd, why I would take it for granted, that you never had read it ... [You have committed] such an Act as to calumniate [your] Neighbor, and willfully misrepresent him in the most atrocious Manner."[8] Mandeville did not like the fact that the rabid atheist, Lysicles, articulates a version of the Mandevillean hypothesis (private vices are public benefits), while weaving that position together with extreme republican and anarchistic views not present in the *Fable*. But Berkeley is not interested in faithful synopses of rival systems: the "author hath not confined himself to write against books alone," he responds. What matters to him are the intellectual and emotional *dispositions* that weave writings together into identities. Lysicles combines an exaggerated version of Mandeville's theory of vice with extreme republican views with elements of Shaftesbury on wit and Collins on atheism. Alciphron, by contrast, has read many of the same texts as his cohort in disbelief, but has turned out a gentler atheist. He leans towards the beautifying, not the critical side of Shaftesbury and takes no part in the defense of Mandeville's *Fable*. In each case we are surely meant to disagree with the views of Shaftesbury,

[7] *Thoughts of Cicero, translated from the French of the Abbé d'Olivet with the Latin Original* (Glasgow: R. Urie, 1754), pp. viii–ix.

[8] Mandeville, *A Letter to Dion occasion'd by his book called Alciphron, or the Minute Philosopher* (London: J. Roberts, 1732); rprt. *Augustan Reprint Society* 41 (Los Angeles: William Andrews Clark Memorial Library, 1953), p. 2.

Collins, and Mandeville. But we are also meant to make distinctions between Lysicles and Alciphron much like those we make between Lovelace and Belford in Richardson's *Clarissa*. The reader is meant to differentiate not only positions, but also characters.

In this case, however, a work whose purpose was to balance entertainment and instruction actually required the reader to make judgments based not on ideas *per se*, but on an evaluation of lively characters. Though philosophy should predominate, the fuller representation of a greater variety of opinion shifts the balance towards a mode of interpretation more akin to the way one reads novels. Berkeley, like the mid-century translators and imitators of Cicero, faced a problem of the following sort: determined to fight the heretics for the soul of common humanity, Berkeley found it necessary to depict more fully realized characters whose very force of personality began to compete with philosophical doctrine for the readers' attention. As the representation of individual characters and their sentiments became more vivid, the efficacy of any transcendental criterion for arbitrating philosophical dispute, such as that adduced at the end of *Hylas and Philonous*, becomes more and more attenuated. Berkeley fought to retain such a criterion; yet by the end of the dialogue he finds it necessary to equip his readers with a new set of criteria for assessing the value of characters and actions in the absence of agreement about a standard of judgment. Reluctantly, he writes a kind of moral philosophy undergoing novelization. Reluctantly, too, he develops protocol of interpretation more appropriate to complex prose fictions than to metaphysics. *Alciphron* and other mid-eighteenth century imitations of Cicero provide yet another venue where a native theory of the novel developed.

The extension of Pyrrhonism to rational standards of judgment

In each of the seven dialogues of *Alciphron*, regardless of the specific topic under discussion, characters cannot escape the suspicion that there exist no shared rules of public disputation in light of which assertions may be proven true or false. The list of logical fallacies ending *Hylas and Philonous* is proffered in *Alciphron*, but there it only evokes Alciphron's "You do not know what to make of us! I should be sorry you did" (III, p. 320). It is too easy to assume that such doubts merely reflect the obfuscating tactics of the atheists and are rejected out of hand by Berkeley.[9] For one of the most striking features of *Alciphron* is the transference of Pyrrhonian arguments from the voice of Berkeley (in the *Principles*) and Berkeley's spokesman (Philonous in *Hylas and Philonous*) to the voices of the atheists, who call into question the value and norms of rational disputation.

Philonous' references to telescopes and microscopes had relativized the phenomenal world:

[9] Such is Peter Walmsley's view. See *The Rhetoric of Berkeley's Philosophy*, pp. 105–122.

PHIL. I think it may evidently be concluded from your own concessions, that all the colours we see with our naked eyes, are only apparent as those on the clouds, since they vanish upon a more close and accurate inspection, which is afforded us by a microscope ... Even our own eyes do not always represent objects to us after the same manner. In the jaundice everyone knows that all things seem yellow.   (II, pp. 184–185)

As has been seen, this argument supports the credo of *esse percipi*, from which Berkeley's "simple" affirmation of the Deity follows. But what if perspectivalism disregarded the certain point insisted upon at the end of *Hylas and Philonous*? Alciphron only follows out more rigorously the theological implications of Philonous' reasoning when he describes his own development from Latitudinarianism to atheism, a progress that might stand for a short history of religion during the period:

Having observed several sects and subdivisions of sects espousing very different and contrary opinions, and yet all professing Christianity, I rejected those points wherein they differed, retaining only that which was agreed to by all, and so became a *Latitudinarian*. Having afterwards, upon a more enlarged view of things, perceived that Christians, Jews, and Mahometans had each their different systems of faith, agreeing only in the belief of one God, I became a *Deist*. Lastly, extending my view to all the various nations which inhabit this globe, and finding they agreed in no one point of faith, but differed one from another, as well as from the forementioned sects, even in the notion of a God ... I thereupon became an *Atheist*; it being my opinion that a man of courage and sense should follow his argument wherever it leads him, and that nothing is more ridiculous than to be a free-thinker by halves.   (III, pp. 43–44)

The claim that Berkeley parodies the views of the atheists fails to account for the striking similarity between the reasoning which before brought us *esse percipi* and that which here brings us atheism.[10] The more enlarged view possible through a telescope or microscope leads to doubts about the inherent substance of objects; the more enlarged view possible through historical scholarship and travel leads to doubts about the universal appeal of the Christian religion. One can imagine Berkeley asking himself, "did I in the *Principles* and Philonous in *Hylas and Philonous* follow perspectivalism by halves?"

When, in *Alciphron*, attention shifts to the specific dispositions that weave ideas and texts together into modern characters, Berkeley cannot help but acknowledge that *esse percipi* is one of those strains of Enlightenment thought

---

[10] For the view that Berkeley parodies his atheists, see John Richetti, *Philosophical Writing: Locke, Berkeley, Hume*. "The polemic against freethinking [in *Alciphron*] is a dramatization of its style, an elaborate mimicry and parody designed to reveal its moral, theological, and philosophical falsity by literary means" pp. 164–165. Berkeley no doubt mocks the verbal excesses of the atheists ("We have among us moles that dig deep under ground, and eagles that soar out of sight," says Alciphron, complimenting himself and his cohorts). But if one agrees that there exists continuity between Berkeley's early immaterialism and the full-blown atheism of Lysicles and Alciphron, then the author's attitude cannot be one of mere ridicule unless he is practicing philosophical amnesia.

that was tending to be amalgamated into the character of the modern atheist! That is why the stirring defense of immaterialism occurs in the Fourth Dialogue, to be superseded by the philosophers during their next three days' conferences.[11]

The relativism of the atheists does not stop with beliefs and institutions reflected on in dialogue; it questions the grounds of rational discourse itself, the distinctions between good and bad argument, logic and rhetoric, reason and emotion, whose self-evidence had supported the demonstration at the end of *Hylas and Philonous*. "It is natural," Alciphron explains to Euphranor, "for men, according to their several educations and prejudices, to form contrary judgments upon the same things, which they view in very different lights" (III, p. 189). These judgments are, paradoxically, all supported by sound logic and exact reasoning. Alciphron concludes: "I lay it down for a certain truth, that by the fallacious arts of logic and criticism, straining and forcing, palliating, patching, and distinguishing, a man may justify or make out anything" (III, p. 257). Alciphron reduces all philosophy to an expression of will and desire. Truth is no longer the issue; rather, as in Nietzsche, philosophy stands as a kind of symptomatology, telling us what a mind needs most to justify about its body. This skepticism about the conditions of argument leads Alciphron to doubt whether the lyric of private opinion can ever be transformed into a public dialogue ending in consensus:

After all, say what you will, this variety of opinions must needs shake the faith of a reasonable man. Where there are so many different opinions on the same point they cannot all be true, but it is certain they may all be false. And the means to find out the truth! When a man of sense sets about this inquiry, he finds himself on a sudden startled and amused with hard words and knotty questions. This makes him abandon the pursuit, thinking the game not worth the chase.   (III, p. 275)

Berkeley sets an even stronger expression of the same point in the voice of Lysicles:

But I can never hope, Crito, to make you think my schemes reasonable. We reason each right upon his own principles, and shall never agree till we quit our principles, which cannot be done by reasoning. We all talk of just, and right, and wrong, and public good, and all those things. The names may be the same, but the notions and conclusions very different, perhaps diametrically opposite; and yet each may admit of clear proofs, and be inferred by the same way of reasoning.   (III, p. 212)

Hume will repeat this point, though more moderately. "Every voice is united in applauding elegance, propriety, simplicity, spirit in writing ... but when critics come to particulars, this seeming unanimity vanishes; and it is found,

---

[11] For the opposite view, the claim that Berkeley establishes the existence of God in the Fourth Dialogue in order to pass on to the question of God's attributes and our obedience to Him in the Seventh Dialogue, see David Berman, *George Berkeley: Idealism and the Man* (Oxford: Oxford University Press, 1994), chapter 6.

that they all had affixed a very different meaning to their expressions."[12] Hume recognizes yet seeks a way to minimize variation. The atheists in *Alciphron*, on the other hand, revel in and seek to magnify their differences. Whereas Philocles in Berkeley's previous dialogue had sought to join logic and dialectic within the literary embodiment of philosophical dialogue, Lysicles uses dialogue to subvert this bond. Logic and dialectic become species of rhetoric; and rhetoric, divorced from the humanist ideal of joining virtue and persuasiveness, becomes a device for masking the will to self-empowerment. No wonder, then, that Berkeley's atheists express some of the most extreme strains of atheism and anarchism to be found anywhere in eighteenth-century letters. "A man of great soul and free spirit delights in the noble experiment of blowing up systems and dissolving governments, to mould them anew upon other principles and in another shape," Lysicles proclaims. "We are for thorough, independent, original freedom. Inward freedom without outward is good for nothing but to set a man's judgment at variance with his practice" (III, p. 100).

Up to this point, I have, it is true, devoted inordinate attention to the cavils of the atheists and have ignored the serious and often compelling arguments of the theists. My purpose in doing so has been to raise this question of a standard of judgment in the sharpest possible way. "The highest arrogance and self-conceit is at last startled," writes Hume about the variety of taste, "on observing an equal assurance on all sides, and scruples, amidst such a contest of sentiment, to pronounce positively in its own favor."[13] In *Alciphron* we witness an often violent "contest of sentiment," in which the participants have fewer and fewer scruples about pronouncing positively in their own favor as the debate drags on. When they find themselves at loggerheads, they appeal to supposedly shared assumptions about what it means to engage in a philosophical dialogue. Yet even – and especially – here, they discover no basis of agreement. The atheists consider wit and interruption important components of dialogue; their aim is more to express extreme opinions than to communicate and convince. The theists desire a calmer, more rational discussion; their aim is to convert the atheists to theism. As in Shaftesbury, two conceptions of dialogue stand at an impasse. It is not in the interest of either party to validate the other's interpretation of the very discourse in which each is engaged.

Given the loss of the structural and thematic conditions that (in *Hylas and Philonous*) had favored Berkeley's "successful" appropriation of philosophical dialogue, the question then becomes why Berkeley chose to retain the genre in writing *Alciphron* and how he transformed the Ciceronian dialogue into a form still capable of conveying his "apology for the Christian religion, against

---

[12] Hume, *Of the Standard of Taste and Other Essays*, ed. John W. Lenz (Indianapolis: Bobbs-Merrill Co., 1981), p. 3.

[13] *Ibid.*, p. 3.

those that are called free-thinkers" (title-page). In the previous chapter, I held
that Berkeley was engaged in a struggle with skeptics over who would control
the implications of perspectivalism in theological dispute. That struggle
continues throughout Berkeley's entire life. It is reflected once again in his
decision to continue writing dialogues even after Pyrrhonian arguments have
threatened to destroy the basis for religious dialogue. Whereas before the
relativity of sense perception was the category to be fought over and
transformed into the basis of a theology, now it is the relativity and isolation
of individual desire in particularized characters that must be reclaimed as the
basis for sound theological conclusions. In other words, Berkeley refuses to
allow philosophical dialogue to fall without a fight into the hands of deists like
Matthew Tindal and skeptics like Hume.

Two years before *Alciphron*, Tindal had composed his own dialogue,
"Christianity as Old as the Creation" (1730). Although lacking all signs of
dramatic interaction between individualized characters ("B" only asks
leading questions so that "A" can elaborate the doctrines of deism), the
dialogue is an appropriate form for Tindal because the deist takes the
multiplicity of theological sentiments as an axiom:

B. If men, having done all in their power to find out his [God's] will, should fall into
   opposite sentiments, must it not be the will of God that it should be so?
A. There is, I think, no way to avoid this objection, of God's willing contrarieties, but
   by supposing he requires nothing of men but what is founded on the nature of
   things, and the immutable relations they bear to one another.
B. This seems to my bewildered reason to imply that there was from the beginning
   but one true religion, which all men might know was their duty to embrace; and
   if this is true, I can't well conceive how this character can consist with
   Christianity, without allowing it, at the same time, to be "as old as the
   Creation."[14]

B's bewildered conclusion is, of course, exactly the implication A wishes him
to draw from the irreducibility of theological sentiments. We are to stop
looking to any special Christian revelation as a basis for consensus in the
community and to heed instead "the law of nature ... founded on the
unalterable reason of things."[15] In his ongoing confrontation with skeptics
and deists of every stripe, Berkeley had to show why this line of reasoning was
defective, just as he needed to offer an alternative to Alciphron's biographical
account of his irresistible progress from Latitudinarianism to atheism by
means of an expanding perspective. He therefore sought to dramatize the
way in which a free, skeptical inquiry (dialogue) may be transformed into an
instrument of sound theological teaching. This renovation of dialogue would
depend upon the possibility of establishing a standard for judging the atheists

[14] Tindal, "Christianity as Old as the Creation," in *Deism and Natural Religion, a Source Book*, ed. E.
     Graham Waring (New York: Ungar, 1967), p. 111.
[15] *Ibid.*, p. 118.

in a climate of uncertainty about a standard of judgment. If the atheists are to be converted, it will be in light of principles they themselves do not accept. Berkeley's solutions – there are several, not always consistent – depend largely upon the fictional elements of the dialogue and fall into two classes: those that reassert the efficacy of a fixed, rational standard, despite the blindness of the atheists to it; and those that appeal outside strict philosophical reason to a new standard based upon the behavior of characters.

In one sense the threat posed by the extension of Pyrrhonian tactics to rational disputation is less than I've made out. The dialogue recounts a contest to determine which figure, atheist or theist, deserves the title of "free-thinker." To engage in such a game, both sides must acknowledge certain rules, in particular a willingness to subject their ideas to close examination. The atheists accept and obey these rules when things are going their way, but when the theists gain the upper hand, out come the tactics cited above. When, for instance, Euphranor backs Lysicles into a particularly disadvantageous position, the atheist responds,

If I say *yes*, you will make an inference; and if I say *no*, you will demand a reason. The best way is to say nothing at all. There is, I see, no end of answering.

And Euphranor replies,

If you give up the point you undertook to prove, there is an end at once: but, if you hope to convince me, you must answer my questions, and allow me the liberty to argue and infer.   (III, p. 80)

In addition, Alciphron seems to recognize the force of reasoned argument even when it requires him to abandon his atheism. In perhaps the most humorous passage of the work, Alciphron must explain the results of the fourth day of discussion to Lysicles, who has been absent:

I am glad, said ALCIPHRON, that I have found here my second, a fresh man to maintain our common cause [atheism], which, I doubt, Lysicles will think hath suffered by his absence.

LYS. Why so?
ALC. I have been drawn into some concessions you will not like.
LYS. Let me know what they are.
ALC. Why, that there is such a thing as a God, and that His existence is very certain.
LYS. Bless me! How came you to entertain so wild a notion?
ALC. You know we profess to follow reason wherever it leads. And in short I have been reasoned into it.
LYS. Reasoned! You should say, amused with words, bewildered with sophistry.
                                                                  (III, p. 162)

A case can be made, then, for Berkeley's introducing the atheistic attacks on dialogue as a way of underscoring the theists' rightful claim to the title of free-thinker. The same system of logic and reason obtains here as in *Hylas and Philonous*, only now it is asserted *via negativa*, through the evasions of the atheists. The dialogue might then be said to operate as a kind of satire. Its standard of judgment is proffered negatively, in much the same way that *The Tale of a Tub* and *The Dunciad* convey a positive norm by excoriating the hacks and dunces. Along these lines, Gregory Hollingshead has argued that "Pope looked to the argument of *Alciphron* for an orthodox model upon which to base his satire on deism lest inadvertently he make the same doctrinal mistake that led him to be charged with deism on the basis of the *Essay on Man*."[16]

The question of how in *The Dunciad* an exhaustive representation of anarchy could possibly suggest stable religious and cultural values parallels the question of how in *Alciphron* an apparently unresolved "contest of sentiment," including a full articulation of atheism, might result in an apology for the Christian religion. The work shifts from an attempt to achieve internal agreement among the members of a fictional community to a spectacle of disagreement, which the reader is nevertheless expected to resolve in favor of the theists. The reader knows which standards to apply, and, as a silent participant in the dialogues, condemns the atheists for their evasions, recognizing the force of Berkeley's earlier positions even though they do not now produce the conversion of the skeptic. Crito sums up this point: "Arguments, therefore, which carry light have their effect, even against an opponent who shuts his eyes, because they shew him to be obstinate and prejudiced" (III, p. 143). The "show" is for someone outside the dialogue, an ideal reader, whose agreement with the theists re-establishes the community of reason. Nevertheless, the difference between a dialogue that includes its own ideal reception (like the chorus of a Sophoclean tragedy) and a dialogue that leaves the determination of truth up to the reader is an important one. Dion, whose position as the silent transcriber of the dialogue stands closest to that of Berkeley's imagined reader, remains dissatisfied at the end of the work. Although he had expressed the hope that the dialogue would lead to a resolution of differences – "so many points [had] been examined, discussed, and agreed ... that I hoped to see them come to an entire agreement in the end" (III, pp. 219–220) – the rude departure of the atheists (called away suddenly on business after partaking of Euphranor's hospitality for a full week) leaves him with the disquieting sense that nothing has been accomplished, since the atheists have not been brought to renounce their heresies. Dion remarks "how unaccountable it was that men [atheists] so easy

16 "Pope, Berkeley, and the True Key to the *Dunciad in Four Books*," *English Studies in Canada* 10 (1984) 146–147.

to confute should yet be so difficult to convince" (III, p. 323). He differentiates between confutation, which at this time connoted silencing an adversary by unfair means, and conviction, which implied the victory of one party over another based upon rational standards the contending parties shared.[17] Dion wants to know how a dialogue like the one he has just witnessed could possibly supply other observers (i.e. common readers) with an edifying lesson. His concern is with interpretation *per se* in a climate of epistemological uncertainty and rhetorical excess.

Crito tries to reassure Dion. He first tells him that those who remain unconvinced by the arguments of the Christians must have been improperly educated. Citing the authority of Aristotle, he holds that true arguments will persuade only those "whose minds are prepared by education and custom, as land is for seed" (III, p. 323).[18] Had the atheists been properly educated, for instance, they would not have argued that the multiplicity of religious convictions negates any means of determining which is truest. Crito explains,

The most general pretext which looks like reason is taken from the variety of opinions about religion. This is a resting-stone to a lazy and superficial mind. But one of more spirit and a juster way of thinking makes it a step whence he looks about, and proceeds to examine and compare the differing institutions of religion. He will observe which is the most sublime and rational in its doctrines, most venerable in its mysteries, most useful in its precepts, most decent in its worship? which createth the noblest hopes, and most worthy views? . . . and upon the whole form his judgment like a reasonable free-thinker.   (III, pp. 326–327)

When Montaigne performed a similar operation, he decided the case in favor of the cannibals; Tindal made the same premise the basis for a natural religion obviating need for any specifically Christian doctrine. Yet Crito feels certain that only one answer, the Christianity of the established Church of

---

[17] In late seventeenth- and early eighteenth-century usage, to stand confuted did imply an intellectual defeat, but the word also carried connotations of one's having been silenced by physical (i.e. unfair) means. *The Oxford English Dictionary* provides the following instances of "confute" used as a synonym for repression or silencing: 1614, T. Adams in Spurgeon *Treas. Dav.* Ps. lxxx. 20 "Goliath . . . shall be confuted with a pebble"; 1660, R. Coke *Justice Vinc.* 15 "He . . . ought . . . to be confuted with clubs and hissing." Alciphron's question emphasizes the difference between the words: "It is one thing to silence an adversary, and another to convince him" (III, p. 323). It is not enough, in other words, for the theists to mock, satirize, or caricature their adversaries. They wish to convince them, which meant, in the terms of Johnson's *Dictionary*, "to cause a person to admit, as established to his satisfaction, that which is advanced in argument." Yet, as we have seen, *Alciphron* is in part about the loss of common grounds of rational deliberation that would make such an admission possible.

[18] Berkeley refers to Aristotle's *Nicomachean Ethics*, bk. 10, section 9. A similar argument can be found in Aristotle's *Rhetoric*: "Moreover, before some audiences not even the possession of the exactest knowledge will make it easy for what we say to produce conviction. For argument based on knowledge implies instruction, and there are people whom one cannot instruct. Here, then, we must use, as our modes of persuasion and argument, notions possessed by everybody, as we observed in the *Topics* when dealing with the way to handle a popular audience." *The Complete Works of Aristotle*, II, p. 2154 (I, 1355a 24–29).

England, is possible to the questions he poses. Just as making too much of the variability of opinion is the sign of an uneducated mind, so education becomes the means to restrict variety. "The real cause," he says, "of whatever is amiss may justly be reckoned the general neglect of education in those who need it most – the people of fashion" (III, p. 328). Were privileged British youth properly educated, "we should soon see that licentious humour, vulgarly called *free-thinking*, banished from the presence of gentlemen, together with ignorance and ill taste" (III, p. 329).

Dion himself is not satisfied with the response. To his question of why intelligent men become atheists, Crito seems only to have offered the circular reply that their atheism bespeaks a want of intelligence: "This answer might hold with respect to other persons and other times," says Dion, "but when the question was of inquisitive men, in an age wherein reason was so much cultivated and thinking so much in vogue, it did not seem satisfactory" (III, p. 323).

The rejoinder agitates Crito and leads to a second explanation, the anecdote of one "Honest Demea," who "having seen a neighbour of his ruined by the vices of a free-thinking son, contracted such a prejudice against thinking that he would not suffer his own to read Euclid, being told it might teach him to think" (III, p. 325).[19] The anecdote makes clear that the atheists are considered as much social as intellectual threats. Strictly speaking, however, Crito has answered a philosophical question with a literary anecdote. The reader is meant to call to mind instances in his or her own experience when atheistic characters drove good sorts to bad actions. Crito proceeds to explain why his anecdotal logic provides an accurate way of reading the modern atheist. "In order to cure a distemper," he argues, "you should consider what produced it":

Little incidents, vanity, disgust, humour, inclination, without the least assistance from reason, are often known to make infidels. Where the general tendency of a doctrine is disagreeable, the mind is prepared to relish and improve everything that with the least pretence seems to make against it. Hence the coarse manners of a country curate, the polite manners of a chaplain, the wit of a minute philosopher, a jest, a song, a tale, can serve instead of reason for infidelity. Bupalus preferred a rake in the church, and then made use of him as an argument against it. Vice, indolence, faction, and fashion produce minute philosophers, and mere petulancy not a few. Who then can expect a thing so irrational and capricious should yield to reason? It may, nevertheless, be worth while to argue against such men, and expose their fallacies, if not for their own sake, yet for the sake of others; as it may lessen their credit, and prevent the growth of their sect.   (III, p. 326)

Although Crito says it is worthwhile to argue against atheists, his account of the genesis of atheistic sensibilities suggests that the cure is not to be found

---

[19] I shall argue in the next chapter that Hume had read *Alciphron* by 1748 and derived the name for his fideist (Demea) from this anecdote.

in the realm of philosophical exchange, but rather in the exposure of bad conduct to public ridicule and punishment. "Little incidents" produce big infidels; and if one wishes to disprove their philosophical bent, one had better establish the existential links between ideas and actions. As the force and vividness of Crito's anecdotes makes clear, the conflation of wrong thoughts and bad conduct is nothing if not seconded by fictions in which characters betray the sinfulness of their ways. It is not enough, in other words, that a reader who already agrees with Crito should condemn the atheists based on a standard the atheists do not share; the atheists must be brought by other means to "expose their fallacies" and so to uphold a standard of judgment despite themselves.

This strategy can be described most succinctly as a shift from the question, "which opinion is most compatible with right reason?" to the question Euphranor asks Crito: "What hinders them [minute philosophers] from putting an end to their own lives?" (III, p. 92). Here is Crito's answer:

Their not being persuaded of the truth of what they profess. Some, indeed, in a fit of despair, do now and then lay violent hands on themselves. And as the minute philosophy prevails, we daily see more examples of suicide. But they bear no proportion to those who would put an end to their lives if they durst. My friend Clinias, who had been one of them and a philosopher of rank, let me into the secret history of their doubts, and fears, and irresolute resolutions of making away with themselves, which last he assures me is a frequent topic with men of pleasure, when they have drunk themselves into a little spirit. It was by virtue of this mechanical valour the renowned philosopher Hermocrates shot himself through the head. The same thing hath since been practiced by several others, to the great relief of their friends.[20]   (III, p. 92)

Amidst the babble of competing reasons, a new standard of judgment emerges: the behavior of characters. We know Lysicles does not believe his own claims because if he did he would not be alive: atheism is false because it leads to destructive behavior. Recourse to such an argument, which I shall refer to as *ad hominem* in the largest sense, as much as acknowledges the impotence of any established authority to enforce limits upon thought and conduct.[21] The reader must believe that something else in the nature of things, a marvelous homology between thought and just reward, keeps the

---

[20] Fraser notes that the reference here may be to Charles Blount, one of the early representatives of English minute philosophy, who took his own life in 1693. His thoughts were later developed by Charles Gildon in *Oracles of Reason* (1695).

[21] Peter Suber defines the *ad hominem* appeal as "any argument whose conclusion is a disparaging assessment of the character or capacities of a person," in "A Case Study in *Ad Hominem* Arguments: Fichte's Science of Knowledge," *Philosophy and Rhetoric* 23 (1990) 12. Although philosophers normally think of this tactic as a scoundrel's recourse, I am arguing here that the *ad hominem* argument emerges as a necessary means of upholding rational Christianity once it is threatened by competing claims made upon the standard of reason. In the absence of clear standards of determination, matters are decided on an *ad hoc*, *ad hominem* basis, with the rhetorical force of one *ad hominem* anecdote set against the rhetorical force of others.

atheists in check: they punish themselves. For the homology to be brought home to the reader, who perhaps knows some atheists who seem free of anguish, one needs to witness a compelling sequence of actions – secret histories, anecdotes, cautionary tales, rakes' progresses – wherein the drama of retribution is played out.

Crito, whom Dion describes as a "zealous Protestant," is the master of this philosophical story-telling. "It puts me in mind of my friend Lamprocles, who needed but one argument against infidels. I observed, said he, that as infidelity grew, there grew corruption of every kind, and new vices. This simple observation on matter of fact was sufficient to make him ... imbue and season the minds of his children betimes with the principles of religion" (III, p. 139). Stories about the foresight of true believers are matched by brief histories of the eventual justice visited upon recreants. Crito tells the anecdote of a rake who tutored the son of one Crates. The same libertine "soon after did justice on himself. For he taught Lycidas, a modest young man, the principles of his sect. Lycidas, in return, debauched his daughter, an only child: upon which, Charmides (that was the minute philosopher's name) hanged himself" (III, p. 98).

At the end of *Hylas and Philonous*, the characters appeal first to logic and then to the laws of nature to reconcile their differences. Characters look elsewhere for justice. But here character does justice on itself. The evil of Charmides' mind has become a noose around his neck. The falsehood of Hermocrates' thoughts becomes a bullet through the brain. The greater realism of Berkeley's later dialogue (in comparison to *Hylas and Philonous*), the representation of a more wide-ranging, skeptical exchange taking in any number of philosophical, political, and theological controversies, deprives Berkeley of the comedic, dialectical structure of *Hylas and Philonous* and leads in turn to an increasing reliance upon fictional anecdotes as a means of administering justice.

The probable as criterion: Cicero and the turn to character

At this point it is difficult not to hear the objection of philosophers and critics familiar with *Alciphron*. It might go something like this: it is willful and inexact to argue that Crito's *ad hominem* tirades occupy a position of philosophical importance. These anecdotes are marginal to the central philosophical arguments set forth especially in the Fourth and Seventh Dialogues. To make the *ad hominem* appeal the stopping point of *Alciphron* is just the move one might expect from someone who seeks to relate philosophical dialogue to the development of the novel.

Philosophers are trained not to take fictional supplements seriously; literary critics are trained to reduce serious philosophical arguments to rhetorical displays. Together, they seem to be in no position to understand the dynamic interaction between poetic and philosophical elements in a complex work such as *Alciphron*. But the question Dion asks the theists is important: how is one to adjudicate a contest of opinion in which sides are upheld equally? Crito's first answer (educate the heretics) skirts the issue by claiming that neither the debate at hand nor any debate regarding the truth of Christianity could be undecidable. But his second response, the shift from philosophical argument to *ad hominem* attack, is more significant. The *ad hominem* needs to be viewed here not as a scoundrel's recourse but as the quite plausible accompaniment of serious philosophical positions.

In order to develop this point, let us turn briefly from *Alciphron* to a group of writers who confronted the same problem in Berkeley's day. I refer to the eighteenth-century translators and imitators of Cicero, with whom this chapter began. Cicero, of course, was both famous and notorious for his rhetorical ability to construct dialogues that upheld all sides of the question equally (*in utremque partem dicere*). Christian apologists for Ciceronian dialogue were thus forced to answer Dion's question: how were such works to be adjudicated; why should Ciceronian skepticism be distinguished from a more outrageous Pyrrhonism? William Guthrie, one of the most prolific of the eighteenth-century translators, acknowledges the problem: "It cannot be dissembled, that the Contiguity of Doctrines, with regard to the Criterion of Truth, which arose among the followers of Socrates, is so great as to create Confusion, and it requires the nicest acquaintance with our Author's Manner, and the Philosophy of the Ancients, to separate them."[22] He then sets about teaching the reader that "nice acquaintance":

Philosophers of the New Academy recommended moderation through their Unwillingness to give their positive Assent to any Proposition; because of the great Difficulty in discerning the Truth, thro' the Arguments which might be offer'd on contrary Sides. This was a Doctrine in common with the Academics both new and old, and the Skeptics; but with the following Difference: A Skeptic, who was a kind of intellectual Prize-fighter, laid himself out to invent Arguments, which might balance the Assent so equally on both Sides, that it would preponderate to neither. Hence it is that Cicero's Character of Arcesilas, agrees with a Skeptic rather than an Academic, who allow'd that the Arguments on one Side might admit of Probability. Thus the New Academic, by admitting a Degree of Comprehension, preserv'd a Principle of Agency, whereas the Skeptic, by the equal Balance he affected, took away both Comprehension and Probability, by which Means he rendered Volition inert, and thereby destroy'd every Principle of moral Agency.   (p. v)

Guthrie finds it necessary to distinguish the radical skepticism of the Pyrrhonists from the moderate skepticism of the New Academy in 1744 because a similar blurring of categories has occurred in the British Enlighten-

22 *The Morals of Cicero, containing I. His Conferences De Finibus II. His Academics, Conferences concerning the Criterion of Truth, and the Fallibility of Human Judgment*, trans. William Guthrie (London: T. Waller, 1744), p. vi.

ment by the middle of the eighteenth century. One might parse the passage above in the following way: philosophers of the late seventeenth century (for example, Locke) responded to the excesses of the Civil War period by developing the philosophical principles of moderation. Consequently, as in the time of the New Academy, extreme skeptics misunderstood the willingness to suspend conviction for the sake of peace as an invitation to relativism, or worse.

Guthrie responds by transferring the point of dispute from the existence or non-existence of a standard of judgment to the obligation moral agents live under to identify the highest degree of certainty possible in given cases (i.e. probability). The philosopher of the New Academy decides ahead of time to admit a "Degree of Comprehension," thus imposing a limit upon skeptical questioning. That limit marks a turn from the free-play of ideas to conduct (moral Agency) as the primary test of philosophical value. Even if skeptic and academic agree about the difficulty of locating the criterion of truth, the standard now supplied by the existential requirement that one *act*, that the principle of agency be preserved, shows that they have little in common.

According to Guthrie, Cicero's escape from a debilitating skepticism begins with a conception of character: it is better to act than to remain passive, and better still to act well than to act ill. Even in the absence of Truth, it will therefore be necessary to determine the true in given cases; and even in the absence of Goodness, it will still be necessary to choose the better of two courses of action. Thomas Francklin, the eighteenth-century translator of Cicero's most notorious work, *De Natura Deorum*, defends himself and Cicero in the following terms: "I assure them [readers] we do not assert that nothing has the appearance of truth; but we say that some falsehoods are so blended with all truths, and have so great a resemblance to them, that there is no certain rule for judging and assenting; on which is founded this tenet, that many things are probable, which tho' they are not evident, have so persuasive and beautiful an aspect that a wise man chuses to direct his conduct by them."[23]

The problem that next confronts Guthrie and the apologists for Cicero is how to provide a philosophical elaboration for the doctrine of probability. As Douglas Patey has shown, this was a question that exercised not only philosophers but also literary critics, historians, theologians, scientists, and artists throughout the eighteenth century.[24] Patey explains that "'conjec-

---

[23] Cicero, *Of the Nature of the Gods in Three Books*, trans. Thomas Francklin (London: T. Davies, 1775), p. 11.

[24] Writes Patey, "'Probable signs' are effects which lead the mind to infer to their causes; probable signification, we might say, is a causal relation in reverse. Until well into the eighteenth century, it was through probable signs that reasoning from effect to cause, from the 'manifest' (outer) properties of objects to their 'occult' or 'hidden' (inner) properties was understood. Probable signs licensed inferences from macroscopic nature to what was called 'the internal constitution' of objects; from body to mind; and, at a variety of levels, from literary form to meaning ... In the Augustan age probable signs were a staple not merely of rhetoric and the sciences, but of the theory of education, history, and even theology, where they formed the groundwork of the enterprise known as physico-theology" (*Probability and Literary Form*, p. 35). See also the chapter entitled

turing,' as probable inference was called, came to be subject to explicitly
formulated rules, rules especially concerning signs: conjecturing must take
account not only of the clear signs that might indicate a conclusion, but also
of the modifying 'circumstances' of each case."[25] Yet great difficulties
attended the formulation of rules for conjecture: "To be able to reduce the
vagaries and diversities of testimony to a science would be to erect
demonstration where, *ex hypothesi*, there are only probabilities."[26]

It is not surprising that this problem arises with special vividness in the
philosophical dialogues of the age. For in the most skeptical and probing
dialogues – Shaftesbury's *The Moralists* and Berkeley's *Alciphron*, for instance –
disagreement about substantive matters very quickly extends to disagreement
about the rules or criteria in light of which differences of opinion should be
adjudicated. Dion's question to the theists becomes unavoidable, as does the
realization that for every rule proposed to govern probability it is probable
that disputes will arise, making it necessary to establish a new criterion to test
the old criterion. How does one provide rules for a mode of deliberation
premised upon the absence of certain grounds? Guthrie, prefacing Cicero,
cannot decide how to solve the dilemma. Part of him wants to dismiss the
whole issue by redescribing Cicero's dialogue as a mode of satire: the
"mixture of Childishness and Impertinence" the dialogues contain "leaves no
room for us to doubt that he intended them as a Banter upon all Logic ...
Whoever considers the good Sense of Cicero, can view all the Arguments ...
in no other Light than that of Ridicule" (p. xxxiii). Elsewhere, however,
Guthrie does attempt to ascertain the highest degree of probability in matters
of ethical choice:

Arcesilas made it a Rule in Life to follow what is judged to be most probable; and
that a Person who acts himself according to the Dictates of Prudence (or sound
Judgment) attains Happiness in Life. That this Prudence consists in the moral Fitness
of things, and that moral Fitness is agreeable to Probability and Reason. That,
therefore, whoever follows Probability, acts according to moral Fitness, and arrives at
Happiness.   (p. xx)

The passage makes clear why satire was an attractive alternative to situational
ethics (casuistry). How should this interlocking set of equivalancies be
verified? Have we not entered the realm of tautology? In life one follows the
rule of what is most probable. But in order to determine the rule, one looks to

---

"Scattered Atoms of Probability," in Hoyt Trowbridge, *From Dryden to Jane Austen: Essays on English Critics and Writers, 1660–1818* (Albuquerque, New Mexico: University of New Mexico Press, 1977).

[25] Patey, *ibid.*, p. 35.

[26] *Ibid.*, pp. 33–34. The comment follows citation of Locke's *Essay* (bk. 4, ch. 16, section 9), in which Locke observes that testimonies "are liable to so great variety of contrary Observations, Circumstances, Reports, different Qualifications, Tempers, Designs, Over-sights, etc. of the Reporters, that 'tis impossible to reduce to precise Rules, the various degrees wherein Men give their Assent."

the moral fitness of things, and one knows moral fitness by its consistency or accord or agreement with probability and reason, all of which conduce to happiness. Probability as a guide was meant to substitute for a metaphysically informed ethics grounded in an a priori principle of truth and virtue; yet, in the above formulation, unless one begins with an a priori understanding of one of the crucial terms – happiness or prudence or the moral fitness of things – the chain of assertions becomes circular.

In order to break out of circularity, one must assume a change in the fundamental unit of philosophical analysis (much like the change already noted in Berkeley's *Principles*). The whole human character must be thought the desideratum of ethics, not some reasoning faculty that has the capacity to disprove itself and its connection with the body. Looked at philosophically, Guthrie's magical circle of probability, moral fitness, and happiness may seem to beg the question; looked at in terms of a prudential ethics that takes the whole character as its starting point, the same argument carries force. One escapes Guthrie's circles by picturing his equivalancies less as a rigorous philosophical argument and more as a call for a kind of narration – the kind *Alciphron* begins to provide and Austen's novels supply in full – that *would* verify the intimate connection between the ideas characters hold, their conduct in the world, and the extent to which they realize happiness.

Ad hominem, utility, and the emotive force of language

Now it is possible to return to my claim that *ad hominem* arguments in *Alciphron* are part of a serious philosophical position. In Berkeley, too, we find a transition from strict philosophical reason (*esse percipi*, immaterialism) to an argument that hinges upon fictional constructs of character, acting in light of probabilistic criteria. In the Seventh Dialogue, Euphranor, ever patient, offers one final defense of Christianity against the stubborn atheists. Alciphron has just finished arguing, following Locke and Toland, that words which do not connote clear and distinct ideas are meaningless. Such concepts as "grace" evoke no determinate idea, and "there can be no assent where there are no ideas: and where there is no assent there can be no faith" (III, p. 291). Euphranor answers that Alciphron has not consistently ruled out all terms that connote no clear and distinct meaning. Force, a favored term of atheistical mechanists, also connotes no clear and distinct idea, "and yet," says Euphranor, "I presume, you allow there are very evident propositions or theorems relating to force, which contain useful truths" (III, p. 295). Though vague, certain terms are useful. Euphranor derives the lesson:

Shall we not admit the same method of arguing, the same rules of logic, reason, and good sense, to obtain in things spiritual and things corporeal, in faith and science? and shall we not use the same candour, and make the same allowances, in examining the revelations of God and the inventions of men? For aught I see, that philosopher cannot be free from bias and prejudice, or be said to weigh things in an equal balance, who shall maintain the doctrine of force and reject that of grace; who shall admit the abstract idea of a triangle, and at the same time ridicule the Holy Trinity.

(III, p. 296)

Without quite stating the point directly, Euphranor has shifted to a theological position based upon the pragmatics of utility. He has stopped talking about truth and falsehood of propositions and is interested instead in the "allowances" human agents routinely make for concepts that help them get things done. Allowing for the impossibility of absolute verification makes "force" and "grace," "triangle" and "Trinity," equally truthful – which is to say, equally useful.

While Berkeley allowed the argument to stand unopposed in the first edition, by the second he had developed its counter, which he placed in the mouth of Alciphron. "According to this doctrine," Alciphron replies, "all points may be alike maintained. There will be nothing absurd in Popery, not even in transubstantiation" (III, p. 309). He sees that all Euphranor has done is to shift the point of disagreement from the real existence of entities represented by abstract terms to the utilitarian value of forming abstract ideas. To say that force and grace are both "significant" is only to say that one group of people thinks one abstract idea useful and another group of people thinks another abstract idea useful, though their favorite abstract ideas be diametrically opposed. Although both Alciphron and Euphranor dislike the Catholics, according to the argument from utility, there can be no basis for distinguishing their useful abstract terms from anyone else's. Further, Euphranor's argument says nothing about the reality of grace or even of force. Each term offers a useful conscious fiction.

The objection forced Berkeley to address, albeit in a more complex form, the same problem that troubled Guthrie: how is one to distinguish between good and bad ideas (concepts) once one allows that unprovable abstractions like force and faith serve concrete existential needs? How should philosophy pass judgment on such needs? Berkeley's answer, delivered through the character Euphranor, provides the high-level philosophical justification for Crito's low-level *ad hominem* tirades. Euphranor answers that those abstract ideas are good that produce "a lively operative principle, influencing [one's] life and actions, agreeably to that notion of saving faith which is required in a Christian" (III, p. 297).[27] This view, which David Berman rightly identifies as

---

[27] In *George Berkeley: Idealism and the man*, David Berman calls this argument, the "emotive language" position, a belief in the power of language to produce non-cognitive meaning directly influencing moral action. He does not mention that the position arises in a dialogue and is attacked – effectively, I think – by Alciphron, in a counter that Berkeley added to the second edition. For another objection to the emotive language argument see Fraser's editorial notes at II, p. 173, n. 1; and II, p. 178; n. 1.

the central claim of the concluding dialogue of *Alciphron* – what he calls the
"emotive language" position – holds that if we seek to distinguish between
one abstract idea and another, we must consult the implications of each for
conduct. Useful abstract ideas lead to Christian behavior; Christian behavior,
to round out the tautology, generates useful abstract ideas. We choose our
final vocabularies carefully not because logic or reason provides a guide, but
because they produce "certain dispositions or habits of mind, and [direct] our
actions in pursuit of that happiness which is the ultimate end and design, the
primary spring and motive, that sets rational agents at work" (III, p. 307).
Here Berkeley is at one with the eighteenth-century apologists for Ciceronian
dialogue.

What *kind* of philosophical exposition would be adequate to such an
assertion? Would it not be a writing that made the *ad hominem* move an
integral part of the exposition of ideas? The emotive language argument
depends upon the same homology of thought and behavior as marks Crito's
ad hominem assaults. And so it is not surprising that Crito again provides the
general rule: "Whether the principles of Christians or infidels are the truest
may be made a question; but which are safest can be none" (III, p. 322). The
assertion had better be seconded by lively and moving representations; for
otherwise it does not avail: theists think atheism dangerous because it disposes
people to suicide; atheists think theism dangerous because it brings on
intellectual torpor. Both believe they understand the behavioral consequences
of thought.[28] All parties seem to agree with Nietzsche that philosophical and
religious opinions cover physiological demands for the preservation of a
certain kind of life, though, of course, they do not extend this insight to their
own principles:

CRI. The conduct we object to minute philosophers is a natural consequence of their
principles. Whatsoever they can reproach us with is an effect, not of our
principles, but of human passion and frailty.
ALC. This is admirable. So we must no longer object to Christians the absurd
contentions of Councils, the cruelty of Inquisitions, the ambition and usurpation
of churchmen?
CRI. You may object them to Christians, but not to Christianity. If the Divine
Author of our religion and His disciples have sowed a good seed, the enemies of
His gospel (among whom are to be reckoned the minute philosophers of all ages)
have sowed bad seeds whence spring tares and thistles; is it not evident, these
bad weeds cannot be imputed to the good seed, or to those who sowed it?

(III, p. 194–95)

[28] We are familiar with the passions this kind of question can raise. In light of the disclosures about
Paul de Man, those who never liked deconstruction suggest there is a necessary parallel between
theories of linguistic indeterminacy and the unrepentant behavior of a collaborationist. Another
school proclaims personal biography irrelevant to the realm of intellectual production. These
groups tend to have little to say to each other.

Each character would like to be the author of a fiction in which he controls the distribution of justice, but when sentences are meted out by so many authors, we have a formula for unbridled conflict, and even violence. At one point Lysicles and Crito seem close to an outright challenge. "Our curate is of the opinion that all you free-thinking rakes are either fools or cowards," states Crito. To which Lysicles responds, "As for their courage, they are at all times ready to give proof of it; and for their understanding, thanks to nature, it is of a size not to be measured by country parsons" (III, p. 93).

Alciphron's objection to the argument from utility forces us to modify the claim that we have moved in philosophical dialogue to a test of truth based upon the behavior of characters. While characters illustrate the just reward of right thinking, the basis of that correspondence is not itself located in a conception of character but in an overriding narrative principle: the moral fitness of things. The philosophical significance of the *ad hominem* argument, as Crito uses it, is that it presents us with a scene of justice in which we come to know the truth about an invisible source of judgment. When Charmides does justice upon himself, as when Lovelace confesses his sin and then meets the sword of Colonel Morden, the reader witnesses a material incarnation of an active though invisible spirit, acting to justify the ways of man to man to God.

The literary force organizing these narratives, the entelechy that gives direction to the plot, is poetic justice. And the metaphysical force behind poetic justice is what gives Euphranor the confidence to found a theological argument upon the utility of certain ideas. In *The Origins of the English Novel*, Michael McKeon points out that the increasing importance of poetic justice at the end of the seventeenth century parallels the declining significance of providence as a persuasive idea after the Restoration:

The impulse to detect God's immediate and tangible effects might be thought to convey not only a conviction of, but also an uncertainty about, his presence. But such an argument becomes fully plausible only when the doctrine of providence becomes concentrated, as it were, into the doctrine of poetic justice ... The doctrine of poetic justice will become important for a culture in which divine presence is felt to be in jeopardy ... What is therefore unusual about the Restoration is that it should have elaborated this special method – poetic justice – of compensating for the deficiencies of providential justice, rather than having continued to rely on the traditional and orthodox view of the afterlife.[29]

In that one of the characteristics of Protestant theology after the establishment of the Royal Society was the attempt to provide a rational justification for religion, bracketing reference to the afterlife is not all that surprising. What is remarkable is the moment in the history of rational theology when the design argument, endangered by too much evidence from the senses,

---

[29] McKeon, *The Origins of the English Novel*, pp. 124–125.

makes a conscious appeal to fiction (poetic justice) in order to verify its claims about ultimate design. The physical manifestation of a transcendental authority has been relocated in a construct avowedly "poetic" (for which McKeon will use the term "aesthetic"), namely character and plot. The irony is that as a form of compensation, poetic justice supplies the place of truth, which is to say, it must be unpoetical, real. What gives a person, whether character, narrator, or author the penetration of other minds, the ability to say, though you appear satisfied in your atheism, you are really sick? Poetic justice supplies this sense of inevitability.

What the anecdote describes, then, is not a more modest relation to transcendence, but an even more concrete grasp of revelation, still known through the evidence of the senses, but mediated through the realism of characters and plots. In the "pineal gland" essays Berkeley contributed to the *Guardian*, we find a fantasy of space travel that literalizes this revelatory structure of anecdote. Berkeley writes in the persona of a man who has acquired a quantity of "Philosophical Snuff." The magical powder gives the writer "the faculty of entering into other men's thoughts." Invading a free-thinker through the conduit of his pineal gland, the philosopher pauses to describe conscience: "I saw a wretch racked, at the same time, with a painful remembrance of past miscarriages, a distaste of the present objects that sollicite his senses, and a secret dread of futurity" (VII, p. 187). Thus seen, the free-thinker is conquered, even if it took some magical powder, the pineal gland, and metempsychosis to narrate his self-betrayal.

The philosophical elaboration of an ethical standard based on utility, the emotive language position, the deployment of *ad hominem* insults, and the claim to control the distribution of poetic justice thus work together by the end of *Alciphron* to effect Berkeley's "apology for the Christian religion." The combination of strategies gives representational life to a mere aside from the *Principles*:

In the ordinary affairs of life, any phrases may be retained so long as they excite in us proper sentiments or dispositions to act in such a manner as is necessary for our well-being, how false soever they may be if taken in a strict and speculative sense.

(II, 52, p. 63)

What are these dispositions and proper sentiments? If they are fed or created or activated by claims that have no speculative status (which is to say, by claims that are false, contradictory, emotive, or unprovable), then how are they to be explained and defended within the elevated discourses of moral philosophy? The novel, I would argue, becomes the genre that concerns itself with "the ordinary affairs of life" once philosophical speculation turns from mind to sentiments and dispositions as the locus of moral authority.

From philosophical dialogue to metaphysical novel

In this and the preceding chapter I have offered an account of why the author of the *Principles* moves first from the treatise to a formal philosophical dialogue ending in a point of demonstration, and then to a free-wheeling fictional dialogue. The unifying thread has been Berkeley's confrontation with the Pyrrhonian implications of the New Science, as applied first to our perception of phenomena, but as extended later to the conditions of understanding and reasoning themselves. In the simplest terms, the inadequacy of a philosophical response to Pyrrhonism gives rise to a fictional response, to a portrait of characters whose behavior is tested by an invisible yet efficacious standard. We move, accordingly, from a dialogue in which the reader remains relatively passive, observing a conversion assented to by the participants in light of mutually agreed upon canons of reason, to a dialogue in which the reader must, in the absence of such internal agreement, actively sort out the values of competing claims, based upon a combination of rational and *ad hominem* appeals.

These observations bring us back to Hervey's hostile description of Berkeley as a metaphysical novelist. Hervey's attack was no doubt motivated by political animosity.[30] Nevertheless, the terms of the criticism remain interesting. Unlike other early replies to Berkeley that ridiculed either Berkeley himself or his paradoxical theory of immaterialism, Hervey concentrates on the incompatibility between the genre of dialogue and the aims of a would-be defender of Christianity.[31] In effect, Hervey turns the practice of *Alciphron* against the theory of *Hylas and Philonous*, with the result that the special suitability of philosophical dialogue to theological inquiry is explicitly denied:

Let his Intention therefore have been never so good, I cannot help feeling a very

---

[30] Hervey was a Whig of the Court Party, loyal to Walpole against Pulteney, and a staunch enemy of Bolingbroke and (eventually) Pope. Thus, Hervey would have opposed Berkeley on political grounds. He would have had little reason to object to dialogue in principle, and, in fact, Hervey composed his own a few years later (*A Satire in the Manner of Persius in a Dialogue between Atticus and Eugenio* ... [London: J. Clarke, 1739]). Hervey probably saw in Berkeley's appropriation of philosophical dialogue an attempt to add rational rigor to Tory and High Church views, to him a paradoxical and false position. See Robert Halsband, *Lord Hervey: Eighteenth-Century Courtier* (Oxford: Oxford Unversity Press, 1973), especially pp. 139–144. Halsband notes that Hervey's response to *Alciphron* met with the approval of Voltaire.

[31] It is possibly for this reason that Bracken does not mention Hervey in his study of Berkeley's early reception. Although Hervey's *Some Remarks* runs to sixty-six pages and was published as an independent pamphlet, Bracken holds that "the first extended criticism in English of Berkeley's philosophy" does not appear until Andrew Baxter's *An Enquiry into the Nature of the Human Soul* (1733), which takes up the ideas of Berkeley's *Principles*. Bracken's interest, however, is solely with the reception of Berkeley's philosophical views, in particular the doctrine of immaterialism. See Harry M. Bracken, *The Early Reception of Berkeley's Immaterialism 1710–1733*, p. 62. On the early reception of Berkeley's philosophical views, see also Richard Popkin, *The High Road to Pyrrhonism*, pp. 319 (especially n. 2) and p. 320.

great Resentment against him, for publishing such an Apology (as he calls it) for our
Religion, as, according to my firm Belief, will go further towards discrediting it, and
hastening its Decay, than anything that ever was the most avowedly and imprudently
written against it. The *Tale of a Tub* ... and *Fable of the Bees* ... are books from which
Christianity has not received half so dangerous a Wound, as it will do from the Hand
of this Friend. Those Wags [Swift and Mandeville] only shew there are a great many
ludicrous things to be said against Christianity; but this puzzling Zealot will tempt
People to believe, there is nothing seriously and argumentatively to be said for it.

(p. 5)

Hervey reserves special invective for Berkeley's decision to cast religious
apology in the form of philosophical dialogue. "I must own," his country
parson writes, "I conceived some Prejudice against his Book, from the
Moment I found it was written in Dialogue" (p. 11). Although recognizing the
ancient sanction of the genre, the parson insists, "there never was anything
written in that way ... but what appears to me stiff, forced, and unfair." His
concern with fairness is, however, beside the point. Dialogue fails because it is
not unfair enough. "It can never be their [the Priesthood's] interest to join
Issue with heretical Skeptics, and plead *pro* and *con* on Points that leave all at
stake, and bring the *Whole* into Dispute ... There are some Points that ought
never to come into Play, any more than the King at Chess: Whenever they
give him a Check, your only Recourse is to Cover it; and when you cannot
Cover it any longer, the Game is lost" (pp. 7–8). Hervey's parson denies, in
other words, the dominant argument of Protestant theology that had made
dialogue a valuable mode of exposition: religion and reason are incompatible,
a point proven by *Alciphron* itself. "Men were willing to submit to 'reason,' "
writes Roland Stromberg, "because there was on all hands a sublime
confidence that reason and religion were in harmony."[32] But Hervey's
parson, even if he had this confidence before, lost it when he read *Alciphron*.
The parson does not believe anyone, least of all the common reader, will be
capable of interpreting the unified argument emerging from the multiplicity
of doctrines; a tragic undecidability will replace the comedic marriage of
minds. Whether or not Hervey himself shares the views of the country
parson, the position he ventriloquizes becomes more and more important
towards the middle of the century. It is the voice that negates the entire
project of metaphysical dialogue, that sees the rational approach to faith as a
formula for religious and political disaster.

   Berkeley finally seems to have come to the same conclusion. As Walmsley
notes, Berkeley refused to send copies of *Alciphron* to America, fearing it might
do mischief.[33] And in *A Discourse Addressed to Magistrates*, written in 1738, six
years after *Alciphron*, Berkeley stated that such philosophical investigations
must be limited to the eyes of the few. "Those who are not qualified by Age

---

[32] Stromberg, *Religious Liberalism in Eighteenth-Century England*, p. 10.
[33] Walmsley, *The Rhetoric of Berkeley's Philosophy*, p. 118.

or Education," he writes, sounding exactly like Crito, "those who have neither Disposition nor Leisure, nor Faculties to dig in the Mine of Truth themselves, must take it as retailed out by others. I see no Remedy."[34]

Although Berkeley found no remedy for the rampant relativism of his age within the context of formal philosophical dialogue, he, like Shaftesbury, suggested to other writers, whom we now call novelists, how the resources of prose fiction might be employed to teach readers to "follow what is judged to be most probable," most conducive to "moral fitness" and "happiness," even in the absence of theological norms or philosophical criteria. Fielding's *Joseph Andrews*, for instance, repeatedly stages the crisis in the standard of judgment at the heart of *Alciphron*. The problem is repeated in one short fictional parable after another. In the third chapter of the second book, we read "The Opinion of Two Lawyers concerning the same Gentleman, with Mr. Adams' Enquiry into the Religion of his Host." The incident concerns a difference of opinion between two men regarding the same character, a difference so great that Adams is forced to consult a third figure, a supposedly impartial bystander:

Adams, who was in the utmost Anxiety at those different Characters of the same Person, asked his Host if he knew the Gentleman: for he began to imagine they had by mistake been speaking of two several Gentlemen. 'No, no, Master!' answered the Host, a shrewd cunning Fellow ... 'I know the Gentleman very well.'[35]

Although more lively and vivid, the scenario raised here is much the same as that confronted at the end of *Hylas and Philonous* and throughout *Alciphron*. If the authority of characters to evaluate an absent figure is suspect, and if the higher authority of the supposedly impartial judge is also suspect, then where is the reader to turn for guidance?

Again at the end of *Joseph Andrews*, as if to stress the centrality of this problem to the novel, Adams' son Dick reads "The History of two Friends." The story purports to be a warning to "those Persons, who happen to take up their Residence in married Families," but it is really another fictional encounter with epistemological uncertainty, the damaged criterion. Paul comes to stay with his friend Lennard and his wife, but soon becomes embroiled in their endless debates, the pair throwing out arguments that "would hold equally on both sides" (p. 316). Eventually, Paul is asked to render his judgment. For a time, his edicts re-establish matrimonial harmony, and so Paul becomes "eternally the private Referee of every Difference." But he finds it extremely difficult to remain neutral and equally trusted by both parties. While preaching a "Doctrine of Submission" in public, he "never

---

[34] Berkeley, *A Discourse Addressed to Magistrates*, p. 35.

[35] *Joseph Andrews*, ed. Martin C. Battestin (Middletown, Connecticut: Wesleyan University Press, 1967), pp. 98–99. Subsequent citations refer to this edition and will be given by page number in my text.

scrupled to assure both privately that they were in the right in every Argument" (p. 319). Eventually, the husband and wife discover that Paul has been placating both of them. "They then proceeded to produce numberless other Instances in which Paul had, on Vows of Secrecy, given his Opinion on both sides." They turn on Paul, accusing him of being the source of their disputes. Finally, the third figure is kicked out of the happy household. The impartial judge becomes, in the world of Fielding's fictions, an unfortunate go-between, torn by the competing demands of interested characters, and himself guilty of abusing the authority vested in him.

Berkeley's attempts to solve the problem of the contested third in philosophical dialogue led first to the beautiful image of the fountain, which reasserted the efficacy of transcendental dialectic, but later, under further skeptical challenge, it led to the abandonment of rational disputation in favor of a strange mixture of *ad hominem* devices: anecdotes, assaults, emotive claims, and the doctrine of utility. Fielding's effort to solve the same problem leads to a more extensive depiction of characters set within concrete circumstances, whose actions provide a basis for determining the value of their ideas.

In the "Preface," Fielding defines this fictional standard as "the true Ridiculous." Without seeming to impose an arbitrary moral authority from outside the narration, fictional representations of characters betraying a gap between word and deed, self-image and conduct towards others, offer the reader a probable guide for determining the value of ideas. More than one parson, more than one lover, more than one innkeeper, more than one aristocrat respond to a shared set of experiences. The representational dimension, setting ideas in characters and characters in circumstances, gives the reader a constant source of comparison.

The threat of philosophical skepticism and the counter-assertion of a fictional test of truth (the true Ridiculous) come together in Mr. Wilson's account of the "rule of right men." In this scene Fielding takes aim at the same free-thinkers who had bothered Berkeley, and his tactics are strikingly similar. "These Gentlemen were engaged in a Search after Truth," explains Mr. Wilson, "in the Pursuit of which they threw aside all the Prejudices of Education, and governed themselves only by the infallible Guide of Human Reason" (p. 212). They abandon God, embrace the rule of right, and so lose any transcendental standard for ethics. The reader is not allowed to think even for a minute that such godless souls might light their own way to a workable ethics. Wilson proceeds to narrate a series of anecdotes recounting the vile behavior of the rule of right men towards each other (they commit adultery, they lie, they steal). The narrative makes the slide from the rejection of a Deity to criminal conduct seem a *necessary* consequence of philosophical relativism. Here Berkeley's philosophical *ad hominem* gains fictional vivacity. A member of the club, rationalizing the appearance of wrong-doing, tells

Wilson, that "there was nothing absolutely good or evil in and of itself; that Actions were denominated good or bad by the Circumstances of the Agent" (p. 213). The "true Ridiculous" proves otherwise.

My purpose here is not to enter into a lengthy discussion of the way Fielding responds to the threat of Pyrrhonism dramatized within these scenes. His solutions are many: the doctrine of ridicule testing characters' words against their deeds, the genial interventions of the narrator, Adams' classicism, the romance ending, reasserting the connection between birth and merit, chance episodes and providential design. Rather, it is to point out the relevance of *Alciphron* to the history of the eighteenth-century novel. By 1732 Berkeley was already on the way to writing an extended prose fiction in which the threat to the tripartite structure of rational deliberation was answered through fictions of conduct guided by the plotting device of poetic justice. Much as Berkeley would have liked to perfect his apology for the Christian religion through the more dignified appeal to reason emblematized by the fountain at the end of *Hylas and Philonous*; much as he wished to catalog and contain irreligion through an imitation of Cicero; his philosophical rigor, the depth and honesty of his encounter with the rampant Pyrrhonism of his age, led him to adopt the argument from utility and to adjust his philosophical exposition in accordance with its considerable demands.

5

Hume and the end of religious dialogue:
Dialogues concerning Natural Religion[1]

Hume's *Dialogues concerning Natural Religion* has long puzzled commentators. While source studies have established the significance of Cicero's *De Natura Deorum* as an important model, most other aspects of the work have provoked commentary as divided as the dialogue itself.[2] Who, if anyone, speaks for Hume? If Philo does, as many argue, how are we to take the skeptic's apparent conversion to natural religion (Cleanthes' position) by the end? Are Philo's final words – "To be a philosophical skeptic is, in a man of letters, the first and most essential step towards being a sound, believing Christian" (p. 228) – meant to be taken seriously, or are they window dressing for an otherwise indeterminate work that Hume completed in 1751 but was forced to suppress for the rest of his life (it was published in 1779 by his own nephew three years after Hume's death).

In the wake of important efforts by scholars such as Berel Lang and John Richetti to apply the resources of literary critical analysis to our under-standing of philosophical texts, Hume's *Dialogues* has received a number of interpretations based upon the work's rhetorical qualities.[3] These have been fruitful to the extent that they explore what was a given for Enlightenment authors – that style is substance, that political, theological, and philosophical polemics are carried out as much by *how* one writes as by *what* one writes. But too often the seemingly unavoidable competition among disciplines has led literary critics to claim that they now hold the key to the true meaning of

---

[1] A version of this chapter appeared in *Eighteenth-Century Studies* 25 (1992) 283–308.

[2] On Hume's use of Cicero, see A. G. Vink, "The Literary and Dramatic Character of Hume's *Dialogues Concerning Natural Religion*," *Religious Studies* 22 (1986) 387–396; Christine Battersby, "The Dialogues as Original Imitation: Cicero and the Nature of Hume's Skepticism," in David Fate Norton, Nicholas Capaldi, and Wade L. Robison, *McGill Hume Studies* (San Diego: Austin Hill Press, 1979), pp. 239–252. Hume himself cites *De Natura Deorum* (p. 149). All references to Hume's *Dialogues* are to Norman Kemp Smith's edition (Indianapolis: Bobbs-Merrill Co., 1981) and will be given subsequently by a page number in my text.

[3] See, for instance, the following studies of Hume's rhetoric: John Bricke, "On the Interpretation of Hume's *Dialogues*," *Religious Studies* 11 (1975) 1–18; W. B. Carnochan, "The Comic Plot of Hume's *Dialogues*," *Modern Philology* 85 (1988) 514–522; Gary Shapiro, "The Man of Letters and the Author of Nature: Hume on Philosophical Discourse," 115–137; David Simpson, "Hume's Intimate Voices and the Method of Dialogue," *Texas Studies in Literature and Language* 21 (1979) 68–92; A. G. Vink, "The Literary and Dramatic Character of Hume's *Dialogues Concerning Natural Religion*"; Jeffrey Wieand, "Pamphilus in Hume's *Dialogues*," *The Journal of Religion* 65 (1985) 33–45.

serious philosophical works, just as, before, philosophers trained in the history of ideas and oblivious to style made the same claim.

In a recent article on Hume's *Dialogues*, for instance, W. B. Carnochan argues that the actual theme of the work is "the overriding Ciceronian virtue of friendship," which asserts itself once "the struggle over matters of belief . . . has come to a close . . . The *Dialogues* are a drama, ultimately comic, in which Philo and Cleanthes, in league against Demea, drive their adversary from the stage. The plot, that is, rests on the eviction of a disruptive presence and the final comic union of characters . . . that reasserts the social order. On this view, the *Dialogues* become, dramatically, a commentary on the social order of friendship that merges with the discursive commentary on natural religion."[4] As the passage indicates, the new key involves a shift in critical terminology, from a vocabulary that interprets the *Dialogues* within the religious and philosophical terms it contests, to a vocabulary that locates theme in style, and thereby organizes a replacement of philosophy and religion by "literature."

I say "replacement" because in these accounts one finds little discussion of natural religion, or what Philo more sarcastically calls "experimental Christianity." Instead, the claim is that Hume anticipates our own desire to stand "after philosophy," by setting aside, in Shapiro's terms, "the purist model of philosophical discourse" in favor of "the alternative offered by the man of letters" (117), or, as Simpson writes, by jettisoning "the 'rationalist' enterprise" in favor of "a way of holding all options at a distance, of having no engagements" (82). These arguments simplify relations between philosophy, religion, and literature in Hume's *Dialogues*, relations better approached by asking why Hume, in 1751, would have chosen to attack rational Christianity through the composition of a philosophical dialogue.[5]

---

4 Carnochan, "The Comic Plot of Hume's *Dialogues*," 515.
5 Simpson argues that Hume sought to conceal the heterodoxy of his own views. Basing his reading on Strauss' influential essay, "Persecution and the Art of Writing," Simpson states, "any writer . . . who faces one or another kind of censorship and is working within a social context where people can be punished for their ideas will tend to look for a way of putting over his arguments without leaving himself open to obvious attacks" (77). In the valuable introduction to his edition of the *Dialogues*, Norman Kemp Smith also takes the position that Hume conceals his own position behind the persona of Philo (p. 62).

The argument has been well canvassed and will not figure prominently in this reading. I bracket it not only because I find Skinner's well-known critique of Strauss convincing ("Meaning and Understanding in the History of Ideas," *History and Theory* 8 [1969] 21), but more importantly because the argument fails to address a question Hume himself posed to his friends when they refused to see his *Dialogues* through to publication – namely, why Hume would be accused of concealing heterodox views in his *Dialogues* when the most "exceptionable" ideas in that work had already appeared in the directly argued essays of the *Inquiry*. The present argument suggests reasons why Hume chose to repeat those arguments in the form of a dialogue, and also why contemporary readers viewed the *Dialogues* as a greater threat than the earlier essays. I take up Hume's challenge to his friends later in the chapter.

As we have already seen, during the first half of the eighteenth century philosophical dialogue became an important means of religious discourse because it was thought to replicate in formal terms the conceptual movement of rational Christianity. In the words of Shaftesbury's character, Theocles, it is "the province of philosophy alone to prove what revelation only supposes. ... A providence must be proved from what we see of order in things present" (II, 53–54, p. 58). Within religious dialogue, as within a providentially ordered nature, an initial appearance of randomness, multiplicity, and indeterminacy would give way to a final point of unity and order: dialogue would express a theodicy of the social realm through the staging of rational consensus, just as natural religion offered a theodicy of the phenomenal world through the subordination of chance to design.[6] The fictional elements of dialogue thus lent credence to the precarious logic of the design argument.[7] Hume was aware of this tradition of religious dialogue. Not satisfied with his analytical critique of rational Christianity in *A Treatise of Human Nature* (1740) and *An Inquiry concerning Human Understanding* (1748), he doubled his barb by recasting the attack upon analogy, induction, and design within a dialogue whose *failure* to achieve consensus dramatized the deeper structural fallacies of natural religion. The *Dialogues* may thus be considered a dialogue about the irrelevance of dialogue to religious belief. Hume's purpose is not entirely destructive, however; for the fictional dialogue also works to drive a wedge between secular and religious realms of inquiry, thus delineating fields within which experimental method promises better results.

"The literary," then, is not so much the end of Hume's *Dialogues* as the means by which it attacks rational Christianity and adumbrates the limits of hermeneutic investigation. The closest literary tradition to Hume is not that of comedy; on the contrary, Hume uses dialogue to subvert the comedic interpretation of philosophical dialogue as it had passed down to Shaftesbury and Berkeley from Renaissance Neoplatonism and the Cambridge Platonists. Rather, the closest literary parallels to Hume's *Dialogues* are works such as Sterne's *Tristram Shandy* and Diderot's *Jacques le fataliste et son maître*, which, assuming Hume's radical separation of ethics from theology, ask what is left of philosophy in a post-metaphysical world, and what is left of ethics once characters have only each other and common experience to shape their values. I shall argue in the concluding section of this chapter that Hume's *Dialogues* provides a conceptual model for the development of comic prose fiction in the middle of the eighteenth century.

---

[6] For a more detailed treatment of this isomorphism between the design argument (providence) and literary form see Douglas Patey, *Probability and Literary Form*, particularly chapters 1 and 6.

[7] On the "precariousness" of the design argument during the eighteenth century, see Earl Wasserman's formative study "Nature Moralized: the Divine Analogy in the Eighteenth Century," *ELH* 20 (1953) 39–73.

Demea makes a third

In the dream of a perfect theodicy, assurance of ultimate order and purpose is only strengthened as more and more accidents are brought within the framework of representation. The haphazard quality of dialogue (as opposed to the planned execution of a systematic treatise or deductive argument) became the surest indication that order, once realized, was itself natural. Obviously, dialogue so conceived was never as inclusive as authors pretended. Women, the working poor, extreme atheists and the like are not invited into most of these dialogues. But even within works so restricted the problem remained, how an author could make the transition from competing interpretations to consensus believable.

Eighteenth-century religious dialogues before Hume's usually assume a binary structure: they take place between a skeptic and a theist (or, as in Berkeley's *Alciphron*, between two atheists and two theists) and lead to a capitulation of skepticism before the more persuasive arguments of theism. The stability of such works depended upon the efficacy of a standard for distinguishing right from wrong, error from truth. Yet, to the extent theological dialogues remained skeptical, the point of transformation from skepticism to faith, from doubt to determination, inevitably became a topic of discussion *within* the dialogue. Once characters were allowed to question the *telos* hustling them towards closure (the plot), the binary structure produced a third term – logic, reason, gravity, harmony, providence – whose invisibility (and inviolability) had previously overseen the "success" of religious dialogue. Hume's fundamental contribution to the history of philosophical dialogue described here is the addition of a third character, the fideist Demea. The introduction of a third transforms what had been the higher principle of adjudication – the third term – into the fallible character of the dogmatist, thus destroying the paradigmatic structure of religious dialogue.

At several points in *Alciphron* we find anticipations of the tripartite division of Hume's *Dialogues*. At the end of the Second Dialogue, we find this exchange:

EUPHRANOR: I have another scruple about the tendency of your opinions. Suppose you should prevail, and destroy this protestant church and clergy: how could you come at the popish? I am credibly informed there is a great number of emissaries of the church of Rome disguised in England: who can tell what harvest a clergy so numerous, so subtle, and so well furnished with arguments to work on vulgar and uneducated minds, may be able to make in a country despoiled of all religion, and feeling the want of it? ... who can tell, I say, whether in such a juncture the men of genius themselves may not affect a new distinction, and be the first converts to popery?

LYSICLES: And suppose they should? Between friends it would be no great matter. These are our maxims. In the first place, we hold it would be best to have no religion at all. Secondly, we hold that all religions are indifferent. If, therefore, upon trial, we find the country cannot do without a religion, why not popery as well as another?   (II, p. 117)

Euphranor appeals to Lysicles' recognition of shared interests between skeptic and Protestant. Both submit belief to the test of reason; both oppose dogmatism; both call themselves free-thinkers; both emphasize the knowable over the mysterious. But Lysicles is willing to press his skepticism to an extreme. In comparison to the courage of the atheist, all religious belief strikes him as equally cowardly.

More than arrogance informs this leveling. Lysicles claims, as will Philo, that a rational Christianity based on evidence gathered through experience always depends, despite itself, upon a dogmatically held article of faith: "Lysicles, instead of answering Crito, turned short upon Alciphron. It was always my opinion, said he, that nothing could be sillier than to think of destroying Christianity, by crying up natural religion. Whoever thinks highly of the one can never, with a consistency, think meanly of the other; it being very evident that natural religion, without revealed, never was and never can be established or received anywhere, but in the brains of a few idle speculative men" (II, p. 230). Lysicles has divided the world into theists and atheists. Fine distinctions between more and less rational proofs of the Deity do not matter to him. For all religion is finally a version of fideism.

Nowhere is the materializing of the third more evident than at the end of *Alciphron*. In the closing moments of the Seventh and last Dialogue, the two atheists, Alciphron and Lysicles, depart on a moment's notice after sharing the company of the two theists in Rhode Island for a week. They never renounce their apostasy. This leaves the theists alone with the narrator, Dion, who, in a rare contribution to the dialogue he otherwise reports, observes, "how unaccountable it was that men [atheists] so easy to confute should yet be so difficult to convince" (II, p. 361). Berkeley anticipates the objections of incredulous readers such as John Hervey, who would find a dialogue in which the atheists are allowed such wide latitude of expression a work "likelier to make, than to convert Atheists." Thus, Berkeley's narrator asks how we are to know a stable determination has been reached in the absence of consensus among the speakers.

As I indicated in the previous chapter, this question elicits several responses. The one relevant to Hume's *Dialogues* is the anecdote Crito tells of one "Honest Demea," who "having seen a neighbor of his ruined by the vices of a free-thinking son, contracted such a prejudice against thinking that he would not suffer his own to read Euclid, being told it might teach him to think" (II, p. 363). As the anecdotal status of Demea implies, the position of the dogmatic fideist is not central to *Alciphron*. Nevertheless, Hume may well have noticed that Demea stands for the inability of the rational Christian to explicate the hinge between reason and revelation; Crito's anecdote describes the reaction of a Christian to rational dialogue once arguments promising the containment of skepticism fail. Hume had read Berkeley's *Alciphron* as early as 1748 and there found a religious dialogue that had already begun to generate its own refutation.[8] That is why he promoted Demea from a figure in anecdote to a central character in his own work.

The significance of this attribution is not only that it solves a long-standing puzzle about the names of Hume's characters;[9] more importantly it indicates that Hume's dialogue differs from those of his predecessors in its openly tripartite structure, and the crucial addition is a character – Demea – whose position is already anticipated in earlier dialogues at the point where the transition from skeptical method to religious doctrine itself comes into question.[10] Hume, in other words, read the religious dialogues of the early eighteenth century *antithetically* as inadvertent expressions of the fatal weakness of rational Christianity. He exposes the absurdity of analogical reasoning in religious dispute specifically by constructing a dialogue in which the move towards closure is frustrated and consensus is shown to depend upon the *exclusion* of the third party – the dogmatist – who does not belong in a rational dialogue, but who, Hume seems to argue, was present all along in various guises within "successful" religious dialogues.

Hume was aware of the modern tradition of religious dialogue. Through the naive student, Pamphilus, he introduces at the beginning of the *Dialogues* just those assumptions about the compatibility of skeptical dialogue and rational Christianity that writers of the British Enlightenment, Shaftesbury and Berkeley in particular, had taken seriously. The central irony of the work is that the intellectual plot of the *Dialogues* refutes Pamphilus' defense of dialogue, supposedly gleaned from that very discussion. Neither religious dialogue nor rational Christianity survives this devious assertion of their compatibility.

---

[8] In the third edition of *Essays, Moral and Political* (1748), Hume added the essay "Of National Characters," within which appears a reference to "Dr. Berkeley: *Minute Philosopher.*" Apart from this evidence, it should be noted that Demea's first statement in Hume's *Dialogues* is also about the education of youth and repeats the position of Berkeley's Demea:

> To season their [youths'] minds with early piety is my chief care; and by continual precept and instruction, and I hope too by example, I imprint deeply on their tender minds an habitual reverence for all the principles of religion (p. 130).

[9] Vink attributes the names Pamphilus, Cleanthes, and Philo to Cicero's dialogue *De Natura Deorum*, but is less confident about the source of the name Demea. He gives Terentius' comedy, *Adelphi*, as a possibility, or derivation from the Greek, *demos* (common people). See also Kemp Smith (p. 60).

[10] I have figured this moment in various ways thus far: as the myth of Orpheus and Eurydice in Boethius, as Right Reason in Hobbes, as a point of silence in *The Moralists*, as an emblematic fountain in Berkeley's *Hylas and Philonous*, as an elaborate doctrine of probability in *Alciphron*. A history of philosophical dialogue accounts for changes in philosophy and literature in part because it entails a history of the third and efforts to secure its inviolability.

Pamphilus' naive defense of dialogue

The *Dialogues* begins with Pamphilus' extended defense of religious dialogue. Because the work is being narrated in a letter to a friend (Hermippus) after the discussion has taken place, Pamphilus' observations are supposedly derived from the dialogue he has just witnessed. After noting the faults to which dialogue is prone (dogmatism, undue length, lack of system where system is most required), Pamphilus says there are nevertheless some subjects "to which dialogue writing is peculiarly adapted" (p. 127). He mentions three. The first two are these:

Any point of doctrine, which is so *obvious*, that it scarcely admits of dispute, but at the same time so important, that it cannot be too often inculcated, seems to require some such manner of handling it; where the novelty of the manner may compensate the triteness of the subject, where the vivacity of conversation may enforce the precept, and where the variety of lights, presented by various personages and characters, may appear neither tedious nor redundant.

   Any question of philosophy, on the other hand, which is so *obscure* and *uncertain*, that human reason can reach no fixed determination with regard to it; if it should be treated at all; seems to lead us naturally into the style of dialogue and conversation. Reasonable men may be allowed to differ, where no one can be reasonably positive: Opposite sentiments, even without any decision, afford an agreeable amusement ...

(pp. 127–128)

Pamphilus merges the two contradictory claims made for the dialogue form through the early eighteenth century. It offers, on the one hand, a means of conveying important didactic arguments. Like the periodical essay and epistle, it renders potentially dry lessons in a lively, conversational form, thus conveying scientific, historical, literary, philosophical, and religious information to a broader audience.[11] Dialogue in this case is frankly didactic and thus especially appropriate to topics about which there can be no disagreement, such as the existence of God. On the other hand, Pamphilus holds that dialogue supports topics that are obscure, such as the precise attributes of God. Dialogue is suitable to these philosophical questions because its potentially interminable play of opposing voices echoes the indeterminacy of probabilistic topics, while providing an "agreeable amusement." This rationale repeats the arguments for dialogue voiced by the character of Philocles in Shaftesbury's *The Moralists*. He holds that dialogue "goes on no established hypothesis, nor presents us with any flattering scheme, talks only of probabilities, suspense of judgment, inquiry, search, and caution not to be imposed upon or deceived" (II, p. 9).

[11] I discuss the pedagogical aspects of eighteenth-century dialogue more fully in "Literacy and Genre," *College English* 51 (1989) 730–749. See also Ann Shteir's discussion of the pedagogical dialogue in "Botanical Dialogues: Maria Jackson and Women's Popular Science Writing in England," *Eighteenth-Century Studies* 23 (1990) 301–317.

One would think dialogue could be justified by one or the other of these arguments, but not by both together; yet Hume's insight into the formal claim made by rational Christianity was precisely that a "reasoned faith" implied the contradictory conjunction of dialogue as a vehicle of didactic argument with dialogue as a vehicle of indeterminacy. So argues Pamphilus, in naming the third topic ideally suited to dialogue:

Happily, these circumstances are all to be found in the subject of NATURAL RELIGION. What truth so obvious, so certain, as the *being* of God ... But in treating of this obvious and important truth; what obscure questions occur, concerning the *nature* of that divine Being; his attributes, his decrees, his plan of providence? ... Concerning these, human reason has not yet reached any certain determination: But ... we cannot restrain our restless enquiry with regard to them.   (p. 128)

Because itself divided into two parts – the prior acknowledgment of the *being* of a Deity, and the attempt to establish more fully the *nature* of God based upon the analogy with human reason and design in nature – natural religion would seem the best possible topic for dialogue. Just as natural religion would bring together the impartial study of nature with faith in revelation, so this ideal religious dialogue would be skeptical without undermining established doctrine, and doctrinaire without abandoning free inquiry.

According to Stanley Tweyman, Pamphilus' statements about dialogue "do not pose a problem since the main point made, namely, the suitability of dialogue form to an inquiry into the existence and nature of God, appears to be borne out by the text ... It would be strange for Hume to attempt to mislead us on the form the book should take."[12] But why should the reader credit the opinion of Cleanthes' own disciple, who favors an interpretation of dialogue compatible with Cleanthes' position, and who intervenes at the end to pronounce Cleanthes the winner? It should come as no surprise that a writer who consistently attacks the tenets of rational Christianity through discrete analytical arguments would simultaneously invoke and subvert the very genre that was thought to epitomize the religious hypothesis. Tweyman accepts Pamphilus' view that a genre equally appropriate to "obvious" topics (such as the being of God) and to "obscure" matters (such as the debate over attributes) must be all the more suited to a topic that combines self-evidence

---

[12] Tweyman, *Scepticism and Belief in Hume's Dialogues Concerning Natural Religion* (Dordrecht: Martinus Nijhoff, 1986), pp. 21–22. Wieand goes even further, arguing that "if Hume is to be identified with any of his characters, it is Pamphilus ... [who] should be regarded not only as the reporter of a conversation but also as its author. The *Dialogues* present the views of Pamphilus on natural religion" ("Pamphilus in Hume's *Dialogues*," 33–34). My argument here is that in adopting the genre of philosophical dialogue, Hume not only appealed to classical precedent (his debt to Cicero's *De Natura Deorum*), but also evoked the complex debate about dialogue during his own time. Only by ignoring Hume's participation in the argument over the nature and viability of the eighteenth-century dialogue is it possible to equate Pamphilus' naive rehearsal of the received rationale for religious dialogue with Hume's own position.

and obscurity (such as natural religion). Yet the intellectual plot of the *Dialogues* dramatizes the point that clear distinctions between being and attributes cannot be maintained in religious argument. A dialogue that, according to Pamphilus, has set aside the question of God's existence to concentrate on the problem of attributes seems constantly to reopen the first, non-debatable issue: differences of opinion with regard to attributes, one soon realizes, are vital enough to lead Cleanthes to accuse Demea and Demea to accuse Cleanthes of denying the existence of God. Thus, Cleanthes to Demea: "those who maintain the perfect simplicity of the supreme Being ... are complete *mystics* ... They are, in a word, atheists, without knowing it" (p. 159). And Demea to Cleanthes: "Can we reach no further in this subject than experience and probability? I will not say, that this is betraying the cause of a Deity: But surely, by this affected candour, you give advantage to atheists, which they never could obtain, by the mere dint of argument and reasoning" (p. 144). I shall develop these points now through a more detailed reading of the central arguments of the *Dialogues*, as they relate to its literary structure.

The fallacy of induction and the end of religious dialogue

Understandably, the fideist, Demea, makes the strongest case for the existence of God being a subject beyond dispute. He tells Cleanthes, "by the whole tenor of your discourse, one would imagine that you were maintaining the being of a God, against the cavils of atheists and infidels; and were necessitated to become a champion for that fundamental principle of all religion. But this, I hope, is not by any means a question among us ... The question is not concerning the *being* but the *nature* of *God*" (p. 141). Whatever doubts Philo may have on this score are hidden by his tactical league with the fideist and by his willingness to mouth whatever words the situation demands: "where reasonable men treat these subjects," he says, "the question can never be concerning the *being*, but only the *nature* of the Deity" (p. 142). Cleanthes, who is no atheist, does not challenge the claim directly. Yet for the philosophical Christian, nothing rides on the mere assertion of God's existence; it is a contentless proposition, as Philo's protestations of faith imply. Cleanthes insists, "if our ideas, so far as they go, be not just and adequate, and correspondent to his real nature, I know not what there is in the subject worth insisting on. Is the name, without any meaning, of such mighty importance?" (p. 158). Demea's affirmation of the existence of an unknowable being strikes Cleanthes as the worst kind of mysticism. For Cleanthes the attributes of comprehensibility, benevolence, and order must be predicated upon God if statements about "existence" are to carry any relevance for human conduct[13] This convergence of existence and attributes means,

---

[13] Elsewhere Cleanthes asks, "For to what purpose establish the natural attributes of the Deity, while the moral are still doubtful and uncertain" (p. 199).

however, that the distinction Pamphilus draws between "obvious" and "obscure" questions is disregarded by his own teacher.

Comprehensibility for Cleanthes depends upon the method of forming inferences about the unknown cause through observation of known effects. In one of his most extended articulations of the design argument, Cleanthes explains,

The curious adapting of means to ends, throughout all nature, resembles exactly, though it much exceeds, the productions of human contrivance; of human design, thought, wisdom, and intelligence. Since therefore the effects resemble each other, we are led to infer, by all the rules of analogy, that the causes also resemble; and that the Author of nature is somewhat similar to the mind of man; though possessed of much larger faculties, proportioned to the grandeur of the work, which he has executed. By this argument a posteriori, and by this argument alone, we do prove at once the existence of a Deity, and his similarity to human mind and intelligence.

(p. 143)

Demea's response establishes the methodological battle lines between natural and revealed religion: "What! No demonstration of the being of a God! No abstract arguments! No proofs a priori!" (p. 143). While the spokesman for natural religion is linked to inductive procedures, the fideist is characterized by the deductive, a priori assumptions of the ontological argument. He states,

Whatever exists must have a cause or reason of its existence; it is absolutely impossible for any thing to produce itself, or be the cause of its own existence. In mounting up, therefore, from effects to causes, we must either go on in tracing an infinite succession, without any ultimate cause at all, or must at last have recourse to some ultimate cause that is *necessarily* existent . . . We must, therefore, have recourse to a necessarily existent Being, who carries the REASON of his existence in himself; and who cannot be supposed not to exist without an express contradiction. There is consequently such a Being, that is, there is a Deity. (pp. 188–189)

Although Demea expresses this position within a dialogue among friends, it is a position that admits of no dialogical challenge – a frank affirmation of faith set in philosophically respectable vocabulary. Cleanthes' argument is compatible with rational dialogue, by contrast, because it claims to suspend resolution for a time in order to derive the Deity from a reading of phenomena.

Much of the force of Hume's *Dialogues* lies in this reduction of theological dispute, the contest of characters, to a trial of epistemological method. For his part, Philo capitalizes upon the condensation by exposing the underlying similarity between induction and deduction within religious debate. His use of Demea as a foil is meant to show not so much that fideist and skeptic agree, as that the philosophical Christian is a closet fideist. Demea therefore becomes the crucial presence in Hume's *Dialogues*, the figure who allows Hume to break out of the binarism of previous religious dialogues and to

destabilize the basic assumptions of rational Christianity by exposing what
Karl Popper has called "the fallacy of induction."

Philo's strategem appears at several points and is not always noticed by
Cleanthes. After Demea responds angrily to Cleanthes' explication of the
a posteriori position ("What! . . . No proofs a priori!"), Philo offers "so to state
the matter to you [Demea], that you will entertain no farther scruples with
regard to it" (p. 145). Philo explains that the a posteriori argument does not
really locate order in the things of nature, but instead begins with order as a
constitutive principle of thought. Design then refers not to anything
observable in the natural world, but to the assumption that like effects (order
in the mind) must have like causes (the intelligence of an ordering Deity).
"Now according to this method of reasoning, DEMEA," Philo explains, "it
follows (and is, indeed, tacitly allowed by CLEANTHES himself) that order,
arrangement, or the design of final causes is not, of itself, any proof of design;
but only so far as it has been experienced to proceed from that principle."

Philo's assurance that the explanation will set Demea's mind at ease might
have put Cleanthes on his guard; yet when Philo asks Cleanthes if he has
represented the design argument fairly, Cleanthes assents without comment
(p. 146). But *is* this Cleanthes' argument? In part it is, but Philo has subtly
transposed two of its steps. Cleanthes most typically begins with a perceptual
survey of phenomena, which turns up the "order and arrangement of nature,
the curious adjustment of final causes, the plain use and intention of every
part and organ" (163). He then compares this evidence of order to the design
of human productions, and so reasons by analogy to a higher order of
Design. He does not say that nature appears orderly because the mind
cannot help but perceive it so. When Philo redescribes the argument a
posteriori, however, he places the ordering power of mind first. This reversal,
closer to Kant than to Cleanthes, implies that the inductive survey of nature
begins with the prior hypothesis of necessary order.

On another occasion, Philo makes the point more directly:

To say that all this order in animals and vegetables proceeds ultimately from design is
begging the question; nor can that great point be ascertained otherwise than by
proving a priori, both that order is, from its nature, inseparably attached to thought,
and that it can never, of itself, or from original unknown principles, belong to matter.

(p. 179)

The subtext for this passage may well be Berkeley's *Principles*. Philo exposes
the uncomfortable either/or into which a radicalized empiricism falls when it
turns from investigation to theology. Once, with Berkeley's *esse percipi*, one has
relocated existence within the mind's ideas derived from sense perception;
and once, with this relocation, one has rejected such imperceptible entities as
matter or substance, which had previously served as organizing principles for
phenomena; then *either* order becomes a projection of mind, *or* it ceases to

exist at all. As we have seen, Berkeley had an answer for this problem, a theory of the divine language of nature locating God's grammar of natural laws somewhere between the phenomenal and ideal realms, but this is not my concern here. What is important is Philo's point that the turn from investigation to theology requires the abandonment of a posteriori methods in favor of a priori assertions.

The methodological inversion collapses the distinction between Cleanthes and Demea. The one league that is never directly acknowledged, as the skeptic sides first with the fideist against the rational Christian and then with the rational Christian against the fideist, is this unwilling bond between Cleanthes and Demea. Yet their connection expresses the polemical argument of the *Dialogues*, that there is finally no meaningful difference between induction and deduction, rational Christianity and fideism.[14] Saying that Cleanthes' argument begs the question is a polite way of asserting that it depends no less upon an article of faith. The flight up the ladder of being from effects to causes and then to the causes of those causes ends, Philo claims, either in Demea's acknowledgment of utter incomprehension or in pseudo-explanations such as that the nourishing quality of bread is caused by a "nutritive faculty." Seeking out the cause of intelligent design leads us "to trace that ideal world into another ideal world, or new intelligent principle" (p. 161). And where is one to stop? "It were better," says Philo, "never to look beyond the material world. By supposing it to contain the principle of order within itself, we really assert it to be God; and the sooner we arrive at that divine Being so much the better" (p. 162).

For the moment what Philo means by associating God with the material world is less important than his reference to methodological speed: "the sooner ... the better." Shaftesbury held the slow method of dialogue to be preferable to the fast one of declamation, especially in religious dispute. But

[14] Here Popper's affinity to Hume is clear. In *The Logic of Scientific Discovery* (New York: Harper and Row, 1968), Popper argues that "similarity, and with it repetition, always presuppose the adoption of *a point of view* ... But if similarity and repetition presuppose the adaption of a point of view, or an interest, or an expectation, it is logically necessary that points of view, or interests, or expectations, are logically prior, as well as temporally (or causally or psychologically) prior, to repetition. But this result destroys the doctrines of the logical and of the temporal primacy of repetitions" (pp. 421–422). If for "point of view" we read "an unexamined article of faith," and if for "the doctrines of the temporal primacy of repetitions" we read "the apparently neutral method of induction," then Popper's point is identical to the one I am claiming Hume makes by linking Cleanthes and Demea: the rational Christian cannot escape fideism because induction is always premised upon a prior deduction. This is the force of any number of Humean salvos in the *Inquiry*, as when he argues that "when we say ... one object is connected with another, we mean only that they have acquired a connection in our thought and gave rise to this inference by which they became proofs of each other's existence" ("Of the Idea of Necessary Connection," p. 86).

For more detailed examinations of Popper's relation to Hume, see also Arnold Levison, "Popper, Hume, and the Traditional Problem of Induction," in *The Philosophy of Karl Popper: Book 1*, The Library of Living Philosophers, ed. Paul Arthur Schilpp (Le Salle, Illinois: Open Court Press, 1974); and Anthony O'Hear, *Karl Popper* (London: Routledge and Kegan Paul, 1980).

Philo sees no difference. Inductive method sets up false gradations, a pretence of slow but ineluctable progress from the gathering of data to the formation of conclusions. As Philo and Demea both insist, "we have no *data* to establish any system of cosmogony" (p. 177; Hume's emphasis). Finally, Cleanthes will have to describe his own fountain, his prior framework according to which supposedly neutral data has been organized. Goaded by the skeptic, Cleanthes declares, "You ask me, what is the cause of this cause? I know not; I care not; that concerns not me. I have found a Deity; and here I stop my enquiry. Let those go further who are wiser or more enterprising" (p. 163).[15] Demea can afford to be silent at this point: his adversary as much as makes his argument. And Philo also agrees: "I must at last be contented to sit down with the same answer, which, without further trouble, might have satisfied me from the beginning" (p. 163).

Hume uses the dramatic possibilities of the dialogue form to develop characters who are linked to distinct intellectual and methodological positions. The shifting allegiances illustrate not merely Philo's slippery brand of skepticism, and Hume's desire to conceal his heterodoxy, but also the equation of views that the characters want to keep distinct.[16] When the characters stay on point, the pseudo-opposition between induction and deduction tends to devolve into *ad hominem* assaults, as had the debate in *Alciphron*. Cleanthes calls Demea a mystic. Demea calls Cleanthes an anthropomorphite. Such name-calling can only result in impasse, as Ralph Cohen has observed: "In a sly way, Hume points out, as he had in his other works, that religious discussions tend to be reduced to insulting exchanges rather than analysis of arguments."[17]

Dramatic interaction in the *Dialogues* therefore constructs a philosophical and religious position, though by no means a shift from "matters of belief" to "friendship." Hume made the relation between literary structure and intellectual argument explicit in a lengthy passage that he added in 1776, the year of his death. Philo tells Cleanthes that any religious debate that attempts to fix the attributes of an unknowable deity cannot be settled; it does not permit "exact mensuration." Thus, the controversies concerning natural religion are "merely verbal, or perhaps, still more incurably ambiguous"

[15] Cleanthes' dogmatism is repeated on another occasion: "it is by no means necessary that theists should prove the similarity of the works of nature to those of art; because this similarity is self-evident and undeniable" (p. 152).
[16] Alone among recent commentators, Leo Damrosch is sensitive to the philosophical and religious significance of characterization in the *Dialogues*. "Each of the three [characters]," he writes, "represents one of the main directions in which belief was tending in the later eighteenth century: Demea reflects its privatization, Cleanthes its secularization, and Philo its marginalization." *Fictions of Reality in the Age of Hume and Johnson* (Madison: University Press, 1989), p. 130.
[17] *Essential Works of David Hume*, ed. Ralph Cohen (New York: Bantam Books, 1965), p. 297.

(p. 218). Pressing the controversy can only produce the kind of vacillation dramatized by the *Dialogues*:

I ask the theist, if he does not allow, that there is a great and immeasurable, because incomprehensible, difference between the *human* and the *divine* mind: The more pious he is, the more readily he will assent to the affirmative ... I ask [the atheist] whether, from the coherence and apparent sympathy in all the parts of this world, there be not a certain degree of analogy among all the operations of nature ... He will readily acknowledge it. Where then, cry I to both these antagonists, is the subject of your dispute? ... Will you quarrel, Gentlemen, about the degrees, and enter into a controversy, which admits not of any precise meaning, nor consequently of any determination? If you should be so obstinate, I should not be surprised to find you insensibly change sides; while the theist on the one hand exaggerates the dissimilarity between the supreme Being, and frail, imperfect, variable, fleeting, and mortal creatures; and the atheist on the other magnifies the analogy among all the operations of nature, in every period, every situation, and every position.   (pp. 218–219)

Philo's claim that the debate between theist and atheist, if pursued obstinately, will cause an inversion of positions is matched by a dialogue whose characters knowingly and unknowingly change sides. When pressed, the philosophical Christian begins to sound like a fideist, the skeptic like a theist, even a pantheist (as when Philo, in the passage cited above, equates God with the material world). These vacillations have little to do with the value of friendship *per se*. They do, however, dramatize the futility of a dialogue concerning natural religion.

Materializing the third: towards a mundane ethics

Hume's dying wish was that one of his literary friends – he appealed particularly to Adam Smith and William Strahan – agree to help publish the *Dialogues*. No one would, and it was left to Hume's own nephew to bring out the first edition in 1779. Previous attempts to understand the significance of the dialogue form fail to address the question Hume himself set to his friends in the face of their timorousness: "I seriously declare, that after Mr. Millar and You [Willaim Strahan] and Mr. Cadell have publickly avowed your Publication of the *Enquiry concerning Human Understanding*, I know no Reason why you should have the least Scruple with regard to these Dialogues. They will be much less obnoxious to the Law, and not more exposed to popular Clamour" (in Kemp Smith p. 90). Even if the subterfuge of dialogue fails to conceal what is "exceptionable" in the work, Hume seems to ask, why should readers who facilitated the publication of such essays as "Of Miracles" and "Of the Idea of Necessary Connection" want to suppress the *Dialogues*? The present reading offers one explanation for their discretion: far from concealing the polemic against rational Christianity, the dialogue form, as appropriated by Hume, expresses his most extreme assertion – that rational inquiry finally has nothing to do with religion.

The introduction of the third character, Demea, is central to the composition of the *Dialogues*; his angry departure in turn precipitates the decomposition of religious dialogue. If Pamphilus were indeed right about the special suitability of philosophical dialogue to natural religion, the three characters should get along. Their agreement would express in miniature the optimistic program of scientific theologians such as Newton, Clarke, and Wilkins, who sought both to convince skeptics that their methods were sufficiently empirical and to convince the orthodox that their conclusions were sufficiently pious.[18] It is within this context that Demea's angry departure should be understood – not as "the eviction of a disruptive presence" in anticipation of the "comic" marriage between Philo and Cleanthes, but as the destruction of what Martin Battestin calls the comic world view of the Augustans, the belief in a rational universe "not only full and various, but regular, created by a just and benevolent Deity whose genial Providence governs all contingencies."[19] Demea's departure preserves Christian belief from skeptical attack, but only by severing the connection between reason and faith, natural philosophy and religion.

Cleanthes himself seems close to this realization when he observes upon Demea's sudden exit:

Our friend, I am afraid ... will have little inclination to revive this topic of discourse, while you are in company; and to tell you the truth, Philo, I should rather wish to reason with either of you apart on a subject so sublime and interesting.   (p. 214)

Cleanthes describes the breaking apart of an unstable tripartite structure into two possible binary arrangements. The first, despite Cleanthes' claim that he would "reason" with Demea, would permit a coming together of theist and fideist over matters of faith, the realm secured by Demea's rejection of rational dialogue; the second, between philosophical Christian and skeptic, would permit rational inquiry, but only regarding topics not "incurably ambiguous," namely, those within the secular realm. In each case Cleanthes loses, for his desire all along has been to construct a bridge between these realms.

Dividing religious and secular spheres is the point of Philo's own rationale

[18] See James E. Force, "Hume and the Relation of Science to Religion Among Certain Members of the Royal Society," *Journal of the History of Ideas* 45 (1984) 517–536. Force argues that Hume's main object of attack was the first program of the Royal Society, which attempted to place natural philosophy at the service of religion. He bases his argument on a reading of the essays "Of Miracles" and "Of a Particular Providence and of a Future State," which, taken together, refute the attempted synthesis of general providence (the design of nature) and special providence (miracles). In the *Dialogues* this dual attack is brought together into a single work, with Cleanthes standing for general and Demea for special providence.

[19] Battestin, *The Providence of Wit*, p. 141.

for inductive method, which can also be read as Hume's refutation of Pamphilus' defense of dialogue:

So long as we confine our speculations to trade, or morals, or politics, or criticism, we make appeals, every moment, to common sense and experience, which strengthen our philosophical conclusions, and remove, (at least, in part) the suspicion, which we so justly entertain with regard to every reasoning that is very subtile and refined. But in theological reasonings, we have not this advantage ... We are like foreigners in a strange country, to whom everything must seem suspicious, and who are in danger every moment of transgressing against the laws and customs of the people with whom they live and converse. We know not how far we ought to trust our vulgar methods of reasoning in such a subject.   (p. 135)

Bad tourists, according to Philo, assume that their old maps will suffice in alien territory. They are speculative imperialists, rather than versatile hermeneuts. The extension of dialogue to religious dispute strikes Philo as just this sort of bad tourism. Thus, he adds to Socrates' well-known turn from natural to moral philosophy a further delimitation of dialogic inquiry: where inferential reason aims to extend "past observation to any particular phenomenon," it must establish ahead of time the precise similarity of cases. A great disproportion (such as that between a watch and the universe) will "bar all comparison and inference" (p. 147). Such prior homogeneity can only be assured if one abandons metaphysics, shifting the focus of philosophical investigation from theology to the social (or human) sciences. Required, then, would be a fundamental redefinition of the scope of inquiry, as is found, for instance, at the beginning of Vico's *The New Science* – the "never failing light of a truth beyond question: that the world of civil society has certainly been made by men, and that its principles are therefore to be found within the modifications of our own human mind."[20]

In the *Inquiry* Hume calls the differentiation of sacred and secular realms mitigated skepticism, "the limitation of our inquiries to such subjects as are best adapted to the narrow compass of human understanding."[21] By stopping the hasty tourist at the border of the knowable, Hume deprives theology of regulative force in society, ruling out a divinely sanctioned ethics: "measures of conduct and behavior," he writes, "are furnished by reflections on common life ... Nor have the political interests of society any connection

[20] Vico, *The New Science*, trans. Thomas Goddard Bergin and Max Harold Fisch (Cornell: Cornell University Press, 1970), p. 52. One could also argue that the principle of Hume's attack on induction would apply to all rational arguments, whether in the religious or secular realm. For an expression of this view, see J. R. Milton, "Induction Before Hume," *The British Journal for the Philosophy of Science* 38 (1987) 49–74. Hume subscribes to the view, as Milton puts it, that "no inductive arguments, whether to particular or to general conclusions, can be given any rational foundation whatsoever" (62). If Philo's position in the *Dialogues* is any indication, however, Hume here uses the weaknesses of induction as a means of drawing sharper distinctions between secular and religious fields of inquiry.

[21] In "Of the Academical or Skeptical Philosophy," *Inquiry*, p. 170.

with the philosophical disputes concerning metaphysics and religion."[22] His aim, here the same as Philo's, is to dislodge theology from the space between events and their causes, and so to put off, for as long as possible, the investigator's recourse to what Hume elsewhere calls "fairyland" as a means of explaining complex phenomena.[23] Far from providing a bridge between reason and revelation, rational dialogue becomes the measure and limit of investigation in the human sciences. It uses characters not to point to a truth beyond character, but to posit a wholly mundane ethics.

What, then, of Philo's apparent "conversion" to Cleanthes' position, which has caused such divided commentary? In granting the existence of some "inexplicable contrivance" (p. 214) or "inconceivable analogy" (p. 218), does not Philo assent to the position of the rational Christian and so violate his own rule against casual tourism? His acquiescence says nothing more than this: rational inquiry cannot dispense with the logic of cause and effect; but, by the same token, causality cannot be grounded tautologically in Reason, as if Reason gave rise to inference rather than the reverse. Philo cannot deny, therefore, that observed regularities within the chain of mixed phenomena may have behind them Cleanthes' pure, unmixed Cause. But he does not take this default assumption as a pretext for the leap from the known to the unknown. D'Alembert's observation in his *Preliminary Discourse to the Encyclopedia of Diderot* that the problems of hydraulics and statics (when not solved by arbitrary hypotheses) might occupy one's attention for a whole lifetime echoes the real difference between Philo and Cleanthes. The hasty tourist feels uncomfortable in the realm of phenomena; his residence there only serves the larger goal of validating a prior metaphysical hypothesis about the regulation of all chance effects by an ultimate Cause. The skeptic, in all due modesty, cannot deny the possibility of such a Cause; however, he insists upon dwelling in the realm of effects in order to enlarge his understanding of the natural world, now understood to include the field of ethics freed from theology. In this respect, the apparent agreement between Cleanthes and Philo about a vague religious hypothesis is less decisive than the desire of the one to drive discussion to a single, pious conclusion, and the willingness of the other to prolong dialogue interminably.

Critics who exaggerate the significance of Philo's supposed "conversion"

---

[22] In "Of a Particular Providence and of a Future State," *ibid.* p. 155.

[23] The word "fairyland" captures the force of Hume's polemic. "It seems to me," he writes in "Of the Idea of Necessary Connection," "that this theory of the universal energy and operation of the Supreme Being is too bold ever to carry conviction with it to a man sufficiently apprised of the weakness of human reason and the narrow limits to which it is confined in all its operations ... There must arise a suspicion, if not an absolute assurance, that [this theory] has carried us quite beyond the reach of our faculties when it leads to conclusions so extraordinary and so remote from common life and experience. We are got into fairyland long ere we have reached the last steps of our theory; and *there* we have no reason to trust our common methods of argument or to think that our usual analogies and probabilities have any authority" (*Ibid.*, p. 83).

also fail to note the specific terms of his acquiescence. As Kemp Smith has already pointed out, Philo's final acknowledgment of some "inexplicable contrivance" or "inconceivable analogy" as the cause of order simply takes back with the left hand what it appears to give with the right.[24] Cleanthes has tried to argue all along that analogy and contrivance make the Deity *explicable* and *conceivable* to human understanding. When Philo allows for an "inexplicable contrivance" or "inconceivable analogy" he is only having more fun at Cleanthes' expense. The vow of intellectual allegiance is laced with combative irony. Philo's is a "philosophical assent" (p. 227), namely, the allowance a skeptic makes for an argument that is not disprovable but probably vacuous. That is why Cleanthes answers him with the equivalent of a Johnsonian kick of the stone: "Whether your skepticism be as absolute and sincere as you pretend, we shall learn bye and bye, when the company breaks up: We shall then see, whether you go out at the door or the window" (p. 132).

Thus far, I have traced what might be called the negative argument of Hume's *Dialogues*. Hume shows what reason and dialogue cannot do, namely come to a resolution about natural religion. He is then able to suggest several fields where inferential reason may produce knowledge. Yet by sabotaging philosophical dialogue, Hume also points positively to what might be called a post-metaphysical ethics, a transformation in moral philosophy as much expository as conceptual. I believe a clue to answering this development appears at a point in the discussion when Philo, attacking Cleanthes' anthropomorphism, uses the phrase "this little agitation of the brain which we call thought" (p. 148). Now it is already of some interest that in transmitting these words to the present Norman Kemp Smith's edition, wise even in its oversight, makes a small change, substituting "this little agitation of the rain which we call thought." The replacement of brain by rain images the very intent of the line, to place thought on par with metaphor, philosophy with imagination.

This "little agitation of the brain" exceeds its purpose. It voices a transition from a skeptical philosophy barring the rational ascent to the divine to another exercise of the imagination. The greatness of thought will be in its encounter with limitation and the richness with which it can evince a mundane world. The "little agitation of the brain which we call thought" asks thought to step outside "philosophy" while remaining philosophical about its predicament, less than it thought, but also thereby greater. Cleanthes recognizes the difference when he accuses Philo of exercising "too luxuriant an imagination" (p. 155). Philo speaks in a rambling way about all the possible cosmological accounts one might give for the origin of creation: Things might have been spun out of the belly of a spider

---

[24] See Kemp Smith's editorial notes to the edition of Hume's *Dialogues* cited in this chapter (p. 70).

(p. 180); they might be a product of God's dotage (p. 169); there may be as many gods as things, "a numerous society of Deities as explicable as one universal Deity" (p. 175); the world may be one of a billion seeds scattered by an infinitely procreant plant-like urge (p. 177); or things might just be the discharge of a cosmic bowel (p. 180).

Any one of these examples might have sufficed. Their reduplication draws attention away from the final Cause, which they all inadequately illustrate, and towards the imaginative competence of the everyday to provide meaning. But such possibilities of thought, little agitations of the b/rain, remain only the exempla in a philosophical argument against reason. They bear a striking resemblance to the stories Demea also begins to tell at this point in the dialogue, namely, repetitive accounts of human suffering graphic enough to convince us of the vanity of human reasoning: "This world is but a point in comparison of the universe," says Demea, "this life but a moment in comparison of eternity. The present evil phenomena, therefore, are rectified in other regions, and in some future period of existence" (p. 199). While Philo conceals his position by appearing to swap cautionary tales with the dogmatist, his turn from reason to imagination has a different purpose. His vision is neither comedic nor tragic but comic: it evokes a restless plurality of cosmologies, without bestowing final authority on any. For Philo a viable ethics must be located within the vicissitudes of human experience. The productive side of his skepticism calls for "the poet who speaks from sentiment, without a system, and whose testimony has therefore the more authority" (p. 193). One poet who took up this challenge of formulating a mundane ethics in the middle of the century was Laurence Sterne.

Hume and the comic novel: Sterne's *Tristram Shandy*

Sterne, like Hume, subverts the structure of metaphysics by historicizing the third term. His critique of metaphysics is, of course, carried out through indirection, wit, and no hint of a programmatic intent. *Tristram Shandy* then explores the ethical domain left after the departure of theology, just as Hume's *Dialogues* leave us with the certainty, from experience, "that the smallest grain of natural honesty and benevolence has more effect on men's conduct, than the most pompous views suggested by theological theories and systems" (p. 221).[25] In each case, the need for a mundane ethics arises once the logical structure of transcendental dialectic has been destroyed or

---

[25] I am avoiding the obvious complaint that Hume's *Dialogues*, though largely written by 1751 and circulated among friends between then and 1763, was not published until 1779, eleven years after Sterne's death. Hume received his impetus through a strong misreading of Berkeley, who had done the same with Locke. Sterne studied Locke with the intensity of a philosopher and the imagination of a poet. He drew conclusions from this study similar to those Hume derived from Berkeley's radicalization of empiricism.

mocked. For Sterne, the interminable comic novel replaces, corrects, ingests father Walter's aspiration towards a complete, systematic encyclopedia. It transforms metaphysics into gossip.[26]

Walter has many dialogues with Toby, but these bear little resemblance to the works discussed in this book. For one thing, Walter has no real interest in an exchange of ideas: "his aim in all the pains he was at in these philosophical lectures," Tristram explains, "—was to enable my uncle Toby not to discuss,—but *comprehend*—."[27] Adopting the pose of Socrates ("so finely painted by *Raffael* in his school of *Athens*"), Walter would silence his partner with an unassailable sequence of reasonings, "for he holds the fore-finger of his left-hand between the fore-finger and thumb of his right, and seems as if he was saying to the libertine he is reclaiming – '*You grant me this* – and this: and this, and this, I don't ask of you – they follow of themselves in course'" (IV, 7, p. 333). Walter "was all uniformity; – he was systematical, and, like all systematic reasoners, he would move both heaven and earth, and twist and torture every thing in nature to support his hypothesis" (I, 19, p. 61).[28]

Walter aspires to the logical rigor of his favorite author, the noble Slawkenbergius, whose treatment of noses has achieved the perfection of a closed system: "for he has taken in, Sir, the whole subject, – examined every part of it, *dialectically*, – then brought it into the full day; dilucidating it with all the light which either the collision of his own natural parts could strike, – or the profoundest knowledge of the sciences had impowered him to cast upon

---

[26] One of Sterne's most astute eighteenth-century readers was Diderot. In both *Jacques le fataliste et son maître* and *Le Neveu de Rameau*, we find the same pattern of serious philosophical dialogue placed under parody, the third term rendered entirely fallible, and abstract metaphysical discussion transformed into gossip and pantomime. Consider this exchange:

> JACQUES: ... Each of us judges of good and evil in his own manner; and perhaps not two seconds in our whole life do we have the same judgment.
>
> MASTER: Yes, yes, cursed gossip, and then what?

Jacques the Fatalist and his Master, trans. J. Robert Loy (New York: W. W. Norton, 1959), p. 53. Parody of philosophical dialogue becomes a common feature of mid-eighteenth century novels. In Goldsmith's *The Vicar of Wakefield*, one of the defining characteristics of the evil Squire is his ability to smoke Moses "dialogically" in a one-sided exchange beginning, "and firstly of the first. I hope you'll not deny that whatever is, is. If you don't grant me that I can go no further." In Voltaire's *Candide*, Pangloss finds Candide buried under a heap of rubble after the Lisbon earthquake. Candide cries out for oil and wine. Pangloss chooses the moment to begin a philosophical dialogue proving that "the earthquake is nothing new." "'Nothing is more likely,'" said Candide, "'but oil and wine for pity's sake!'" To which the philosopher responds, "'Likely! ... I maintain it's proved!'" About the relation between dialogue and the comic novel, Milan Kundera has observed, "The dominant device of all these individual stories [in Diderot's novels] is dialogue ... but since the narrators tell their dialogues in dialogues ... the novel as a whole is nothing but a big, noisy conversation. Diderot's novel is an explosion of impertinent freedom without censorship." "An Introduction to Variation," in *The New York Times Review of Books*, January 6, 1985, p. 1, 26ff.

[27] Sterne, *The Life and Opinions of Tristram Shandy, Gentleman*, eds. Melvyn New and Joan New, 3 vols. (Florida: University of Florida Press, 1978), III, 40, p. 281). Subsequent citations from *Tristram Shandy* refer to this edition and will be given by Sterne's volume and chapter and the page number from the Florida edition.

[28] I have benefited from conversations with Regina Marz about Walter's systematic philosophy and Tristram's attempt to elude his father.

it" (III, 38, p. 274). Walter's fondness for Slawkenbergius goes beyond his
systematic rigor. For Walter, too, has a thing for the nose. His hopes for his
son, his opinion of other men, his measure of all things depend upon a theory
of the nose. In short, the nose is his third term, the Berkelean fountain to the
elder Shandy's system. And so when Walter reads Erasmus' dialogue *De
Captandis Sacerdotiis*, and finds that a character says "My nose has been the
making of me," he cannot believe that the text contains no further
elaboration on the point, no "speculative subtilty or ambidexterity of
argumentation upon it" (III, 37, p. 271). He cannot believe the dialogue fails
to organize itself around this great idea: "Mayhaps there is more meant, than
is said in it, quoth my father. – Learned men, brother Toby, don't write
dialogues upon long noses for nothing."

Perhaps there is more meant in it, but for the sake of his own aspiration to
system, Walter would be better served by not subjecting the nose to such
close scrutiny. He scratches the letters with a penknife until they say what he
sought. " 'See, my dear brother *Toby*,' " he exclaims, " 'how I have mended
the sense.' " " 'But you have marr'd a word,' replied my uncle Toby." Walter
would be better off observing his own rule: "to come to the exact weight of
things in the scientific steel-yard, the fulcrum, he would say, should be almost
invisible, to avoid all friction from popular tenets" (II, 19, p. 170). That
friction is what happens to the fulcrum in Hume when the third term, the
absolute principle of adjudication, enters history and must defend itself
against attack. And it is similarly what happens to the third term throughout
Tristram Shandy: friction produces fiction. The nose keeps being rubbed,
tweaked, smashed, broken. After the incident with the window sash, Tristram
tells us, "the misfortune of my NOSE fell … heavily upon my father's head"
(IV, 18, p. 349). Tristram proves – to his own misfortune – that the nose is as
subject to accident as any other part of his father's system.

There is a stern side to all of this: the novelist enlarges the territory of *his*
prose fiction by parodying rival claims to knowledge asserted within other
(more systematic, metaphysical) genres. He takes aim, in particular at
transcendental dialectic, first through the parodic incorporation of serious
philosophical dialogue into the novel, and then by lampooning the structure
of dialectical reason itself. In the middle of Walter's praise of Slawkenbergius,
Tristram pauses to explain the structure of his father's thought:

the great and principal act of ratiocination in man, as logicians tell us, is the finding
out the agreement or disagreement of two ideas one with another, by the intervention
of a third (called the *medius terminus*); just as a man, as *Locke* well observes, by a yard,
finds two men's nine-pin-alleys to be of the same length, which could not be brought
together to measure their equality by *juxta-position*.   (III, 40, p. 280)

As Tristram makes clear, the third only works if it stands outside the flux of
ideas, while organizing their coherence through the stability of comparisons

within a system of knowledge. The measure cannot itself be measured (except by another measure deemed superior to it). But Walter's thirds never escape being dragged through the mud of contingency or smashed between the forceps of chance. " ''Tis a pity,' said my father, 'that truth can only be on one side, brother Toby, – considering what ingenuity these learned men have shewn in their solutions of noses' " (III, 41, p. 282). Toby, understanding more than he knows, hears the word "solutions" in its precise etymological sense, deriving not from *explicatio* but from *solutio*, the *dissolution* of particles into fluid. " 'Can noses be dissolved?' replied my uncle Toby." If the hypothesis of noses admits of more than one solution, if two characters do not agree about the status of the criterion for measuring truth, then Walter's third dissolves into the flux. Toby's question provokes a more passionate outburst than the death of Walter's own son.

More intimately than any philosopher of his age (except perhaps Hume), Sterne recognized the implications of Pyrrhonian skepticism for moral philosophy. Walter's nose is Pyrrho's hapless criterion under hobby-horsical redescription. The word Walter chooses to represent that which measures but is beyond measure, that which qualifies but is unqualified, is itself, through the common euphemism, so frequently measured and found lacking, so often qualified and then disqualified, that language ends up undoing the metaphysical labor it has just been asked to perform.

Behind Sterne's proliferation of horses and riders stands the philosophical refutation of a single, metaphysical criterion and the dialectical reduction it validates. Although Walter elevates his standard above those of the other characters, Sterne, like Pyrrho, denies that we have any basis in reason or logic or metaphysics to establish the criterion. For to decide between Walter's nose and Toby's fortifications, we would need a criterion that was neither a nose nor a fortification – a bridge, so to speak – to which both Walter and Toby would agree to refer their differences. Pyrrho already denied the possibility of such agreement:

to judge this controversie of the Criterie it is requisite we have a Criterie acknowledged, by which we may judge it; and to have a Criterie acknowledged, it is necessary, that the controversie concerning the Criterie be first judged; [therefore] it cannot be resolved whether there be a Criterie or no. For we grant them not a Criterie by supposition; and if they judge a Criterie by a Criterie, we force them to go into infinite.[29]

In Pyrrho, "to go into infinite" entails an infinite regress, but Sterne's comic vision interprets loss as gain: the absent criterion transforms the closed system into an open book, the transcendental sign into a pun, the life spent in chronological succession between birth and death into a long series of fruitful digressions (save one). There may be a single right way for the orator to drop

---

[29] Stanley, *The History of Philosophy*, p. 492.

his hat, as he pronounces the words, "are we not here one minute, and gone the next," but the "line of gravity," falling or ascending, is not Sterne's way: "Now – Ten thousand, and ten times ten thousand (for matter and motion are infinite) are the ways by which a hat may be dropped upon the ground" (v, 7, pp. 432–433). Not the striving after perfection, but the ten times ten thousand deflections from the primary opposition – life/death – will be the subject of this novel.[30]

Through Walter, Sterne invokes the character of Socrates and the tradition of Platonic dialogue: "Sir, you could scarce have distinguished him from *Socrates* himself," Tristram tells us as Walter recites the philosopher's oration from the *Apology* (v, 13, p. 442). Only now it makes a great difference that this agent of reason has been set in a fictional world where idiosyncracies of character and the ambiguities of language overwhelm any straightforward appeal to a higher destination for thought. Walter's kind of writing, not dialogue but the finished encyclopedia, the perfect system of knowledge, cannot survive in such a world:

Prejudice of education, he [Walter] would say, *is the devil,* — and the multitudes of them which we suck in with our mother's milk — *are the devil and all.* — We are haunted with them, brother Toby, in all our lucubrations and researches; and was a man fool enough to submit tamely to what they obtruded upon him, — what would his book be? Nothing, — he would add, throwing his pen away with a vengeance, — nothing but a farrago of the clack of nurses, and of the nonsense of old women (of both sexes) throughout the kingdom. (v, 16, p. 448)

Although Walter throws his pen away, Tristram picks it up. For this world of diminished thirds, of gossip, of associations based on sentiment instead of reason, of what Tristram calls "the confusion and distresses of our domestick misadventures," becomes the stuff of his interminable novel.

The loss of an ultimate reference point deprives *Tristram Shandy* of its origin, its end, and a plot connecting them. This, of course, is Sterne's point, just as it was Hume's goal to write a religious dialogue that failed to reach its goal. In the absence of this reference point both Hume and Sterne interrupt the linear plot of ascent from body to spirit. Both wish to redirect attention from the vision traveling down and then up, to the look remaining here, in between:

It is said in *Aristotle's Master-Piece,* "That when a man doth think of any thing which is past, – he looketh down upon the ground; – but that when he thinketh of something that is to come, he looketh up towards the heavens."
My uncle *Toby,* I suppose, thought of neither, – for he look'd horizontally."

(II, 7, pp. 117–118)

Both seek to transform the transcendental standard or criterion for ethical

---

[30] The notion of Sterne's manifold deflections from the primary opposition was brought to my attention by Claire Bergmann in a seminar paper at Boston University.

conduct into a mundane standard existing wholly within the sphere of human relations. Hume's *Dialogues* ends with this point:

It were better, therefore, never to look beyond the present material world. By supposing it to contain the principle of its order within itself, we really assert it to be God; and the sooner we arrive at that divine Being so much the better. When you go one step beyond the mundane system you only excite an inquisitive humour, which it is impossible ever to satisfy.   (p. 162)

Why an orderly system may not be spun from the belly as well as from the brain, it will be difficult for him [Cleanthes] to give a satisfactory reason.   (pp. 180–181)

It is certain from experience, that the smallest grain of natural honesty and benevolence has more effect on men's conduct, than the most pompous views suggested by theological theories and systems. A man's natural inclination works incessantly upon him; it is forever present to the mind; and mingles itself with every view and consideration ... The force of the greatest gravity, say the philosophers, is infinitely small, in comparison of that of the least impulse.   (p. 221)

But the *Dialogues* offers few indications of what such a mundane ethics would look like. It cannot develop these insights because they break the form of both philosophical dialogue and (need one add) systematic metaphysical exposition, to the extent these genres customarily elevate ideas over characters, theory over story. Moral philosophers such as Sterne, Diderot, and Austen were left to determine what *kind* of writing might best take up the challenge of constructing a mundane yet purposeful ethics once the contingencies of circumstance and desire could no longer be referred to an a priori norm.

We do not usually call these novelists moral philosophers because "serious" philosophers of the late eighteenth century continue to seek out a metaphysical reference point for ethics, belittling other writings whose preoccupation with concrete examples appears a small-minded pandering to popular tastes. Kant, for instance, holds that in order to revive a metaphysics of morals, we need to rescue reason from a debased form of dialectic, which he calls "a natural dialectic," and which Walter called the "farrago of the clack of nurses, and of the nonsense of old women":

From this [the turbulent demands of inclination] there arises a *natural dialectic* — that is, a disposition to quibble with these strict laws of duty, to throw doubt on their validity or at least on their purity and strictness, and to make them, where possible, more adapted to our wishes and inclinations; that is, to pervert their very foundations and destroy their whole dignity.[31]

Kant's separation of a good transcendental dialectic (metaphysics) from a bad natural dialectic (quibbling) offers yet another indication that philosophical dialogue, which had always attempted to reconcile these, has been set aside.

[31] Kant, *Groundwork of the Metaphysic of Morals*, trans. H. J. Paton (New York: Harper and Row, 1964), p. 73.

The space between philosophy and fiction therefore widens: just as Sterne mocks transcendental dialectic in order to establish the conditions for his own version of moral philosophy (the comic novel), so Kant feels he must attack a natural dialectic in order to resuscitate the dignity of systematic metaphysics.

In *Tristram Shandy* the historical connections between prose fiction and philosophy are preserved through the relation between father Walter and son Tristram. Sterne represents the two responses to eighteenth-century skepticism as a choice to be made between Walter's book, the encyclopedic system, and Tristram's strange autobiography. As it turns out, however, they go together, if only because the perpetual dissolution of the father's system keeps providing the grist for his son's interminable novel:

This is the best account I am determined to give of the slow progress my father made in his *Tristra-paedia*; at which (as I said) he was three years and something more indefatigably at work, and at last, had scarce compleated, by his own reckoning, one half of his undertaking: the misfortune was, that I was all that time totally neglected and abandoned to my mother; and what was almost as bad, by the very delay, the first part of the work, upon which my father had spent the most of his pains, was rendered entirely useless, — every day a page or two became of no consequence—.

Certainly it was ordained as a scourge upon the pride of human wisdom, That the wisest of us all, should thus outwit ourselves, and eternally forego our purposes in the intemperate act of pursuing them.   (v, 16, p. 448)

As an independent genre, philosophical dialogue after Hume moved in two directions. Those writers who recognized the value of dialogue as a means of disseminating fields of knowledge to an expanding readership still advocated its composition, while stipulating a series of restrictions on its structure and content. The effort to restrict dialogue, which I shall describe in greater detail in chapter eight, is epitomized by Richard Hurd's insistence (given in his own " 'Preface' On the Manner of Writing Dialogue") that "We should forbear to dispute some things because they are such as both for their sacredness, and certainty, no man in his senses affects to disbelieve."[32] Dialogue continued to be written, especially in the sub-genres of dialogues of the dead and dialogues on education, but these generally side-step any sustained encounter with serious metaphysical or theological topics. Another group of works, composed for the most part during the years when Hume's *Dialogues* was being suppressed (1751–1779), continues the project of metaphysical dialogue, now in translations and imitations of Platonic dialogues on beauty. These works contribute to the early philosophical discourse of aesthetics. They provide fictional confirmation of a shared standard of taste. I turn to the dialogues of the Platonic Revival in the next chapter.

[32] Hurd, *Moral and Political Dialogues with Letters on Chivalry and Romance*, 5th edn., 3 vols., (London: T. Cadell, 1776), "Preface, on the Manner of Writing Dialogue," p. xv.

PART 2

Dialogue, aesthetics, and the novel

6

The Platonic revival: 1730–1770[1]

Not that I presume to think it [Platonic dialogue] unworthy of imitation. But the public taste, as appears, is running full fast that way, insomuch, that some may even doubt, if the state of literary composition be more endangered by the neglect, or vicious imitation, of the Platonic manner.

Richard Hurd, *Notes on the Art of Poetry* (1776)[2]

The bridge to idealist aesthetics

For the purposes of this history, it is important that Hume completed the first draft of his *Dialogues concerning Natural Religion* by 1751. His work portrays a disjunction between metaphysical topics and experimental reason. With Hume the interpretation of philosophical dialogue as a form especially suited to the defense of Christianity in an increasingly secular age loses its moment. The work ends, appropriately, with Philo's designation of topics commensurable with dialogic inquiry, those now comprehended by the human sciences. Hume's dialogue, the entire tendency of his thought, is anti-Platonic: the plot of ascent from divided opinion to consensus, from phenomena to noumena, is denied. A skeptical interpretation of dialogue has been turned against its idealizing counterpart, with the result that all of the relics of what Wasserman calls "the divine analogy" of microcosm to macrocosm – typology, a fixed hierarchy of causal relations, the inductive evocation of a priori epistemological claims – lose their naturalizing ground in human exchange.

Nonetheless, during the middle decades of the eighteenth century (and particularly during the years when Hume's work was being suppressed) dialogue continued to be used to further metaphysical arguments. Indeed, there appeared a remarkable proliferation of dialogues translating or imitating Plato, whose purpose was to establish a standard of taste or judgment. These works, until now wholly overlooked in discussions of the

---

[1] Part of this chapter appeared as "The Eighteenth-Century Beauty Contest" in *Modern Language Quarterly* 55 (1994) 251–279.

[2] In Q. Horatii Flacci, *Epistolae ad Pisones, et Augustum: With an English Commentary and Notes*, trans. Richard Hurd, 3 vols. (Printed by W. Bowyer and J. Nichols for T. Cadell and J. Woodyear, 1776), I, p. 250.

origin and ideology of philosophical aesthetics, occupy an important position in English literary history. Proponents of a metaphysical interpretation of dialogue who recognized the difficulty of grounding consensus in reason looked to aesthetic experience as a new means of guaranteeing uniformity of response among diverse characters. Although describing an increasingly private and subjective aspect of human experience (taste), a group of late Platonists (or early aesthetes) continued to favor the form of dialogue because it allowed them to prove the objective universality of aesthetic response. Their proof involved the fictional representation of a scene in which characters experienced the same reaction to an instance of beauty or (later) sublimity. Once again, the realistic give-and-take of competing viewpoints achieves a moment of unity all the more convincing for its depiction as a realizable fact of social encounter. And even if, as the authors of these late metaphysical dialogues continue to suspect, dialogue so conceived belies the actual patterns of social exchange, a better time and better people – Plato's Greeks – provide the model for the way dialogues on beauty should resolve themselves in the middle of the eighteenth century.

In translations, imitations, and critical commentaries, moral philosophers supplement early philosophical expositions on the judgment of art (especially those of Shaftesbury and Hutcheson) with dialogues dramatizing intersubjective agreement among initially divided characters. A naturalized logic no longer controls their dialectical progress towards consensus, as had been the case at the end of *Three Dialogues between Hylas and Philonous*. Rather, the principle of sublimation has been displaced in two directions: it enters the exemplary object of beauty, whose special contrivance, the dialectical reduction of parts to whole, provides an objective correlative for agreement among diverse subjects; and it enters the mind itself (for Kant, the subjective faculty of aesthetic judgment), whose predisposition to apprehend unity amidst the diversity of phenomena explains our immediate sympathy for beautiful objects exemplifying the same. Late Platonic dialogues on beauty were thus placed in the anamolous position of proving through the gradual give-and-take of opinion an experience which, according to Hutcheson, had to be undergone immediately, powerfully, almost intuitively.[3]

The anomaly set form at odds with content, opening the Platonic imitations to parodic attack in their own day and relegating them ever since to critical oblivion. Why include such minor texts in a history of philosophical dialogue? In *The Origin of German Tragic Drama*, Walter Benjamin deals with a similar question. He responds:

---

[3] "It plainly appears," writes Hutcheson, "that some Objects are *immediately* the Occasion of this Pleasure of Beauty, and that we have Senses fitted for perceiving it ... The Ideas of Beauty and Harmony, like other sensible Ideas, are necessarily pleasant to us, as well as immediately so." *An Inquiry into Our Ideas of Beauty and Virtue; in Two Treatises*, 2nd edn. (London: J. Darby, 1726; rprt. New York: Garland, 1971), pp. 11–12.

[This study] will be guided by the assumption that what seems diffuse and disparate will be found to be linked in the adequate concepts as elements of a synthesis. And so the production of lesser writers, whose works frequently contain the most eccentric features, will be valued no less than those of the great writer. It is one thing to incarnate a form; it is quite a different thing to give it its characteristic expression. Whereas the former is the business of the poet elect, the latter is often done incomparably more distinctly in the laborious efforts of minor writers.[4]

There is something about the minor work that betrays the most "characteristic" features of a cultural or philosophical system. In its least successful variants, a genre may embody what Benjamin calls the "necessary tendency towards the extreme which, in philosophical investigations, constitutes the norm in the formation of concepts ... [so that] the form itself becomes evident precisely in the lean body of the inferior work" (pp. 57–58).

So it is in the case of the minor Platonic imitations. George Stubbes may or may not have been short on genius; yet the plot of his *A Dialogue on Beauty in the Manner of Plato* (1731), the story of a young woman named Aspasia, who, in conversation with Socrates, learns to renounce the seductions of lower beauties and embrace the true, intellectual beauty, *literalizes* the claims implicit in philosophical aesthetics from Hutcheson through Kant – that uniform response to aesthetic phenomena provides the basis for agreement among a mixed audience; that more than custom guides preference; that some people possess a greater share of taste, or delicacy, or refinement; that others, to the extent they are moral, are susceptible to being taught this aesthetic discernment; and that, in one way or another, the order announced when competing tastes acknowledge a norm of judgment doubles as a principle for order in the social sphere. However minor and decadent it may be, the *Dialogue on Beauty* is entirely representative in its attempt to prove that "Intelligent Beings, conspiring to promote the common Happiness, can alone furnish the true and genuine Ideas of this supreme Degree of Beauty" (pp. 25–26).

As one might expect, attempts to enlist dialogue in support of early modern aesthetics did not go unchallenged. Writers who opposed what one · called the new "religion of taste" saw that aesthetic theology depended upon the premise of uniform response to the beautiful. Successful dialogue was hardly incidental to the claim; it enacted on the level of mimetic fiction just that kind of world in which parts were always prepared to sublimate themselves to the whole; where a mechanism existed, in nature and in mind, guaranteeing a reading of phenomena that ascended to greater and greater levels of abstraction. If aesthetic dialogues could be made credible as realistic representations, then the late Platonists would have established a philosophical rationale for allegory in the modern age. In a quite conscious way,

---

[4] Walter Benjamin, *The Origin of German Tragic Drama*, trans. John Osbourne (London and New York: Verso, 1977), p. 58.

writers of anti-aesthetic dialogues were engaged not just in opposing the
discrete arguments of early aesthetics but also in redefining representation
itself: in their opposition to the allegorizing tendencies of the late Platonist,
they opened yet another front where a theory of the novel was being
formulated. The struggle that ensued within the minor works of the Platonic
revival to control representation and to define moral philosophy is the subject
of this and the following chapter.

Translating Plato: improving Socrates

While it is certainly true that a Platonic, and to an increasing extent
Neoplatonic (Plotinian), influence remains a constant from the Cambridge
Platonists, through Shaftesbury's response to Lockean empiricism, to the
moral sense philosophers (Hutcheson, Smith) and beyond, during the
middle decades of the eighteenth century, translations and imitations of
Plato and Xenophon, critical essays on Platonic dialogue and philosophy,
apologia for the life of Socrates, first translations of Greek dialogues, and
new editions of older translations, proliferated. The phenomenon I have
referred to as a "revival" of Platonic dialogue, and which Hurd refers to as
"the public taste, running full fast that way," is first and foremost a
bibliographical event.[5]

Plato was called upon to confirm the fact of uniform response to the
beautiful. In one representative instance, George Stubbes' *A Dialogue on the
Superiority of the Pleasures of the Understanding to the Pleasures of the Senses* (1734),
Socrates is invited to the landed estate of one Protarchus, who seeks his
judgment on the lay of his land. Before responding, Socrates asks to be
brought to the "Principal Point of View, from whence only its Beauty can be
understood."[6] When Protarchus responds that he planned no single prospect,
but sought instead to please a variety of tastes, Socrates, skeptic turned
flatterer, responds,

> But can you equally comply with every Taste; or is there some Preference due to
> a Genius of a superior Elegance.
> PROTARCHUS. Some Distinction may be fairly allowed.
> SOCRATES. And those ... are best intitled to this Distinction, whose corresponding
> Sentiments are by a just Sympathy conformed to the rule of Yours? ... Your
> own mind is then the Principal Point of View.   (pp. 10–11)

Socrates' aim is to teach Protarchus that the same virtue that selects the most
refined pleasure (intellectual) for emphasis among competing pleasures

---

[5] I have located approximately thirty separately issued works translating, imitating, or discussing
Plato, Xenophon, and Plotinus between 1730 and 1775. See also the work of K. J. H. Berland.

[6] George Stubbes, *A Dialogue on the Superiority of the Pleasures of the Understanding to the Pleasures of the Senses*
(London: W. Wilkins, 1734), p. 8. The dialogue is dedicated to His Royal Highness, Frederick,
Prince of Wales.

supplies "that Legislative Skill" necessary to govern a state. Addressed to the Prince of Wales, the dialogue conflates political and aesthetic directives in its advice that the landed gentleman discover "the Rule of ... Measures and Proportions" in estate and state.

Socrates-as-man-of-taste was not the only hero of Platonic dialogue summoned during the eighteenth century. As K. J. H. Berland has already shown, the reception of Socrates was also divided between those who viewed him as an ecstatic prefiguration of Christ, miraculously endowed with knowledge of an unwritten gospel; and those who viewed him as a prefiguration of Bacon and the deists, humanly supplied with the ability to reason his way to conclusions coincident with the salient truths of Christian ethics.[7] For the more ecstatic view, the deathbed Socrates culled from the *Apology*, *Crito*, and *Phaedo* was of obvious importance. What the *Phaedo* proves, after all, is that "if a man perfectly righteous should come upon the earth, he would find such opposition in the world, that he would be imprisoned, reviled, scourged, and, in fine, crucified by such, who, though they were extremely wicked, would yet pass for righteous men."[8] The first English translation of the *Apology* appeared in 1675, together with the *Phaedo*.[9] The translators inform us that Socrates "makes the Author of that his Office or Duty of reprehending and informing Men, to be God: by whose certain command he avows he did whatsoever he had done in that kind. And this Command of God he calls ... a Spiritual Intelligence, a Voice, a Sign: By those words, in way of excellency, *designing not any power of Human Wit*, but a certain Divine and extraordinary Signification; and (as we commonly call it) Inspiration."[10]

The interpretation of Socrates as prefigurer of Christ remained important, though not dominant, throughout the eighteenth century. It informed Amyas Bushe's transformation of two Socratic dialogues (the *Crito* and *Phaedo*) into a single lyric poem. An admiring reader introduces the poem with these words:

> The half-evangelicized, inspired store
> Of sacred Socrates – his heaven-taught lore
> Informs with dignity divine your lays;
> There Pagan truths with Christian fervor blaze,

---

[7] See K. J. H. Berland, " 'Bringing Philosophy Down from the Heavens': Socrates and the New Science," *Journal of the History of Ideas* 47 (1986) 299–308.

[8] *Phedon: or a Dialogue of the Immortality of the Soul, from Plato the Divine Philosopher*, with a "Discourse concerning Plato" (London: J. Davidson, 1777). According to this translator, "Plato ... pays homage to Christianity; in piercing by a supernatural light, into a part of those shadows and figures that covered it" (p. vi).

[9] *Plato his Apology of Socrates and Phaedo, or Dialogues concerning the Immortality of Mans Soul, and Manner of Socrates his Death: Carefully translated from the Greek* (London: Printed by T. R. and N. T. for James Magnes and Richard Bentley, 1675).

[10] *Ibid.* p. 4.

> The gospel's harbinger, who shone so bright,
> With more than ethic rays, than nature's light
> His Lamp was rais'd – with more than mortal flame
> His soul was fir'd, from heaven its lustre came.[11]

So "fir'd," Socrates presents us with an explicit refutation of any thin-spun rationalized Christianity.[12] Not reason but a miraculous insight into the future revelation makes Socrates sound so much like Christ. For those who adopted this line, Socrates' dying words in the *Phaedo* posed something of a problem. The modern translation of Hugh Tredennick gives them as follows: "Socrates uncovered his face, for he had covered it up, and said – they were his last words – Crito, we ought to offer a cock to Asclepius. See to it, and don't forget."[13] In John Cooper's *The Life of Socrates, Collected from the Memorabilia of Xenophon and the Dialogues of Plato* (1749), Socrates' request is preserved, but a footnote, running to several pages, accompanies it. Cooper recognized that Socrates' dying reference to the pagan god of medicine might betray an "Uncertainty of the Philosopher with regard to the Unity of the DEITY." He therefore rationalizes the statement with the claim that Socrates chose for the good of the populace to "comply externally with the religious Ceremonies of his own Country."[14] His occasional conformity should not distract us, however, from the more important point that "as a Religionist, he constantly wore the moral Image of God in his Heart, in the Spirit of Mercy and Peace."[15] In Amyas Bushe's poetic redaction of the *Apology* and *Phaedo*, Socrates' dying words undergo a more striking transformation:

> 'Tis heaven itself unfolds – O wider yet
> Unfold that glorious gate, the courts of light –
> I see, I see – no mortal tongue can utter –
> I spring, I soar, I mingle with the blest –
>
> [He grows faint]
>
> Hold, hold me up – ye winged ministers –
> To Thee, thou God supreme – to Thee I give –
> Thou source of life – but O my soul is thine –

---

[11] Amyas Bushe, *Socrates, a Dramatic Poem* 2nd edn. (Glasgow: R. and A. Foulis, 1762).

[12] In another version of this argument, Joseph Priestly will claim that Socrates' uncertainties about monotheism prove the necessity of divine revelation. "I much question," he writes in 1803, "whether any person educated as Socrates was, among polytheists and idolaters, could possibly, by the mere light of nature, have attained to a firm belief of the divine unity ... As this appears to have been all that the most sagacious of the heathens could attain to [in religion] by the light of nature, what reason have we to be thankful for the superior light of revelation, and especially for the gospel, which brings life and immortality to light." *Socrates and Jesus Compared* (London: T. Johnson, 1803), pp. 5, 24.

[13] Plato, *Phaedo*, 118a. *The Collected Dialogues of Plato, Including the Letters*, p. 98.

[14] Cooper, *The Life of Socrates, Collected from the Memorabilia of Xenophon and the Dialogues of Plato* (London: R. Dodsley, 1749), p. 167.

[15] *Ibid.*, p. 170.

Take back this portion of thyself – take back –
Let Socrates be thine – forever –

[Expires][16]

The characterization of Socrates as a type figure for Christ was countered by a more secular interpretation, a Socrates-as-proto-deist, who proved that one could achieve a sufficiently religious and ethical outlook through the exercise of reason unaided by any specific religious doctrine. Friend to the moderns, the Newtonian Socrates appears in James Welwood's translation of *The Banquet of Xenophon* (1710):

Thus was this great Man [Socrates] possess'd of Ideas about the Immortality of the Soul, and the Certainty of a Future State, not only much clearer than those the Jews had under the Mosaik Oeconomy, but such as come not much short of what has been reveal'd to us under the Evangelical Dispensation ... [Socrates] is a remarkable Instance, to what Heights of Religion and Vertue a Man may arrive thro' the meer force of Reason, *without the help of Revelation*.[17]

And he enters Cooper's *The Life of Socrates* (1749):

[Socrates] constantly and invariably taught and believed the Immortality of the Soul, and a future Retribution of Rewards and Punishments: and even in an Age of the grossest Idolatry, without the Assistance of supernatural Agents, collected by human Reason alone from the Nature of Things, the following important Truths concerning God, to establish which he fell a glorious and undaunted Martyr, viz. That he is One, eternal, uncreated, immutable, immaterial, incomprehensible Being.[18]

As the dates of these passages indicate, competing appropriations of Socrates are not peculiar to the middle decades of the eighteenth century. What is more specific to the period 1730–1770 is an attempt to reconcile sacred and secular through a third figure, a Socrates who serves as guide to the beautiful.

Emphasis upon the Platonic itinerary from sensible to supersensible beauty shifts the translators' attention away from the dialogues pertaining to Socrates' last days to those dealing with the judgment of art and the ascent to the Ideal Beauty. More important than the deathbed Socrates will be the representative Platonic *plot*, a pattern of teleological ascent confirmed by the shared responsiveness of characters to objects of beauty.

Between 1759 and 1776 Floyer Sydenham sought to provide a new translation of the Platonic dialogues and supplemented his translations with extensive notes and prefatory essays. He published his translations as they were written, and the first was the *Greater Hippias*, a dialogue concerned

---

[16] Bushe, *Socrates, a Dramatic Poem*, lines 101–112.
[17] *The Banquet of Xenophon, Done from the Greek, with an Introductory Essay to Lady Jean Douglass concerning the Doctrine, and Death of Socrates*, trans. James Welwood, (London: John Barnes, Andrew Bell, 1710), pp. 7–8
[18] Cooper, *The Life of Socrates*, "The Design" pp. vi–vii.

specifically with the judgment of beauty. In his introduction Sydenham describes Plato's purpose in these terms: "the design of this Dialogue is little by little to unfold the Nature of true Beauty; and gradually to conduct our Minds to the View of that Being, who is Beauty itself; and from whose Original Ideas, all of them essential to his Nature, is copied every Particular Beauty."[19] Reading the dialogue, we therefore undergo a gradual induction into the knowledge of absolute Beauty, and based upon this initiation, we are in a position to reverse the process, reinterpreting all lower particulars as copies of the Ideal. No doubt, such an induction into the knowledge of Ideal Beauty has a long history prior to the eighteenth century. Sydenham and the other translators and imitators of Plato can be said to continue the Christian Neoplatonic tradition descending to them through such Renaissance humanists as Firenzuola (*Dialogue on the Beauty of Women* [1548]) and Ficino (*Commentary on Plato's Symposium* [1544]). In this tradition beauty serves as a special kind of sign, a "figura" in Auerbach's sense of the term: "an occurrence on earth signifies not only itself but at the same time another, which it predicts or confirms, without prejudice to the power of its concrete reality here and now. The connection between occurrences is not regarded as primarily a chronological or causal development but as a oneness with the divine plan."[20] Beauty provides the philosophical lover with a conduit from microcosm to macrocosm. Yet during the eighteenth century the appeal to beauty is far less confident. Moral philosophers turn to beauty because the two worlds are coming apart, and only by concentrating the divine hypothesis into a single ecstatic event – the beautiful, the sublime – can they reassert *in principle* our epistemological *access* to an ideal realm. Beauty's first service is to method.

Sydenham uses the occasion of his translations of Plato in order to attack skeptics such as Hume who were in the process of destroying the methodological bases of transcendental induction (analogy, metaphysical dialectic). For him the *currency* of Platonic dialogue itself makes the case for the efficacy of the old plot:

the Philosophy of Socrates is like the Ladder in the Patriarch Jacob's Dream: his Metaphysicks ascend gradually up to the First Cause of Things; from which depend, and from whence come down to Earth, the Sciences of Ethics and Politicks, to bless Mankind.[21]

Sydenham repeats the biblical story in a preface to one of his dialogues because the genre itself stands for the ladder, and the reader the angels ascending and descending. This most important of eighteenth-century travel

---

[19] *The Greater Hippias: a Dialogue of Plato concerning the beautifull*, trans. Floyer Sydenham (London: H. Woodfall, 1759), pp. 5–6.

[20] Erich Auerbach, *Mimesis: the Representation of Reality in Western Literature*, trans. Willard R. Trask (Princeton: Princeton University Press, 1953), p. 555.

[21] The note refers to a work he calls "The Rivals, a Dialogue concerning Philosophy," in *The Dialogues of Plato*, trans. Floyer Sydenham, 2 vols. (London: W. Sandby, 1767), p. 32.

stories is being figured specifically in terms of the dialectical plot of the Platonic dialogue on beauty. Jacob's dream, like Sydenham's, is of a metaphysically grounded ethics and politics. Such grounding requires the patriarch and moral philosopher first to ascend the ladder of being to the first cause, and then, without forgetting the illumination, to descend again to the realm of humanity, where revelation will enforce ethical and political doctrines.

As we have seen, however, Hume spent much of his philosophical career refuting that dialectical plot and the conjunction of ethics and theology it subserves. In "Of a Particular Providence and of a Future State," he writes,

In general, it may, I think, be established as a maxim that where any cause is known only by its particular effect, it must be impossible to infer any new effects from that cause, since the qualities which are requisite to produce these new effects along with the former must either be different, or superior, or of more extensive operation than those which simply produced the effect, whence alone the cause is supposed to be known to us.[22]

The phrase "impossible to infer any new effects from that cause" strikes at the point of reversal in the Platonic model, whereby a *theological* ascent through beauty becomes a pretext for the *political* descent putting the absolute to use inferring "new effects." Hume's critique of necessary connection would abolish the upward, transcendental journey; his ridicule of analogical leaps (whether from part to whole or whole to part) would negate the downward movement. Aesthetic theology seeks to restore the intellectual operation denied in Hume's "maxim."[23] That is why Thomas Stanley's description of Platonic dialectic in his *The History of Philosophy* repeats the same plot as the dialogues on beauty: "as if from that Beauty which is in the Body, we should proceed to that of the Mind, from that to another Conversant in the Offices of Life, thence to that of Laws, and so at last to the vast Ocean of Beauty, that by these Steps, as it were, we may arrive at the sight of the supream Beauty."[24] A transcendental cause (Beauty with a capital B) is inferred from certain of its effects (beauties with small bs). And having moved from low to high, we

---

[22] Hume, "Of a Particular Providence and of a Future State," p. 154, n. 7.

[23] As M. H. Abrams has shown, philosophical aesthetics is radically continuous with the older project of rational Christianity (physico-theology). It merely transfers design from a quality attributed to all of nature to a quality exemplified by certain exemplary aesthetic objects. See his "From Addison to Kant: Modern Aesthetics and the Exemplary Art," in *Studies in Eighteenth-Century British Art and Aesthetics*, ed. Ralph Cohen (Berkeley and Los Angeles: University of California Press, 1985). "The antecedents of heterocosmic theory emerged in critics of literature who, beginning in the late fifteenth century, reversed the traditional comparison of God the creator to a human artisan by making the portentous comparison of the literary artisan to God the creator ... [But] not until the eighteenth century was the divine analogy converted from a topic of laudation into a principle of critical theory, for only then was the concept that a poem is its own world exploited so as to qualify, then to displace, the concept that a poem is a credible imitation of the existing world" (pp. 28–29).

[24] Stanley, *The History of Philosophy*, p. 181.

reverse the process: every figure becomes a *figura*, every person a *persona*, every object an emblem, all of nature once again enchanted, allegorized, under the auspices of the beautiful. The real concern here is not beauty itself or the "realism" of dialogue, but the theoretical possibility of abstraction.[25]

Unlike those who imitated Plato, several of whom I shall discuss below, the translators were relieved of the need actually to represent beauty and the response it instigates because they were, after all, transmitting the wisdom of the wisest and most beautiful of ancients to the modern audience. In his *Synopsis or General View of the Works of Plato* (1759), Sydenham takes the case against Humean skepticism as proven and draws his own moral:

all Virtue is Order and Proportion, whether in the Soul of Man, or in a Civil State ... The Rule, according to which the Mind by [Virtue's] Will then governs, is Beauty itself; and the Science, through which She governs, is the Science of that Beauty. For Truth and Beauty concur in One; and where-ever They are, there is also Good. The Love of Beauty then is nothing different from that First and Leading Motive in all Minds to the Pursuit of every Thing ... the DESIRE of GOOD. Thus the Perfection of Man consists in his Similitude to this SUPREME BEAUTY; and in his Union with it is found his SUPREME GOOD."[26]

In communicating the teaching of Diotima to the guests in the *Symposium*, Socrates had placed lack at the center of his definition of desire, and desire at the center of his definition of the philosophical quest. But these allowances, which retain for philosophy a necessarily ironic relation to its own end (since one cannot philosophize unless one lacks the desired end), have no place in Sydenham's system. Virtue is to be found in order and proportion, not in a striving borne of lack; and the rule we possess for ascertaining this order is "beauty itself," standing now, miraculously, at the beginning of our quest, closing the circle by providing the rule for itself. The science of beauty thus underlies all other sciences, including ethics and politics. "For Truth and Beauty concur in One; and where-ever They are, there is also Good."

[25] At one point in his *Inquiry*, Hutcheson admits that all he really needs beauty for is to disprove chance:

> Let it be observ'd, "That the preceding Reasoning from the frequency of regular Bodys of one Form in the Universe, and from the Combination of Bodys, is intirely independent on any Perception of Beauty; and would equally prove Design in the Cause, altho there were no Being which perceiv'd Beauty in any Form whatsoever: for it is in short this, "'That the recurring of any Effect oftener than the Laws of Hazard determine, gives Presumption of Design.'" (p. 56)

As the passage makes clear, Hutcheson considers beauty just a very good example of a non-random combination of effects (phenomena) – a means of disproving Chance and affirming Design.

[26] Sydenham, *Synopsis or General View of the Works of Plato* (London: S. Richardson, 1759). When stated this programmatically, the Platonic doctrine bears a greater resemblance to the terms of Plotinus' Enneads, I. 6: "Soul, then, when it is raised to the level of intellect increases in beauty. Intellect and the things of the intellect are its beauties ... For this reason it is right to say that the soul's becoming something good and beautiful is its being made like to God, because from Him come beauty and all else which falls to the lot of real beings." *Plotinus*, trans. A. H. Armstrong, 6 vols. (Cambridge, MA: Harvard University Press, 1966), I, p. 251.

But surely the old Platonic dialogues did not lend themselves entirely to the synopsis. There were elements that resisted easy appropriation to the formula. In order to equate Platonic dialogue with Christian Neoplatonic doctrine, the translator had to place himself also in the position of both editor and censor. The end of the *Symposium* posed special difficulties, since here, after Diotima's definitive expression of the process of transcendental induction, Alcibiades enters, drunken and horny, scheming on Socrates' lower parts. Why did Plato allow the fine metaphysical structure of his dialogue to be perverted by this drunken reveler? Sydenham thought Plato had blundered. Unwilling to censure the passage outright, he adduced critical grounds for its suppression:

Plato's Dialogues are by the ancient Criticks justly likened to Theatrical Representations, in that they exhibit alike the Manners and Character of Men, attributing to each Person the Sentiments proper to his Character. As therefore we cannot but condemn Mr. Congreve for introducing into his Comedys such a Villian-Character as that of Maskwell in his Double Dealer, which properly belongs to Tragedy, so we cannot altogether justify and consequently ought not to follow our author [Plato] in introducing to his Banquet the thorowly debauched Alcibiades.[27]

The comparison between dialogue and drama would seem to be obvious, but it is far from simple. Shaftesbury invoked the generic parallel between dialogue and heroic drama, but only in order to conceal the formal ambivalence of his philosophical rhapsody. George Stubbes links his Platonic imitation (*A Dialogue on Beauty in the Manner of Plato*) to a "serious Comedy . . . more just and instructive, as well as more decent & refined than those [comedies] of a lighter sort, which represent Humane Life under its more superficial Appearances." Introducing his translation of Plato's *Republic* in 1763, H. Spens also advertises dialogue in terms of its similarity to drama: "Now, as the following piece is wholly dialogue, where the Author totally disappears, and all is spoken in the characters of the persons of the drama, here represented, it may be considered a philosophic play, where will be found a variety of characters, distinctly marked, and properly supported, with a vein of humour highly agreeable, and no where else to be met with."[28] Yet critics and writers just as often stressed the competition between the genres. In the Renaissance, Tasso defined dialogue as distinct from stage drama: "dialogue is an imitation of reasoning written in prose for the benefit of civil and speculative men, and for this purpose it requires no stage or platform."[29] In Mandeville's *Fable of*

---

[27] *The Dialogues of Plato*, trans. Sydenham, pp. 247–248.

[28] *The Republic of Plato*, trans. H. Spens, p. xv.

[29] Quoted in Paula Sommers, "Agrippa d'Aubigne and the Literary Dialogue," in *The Dialogue in Early Modern France, 1547–1630: Art and Argument*, ed. Colette H. Winn (Washington, DC: The Catholic University of America Press, 1993), p. 225. Sommers adds, "the elimination of any intent to stage or dramatize the dialogue serves to distinguish it from theater, an important distinction, since Tasso notes earlier in his treatise that the literary dialogue may resemble a tragedy in the actions it describes just as it may recall some aspects of farce or comedy."

the Bees, Part II, the distinction between dialogue and drama redounds to the advantage of dialogue. Unlike the more immediate spectacle of an acted drama, written dialogue, Cleomenes argues, places the burden of interpretation upon the reader, who must study the language "not only for nervous Thoughts and Perspicuity, but likewise for Words of great Energy, for Purity of Diction, Compactness of Style, and Fullness as well as Elegancy of Expressions."[30] In the case of Sydenham, reference to "theatrical representations" justifies altering an established model of philosophical dialogue. In other words, the two genres are actually being viewed in oppositional terms. Rather than ask how the end of the *Symposium* comments upon Diotima's teaching, Sydenham, like Nietzsche, assumes that philosophical dialogue is akin to a domesticating comedy, and proceeds to erase all indications of irony and phallic improvisation from the page.

In order to explain such decisions and assert the relevance of Platonic dialogue to aesthetic theology, Sydenham adds an elaborate editorial apparatus to the translation. As a result he presents his readers with supposedly oral dialogue being strangled by written commentary creeping up from below. On some pages, direct dialogue gives way completely to editorial comment. It is therefore sad but not altogether surprising to find this notice at the end of Sydenham's second volume of translations:

Very many [readers], after taking the First and Second [dialogues] ... were pleased to discontinue their Subscription, so many, that whereas the First and Second are now out of Print, a great Number of the subsequent ones lye upon the Author's Hands, which it cannot be expected any Person will purchase without having the former.

(p. 251)

Imitations of Plato: the eighteenth-century beauty contest

Another option open to writers who defended the arguments of aesthetic theology was a looser imitation of the Platonic model. After all, if the angels really were ascending *and* descending the ladder, it should be possible to represent moderns reasoning their way to agreement about the nature of the beautiful and its implications for ethics. Yet imitators of Plato ran into the problem that dogged all writers of philosophical dialogue during the period, namely, Shaftesbury's suspicion that the genre was dead, or nearly so. In his *Remarks on the Life and Writings of Plato* (1760), Ebenezer Macfait observes, "One great beauty of ancient dialogue was its being a picture of real life; but modern manners, as has been observed by Lord Shaftesbury, cannot be seriously intermingled with a philosophical discourse. Modern dialogue must therefore be unavoidably defective in the life and action, the painting and the scenery."[31] Real life for the ancients *was* beautiful; dialogues arriving at the

---

[30] Mandeville, *Fable of the Bees, Part II*, p. 293.
[31] Macfait, *Remarks on the Life and Writings of Plato* (1760), p. 88.

Ideal Beauty were faithful copies of experience; the angels were ascending and descending. But in modern life, beauty has withdrawn; normal conversation appears nothing like a metaphysical dialogue: the angels have scattered, taking their ladder with them. To write a modern dialogue affirming a fixed standard of beauty might then appear a manifest absurdity.

In prefatory remarks to *A Dialogue on Beauty in the Manner of Plato* (1731), George Stubbes acknowledges that dialogues such as his might violate the expectation of a probable imitation of reality. His solution is simply to claim that he himself witnessed conversations of the sort presented in his imitation of Plato: "tho' I am as fond of Plato as any of the ancient Poets, I should not have entertained a Thought of imitating him, had not some Socratic Conversations at Eastbury, in which I had the Pleasure to bear a (very little) Part, first made me conceive it an Attempt not altogether impracticable."[32] The transparency of Stubbes' gesture towards empirical verification conveys the risk he was willing to run for the sake of reframing the arguments of Shaftesbury and Hutcheson in dialogue form. Through the claim that successful Socratic conversations still occur in 1731 in aristocratic enclaves of rural England, Stubbes places the metaphysical certainties of Christian Neoplatonism within the reach of the best modern conversations.

The immediate occasion of *A Dialogue on Beauty* is Stubbes' attempt to gain the favor of the Duke of Dorset and to procure a position as tutor to his daughters. He constructs a dialogue between the teacher, Socrates, and Aspasia, a young woman of high social rank, as a means of doubling in fiction the kind of tutelage he hopes to provide the Duke's family. Moreover, he anticipates a specifically female readership: the work is designed as a "not uninstructive entertainment for young Ladies, even of the highest Rank" (p. vi). In order to engage them to read, Stubbes has "avoided giving her [Aspasia] the least Tincture of Philosophy, the least Degree of Knowledge, unsuitable to her early Age or Sex" (p. vi). The woman, like Plato's slave Meno, will thus be led by Socrates from ignorance to wisdom through the gradual stages of dialectical reasoning. She will serve as the first reader of the dialogue, in that her progress models the reader's own.

Yet the woman also plays another role. She is the example of beauty. As Stubbes and the other Platonic imitators search about for that sign guaranteed to evoke uniform response in the multitude, they fix upon the beautiful woman and proceed to define the qualities that make her beautiful. Unfortunately for the women represented, the requirement of playing both roles, the object of beauty and the student who learns to transcend earthly allures, places her in an awkward and dangerous position. She must *be* a body to initiate the quest for the absolute; she must simultaneously *renounce* her body, if she is to follow Socrates on his intellectual journey. The role of

---

[32] Stubbes, *A Dialogue on Beauty in the Manner of Plato* (London: W. Wilkins, 1731), p. iv. Subsequent references will be given by page number in my text.

beautiful women in aesthetic dialogues concentrates all the illogic of the dialectical reduction of difference to sameness into the body of a woman who must then testify to her self-subordination, or, as Kant will call it, a "willing subordination to the law." Her progress – a "new kind of Chase, unknown to Diana and her Nymphs" (p. 11) – controls the plot of Stubbes' serious comedy: "a mere Readiness of Apprehension, and an ingenuous Desire to be informed, lead her on with Pleasure thro' a System of Beauty entirely new to her, and discover to her View the Secret Foundations of Moral Excellence" (p. vii).

The dialogue begins as Aspasia, a character "as innocent and beautiful as can be formed by Imagination," sits posing for a portrait. Socrates praises the painting, but Aspasia, all modesty, refuses to share in the commendation of her own beauty. Socrates sets about correcting her: it is not her own beauty that the true artist has the power to imitate, but something more ideal, more essential to who she really is. Aspasia responds:

> But if I must (with a Sigh) resign my Title to the pleasing Appearance of the plain Dress ... tell me, what Kind of Creature then am I, who have, it seems been only the weaver of it?
> SOCRATES. You are a Form too refined for Sense, too delicate to be seen unmasqued; a Mind embellished with the various Charms of Thought and Reason, Fancy, Wit and Judgment; capable of disputing, not only with the Shadow of *Socrates*, but even with Socrates himself.   (p. 7)

Ostensibly, Socrates' aim is to liberate Aspasia and women like her from social conventions that assign her worth only on the basis of appearance. To redefine herself as a mind capable of disputing with Socrates, a mind capable of entering into philosophical dialogue, is to reject the view that she has power only through her ability to please men.[33] Yet the education is double-edged. While Aspasia is invited to ascend the great chain of beauty with Socrates, this ascent requires her to accept the fixed hierarchy in which she, as physical woman, occupies a lower place.

The dialogue progresses through all of the expected stages in the Platonic itinerary. Socrates teaches Aspasia that there exist higher and lower senses capable of discerning greater and lesser degrees of beauty. Sight is the highest physical sense, and its difference from physical taste and touch acquaints us, by analogy, with an even higher faculty for apprehending beauty, situated in the understanding, yet responsive to physical form:

Socrates. It is evident, that the Understanding alone has the Power of discerning Beauty, even when discovered by the Medium of the Senses. This appears yet plainer in the Perception of Beauties purely Intellectual: And consequently, the sublime

---

[33] "A Nymph," explains Socrates, "tho' observing in herself so many curious Faculties designed for nobler Purposes, seems very capable of a Mistake ... in imagining herself to be such a pretty useless Toy" (p. 14).

Pleasure arising from Beauty, consists in the Contemplation of just Proportion, Symmetry, and Order, thro' all their several Kinds and Degrees.   (p. 23)

Aspasia's confession that she is not yet sufficiently acquainted with the different orders of beauty allows Socrates to rehearse a version of the great chain of beauties, beginning with "Beauties of Material and Inanimate Beings," ascending through the "blooming Tribes of Vegetables ... more beautiful than Inanimate Beings," to the "Beauties of Sensitive Creatures ... of an yet higher Order," and arriving finally at "a Being supremely fair, and eminently comprehending in itself all inferior Perfections. So transcendently amiable is the Idea of Moral Virtue, that faithful Miniature of the Divine Goodness!" (pp. 25–26).

Aspasia marvels at the vision. She willingly abandons herself to an ascent requiring only that she relinquish her earlier sense of self. It is in mind that true beauty is situated, and the sooner she sloughs off any undue attachment to lower beauties, the sooner she will join Socrates in the consummate vision. But just before acquiescing entirely, Stubbes permits her one small objection, the one philosophers from Hutcheson through Kant avoid. Aspasia asks, "But is every Mind thus beautifully formed, and furnished with the skill of rightly employing this Instrument of displaying its unseen Perfections?" Socrates responds (with some understatement), "Your question is of Moment." But rather than credit her with locating a crucial objection to the entire theory of "moral beauty" (the question of the variety of tastes and the tenuousness of proving taste objective by the uniform operation of Mind), Socrates gallantly suggests that she has no idea what kind of grumbling hive she threatens to set loose: "Your question is of moment, and well deserves to be considered: But you are not perhaps aware what a various Swarm of Reasonings you have provoked by moving it. Methinks I already perceive them, issuing in a long and intricate Train from the Hive and clustering about us: had we not better leave them silent and undisturbed in their peaceful Cells?" (p. 34). After Aspasia offers a verbal curtsy, declaring herself unafraid while Socrates escorts her through the swarm, the teacher explains:

The Endowments bestowed by the Divine Hand are infinitely various, and distributed amongst an infinite Diversity of Creatures, every Kind enjoying something peculiar to themselves. Hence it is observable that the lesser Beauties, belonging to Creatures of an inferior Rank, are often found wanting in those of a higher Order. But that Want is amply recompensed by some different Perfection of a nobler Kind.   (p. 36)

Just as lesser beauties are found wanting in those "of a higher Order," so the higher beauties are also found wanting in those "of an inferior Rank." As in Pope's *Essay on Man*, the description of a great chain of being shades quietly into a rationale for inequality within the human (social) sphere. Although every taste is in principle capable of ascending the chain to the supreme degree of beauty, it is equally necessary that a great plenitude of unequal tastes persists, confirming the election of a nobility.

In *The Great Chain of Being*, Lovejoy draws frequent attention to the two possible interpretations of man's middle position in the scale of being, linking the opposition to two basic tendencies within Platonism. On the one hand, the Platonic scheme of gradual ascent from material to Ideal Beauty implies a rational, causal principle animating the connections among spheres. A cosmic order so conceived offers a principle of mobility within the hierarchy of life-forms: to the extent one understands and subsumes the energy animating connections from bottom to top, one may aspire to Godhead. On the other hand, the image of man occupying a static middle link in the great chain "led to an open and unqualified rejection of otherworldliness which had always been characteristic of the Christian and Platonic tradition ... any effort to ascend the scale must be an act of rebellion against the divine purpose – a crime against Nature."[34]

We find, then, a ladder meant to be scaled *and* a scale meant to be obeyed. During the eighteenth century, according to Lovejoy, the two strains of Platonism – the conception of teleological ascent and the restriction of human enterprise to this world "have become completely sundered; and one of them has overcome the other." Lovejoy describes the dilemma as an absolute contradiction within eighteenth-century versions of the "unit idea" of the great chain of being. Nevertheless, the ubiquity of this metaphor within aesthetic theology and the apparent disconcern writers have for its contra-dictions raises some question as to whether Lovejoy has actually identified the "unit idea," the controlling intellectual concept (if such a thing exists), for the years 1730–1770. In Hutcheson and Burke, as in the dialogues on beauty discussed here, the great chain of being is introduced to exemplify a larger argument about the orderly, rational, designed, and ultimately beautiful nature of God's universe. The idea of beauty embodies the two contradictory elements of Christian Neoplatonism. It subsumes a progressive dialectical ascent to transcendence while it establishes a fixed hierarchy of beauties and tastes. If the great chain of being suffers from a collision between mobility and stasis, the concept of beauty reconciles these through the sign of beauty itself. When Aspasia learns to interpret beauty correctly (thereby participating in a theological ascent), she also learns to subordinate her own interests (thereby accepting the static vision of her place in the social order).

The contradictions noted by Lovejoy have therefore been condensed within the figure of the beautiful woman. In an objective sense, she provides an example of external beauty universally pleasing to all (men); in a subjective sense she willingly abandons the physical referent (herself) to become a figure for a higher beauty, beauty of the soul, of virtue, of the purified intellect. As

---

[34] Arthur Lovejoy, *The Great Chain of Being* (Cambridge, MA: Harvard University Press, 1966), p. 202.

an instance of what Paul Korshin calls an abstract typological sign, that is, a type removed from allegory, the beautiful woman provides the exemplary figure.[35] Body enough to attract and focus the male's attention, transparent enough to redirect his longing to a higher destination, she straddles the divide, bridging nature and revelation.

That, of course, is the positive view of her achievement. Yet throughout the Christian Neoplatonic tradition, male writers also expressed a certain uneasiness about their tendency to transform living women into type figures for the divine. This uneasiness, which travels for centuries under the banner of "Petrarchanism," has to do with the contradictory function of the sign itself within religious allegory. As de Chenu has observed with reference to the "symbolist mentality" of twelfth-century Christian Neoplatonism:

> the symbol, in order to effect the transference for which it is a vehicle, calls for matter which does not disappear in the process of signifying, such, for example, as the reality of history in biblical typology, or the reality of the material used in a liturgical action. On many counts the masters of the twelfth century responded wholly in favor of this law of symbolic values: these values emerge only in proportion as the *res* retains its integrity while functioning as *signum*. [Yet] in turning reality into nothing but a figure, tropology weakens itself ... Moralization, even in the masterly commentary of St. Gregory on Job, ended up in attenuated abstraction, for it dissolved the natural or historical materials upon which it operated.[36]

If we replace the word "symbol" with the word "woman," we will have an accurate explanation for the ambivalent appeal of so many Greek Helens and Christian Lauras throughout the metaphysical tradition. The woman as trope (vehicle) must be body (*res*) enough to retain the integrity of the material sign, while not so earthy that she then distracts the poet or reader from the symbolic value for which she stands. The instability of the typological sign draws attention to the importance of the larger generic context within which such signs appeared. The interpretative cues supplied by allegory itself taught readers how to "effect the transference" from material sign to spiritual signification without reducing the former to an attenuated abstraction. When allegory falters, as it does in the modern period, the idealized figure of female beauty will also fail the male poet in one of two predictable ways: she will divide into two women – the threatening whore, whose body presents an end in itself, and the nurturing mother, whose physicality, abstracted away, can

[35] Korshin explains that signs become "abstracted" when they are "drawn away from the theological field of action," which had previously assigned meaning, and begin to function as autonomous reminders of an entire system of value. "Types are always *signs*," he continues, "whose meanings would be known to those fortunate enough to 'read' the code they embody and of which they are a part ... [Yet the abstracted type] can be shifted about from one text to another, always keeping the same approximate significance." *Typologies in England: 1650–1820* (Princeton: Princeton University Press, 1982), especially pp. 104–106.

[36] Marie-Dominique de Chenu, *Nature, Man, and Society in the Twelfth Century*, trans. Jerome Taylor and Lester K. Little (Chicago: University of Chicago Press, 1968), pp. 132–133.

no longer prompt the pilgrim's ascent. But she will also persist as a torn figure, the Janus-faced female of Shaftesbury's illustration, an object of constant fascination, her predicament repeating the instability of the sign-function itself in the early modern period.

Beauty in distress becomes the dominant theme of much eighteenth-century literature in large part because the beautiful woman is called upon to "effect the transference" strict philosophy is no longer able to assign. Within scenes of aesthetic education, the beautiful female testifies to her willingness to pass from a physical manifestation into a type figure for the divine. The recovery of typology is thematized: her readiness to die in body in order to ascend in spirit confirms the existence of a physical sign both different from and the same as the metaphysical signified. In her torn identity, both realms – the historical and the ideal – are concentrated within a form of material beauty acquiescing in its own abstraction. The cost of this acquiescence is, of course, enormous: she must become a Clarissa, ordering her own coffin; or an Aspasia, no "less desirous to lay hold on the friendly Aid [of Socrates], than the creeping Vine is ambitious to clasp with her Tendrils the supporting Elm, and rear to the Sun her feeble Branches"; or, in Goethe's culminating expression of the entire Petrarchan tradition, she must become the farm-girl, Gretchen, destroyed by Faust's desire to pierce the veil of divine knowledge.[37]

The tendency to objectify and then destroy the female figure reaches its most embarrassing literalization in Joseph Spence's *Crito, or a Dialogue on Beauty* (1752). Here the female character has been transformed into an object for numerical evaluation, a contestant in a beauty contest. Although no women participate in *Crito*, Spence, like Stubbes, has in mind a specifically female readership: "as there were no Ladies here," one of the characters remarks at the end of the work, "I wish Crito would ... be so good as to print it, for the benefit of the Fair Sex in general."[38] The text thus takes its place beside an expanding body of beauty manuals written for the benefit of young ladies entering polite society.[39] It also belongs, as the author makes clear, to the development of philosophical aesthetics. Its purpose in quantifying female

---

[37] Faust calls upon Mephistopheles to reveal absolute knowledge to him and, in turn, is shown first a mirrored Helen ("Do I see in her recumbant shape / the form and essence of the heavens?") and then the unfortunate Gretchen, whose veil will indeed be penetrated when Faust reads her as a sign for the absolute. *Faust, Part I*, trans. Peter Salm (New York: Bantam, 1988), p. 159. I am suggesting, therefore, that the centrality of "virtue in distress" during this period (especially in the novel) needs to be understood in terms of the role female figures play within attenuated versions of Christian Neoplatonism.

[38] Sir Harry Beaumont [Joseph Spence], *Crito, or a Dialogue on Beauty* (London: R. Dodsley, 1752), p. 60. Subsequent references will be given by page number in my text.

[39] See, for instance, John Cosens, *The Economy of Beauty; in a Series of Fables Addressed to the Ladies* (London: J. Wilkie, 1772). The inscription to the work states: "I claim the Attention of the Ladies, and profess to teach an Art by which all may obtain what has hitherto been deemed the Prerogative of a few; an Art by which their predominant Passion may be gratified, and their Conquests not only extended but secured; – THE ART OF BEING PRETTY."

beauty is to reveal the "real Beauty of the other Works of Nature ... one great universal Beauty, of all created Matter taken in one View ... the Goodness of God, as displayed in the Works of the Creation" (p. 57).

The dialogue is actually an extended dissertation on beauty set within a spare dialogic frame. Although the fiction of interaction drops away, what instigates the set piece is of particular interest. The topic takes shape after Milesius enters the conversation between the host (Timanthes) and Crito. Timanthes somewhat unfairly betrays Crito's earlier confession of a depressed state of mind. Both Timanthes and Milesius then pressure Crito to explain the source of his sadness.

Whatever you saw in me of that kind [sorrow], must have been occasioned by the Visit I made this Morning. You both know the Beauty and Merits of Mrs. B * * *, as well as what a Brute of a Husband she has the misfortune to be married to. I just called there, before I set out; and on the Servant's telling me, that his Lady had been up some time, and was sitting in the Room next the Garden; as my near Relation to her gave me the Liberty of going on without sending in my Name, I walked towards the Room; and found the Door only just open enough, to let me see her leaning on a Couch, with her Head rested negligently on one Hand, whilst with the other she was wiping away a Tear, that stole silently down her Cheek. The Distress in her Countenance, and the little Confusion that appeared about her Eyes ... added so much to the other Beauties of her Face, that I think I never saw her look so charming in my Life.   (pp. 3-4)

Milesius responds:

... but pray, how come you to think that her sufferings add to her Charms? or that a Distress like hers, could ever be pleasing to the eye? Some people get such strange, unintelligible notions of Beauty!   (p. 5)

As will be the case in numerous novels of the period, the beautiful woman in distress takes center stage. The question she poses to the aesthetician peeping through the crack in the door is as follows: if, as Hutcheson and Smith claim, our innately benevolent and sympathetic constitution predisposes us to enter into the pains and delights of our fellow human beings, then why, in the *aesthetic* contemplation of pain (as in tragedy), do we take delight in suffering? Why do the woman's "sufferings add to her Charms?" Hume posed just this question to Adam Smith upon reading a draft of his *Theory of Moral Sentiments*: "It is always thought a difficult problem to account for the Pleasure, receiv'd from the Tears and Grief of Tragedy; which would not be the Case, if all Sympathy was agreeable ... You say expressly, *it is painful to go along with grief and we always enter into it with Reluctance*. It will probably be requisite for you to modify or explain this Sentiment, and reconcile it to your System."[40]

---

[40] Cited in Luigi Bagolini, "The Topicality of Adam Smith's Notions of Sympathy and Judicial Evaluations," in *Essays on Adam Smith*, eds. Andrew S. Skinner and Thomas Wilson (Oxford: Clarendon Press, 1975) pp. 102–103; n. 7. The date of the letter to Smith is 28 July, 1759.

Crito offers to solve the puzzle through a dissertation of not more than a few hours; and, despite Milesius' skeptical retort, "I should as soon think of dissecting a Rainbow as of forming grave and punctual notions of Beauty" (p. 5), Crito speaks without interruption through to the end of the dialogue. He begins by distinguishing between false and true beauty. False beauty has to do with custom. Crito's understanding of beauty will confine itself to "such [beauty] as is natural or real, and not such as is only national or customary . . . for I would not have you imagine that I would have anything to do with the beautiful thick lips of the good people of Bantom, or the excessive small Feet of the Ladies of Quality in China" (p. 110). Not that Crito has in mind some abstract conception of beauty (as in the priority Hutcheson assigns to squares over triangles because they contain more diversity in unity). His example of universal beauty will be specific to "visible Beauty; and of that to such only as may be called personal, or human Beauty." Here one will find a standard for agreement transcending the relative preference some have for thick lips, small feet, and the like.

Once the distinction between real and false beauty has been made, Crito divides the attributes of beauty into four categories: "Color, Form, Expression, and Grace. The Two former of which I should look upon as the Body, and the Two latter as the Soul, of Beauty" (p. 7). These divisions are actually drawn from Renaissance and seventeenth-century discussions of painting and sculpture.[41] The four heads are treated in order of ascending importance, and are exemplified at each point by a reference to female beauty.

The ideal color, we learn, is a mixture of red and white. The tint conveys a "natural liveliness" and the idea "of good Health." The basis for this ideal remains what it had been for Hutcheson, a measure of diversity (the darker tints – redness) blended into the harmony of an ordered whole (whiteness). The pleasure afforded by the synthesis helps explain why the sight of a beautiful woman in pain causes delight: the uniformity of a beautiful face (threatening to become only a white lifeless abstraction) is humanized (diversified) by the traces of red suffering, and although *she* is not aware of her greater appeal at that moment, the man of taste is. He has a preference for "Magdalens" in whom "you would see, by the humid Redness of the Skin, that she had been weeping extremely." Their grief gives the complexion a "Softness or Sulkiness."

"Form," continues Crito, "takes in the Turn of each Part, as well as the Symmetry of the whole Body" (p. 12). Here again, the determining principle is diversity held in unity. The word "turn" brings verbal action into nominative stasis. It applies to a curved or bent part of the body, so that one

---

[41] Spence refers to Felibien's *Entretiens sur les vies et sur les ouvrages des plus excellens peintres anciens et modernes*, 2nd edn., 2 vols. (Paris: Denys Mariette, 1696), and to Roger de Piles *Cours de peinture* (Paris: Jacques Estienne, 1708). This latter work ends with a chart ranking painters numerically on the basis of composition, design, colors, and expression.

can speak of the "turn of the arms." But it conveys also a sense of conscious artifice, as in reference to an artful "turn" in the argument. The turn of an arm or leg thus represents spontaneous action and self-conscious artifice simultaneously. The connoisseur who reflects upon the "turn" of this or that part has thus complimented himself with locating a material analogue to the contradictory demands of ideal beauty: motion brought to a stand, multiplicity brought into harmony. In a lengthy footnote added to this section, Spence sets down guidelines for evaluating the turn of the following body parts: head, forehead, hair, eyes, eyebrows, cheeks, ear, nose, mouth, teeth, chin, neck, skin, shoulders, arm, hand, fingers, bosom, sides, hips, legs, and feet.

Crito moves next from aspects of beauty pertaining to the body to those pertaining to the soul. "Expression" he defines as "the Expression of the Passions; the Turns and Changes of the Mind, so far as they are made visible to the Eye, by our Looks and Gestures." One's ability to interpret correctly these physical signs of invisible qualities (physiognomy) assumes the truth of the fundamental claim of aesthetic theology – that "all the tender and kind passions add to Beauty, and all the cruel and unkind ones add to deformity." Grace, the last of Spence's four categories, conveys the specifically religious aura of expression. While difficult to define, it is "the chief of all the constituent Parts of Beauty; and so much so, that it seems to be the only one that is absolutely and universally admired." Diversity in unity remains the determining principle of expression and grace. "There is no Grace without Motion," says Crito. And for this reason, grace is difficult to fix: "it steals from under the Eye of the Observer" (p. 29).

The difficulty in fixing grace raises a problem for Spence. Although he promises to discuss "personal, or human Beauty" as part of a larger ethical argument, his best examples of the sought-after beauty-effects occur, as one might expect, in the plastic arts. "In the pictured Angel, one has full Leisure to consider it [grace]; but in the living one, it would be too transient and changeable to be the Subject of any steady Observation ... It is on this Account that Grace is better to be studied in Corregio's, Guido's, and Raphael's Pictures, than in real Life" (p. 29). A science of beauty would appear, then, to draw the connoisseur further and further away from living subjects, whose existence in history, whose ever changing minds and bodies, resist any static idealization.[42] But Spence wants his scale for beauty to apply to living subjects, just as he retains the connection between aesthetics and ethics.

Therefore, he needs live human contestants. Spence superimposes the mechanical scale previous critics used to evaluate paintings and sculpture

---

[42] Spence argues, however, that statues move: "the most graceful Statue in the World (the Apollo Belvedere) is so much so [in motion], that when one faces it at a little Distance, one is almost apt to imagine, that he is actually going to move on towards you" (p. 36).

over the living bodies of known women. Out of a serious philosophical dialogue on beauty is born the modern beauty contest. "Now, I should think, that a Scale might be settled in the same manner [as de Piles], by which one might judge tolerably well of the proportional excellence in any of our most celebrated beauties" (p. 50). In this scale, Spence allows a maximum of ten points to color, twenty to shape, thirty to expression and forty to grace. The weighting system thus preserves the theological component within quantitative analysis by assigning seventy points out of a possible hundred to factors influenced by the soul. With great assurance (and no interruption from his friends), Crito then proceeds to rate "particular Ladies":

I should assign to Lady B * * * Eight for Color, Four for Shape, Twenty-Five for Expression, and Ten for Grace; in all Forty-seven; not quite half-way in the complete Sum of Excellence: – To Mrs. A * * *, Eight for Color, Seventeen for Shape, Fifteen for Expression, and Twenty for Grace; in all, Sixty Degrees of Excellence: –And to Mrs. B * * *, Eight for Color, Ten for Shape, Twenty-five for Grace; in all Seventy-three. And that is the highest Sum, that I could in Conscience allow to any Woman that I have ever seen.   (p. 44)

The assignation of numbers to bodies constitutes a kind of symbolic violence that justifies, in turn, more direct forms of violence, when bodies and spirits turn out to be resistent to the grid. But it is worth remembering that the philosophical justification for this violent inscription arises within a body of thinkers (the moral sense school) that asserts an essentially sociable, benevolent view of human nature. We would not share an innate love of beauty (verified by the contest itself) were there no inner predilection to love virtue, order, proportion, fitness, and the like. The calculus of beauty makes it clear that although a small coterie of gentlemen fix a standard of taste, they judge disinterestedly and establish norms valid for humanity in the widest sense. The eighteenth-century rating system confirms the distinction between natural and merely national concepts of beauty. It permits the refined judges who possess knowledge of the perfect one hundred then to make the political turn, descending the Platonic ladder to pass judgment upon all lesser forms.[43]

Because beauty is, finally, an intellectual ideal, those who possess the standard (the male panel of judges) are *always beautiful*, regardless of their age or physical appearance. Those, on the other hand, who provide the objective

---

[43] By the early nineteenth century the science of beauty will be detached from concepts of sympathy, the moral sense, innate benevolence, and the like in order to supply a rationale for frankly imperialistic and xenophobic policies. Alexander Walker's *Beauty: Illustrated Chiefly by an Analysis and Classification of Women* (London: Effingham Wilson, Royal Exchange, 1836) uses the premise of uniform response to beauty to construct what the author calls an "anthropological science in modern times." According to his "science," "in the case of the African, he is born whitish, like the European, but he speedily loses such beauty for that of adaptation, by his color, to the hot climate in which he exists ... The climate of Africa, the cerebral structure of its inhabitants, and the degree of their civilization are as unfavourable to the existence of beauty, as to the power of judging respecting it" (p. 199).

examples of physical beauty are beautiful only so long as their bodies, like
their faces, express the ideal balance between change and permanence. It
becomes painfully clear in Spence that the beautiful woman cannot serve as
both enlightened intellect and attractive body: the one must be sacrificed for
the sake of the other. When, for instance, Crito seeks to explain how any
scale of beauty could apply to living beings who are constantly changing (i.e.
ageing), he must add the stipulation that the ideal of beauty refers only to the
briefest moment in a woman's lifetime. Just as each component part of
beauty is governed by the principle of diversity held in unity, so female
beauty as a whole stands at its highest verge when change (mortality) and
permanence (immortality) reach a fragile moment of equilibrium. It follows,
for Spence, that a woman is most beautiful when her body first suggests a
readiness for procreation, but before pubescence can degenerate into
womanhood. A woman should be, like Denham's Thames, "without
o'erflowing full," or, like Fielding's Fanny, "so plump that she seemed
bursting through her tight stays, especially in the part which confined her
swelling breasts."[44] The peak of female beauty must be shortlived, the
ripeness all:

It might sound odd to you, if I should say, that a Woman is like a Pineapple; yet the
Similitude would hold much farther, and in more Particulars, than anyone would at
first imagine. She has her Season of growing to her greatest State of Beauty, of
Continuance in it, and of a Decay from it, as well as that; and the highest Season of
their Beauty is just as properly timed in the one Case, as in the other.   (p. 43)

The similitude becomes more apt than Spence could possibly wish, assuming
that, like all aesthetic theologians, he wants to keep the metaphor of "taste"
from becoming re-entangled in the cluster of terms evoking salivation,
mastication, swallowing. We draw a habitual connection between the
appearance of a pineapple of a certain hue and the deliciousness of its ripe
fruit. Salivation assures us of a bridge between stimulus and response, cause
and effect, the same for all. Similarly, the appearance of a woman of a certain
age, showing traces of childhood but a readiness (as the man imagines it) for
intercourse (of course for the purpose of procreation), evokes the equivalent
of salivation in the male. Sensual arousal becomes the bridge between
stimulus and response. Within this aestheticized short-circuit, transcendence
is being nudged out of the picture: sublimation of desire has been replaced by
its gratification. It becomes increasingly difficult to hear the connoisseur's
definition of grace – "a certain Deliciousness that almost always lives about
the Mouth" (p. 29) – in quite the sense he intends it.

    The only way to uphold the philosophical and theological relevance of the
similitude between women and pineapples is to claim that Spence has
identified the standard of beauty with a standard of utility (the woman is most

[44] Fielding, *Joseph Andrews*, p. 128.

beautiful when most useful to the man). But this position, apart from being anathema to aesthetic theologians such as Hutcheson, is refuted in the conclusion of Crito's own dialogue. After going to such great trouble to prove through the beauty contest that a single standard can be used to evaluate different women, and after linking this standard to the utility of procreative need, Crito acknowledges that "there would be nothing more wanting than this universal right judgment of Beauty, to render the whole world one continued scene of blood and misery" (p. 59). Utility now demands a great diversity of tastes for beauty in order to keep men from killing each other over a single Helen. Spence arrives at a conclusion diametrically opposed to his own thesis: "there is an Infinity of Tastes, and consequently an Infinity of Beauty ... In short, the most opposite Things imaginable may each be looked upon as beautiful in whole different Countries or by different People, in the same Country" (p. 54). Back come fat lips and small feet.

If Crito retracts his thesis, what then becomes of the opening description of the woman in tears, which set the whole thing going? Might it not be that Crito is right about the scene exerting an irresistible fascination (at least on him), but wrong about the source of his delight in suffering? What is the voyeur feeling as he stares at suffering beauty from a distance; what causes his disinterested pleasure when he first perceives her shame, after she turns towards the door and is shocked to find her grief has become a spectacle for a man peering through the crack? Might not a better explanation (better than the mixture of white and red in her face) be that he enjoys watching her pain because aesthetic detachment constitutes an experience of sudden power?

Mid-century dialogues fixing a standard of taste or beauty become self-parodying once their intended plots – schemes of ascent from matter to spirit – suffer an embarrassing reversal. The dialogue ends up telling us more about Crito's voyeuristic tendencies and his preference for young girls than about the universal standard of beauty. Although no character interrupts Crito's speech, his anticipation of a skeptical listener leads him to identify beauty with what he takes to be a more and more immediate stimulus triggering a less and less rational response. An aesthetic short-circuit results, whereby consensus has only become possible through appeal to the lowest drives and desires. There is no question here of endorsing such an inversion, but only of observing that in an important sense the Platonic dialogue on beauty finds its culmination in the Marquis de Sade's *Philosophy in the Bedroom* (composed of seven dialogues). In Sade the high-minded search for objective phenomena provoking uniform response will turn to physical stimulants that trigger involuntary shame and arousal. The bridge between the eighteenth-century Plato and Sade is supplied by Benjamin Buckler's *A Philosophical Dialogue concerning Decency* (1751), a work that hovers indeterminately between unwitting and conscious parody.

In this dialogue three characters, Philoprepon, Eutrapelus, and the narrator take a walk together before supper. The narrator tells us he was "seiz'd upon an open down, where there is a publick road, with the gripes attended with a necessity of going to stool. Oh these horrid gripes! (said I) they plague me every day of my life. I wish I was now at home; that I might ease myself in the neat apartment I have lately made in my garden."[45] He apologizes for having to relieve himself in public, and, after assuring his comrades that *nihil violentum est diuturnum*, separates himself some distance from them. Seeing that their friend has taken pains to hide himself, Philoprepon and Eutrapelus begin a philosophical disquisition on shame. Philoprepon asks Eutrapelus, "Don't you think *decency* is founded in nature? And don't you observe that there is a desire in almost every one of retiring from company to do several things, which are not only lawful, but necessary? which desire seems to me to be a natural instinct or (perhaps to speak more properly) a dictate of nature, and the shame of doing such things in publick, or before other persons is a natural shame, what nature and reason produce in us?" (p. 4). When the narrator returns, Philoprepon thanks him, "your accident, Sir, has almost led Eutrapelus and me into a philosophical dispute."

Almost is not the word. The discussion continues in earnest with extensive citations of classical and early Christian writings, for twenty-two pages, and is followed by Benjamin Buckler's *magnum opus* "A Critical and Historical Dissertation on Places of Retirement for Necessary Occasions, Together with an Account of the Vessels and Utensils in Use among the Ancients ... " Buckler's use of the dialogue to advertise his scholarly work makes it doubtful that he meant his *Philosophical Dialogue concerning Decency* as a parody. Yet in identifying the universal norm of response with the shame we feel defecating in public, Buckler exposes the contradictions implicit in the revival of Plato for aesthetic theology. In an increasingly skeptical age, the desired move to transcendence by means of the material sign (female beauty) situates transcendence increasingly within the material sign. In a positive sense, the solution revives allegory by re-enchanting nature; in a negative sense, however, the identification of transcendence with the image threatens to degrade transcendence by making the image its own end, which is to say, by creating a fetishized object of worship (the perfect Helen). Worse still, the requirement of an assured uniformity of response will call for an image more and more powerful in its imagined effects: beauty gives way to the sublime, the sublime gives way to an eroticized gothic, the gothic gives way to the

---

[45] Buckler, *A Philosophical Dialogue concerning Decency* (London: James Fletcher, 1751), p. 3. Subsequent references will be given by page number in my text. There exists some doubt about the authorship of this dialogue. It is assigned to Buckler on the strength of his having written the *Critical and Historical Dissertation on Places of Retirement for necessary Occasions*, for which *A Philosophical Dialogue concerning Decency* serves as a preface.

decadent, the decadent to death. We end with a polite philosophical dialogue on shit and shame.

Platonism and decadence

However significant the revival of Platonism may be for the cultural history of mid-eighteenth-century England, its textual embodiment occurs in works now considered minor.[46] Intellectual and literary historians have not had much to say about the "tribe" of writers translating and imitating Plato in the middle of the eighteenth century. Even at the time, moreover, efforts were underway to bury the embarrassments discussed above. Friends and foes of philosophical aesthetics viewed the Platonic imitations as symptoms of cultural decadence.

Richard Hurd was alert to the danger that decadent works pose to high culture:

But when this humour of platonizing seizes on some minuter spirit, bent on ennobling a trivial matter, and all over-run with academic delicacy and affectation, nothing, to a just and manly relish, can be more disgusting ... There is no need, in such a crowd of instances, to point to particulars. What I would rather observe is, that this folly, offensive as it is, may perhaps admit of some excuse from the present state of our literature ... When a language, as ours at this time, hath been much polished, and enriched with perfect models of style in almost every way, it is in the order of things that the next step should be to a vicious affectation. For the simplicity of true taste, under these circumstances, grows insipid. Something better than the best must be aimed at; and the reader's languid appetite raised by the provocatives of an ambitious refinement.[47]

Hurd would rather attribute the fault of the Platonizing imitations to lack of literary talent than to their fundamental positions because he shares those positions. His literary values are even more Platonic than Plato's, for while Plato doubted that poetry could move beyond appearance to truth, Hurd makes art the primary embodiment of the ideal: "For by abstracting from existences all that peculiarly respects and discriminates the individual," Hurd writes, "the poet's conception, as it were neglecting the intermediate particular objects, catches, as far as may be, and reflects the divine archetypal idea, and so becomes itself the copy or image of truth."[48]

According to Hurd, English culture in its Augustan moment has already perfected the art of refined abstraction. The imitations of Plato belabor what has already been accomplished; they try to better the best, and the result is

---

[46] As careful a historian as Pat Rogers concludes that English "literature before the time of Blake ... scarcely makes a nod at Platonism." *Platonism and the English Imagination*, eds. Anna Baldwin and Sarah Hutton (Cambridge: Cambridge University Press, 1994), p. 184.

[47] Hurd, *Notes on the Art of Poetry*, in *Epistolae ad Pisones et Augustum*, I, p. 251.

[48] *Ibid.*, p. 254.

overrefinement, insipidness, affectation, failure. It is therefore not necessary in 1776 to single out any one dialogue for criticism. I suspect, however, that what Hurd actually objects to is the tendency of these works to literalize the conceptual process by which particularized characters undergo abstraction in the name of the absolute. He would prefer not to discuss any dialogue in particular because its faults would also have to be his, if he were ever to become more explicit, that is, more vivid, about what justifies the poet or moralist in "abstracting from existences all that peculiarly respects and discriminates the individual." Does not Spence's beauty contest provide a concrete fulfillment of the process whereby all that respects and discriminates the individual is judged by "the divine archetypal idea, and so becomes itself the copy or image" of this same ideal? "The poet's conception, as it were neglecting the intermediate particular objects, catches, as far as may be, and reflects ... " But reflects what? What does it catch and reflect once the "intermediate particular objects have been removed"? I stop Hurd in mid-sentence in order to suggest that he, too, has the Platonic itinerary in mind. The problem with the Platonic imitators for him is not so much that they are decadent, but that their fictional representations are too explicit about what must be trimmed or lopped from existence – the intermediate particular objects – to guarantee the upward flight. We would need talking statues – or statutes talking.

Hurd attacks the Platonic dialogues because he is a friend to Platonism. Other writers, who are by no means friends to Platonism, will again set dialogue against dialogue, attempting to subvert both the leading arguments of aesthetic theology and the vestiges of an idealized concept of representation. If late Platonic dialogues on beauty attempt to preserve a fundamentally allegorical approach to mimesis, anti-Platonic, anti-aesthetic dialogues establish the conceptual basis for a mode of representation we now call "novelistic."

7

Anti-Platonism and the novelistic character

If we would know the World, we must look into it. You take no Delight in the Occurrences of low Life; but if we always remain among Persons of Quality, and extend our Enquiries no farther, the Transactions will not furnish us with a sufficient Knowledge of every thing that belongs to our Nature.

Bernard Mandeville, *Fable of the Bees, Part II*

Hold up, for a moment, the mirror of experience to this metaphysical phantom, and it shrinks into the nothing from whence it sprung.

Allan Ramsay, *A Dialogue on Taste*

Allan Ramsay's *A Dialogue on Taste*: from the beauty contest to formal realism

The first sustained critique in English of what came to be known as philosophical aesthetics is Allan Ramsay's *A Dialogue on Taste* (1755). Ramsay, a friend of Hume's and fellow Scotsman, turns an anti-aesthetic interpretation of dialogue against late Platonists such as Hutcheson, Stubbes, and Spence, just as Hume had turned an anti-metaphysical interpretation of dialogue against the Christian Neoplatonism of Shaftesbury and Berkeley.[1] As one might expect, Ramsay's attack strikes at both the conceptual underpinnings of early aesthetics and the compositional practices that support them. While textual embodiments of early aesthetics seek to restore allegorical modes of interpretation, eighteenth-century critics of the aesthetic counter by defending approaches to representation we now call novelistic. Their anti-Platonism provides a basis for understanding the development of the novelistic character.

Early in Ramsay's *A Dialogue on Taste*, the central character, Colonel

---

[1] See Alastair Smart, *Allan Ramsay: Painter, Essayist, and Man of the Enlightenment* (New Haven and London: Yale University Press, 1992), pp. 139–149. "It [is] more than probable that Ramsay's *Dialogue* and Hume's own essay *Of the Standard of Taste* (published two years later) have a common origin in conversations between the two friends in Edinburgh during the painter's long visit there in 1754" (p. 139).

Freeman (quite possibly modeled on Hume himself), tells his companions about an encounter he recently had with the author of *Crito, or a Dialogue on Beauty*:[2]

Col. Freeman: I happened to be walking in the Mall with Sir Harry Beaumont [Spence], about a week after Crito was published, when Sir Roger came up to us, and, after congratulating his brother Baronet upon the success of his performance, and the figure it was like to give him in the eyes of the Misses, as an arbiter of beauty, Sir Harry, says he, I observe that in your distribution of grace you give twenty degrees to Mrs. A * * *, and thirty to Mrs. B * * *. Now I do not find fault with your tables, but I should be glad to know by what scale, weight, or measure you compute their several shares with so much precision. You certainly, answered Sir Harry, did not read my paper with much attention, or else you would have seen that I did not pretend to have made my calculations exactly; but rather to point out what might be done by more exact judges of beauty. Ay, but, Sir Harry, says the old Knight, let who will calculate those tables of beauty, it will have but a very unscholarlike appearance, if, when the exactness of their calculations happens to be called into question, they should have nothing better to appeal to, than the infallibility of their own judgments. I am afraid that method would hardly pass muster at the Royal Society.[3]

By framing this attack in a dialogue within dialogue, Ramsay in effect reimagines the dialogue on aesthetic judgment as one in which the skeptic, virtually absent in Stubbes and quickly silenced in Spence, gains the leading voice. Within this competing interpretation, the attempt to combine scientific and religious vocabularies, to provide a calculus of beauty, becomes self-parodying. By what precise formula has the extent of grace in a face been determined? To what criterion did the judge of beauty appeal beyond his own whim? Freeman offers to help Beaumont with his figures:

I have ... been thinking that the rule of three or rule of proportion, might be applied so as to become a golden rule in comparing beauties as much as any thing else. It is performed, you know, by multiplying the first by the second, and dividing by the third; and being curious this morning to know with exactness how much Mrs. D * * * excelled in beauty Mrs. C * * *, I thus stated the question, as a cat is to a wheelbarrow, so is Mrs. C * * * to Mrs. D * * *; but though I tried till my brain was ready to crack, I could never contrive how to multiply a cat by a wheelbarrow ... Now if you, or any other virtuoso, could fall upon the method of multiplying and dividing such matters; I am persuaded you ... would prevent it [the judgment of beauty] from being any longer left, as you justly complain, to the particular whim of ignorant people.   (p. 31)

Borrowing a page from Swift, Ramsay eagerly takes over the project of

---

[2] *Ibid.*, p. 139. "It may not be inconsequential that some years earlier [than the publication of Ramsay's *Dialogue*] Hume had been attached to General St Clair's military mission to Vienna and Turin, when, to his friends' amusement, he had worn a kind of uniform."

[3] Allan Ramsay, *A Dialogue on Taste*, 2nd edn. (London, 1762), pp. 30–31. The first edition appeared in *The Investigator*, no. 322 (London: A. Millar, 1755). Subsequent citations refer to the 2nd edn. and will be given by page numbers in my text.

quantifying beauty, suggesting improvements of his own. The "rule of three" (or law of averages) is not an arbitrary contribution. Although Freeman's mention of the rule in this context probably draws upon the notorious difficulty and murkiness involved in applying the formula, the mockery is also more pointed. For something like that calculation is involved in Spence's attempt to derive the ideal of female beauty through comparisons of known beauties. If we can determine by how much Mrs. D excells Mrs. C in beauty, then it must be possible to compute the unknown value, the third term or perfect one-hundred, in light of which the comparison has been carried out. Spence, Hutcheson, and all of early aesthetics apply versions of the rule of three in their derivations of a standard of taste. For the rule of three also provides the logical basis for the Platonic itinerary from beauties to Beauty, matter to spirit, appearance to reality. It is the dialectical key to abstraction.

Ramsay's parody of Spence goes beyond his local objection to the absurdities of the beauty contest and ridicules the structure of metaphysics itself. The consolidating mirror of Christian Neoplatonism transforms two into one. Its mechanism, which I have referred to variously as a comedic or transcendental dialectic, requires a third term mediating temporal differences. But in Ramsay the mechanism of dialectic fails in the absence of any stable basis of comparison between Mrs. C * * * and Mrs. D * * * yielding knowledge of the divine whatness making the concord of discords, the ranking of unrankables, possible. Freeman's inability to locate the third term implies that the flux of faces cannot be averaged – there is no way to multiply a cat by a wheelbarrow or the beauty of Mrs. A * * * by the beauty of Mrs. D * * * because they belong to non-intersecting sets.[4] Freeman's conclusion, that "there is no standard of female beauty, to which all the various degrees of it may be referred" (p. 21), turns our attention to the mundane, political interests served by cultural events like the beauty contest. Ramsay's philosophical dialogue on taste, while parodying a more allegorical (beautiful) interpretation of the genre, becomes a sociological critique of distinction, in many ways worthy of Bourdieu.

The dialogue occurs at Lord Modish's country seat among Lord Modish, his wife Lady Modish, Lady Harriot (probably Lady Modish's sister), and Colonel Freeman. The main figures in the debate are Colonel Freeman, a free-thinker critical of aesthetic theology, and Lord Modish, apparently a new convert to the "modish" science of taste. The dialogue begins *in medias res*. Lord Modish asks Freeman if it's really true that he prefers Hudibras to Virgil. When Freeman affirms his preference ("he gives me most pleasure"), Modish replies, "Then allow me to tell you, George, you are with all your reading an absolute Goth, and have no manner of taste" (p. 4). The night

---

[4] As Smart notes, Ramsay's own practice as one of the most gifted painters of his age emphasized particularity over abstraction and therefore opposed the aesthetic Platonism underlying Reynolds' defense of the "Grand Style."

before Modish had admonished Freeman for preferring "Canary to Champaign." Freeman reminds Modish of this, hoping the Lord will agree there is a similarity of cases. When Modish does assent, Freeman adds,

I agree with your Lordship that the cases are very parallel, and for that reason I mention your last night's observation. The word *taste* originally belongs to the palate, and it is not amiss to have that always in view, when we suspect a misapplication of it in the way of metaphor ... But allow me to ask your Lordship, why you said I had no taste in wine, when it was plain, by my preference of one of the bottles, that I could very well distinguish it from the rest.   (p. 4)

Modish complains of being misunderstood, since he meant taste not as the capacity to make distinctions pure and simple but to form value judgments of better and worse. Freeman points out that this application of the term, though fashionable, "deviates from its original and proper sense" (p. 5).

Freeman suspects that Lord Modish has adopted the new discourse of taste because it allows him to equate his new wealth with something ancient and eternal. By adopting an antic disposition (preferring Canary to Champaign and Hudibras to Virgil), Freeman insists that statements of aesthetic value are either too subjective to legitimate social standing or so patently objective (salt tastes different from pepper) as to rule out valuation altogether (salt is not thereby better or worse than pepper). Freeman is being purposefully obtuse, for, by 1755, many suspect that taste has begun to supply a substitute theology. In aesthetic theology codes of conduct are based upon an assumed analogy between the exercise of good taste and virtue. But Freeman, speaking as Lord Modish's equal, refuses the analogy, ascribing Lord Modish's preferences to the whims of a rich landowner.

Throughout the dialogue the spontaneous progress of discussion turns the question of taste in directions Shaftesbury, Hutcheson, and all of aesthetic theology had tried to avoid. Taste is referred either to a bodily sense, with no analogy to higher operations, or to an explicitly political and violent imposition of value. Lord Modish understands that his adversary has not committed a *non sequitur* when Freeman responds to the claim that "the few should yield in the choice of liquor to the many" with these words: "For my part, I profess myself an entire friend to toleration and liberty of conscience, and think it little better than popery and inquisition to compel any man to swallow against his stomach, on pretence of preserving unity in public drinking" (pp. 7–8). Modish understands the quip as an explicit attack on Shaftesbury and the blurring of taste and conduct: "Then you don't allow the moral duties to be the objects of taste. My Lord Shaftesbury is of a very different opinion" (p. 9). Freeman answers: "That may be; but his Lordship stands not for divine authority with me. I know, my Lord, that there has been much unfortunate pains employed, by many authors from Plato down to Sir Harry Beaumont, in order to confound the objects of judgment with those of taste and feeling; than which nothing can be more vulgar and unphilosophical" (p. 9).

Ramsay described himself as an "absolute Whig," and although a Scotsman, he supported the Act of Union (1707).[5] How, then, should one explain his opposition to early aesthetics, which, as Bourdieu, Eagleton, Markley, Klein, and McKeon all hold, served the nascent interests of a new Whig hegemony and an emerging bourgeoisie? Freeman's reference to "many authors from Plato down to Sir Harry Beaumont" provides one clue: his attack is directed against Platonism (metaphysics), manifested most recently in the new cult of taste. His reasons for attacking Platonic metaphysics are probably manifold: as a Scot, he may oppose any formula that permits an abstract, idealized authority to rule over a passive citizenry lacking access to power (because lacking in "taste"); as an Enlightenment skeptic, he opposes the perpetuation of Church authority within the secular realm (that is, he resists a "state religion"); finally, as perhaps the finest portrait artist of his age, Ramsay understood the new discourse of taste to be a covert defense of the abstract and idealizing modes of representation that he opposed: against Reynold's contemporaneous return to Platonism through the "Grand Style," Ramsay developed a "natural style" that expressed the particularities of the individual. Whatever its motives, *A Dialogue on Taste* is remarkable in its heterodoxy. One of Ramsay's early readers, Giovanni Piranesi, called the work "an infinitude of botched-up calumnies."[6]

Like Hume, Ramsay uses philosophical dialogue to dislodge theology from what we now call the social or human sciences. In doing so he tries to distinguish rigorously between judgment and taste. When Modish asks Freeman what serves as the criterion for this distinction, Freeman replies, "Whatever has a rule or standard to which it may be referred, and is capable of comparison, is not the object of taste, but of reason and judgment. On the other hand, the proper objects of taste, or feeling, are such as are relative to the person only who is actuated by them, who is the sole judge whether those feelings be agreeable, or otherwise; and being informed of this simple fact from himself, no farther consequence can be drawn from it, neither does it admit of any dispute" (p. 10). The operative clause, Humean in tone and substance, is "no farther consequence." There are no larger political or religious conclusions (mandates) to be made on analogy with the preference one has for one object of taste over another. The fact that such consequences are routinely drawn – especially in the middle of the eighteenth century, when reason and judgment no longer seem capable of grounding ethical universals or traditional hierarchies of value – directs our attention back to the temporal interests served by disinterested pronouncements of taste. And

[5] Smart, *Allan Ramsay*, p. 8.   [6] *Ibid.*, p. 148.

that is precisely the direction in which Freeman takes his auditors, discussing one cultural icon after another, discounting each through historical analysis.

The dialogue turns from drinking to female beauty and from female beauty to architecture, sculpture, fashion, and literature. In each case, Freeman tries to convince his auditors that every standard for creating distinctions of value is contingent upon historical accident and local convenience. In Ramsay's hands the beauty contest becomes a history lesson, directed particularly to the women. When Lady Harriot asks Freeman to agree that "there are some women whom all the world allows to be handsome" (p. 13), he responds:

> let us suppose that two or three of these worthies [men of taste], who are by fate appointed to set fashions in our great city, should, from amongst five thousand young women, equally free of deformity, pick out Miss Thingum, at random, and toast her upon all occasions for a burning beauty. What will be the consequence? Those [men] who are an inch below them in fashionability, if you will allow me the word, will catch the sound, and convey it like the watch-word of a camp from the Generalissimo to the centinel [sic]. The machine being once set in motion, there is nothing to obstruct its progress ... Amongst the fools there is here and there one to be found, who will engage in the wise controversy, and will say, *Indeed I don't see anything so superlatively handsome in Miss Thingum, that there should be all this rout made about her*, but the greatest part of them are such poltroons as to be afraid of opposing the prevailing cry for fear of shewing their ignorance, always supposing beauty to be a science which it is incumbent upon every gentleman to understand ... As for the Ladies, tho' none of them can be supposed much smitten with Miss Thingum, yet they are all unanimous in allowing her to be handsome, and this from a very obvious motive. They all know that any hesitation from them would be ascribed to envy.   (p. 15)

This natural history of taste asks us to reread the cult of beauty in light of the contingencies of social empowerment and affectation. Central to the analysis is the arbitrariness of the entire process of value formation. Such arbitrariness turns our attention from the face of Miss Thingum and from any possible a priori faculty of aesthetic judgment to the social advantage (the utility) enjoyed by those men of taste who confer the prized ascription, and the reflected glory cast upon those lesser luminaries who echo the rumor. Freeman wants to transform pineapples into social critics.

When asked to acknowledge that at least in Greek sculpture one finds evidence of a universal criterion of Beauty, Freeman performs a similar anthropological analysis:

> No sooner were the arts of painting and sculpture brought to some degree of excellence, but the artists, in representing a Venus, an Helen, or any other personage, from whom beauty was expected, must have found all their endeavors to please rendered ineffectual by the variety of sentiments which different men, by the various structures of their nerves and organs, have of beauty ... Here necessity, the mother of invention, would come to his assistance, and set him upon a method that, although it

might charm few, would disgust no body; that is, to form a face that should affect a medium in all its features and proportions, carefully avoiding anything extraordinary.

(p. 24)

The ideal of Greek beauty is here redescribed as a necessary response to the irreducible variety of tastes among the buyers of sculptures and paintings. Unwilling to offend any, the artist tries to please all by seeking out the most mediocre expression: "all the antique statues now remaining ... by their great similarity, plainly appear to be all copies, more or less exact, of one original, framed upon this cautious principle" (pp. 24–25). That principle, formerly the artist's ability to copy the Platonic ideal of a pure intellectual beauty, now becomes the pure calculation of profit.

When, similarly, Lord Modish asks Freeman to acknowledge that "there are rules for the beauties in architecture" (p. 33), Freeman replies,

I should be exceedingly glad to hear a reason why a Corinthian capitol clapt upon its shaft upside down should not become, by custom, as pleasing a spectacle as in the manner it commonly stands ... The fashions in building, tho' more durable than those in dress, are not for that the less fashions, and are equally subject to change. As stones and bricks are more lasting than silk and velvet ... we must have recourse to history for the knowledge of those changes, which we can learn but very imperfectly from our own proper experience. In history we shall find that every nation received its mode of architecture from that nation which, in all other respects, was the highest in credit, riches, and general estimation ... To [the Chinese] the simplicity of the antique [style] would appear mean and rustic; and Convent-Garden church, the pride of English architecture, would be judged fitter for a barn than a temple.   (pp. 36–39)

Here again, a dialogue parodying an imitation of Plato makes change rather than permanence its central preoccupation. In place of a work whose plot seeks out greater and greater degrees of abstraction based upon a preliminary survey of empirical data, Ramsay writes a dialogue that moves in the other direction, towards a more and more detailed encounter with historical phenomena. The student of history attempts to recover those mundane connections between environmental influences, local customs, received traditions, and the manipulation of available material shaping social forms and preferences. Freeman's sociological analysis of taste can be understood as a rewriting of Hume's *Essay of the Standard of Taste* in light of his essay "Of the Idea of Necessary Connection"; that is, the quest for a uniform standard of judgment is being viewed as yet another attempt to impose a fiction of "necessary connection" in nature, when, in fact (according to Hume and Ramsay), all we ever perceive are habitual conjunctions of ideas (such as the link between a certain style of architecture and perfection).

Freeman's lectures about taste transform the pedagogical situation of Stubbes' *Dialogue on Beauty*. Although the male still educates the female, that education is now one of de-sublimation and de-idealization. Freeman seems aware that this lesson to the ladies may violate the decorum of conversation in mixed company. He apologizes after another extended speech, noting that this "Professorial kind of discourse ... will be little agreeable, I am afraid, to the Ladies" (p. 26). And then he adds, "Pray, Lady Modish, has your Ladyship seen the two new dancers that Rich has brought over." Lady Modish expresses anger at this interruption: "you ought to make us some apology for breaking off a serious conversation upon our account; as if we were incapable of being entertained by any thing but trifles. It is true we are seldom tried with anything else, but that is not so much our fault as that of you men; who think, no doubt, to preserve your authority the better by keeping us in ignorance" (p. 27). Lady Harriot seconds this complaint.

Freeman gladly accedes to their demand. He wants Lady Harriot to unmask pretenders to the throne of absolute authority by extrapolating from the example of Miss Thingum and Greek sculpture and architecture a larger guideline for reading all claims to transcendence. His watchword is not taste or beauty, but history:

Mankind upon many such occasions become their own dupes, and fall prostrate before the idols which themselves have set up; but history, Lady Harriot, and the investigation of facts will always enable us to set the true stamp upon such sublime pretensions. Whatever is natural is of divine origin, and the first source of it will be forever hid from our vain curiosity; but all sham claims to divinity are easily exposed, whenever the proper means are employed. Would you, for instance, be certified whether any particular race of Kings are by divine appointment, you need only trace their steps, and it is ten to one but you will find the first of them at the head of a gang of rebels, murderers, and banditti. (p. 16)

Historical method, not Platonic sublimation of desire, is now being presented as a means of liberating women from their secondary role in the discussion of taste. As students of history rather than objects in a beauty contest, the women preserve themselves from their own idealization into invisible spirits or typological characters. They learn that cultural norms such as the superiority of men over women reflect local customs, which may be criticized, mocked, and replaced.

This pedagogy drives Freeman towards an extreme skepticism that seems to leave little room for *any* ultimate value. Like Shaftesbury, Ramsay pays lip-service to "a divine origin" or "first source" even though his historicizing method would seem to do away with all such things. Aesthetic theology, as I have argued, was in large part an attempt to save rational Christianity from the implications of Enlightenment skepticism (radical empiricism, historicism). By mocking the beauty contest, Ramsay also attacks a surviving expression of Christian Neoplatonism in mid-eighteenth-century Britain. Freeman is now prepared to include even the new religion of taste in his list of topics explicable by means of historical narration:

For many ages had bishops and barons, monks and knights errant, kept the people of Europe in slavery and dissention, sloth, ignorance and misery. All the arts which tended to render life more humane and agreeable, were utterly discountenanced and forbid; and those alone kept up and practiced, which were of use in supporting the pride and power of those tyrants. Canon law to defend the worldly pretensions of church-men, and metaphysics to promote and defend their spiritual absurdities, for the same gainful purpose, were what passed currently by the name of learning. When these failed, in determining the truth or falsehood of a proposition, recourse was had, legally and cooly, to single combat; a kind of logic, absurd enough in all conscience, and yet not perhaps the most absurd kind then in use. Painting and sculpture were not yet found necessary to be called in aid of these holy cheats; so no man, as may well be supposed, presumed to carve or draw the resemblance of any thing upon earth.   (p. 44)

Freeman, like others of his day, describes aesthetics as a substitute theology. It arose when a metaphysically sanctioned religion was losing its hold over the people of Europe. Debates about art then replaced the duel in the panoply of persuasive devices. In 1744, Philip Skelton, a country vicar who twice sold his personal library to feed his parishioners in times of famine, offered a similar analysis: "Our great Folks, not liking the vulgar Religions, with which these Countries abound, as being both expensive and inconvenient, were on the point of renouncing all Religion, when his Lordship [Shaftesbury], who knew what they wanted, revealed to them the Religion of Taste ... This Religion sits easy, and breaks no Squares. It neither shocks nor offends. It neither hampers, nor restrains. It can never occasion either Disputes, or Wars. It distinguishes the polite Part of the World from the Vulgar, who cannot participate in it. But it may be, thou wilt ask me what it is? I tell thee again, It is Taste and good Breeding."[7] According to Freeman, the conflation of politics, theology, and aesthetics explains why those who set themselves up as arbiters of taste are often ready to second their preferences with a more direct exercise of violence. Freeman closes the dialogue with this point: "It has sometimes, too often, happened that in default of reasons, force, and terror have been applied, in order to produce an uniformity of thinking, and to render the taste and opinion of the strongest, the catholic, or universal. And then, woe! to the wretched sons of Adam!" (p. 76).[8]

[7] Skelton, *The Candid Reader: or a Modest, yet Unanswerable Apology for all BOOKS that ever Were, or possibly Can be Wrote* (Dublin, 1744; rprt. London: M. Cooper, 1744), p. 29.

[8] Again, Ramsay expresses a critique of the aesthetic that strikes us as peculiarly current; yet the basis for this critique was already evident through a careful reading of primary texts themselves. In Hutcheson's *Inquiry into the Original of our Ideas of Beauty and Virtue* (2nd corrected edn., 1726), the connection between aesthetic value and political utility had already been stated in explicit terms: the "ordinary Connexion in our Imagination, between external Grandeur, Regularity in Dress, Equipage, Retinue, Badges of Honour, and some moral Abilitys greater than ordinary ... may possibly be a great, if not the only Cause of what some count miraculous, viz. That Civil Governors of no greater Capacity than their Neighbours, by some inexpressible Awe, and Authority, quell the Spirits of the Vulgar, and keep them in subjection by such small Guards, as might easily be

Freeman turns the techniques of Enlightenment skepticism against the nascent discourse of aesthetics (which he takes to be a continuation of allegory and metaphysics). But here he faces the same sort of problem Shaftesbury confronted in *Characteristics*. Wielding a method of historicist analysis that potentially "annexes" *every* expression of artistic, political, or religious value to a mere custom or interest, the skeptic must decide how and when the dialectical engine should stop grounding up ideals and affirm something. Although Freeman adds a proviso here and there to fend off the charge of atheism – "whatever is natural is of divine origin," "it is the nature of all fashions (I except only those of a religious kind) to take their rise from the sovereign will and pleasure of the rich and powerful" (p. 34) – Lord Modish would seem to be entirely justified in accusing Freeman of uttering a "complication of heresies." Where, then, does Freeman's relativizing of values stop? As I suggested at the end of chapter 5, this question, which writers of metaphysical dialogue face reluctantly and writers of anti-metaphysical dialogues pose incessantly, becomes a paramount concern for novelists as different as Defoe, Fielding, Richardson, Sterne, Johnson, Burney, and Austen, who seek to recover a basis for ethics from the ruin of a metaphysically grounded theology. It is significant, then, that when Freeman attempts to answer this question towards the end of *A Dialogue on Taste*, he produces a defense of formal realism.

Freeman narrates this history of progress in the arts:

Soon after this importation [into England] of this Italian taste, the power and majesty of the Commons of England began to shew itself; and as the contests concerning the liberty and rights of Christians had introduced a spirit of inquiry into Europe, so that spirit was carried still further in England, by a new contest concerning the peculiar rights of Englishmen. Along with liberty all manner of property was farther ascertained ... At last the Revolution, by establishing the rights of the several orders of the commonwealth upon a clear and solid basis, made way for an entire dissolution of that alliance, which had been so stupidly and villainously cemented betwixt religion and politics. Metaphysics, now no longer necessary in support of opinions which were now no longer useful in the acquisition of power and riches, sunk by degrees into contempt; and Nature having at last shewn her true and beautiful face, poetry from acting the part of a magic lanthorn teeming with monsters and chimeras, resumed her genuine province, like the camera obscura, of reflecting the things that are.

(pp. 63–67)

Having projected the genealogy of a false aesthetic back into the Middle Ages, Freeman now narrates his preferred history of advancement in the arts and sciences, a history that conveniently bypasses the continuation of metaphysics (in the Platonic Revival) and the rejuvenation of allegory (in

---

conquer'd by those Associations which might be rais'd among the Disaffected, or Factious of any State" (p. 235). Here, beauty functions, as does the sublime in Burke, to create an "inexpressible Awe" and thus to "quell the Spirits" of the crowd.

Gothic romance and Spenserian imitations) taking place in Ramsay's own day. Freeman links progress with the rise of a middle class during the Commonwealth, with the extension of experimental philosophy to all fields of human endeavor after the founding of the Royal Society, with the moderation of individual freedom after the Restoration, when "liberty was tempered by a certain degree of fixed dependency," and with the establishment of "rights" after the revolutionary settlement of 1688.[9]

Political solutions having effected an "adjustment" between individual liberty and "a certain degree of fixed subordination" (p. 64), artists were left free to portray social life and nature in more realistic terms. Nature itself, as immediately perceived, without idealization or mythic overlay, will be art's standard. Holding mirror to mirror, Ramsay wants to replace allegorizing modes of representation with another device, the camera obscura, which allows the artist to trace representations of life in its complexity and materiality.[10] "Bring in one of your tenant's daughters," Freeman boasts, "and I will venture to lay a wager that she shall be struck with your picture by La Tour, and no less with the view of your seat by Lambert, and shall, fifty to one, express her approbation by saying they are *vastly natural*. When she has said this, she has shewn that she knew the proper standard, by which her approbation was to be directed, as much, at least, as she would have done, if she got Aristotle by heart and all of his commentators" (p. 57).

The reference to Aristotle is not superfluous; for Aristotle based his *Poetics* upon the view that all artistic expression, even forms as different as epic poetry and flute-playing, are modes of imitation. Taken literally, the emphasis on imitation implies that those arts are best that imitate observed reality most exactly, though this was not Aristotle's view. Nevertheless, according to Freeman, Aristotle's discussion of literary genres in terms of likeness to reality (probability) justifies the claim that the value he places

[9] Eight years earlier Nathaniel Lancaster, staunch defender of the new cult of taste, had narrated just the opposite history: taste was absent from England during the Commonwealth, as it will always be absent when the tastes of the multitude gain ascendency, but "when Monarchy was restored, Taste emerged from her Obscurity, and shone with some degree of Lustre." Nathaniel Lancaster, *The Pretty Gentleman: or Softness of Manners Vindicated from the false Ridicule exhibited under the Character of William Fribble, Esq.* (London: M. Cooper, 1747), p. 7. Lancaster's *Pretty Gentleman* was a response to David Garrick's *Miss in Her Teens*, a farce which Lancaster assumed to be aimed at his own ideas about taste, published the following year in his *Plan for an Essay Upon Delicacy, With a Specimen of the Work in Two Dialogues* (London: R. Dodsley, 1748). In his dialogue Lancaster defends the character of the delicate, refined men of taste. In the farce, Garrick's Fribble claims to be a member of that club, "all young Batchelors, the sweetest Society in the World; and we meet three times a Week ... invent Fashions for the Ladies, make models of 'em, and cut out Patterns in Paper." (London: J. and R. Tonson and S. Draper, 1747), pp. 20–21.

[10] The *Oxford English Dictionary* provides the following definition of the camera obscura, dating from the late seventeenth to early eighteenth century: "an instrument consisting of a darkened chamber or box, into which light is admitted through a double convex lens, forming an image of external objects on a surface of paper, glass, etc. placed at the focus of the lens."

upon formal realism is not a preference of taste but a determination of judgment. Because art imitates reality, a normative standard of excellence (accuracy of depiction) generates a concrete system of rules, which can be acquired by study, and put into practice for a useful purpose. While the critical standard, "the mathematical part" that forms an art (p. 55), may be known only to a few, the universal relevance of this standard can be determined through the simplest of tests: bring in one of your tenant's daughters.

Although Freeman establishes a classical precedent for his literalistic view of mimesis, the more relevant context is the contemporary struggle to define the nature of representation within genres (such as dialogue and romance) that hover between late allegory and new prose realism. Shaftesbury, Hutcheson, Johnson, and Hurd all believe that nature is most faithfully copied when its general properties, its universal truths are represented; they also cite ancient authority in support of this view; they fault the artist who takes as his or her model a too enlarged view of real life. Hurd describes "the kind of censure we pass upon the Flemish school of painting, which takes its model from real nature, and not, as the Italian, from the contemplative idea of beauty."[11] Shaftesbury, as we have seen, vacillates between two different views of mimesis. And in Hutcheson, Shaftesbury's great disciple, the yoking together of opposed concepts of imitation is yet more pronounced. Empirical observation leads Hutcheson to grant the existence of what he calls "relative Beauty," a kind of imitation "founded on a Conformity, or a kind of Unity between the Original and the Copy" (p. 35). The pleasure we take in comparing the artifice to the original is universal, according to Hutcheson. Thus, even the ugly might be beautiful: "It is not necessary that there be any Beauty in the Original; the Imitation of absolute Beauty may indeed in the whole make a more lovely Piece, and yet an exact Imitation shall still be beautiful, tho the Original were entirely Void of it" (p. 35). Nevertheless, Hutcheson's entire argument asserts a natural basis for a universalist ethics, which basis he locates in our uniform response to certain select representations of Beauty that acquaint us with the archetype of virtue. Thus, Hutcheson also stresses an "absolute Beauty," whose representation is simultaneously realistic and idealized.[12] In the generic terms through which all of these questions were being debated, Hutcheson's ultimate preference for "absolute" over "relative" beauty leads him to defend the prosopopoeia

---

[11] Hurd, *Notes to the Art of Poetry*, p. 253.

[12] As Peter Kivy has noted, Hutcheson, like Shaftesbury, advances two inconsistent views of representation. "It is an odd thing," writes Kivy, "to find a moralist encouraging the representation of the immoral in art. But this is exactly what we find Hutcheson doing in the name of greater realism." *The Seventh Sense: a Study of Francis Hutcheson's Aesthetics and its Influence in Eighteenth-Century Britain* (New York: Burt Franklin & Co., 1976), p. 104.

and not prose realism as expressing the highest purpose of art: "Upon this same [moral] sense is founded the Power of that great Beauty in Poetry, the Prosopopoeia, by which every Affection is made a Person; every natural Event, Cause, Object, is animated by moral Epithets. For we join the Contemplation of moral Circumstances and Qualitys, along with natural Objects, to increase their Beauty or Deformity; and we affect the Hearer in a more lively manner with the Affections describ'd, by representing them as Persons."[13]

Freeman's literalization of mimesis needs to be understood in terms of this split view of representation. Aesthetic theology attempts to reconcile two views of imitation as part of the larger claim that an accurate and inclusive survey of natural phenomena confirms our hope that providence has ordered things for the best. The great advantage of dialogue early in the century was that it was thought to offer just such a synthesis: while taking in an indiscriminate survey of natural phenomena (mimesis as exact, inclusive imitation), its magical mirror gave back the better image, nature improved (mimesis as a reflection informed by the beautiful). When Ramsay uses dialogue to attack dialogue, however, the contest to determine the true meaning of the genre leads the skeptic to drive a wedge between the two concepts of imitation. Freeman is relentless in his attack:

ask Bossu, or any of the rest of the Aristotelians, how the Severn came to be so hen-hearted, as to turn tail and hide itself, on the sight of Glendower's and Mortimer's bloody faces, he will tell you that it is by a figure called prosopopoia. This it is to understand Greek. A soundheaded, though less learned critick, would probably have said, that it was by a figure called nonsense.   (p. 72)

Freeman exaggerates the appeal of strict realism in order to emphasize an incommensurability between things as they are and things as they are seen through the lens of the beautiful. And he then politicizes the division, inverting the hierarchy of high and low genres by calling the best literature that which appeals immediately to common readers: "It is only middling poetry that the illiterate do not understand and admire; when it arrives at a supreme degree of excellence it is adapted to the lowest class" (p. 58).

Ramsay, like Philip Skelton, wages his campaign against aesthetic theology through a defense of common readers, untutored tastes, and low, miscellaneous genres. Skelton subtitles *The Candid Reader "a Modest, yet Unanswerable Apology for all BOOKS that ever Were, or possibly Can be Wrote."* He thinks democracy should prevail in the great fields of learning. Speaking for "the Poor, the Disappointed, the Discontented, the Whimsical Part of Mankind" (p. vi), Skelton would "vindicate Thy Taste against the impudent Attempts of a few, who would impose their Own upon Thee" (p. iii), a vindication carried out through a defense of every book ever written! "All Books being wrote, if I

<hr />

[13] Hutcheson, *An Inquiry into the Original of our Ideas of Beauty and Virtue*, p. 263.

mistake not, in order to Perusal.... and there being such an infinite Variety of Tastes and Capacities among Men, prodigious numbers would be excluded from the great and delectable Exercise of Reading, were it not for the plentiful Provision made, and laid in, by the Writers of past and present times" (p. 9).

By the middle of the eighteenth century, a native critique of the aesthetic had emerged in England, one which linked the discourse of taste to political and economic interests and to the attempt to establish and control a vernacular literary canon after the breakdown of Neoclassical hierarchies for ranking genres and individual works.[14] While the Platonists use dialogue to foster an escape from history – from the contingencies of character, setting, and time – Ramsay uses dialogue to escape the escape from history, to redirect philosophical inquiry to the socio-political contingencies that shape human values. His anti-Platonism entails an opposition to any revival of allegory, an opposition that introduces into philosophical commentary a defense of realistic prose fiction.

Mandeville's *Fable of the Bees, Part II*: from characters in dialogue to a dialogue on character

Ramsay's dialogic response to the mid-century Platonists repeats a strategy Mandeville had used against earlier manifestations of philosophical aesthetics in Shaftesbury's *Characteristics* and Hutcheson's *Inquiry*.[15] I have delayed discussion of Mandeville's *Fable of the Bees, Part II*, written entirely in dialogues, in order to group together those writers whose *anti-Platonism*, expressed through a rival interpretation of dialogue, offers both formal and philosophical rationale for the turn to prose fiction as the dominant genre of moral philosophy. Mandeville, like Hume, attacks his adversary on all fronts simultaneously. He views aesthetic theology as bad politics; and thus he mocks the tendency for aesthetic dialogues to exclude women and the poor from their field of representation. He views aesthetic theology as a false system of ethics; thus he interrogates an idealistic view of character and

---

[14] On the development of literary canons concurrent with the emergence of philosophical aesthetics, see Douglas Lane Patey, "The Eighteenth Century Invents the Canon," *Modern Language Studies* 18 (1988) 17–37.

[15] The first edition of Hutcheson's *Inquiry* was followed four years later in 1729 by Mandeville's second volume of *Fable of the Bees*, a work composed of six dialogues. Mandeville refers to the *Inquiry* by name in his Sixth Dialogue:

> Mr. Hutcheson, who wrote the *Inquiry into the Original of our Ideas of Beauty and Virtue*, seems to be very expert at weighing and measuring Quantities of Affection, Benevolence, &c. I wish that curious Metaphysician would give himself the Trouble, at his Leisure, to weigh two things separately: First, the real Love Men have for their Country, abstracted from Selfishness. Secondly, the Ambition they have, of being thought to act from that Love, tho' they feel none.
>
> . *The Fable of the Bees* II, pp. 345–346.

conduct. And he sees aesthetic theology as a false theory of art; thus, he exposes the split conception of mimesis that none of the eighteenth-century Platonists was able to reconcile. Broadening the field of representation, making character the center of philosophical analysis, and insisting upon realism in the depiction of social behavior, Mandeville wrote an imitation of classical dialogue whose purpose was once again to fail. The failure of philosophical dialogue provides the impetus for a contemporary theory of the rise of the novel.

As we have seen, women rarely participate in any of the major philosophical dialogues written during the eighteenth century. When they appear in the mid-century Platonists, they are likely to become objects in a beauty contest. Mandeville's first dialogue in *Fable of the Bees, Part II* turns incessantly to the status of women in discussions of beauty. In its parody of aesthetic theology, it dramatizes scenarios in which female characters who either hold the wrong view of mimesis or embody ugliness must be driven from the stage of philosophical representation before the search for truth can progress.

As the First Dialogue begins, the characters stand in a gallery and discuss the paintings on the walls. Cleomenes, Mandeville's spokesman who pretends to support Shaftesbury and Hutcheson, praises "that *Dutch* Piece of the Nativity," except for the fact that the "fool," its painter, had drawn "Hay and Straw and Cattle, and a Rack as well as a Manger: it is a Wonder he did not put the Bambino into the Manger" (p. 32). At this point Fulvia, a young woman of independent intelligence, speaks up in defense of the painting. "I have no Skill in Painting, but I can see whether things are drawn to the Life or not ... sure nothing in the World can be more like Nature." Cleomenes, still mimicking Shaftesbury, but sounding more and more like Wilde, responds:

Like Nature! So much the worse: Indeed, Cousin, it is easily seen that you have no Skill in Painting. It is not Nature, but agreeable Nature, *la belle Nature*, that is to be represented; all Things that are abject, low, pitiful and mean, are carefully to be avoided, and kept out of Sight; because to Men of the true Taste they are as offensive as Things that are shocking and really nasty.   (II, p. 33)

Mandeville writes a dialogue whose debate concerns the nature of representation and the representation of nature. The polite conversation about art barely conceals a more serious discussion of political participation: the female figure, traditionally excluded from the domain of male philosophical inquiry, complains that their view of mimesis leaves too much outside the legitimate frame of representation. By arguing for straw in the manger scene, she is, in effect, arguing for herself in learned discourse.

Once again, Mandeville uses dialogue not to portray a dialectical synthesis of particulars within a beautiful scheme, but to introduce the exceptions, the anomalies, into a social system modeled on the beautiful. Cleomenes goes on to praise a second depiction of the manger scene which includes "fine Architecture," "a noble Space," all of which "concur to express the majestic Grandeur of the Subject" (II, p. 33). Fulvia asks, "pray Cousin, has good Sense ever any share in the Judgment which your Men of Taste form about Pictures?" The question shocks Horatio, but Fulvia continues her objection, likening the transformation of a stable into a palace to the parodic metamorphosis in Swift's "Philemon and Baucis." When Horatio, the Shaftesbury stand-in, defends the representation of "vast Piles, stately Buildings, Roofs of uncommon Height," and so on, as a means "to raise Devotion and inspire Men with Veneration and Religious Awe" (II, p. 35), Fulvia responds, "I believe there is a Mechanical Way of raising Devotion in silly superstitious Creatures ... " Cleomenes interrupts her, insisting that she say no more in defense of low taste; and then he articulates the bland elitism Mandeville no doubt thought Shaftesbury and Hutcheson endorsed: "Great Masters don't paint for the common People, but for Persons of refin'd Understanding." Fulvia replies: "Why then is it pretended that Painting is an Imitation of Nature?" Both men say that imitation is always of nature "as we would wish it to be." And at this particular moment, the part of nature they wish to exclude is Fulvia herself. After Horatio's lengthy discourse on opera and the *ad hominem* charge that the woman's views on art are defective, Fulvia takes her leave: "I am convinced," she says, "of the Narrowness of my own Understanding, and am going to visit some Persons, with whom I shall be more on the Level" (II, p. 41).

Mandeville has thus placed one of the most telling critiques of the dominant eighteenth-century concept of mimesis in the mouth of a woman whose physical exclusion repeats on the dramatic level the force of her intellectual position – namely, that the "nature" the men of taste praise excludes everything disagreeable, including her.[16] Mandeville cannot be accused of subtlety on this point. In case the reader missed it the first time, he repeats the strategy, again with reference to another excluded female. As Cleomenes, still ventriloquizing Shaftesbury, explains his rule for how to judge "of Mens Actions by the lovely System of the Lord Shaftesbury, in a manner diametrically opposite to that of the *Fable of the Bees*," he raises the example of a "poor industrious Woman,"

who has pinched her Belly, and gone in Rags ... to save forty Shillings, part with her Money to put her Son at six Years of Age to a Chimney-sweeper; to judge of her charitably according to the System of the Social Virtues we must imagine, That though she never paid for the sweeping of a Chimney in her Life, she knows by Experience that for want of this necessary Cleanliness the broth has been often

---

[16] Richard Hurd provides a succinct statement of this view: "truth may be followed too closely in works of imitation ... the artist, when he would give a copy of nature, may confine himself too scrupulously to the exhibition of particulars, and so fail of representing the general idea of the kind." *Notes on the Art of Poetry*, in *Epistolae ad Pisones, et Augustum*, I, p. 253.

spoyl'd, ... and therefore to do good in her Generation ... she gives up her All, both Offspring and Estate ... and, free from Selfishness, sacrifices her only Son to the most wretched Employment for the Publick Welfare.   (II, p. 44)

Horatio responds:

You don't vy I see with Lord Shaftesbury, for Loftiness of Subjects.

To which Cleomenes answers:

When in a Starry Night with Amazement we behold the Glory of the Firmament, nothing is more obvious than that the Whole, the beautiful All, must be the Workmanship of one great Architect of Power and Wisdom stupendious; and it is evident that everything in the Universe is a constituent Part of one entire Fabrick.

Soot and silk. It is a cruel and telling juxtaposition, a jarring collision of the slum and the drawing room, the experience of a Moll Flanders and the discourse of a hereditary peer. Just as in Shaftesbury's *The Moralists* we found the opposition of two interpretations of dialogue marked by a point of silence, so here the Platonic and anti-Platonic, the aestheticizing and the materializing, the theological and the political strains of Enlightenment have resulted in a radical incommensurability of discourses. Allegory and prose realism stare at each other from a widening distance. The failure of dialogue to reconcile these oppositions (a failure Mandeville would identify as his success) repeats the failure of aesthetic theology to contain and order the diversity of social and natural phenomena.

As the passage indicates, the attempt to yoke the slum and the drawing room together under the sign of providence may yield a formula for reverse bathos but hardly a satisfactory justification of the ways of God to poor women. Horatio tries to dispense with the example: "Can anyone in his Senses imagine, that an indigent thoughtless Wretch, without Sense or Education, should ever act from generous Principles?" But Cleomenes corrects him: "Poor I told you the Woman was, and I won't insist upon her Education; but as for her being thoughtless and void of Sense, you'll give me leave to say that is an Aspersion, for which you have no manner of Foundation" (II, p. 47). He concludes: "if the Vulgar are to be all excluded from the Social Virtues, what Rule or Instruction shall the labouring Poor, which are by far the greatest Part of the Nation, have left to them to walk by, when the *Characteristicks* have made a jest of all reveal'd Religion, especially the Christian?"[17]

[17] As the reference to revealed religion indicates, Mandeville attacks aesthetic theology because it would deprive the High Church of supervisory capacity over the lower orders. Mandeville, who opposed charity schools, returns to the theme of his own greater piety again at the end of *Fable of the Bees, Part II*: Cleomenes assures Horatio that his [Mandeville's] doctrine "points indirectly at the Necessity, not only of Revelation and believing, but likewise of the Practice of Christianity, manifestly to be seen in Men's Lives" (II, p. 356). Shaftesbury, on the other hand, would "sap the foundation of all reveal'd Religion, with Design of establishing Heathen Virtue on the Ruins of Christianity" (II, p. 357).

In the First Dialogue of *Fable of the Bees*, the question of good and bad art
leads to an examination of portraits, but not the ones Horatio wanted to
evaluate. We have instead portraits of difficult characters, the woman of keen
intelligence and the indigent wretch. Horatio would like to exclude these
characters from philosophical dialogue, just as he wishes to ban overly
particularized details from the paintings. In the Second Dialogue the
apparently haphazard shift to a new topic actually stays on the same point,
only now discussion turns upon the nature of a seemingly less ambiguous
character, the refined, benevolent, sociable gentleman. As before, Horatio,
defending the moral sense theorists, hopes to show that this character offers a
model for others: he is motivated by an impartial love for beauty and society.
Cleomenes proposes that he be read differently.

"A Complete Gentleman," says Cleomenes, makes "a very handsome
Picture ... a very fine! A very godly Gentleman! Admirably good! How
entirely well hid are his greatest Imperfections! Tho' Money is his Idol, and
he is covetous in his Heart, yet his inward Avarice is forc'd to give way to
his outward Liberality, and an open Generosity shines through all his
Actions" (II, p. 63). Horatio objects to the transformation of the noble
character into a base *Caricatura*. Spurning Cleomenes' irony, he asks, "how
do you know a Foundation to be rotten that supports the Building, and is
wholly conceal'd from you? ... You must have a prodigious Sagacity in
detecting abstruse Matters beyond other Men" (II, pp. 64, 80). Cleomenes
hears the criticism as a question about interpretative method. He responds:
"You wonder, I know, which way I arrogate to my self such a superlative
Degree of Penetration, as to know an artful cunning Man better than he
does himself, and how I dare pretend to enter and look into a Heart, which
I have own'd to be completely well conceal'd from all the World; which in
strictness is an Impossibility and consequently not to be bragg'd of but by a
Coxcomb" (II, p. 80). His answer avoids the trap of simply replacing one
idealization of human nature (Shaftesbury's view of ultimate benevolence)
with its equally essential de-idealization (Hobbes' view of ultimate
depravity). Instead, Cleomenes sets the static portrait of the gentleman into
fictional motion, asking the reader to judge character based upon a plausible
sequence of thoughts and actions.

Suppose, Cleomenes says, this fine gentleman were to find himself insulted
by another gentleman "equal in Birth and Quality":

CLEO. Let this Adversary, *mal a propos*, grow warm, and seem to be wanting in the
    Respect that is due to the other, and reflect on his Honour in ambiguous Terms.
    What is your Client to do?
HOR. Immediately to ask for an Explanation.
CLEO. Which if the hot man disregards with Scorn, or flatly refuses to give,
    Satisfaction must be demanded, and tilt they must ...
HOR. Without a doubt such a thing may happen.   (II, pp. 81–82)

The portrait steps out of the frame and enters a fictional narrative. As soon as he is placed in a specific circumstance and confronted by a difficult choice, a means of interpreting character unfolds. The refined gentleman willing to fight a duel proves himself a deeply divided individual. Cleomenes asks Horatio this question about his hero:

CLEO. But what makes so just and prudent a Man, that has the Good of Society so much at Heart, act knowingly against the Laws of his Country?

HOR. The strict Obedience he pays to the Laws of Honour, which are superior to all others ...

CLEO. If the Gentleman I described was as sincere in his Religion, as he appear'd to be, he must have been of an Opinion contrary to yours; for Christians of all Persuasions are unanimous in allowing the Divine Laws to be far above all other; and that all other Considerations ought to give Way to them.

(II, pp. 82–83)

Horatio's response, "I am no Casuist: But ... " indicates the kind of analysis he thinks he is being asked to perform on the previously self-evident character of the polite gentleman. The only way Horatio will be able to vindicate his character is to locate those special circumstances that warrant the suspension of one set of ethical maxims (Christian) in favor of another (courtly-aristocratic). But as soon as he wades into the treacherous current of casuistry, he abandons the expectation that his hero can be understood as a pure type. To read character would be to understand the mind as a site of competing, often irreconcilable drives and interests.[18]

While defending *The Fable of the Bees*, Cleomenes tells Horatio that it contains "a plain Demonstration, that the same Passion may produce either a palpable Good or a palpable Evil in the same Person, according as Self-love and his Circumstances direct" (II, p. 124). In light of such complexity, interpretations of character will need to be based upon "reasoning from Facts, *a posteriori*" (II, p. 175). The same point arises in Ramsay's *A Dialogue on Taste*. Having historicized aesthetic theology, Ramsay leaves us either with absolute relativism or with a new standard for testing the value of characters and concepts. This new standard, if it can be called a standard, is the same as Mandeville's – utility. Given the conditions of a violent battlefield, Freeman notes, a sword will always be preferable to a pair of scissors, but "vary the circumstances of the intended combat, and explain that it is not to be fought in a field, but in a post chaise or a centry box [*sic*], and you will ... infallibly

---

[18] In *Defoe and Casuistry* (Princeton: Princeton University Press, 1971), G. A. Starr cites George Eliot's claim that "moral judgments must remain false and hollow, unless they are checked and enlightened by a perpetual reference to the special circumstances that mark the individual lot" (p. 1). He relates this view in particular to Defoe's use of dialogue in such works as *Religious Courtship* and *The Family Instructor*, the purpose of which was to temper didactic authority and to allow "a more inductive spirit to prevail" (p. 37). In *Fable of the Bees, Part II*, Mandeville shows how casuistry provides a way of reading character and conflict in the absence of any more "philosophical" or idealized criteria.

declare a pair of scissors to be a more fatal, and consequently a better, weapon than any Toledo in the world" (pp. 10–11).

Even if Horatio does not agree with Mandeville's hypothesis that the polite gentleman's motives can finally be reduced to self-interest, the move into casuistry opens the door to an equally damaging multifariousness in the hero's character. Cleomenes realizes that this topic leads in dangerous directions. Previously, he offered to abandon the point altogether. "I'll be satisfied with having given you some small Entertainment in the Description ... Pray let us do in this as we do in another matter of Importance, never touch upon it: Friends in Prudence should avoid all Subjects in which they are known essentially to differ ... Have you heard any thing from Gibraltar?" (II, pp. 72–73). Mandeville shifts the usual concern of metaphysical dialogue – theology and ethics – into a debate about the nature of human psychology. And then, coyly, Cleomenes offers to suspend discussion. Why character should take on this importance is already clear from the first dialogue: the entire system of benevolent, rational Christianity hinges upon how one interprets the character of the indigent woman. Is she a necessary shade in the predominantly beautiful tapestry of the social order? Or is she the exception that proves the rule, the requisite victim of a society built on principles of arbitrary hierarchy, misogyny, and unchecked greed? The analysis of the refined gentleman (elsewhere called a "Landlord" [II, p. 74]) presents the same question from the opposite end of the social scale. Here the politically relevant issue is phrased in terms of literary characterization; and the offhand reference to a concrete political event – the siege of Gibraltar by Spain in 1727–1728 – provides a distraction.

By bringing character to the center of philosophical dispute, Mandeville targets the conditions of possibility that had informed a metaphysical interpretation of dialogue. The expectation that characters typed according to their leading ideas will wage an intellectual duel leading to the hero's victory has been replaced by a dialogue investigating what it means to be a character. The duel is used not as a framing device for dialogue, but as a metaphor for mixed identity. In this respect, Mandeville, like Hume, attempts to write a failed dialogue. Dialogue cannot be an abstract contest of ideas producing knowledge because the bodies who hold those ideas constantly betray their lower motives for dwelling in abstraction. Character cannot be linked to a single defining idea (materialist versus immaterialist; theist versus atheist) because two different characters may hold the same idea for completely different reasons, and the same character may be torn by incommensurable interests.

As if to place a final exclamation point upon this elevation of mixed character over pure idea, Mandeville rigs things so that Horatio himself, the defender of an idealized view of character, turns out to be the very Christian gentleman who accepted the challenge to a duel!

CLEO. I saw you that very Morning, and you seem'd to be sedate and void of Passion: You could have no Concern.

HOR. It is silly to shew any at such Times; but I know best what I felt; the Struggle I had within was unspeakable.   (II, p. 84)

The advocate of unmixed character is forced to admit that his character is hopelessly mixed. No prosopopoeia or soliloquy will solve the contradiction; sound Christian and man of honor remain hopelessly at variance, a figure for an identity that remains non-identical with itself. "You have now a very fine Opportunity, Horatio, of looking into your Heart," says Cleomenes mouthing Shaftesbury. The self-examination will only confirm the view that people rarely, if ever, act from pure motives, but rather from a calculation of utility. "To speak without Disguise," concludes Cleomenes, "the Struggle in your Breast was between the Fear of Shame and the Fear of Death" (II, p. 92).

Almost two hundred years before Nietzsche, Mandeville constructs the philosophical sequence that culminates in an aphorism: "Behind all logic and its seeming sovereignty of movement, too, there stand valuations or, more clearly, physiological demands for the preservation of a certain type of life."[19] In Mandeville's dialogue, philosophical inquiry can go no further than character on philosophical grounds. Although Mandeville does not write a novel, his dialogue dismantles yet another of the structural features that *distinguished* the high, philosophical conception of dialogue from lower imitations of social converse. Mandeville writes a philosophical dialogue in which characters discuss the impossibility of behaving as they should were they characters in a respectable philosophical dialogue.

One of the best examples of the transformation I am describing here occurs in another dialogue from the middle of the eighteenth century, *Knowledge of the World, or Good Company* (1752).[20] In this work, A and B have just been speaking with a third character, probably an upwardly mobile tradesman, who has departed. The dialogue begins with A asking B, "What strange man, I beseech you, is this?" When B answers that the character is a man who possesses an "exquisite Knowledge of the World," A chooses to misunderstand B by hearing this appellation as a compliment. B, who claims to know more of the world than the philosopher, tries to explain why this new character has knowledge of the world but is not a philosopher. A spurns the suggestion that knowledge of the world could have an unphilosophical meaning:

[19] Nietzsche, *Beyond Good and Evil: Prelude to a Philosophy of the Future*, trans. Walter Kaufmann (New York: Vintage Books, 1966), p. 11.
[20] The dialogue was taken "from the MSS. of J. H. of S. in the County of W.," possibly a reference to James Harris. The work appears in James Harris, *Upon the Rise and Progress of Criticism* (New York: Garland Publishing Inc., 1971). Subsequent references to this work are given by page numbers in my text.

there must be some physics, some metaphysics, and previous to these dialectic and geometry. Add to this, if he [the man of the world] be really what you describe, he must not have contented himself with modern philosophers only; he must have examined and well weighed the several sentiments of antiquity; the watry principle of Thales; the fiery one of Heraclitus; the ideas of Plato; the matter, form, and privation of the Stagirite.

To which B can only respond,

My good friend, what are you talking about?   (p. 28)

The entire dialogue turns upon this misunderstanding and the paradox that, to the philosophical A, knowledge of the world imposes requirements that the tradesman with knowledge of the world does not meet. A pretends not to understand that people of fashion and birth define good company, that goodness is not a philosophical but rather a social construct. For his part, B wants A to give up his philosophical sophistries and to accept the common usage of the phrase "man of the world." A insists that B test such characters against a higher standard, provided by moral philosophy. Although their exchange leads to a long speech delivered by A on the true (philosophical, ancient) meanings of "knowledge" and "mankind," the dialogue actually stages a scene from the twilight of civic humanism:

B. Very fine, truly! – And so you really imagine that by a few trifling questions, and a little sophistical cavilling upon words, you have gained over your friend a complete logical triumph.
A. How well not long ago did I foretell my own fate? Did not I say that I should be arraigned for an idle sophist, a minute refiner upon verbal niceties?
B. And do you not justly deserve the character? Is the whole, you have been saying, at best anything more, than a contradiction to the common language of all mankind?
A. I never heard before that all mankind had a common language.
B. Why there again? – As if by mankind, I meant every human creature, now existing in the world. –
A. Existing in the world? – In what world?
B. Nay this is worse than ever – I am sure, if I had not more philosophy to bear being thus questioned, than you on your part have shewn in questioning, I should long ago not have vouchsafed you an answer.   (p. 36)

Philosophical dialogue has become a suspect mark of character, a mere rhetorical gesture identifying one who refuses to have commerce with the real world. For A, B's understanding of "the world" covers only "a three or four hundredth part" of the eight hundred thousand people supposed to populate the town of London. For B, A's unwillingness to acknowledge "the common language of all mankind" isolates him within an even smaller segment of humanity, the little band of minute philosophers who understand each other (perhaps) and no one else. The cultural and intellectual divisions that philosophical dialogue had been called upon to bridge – between the learned and fashionable worlds, between metaphysics and morals, between ancients and moderns – are now *exacerbated* by that very genre. Anger develops between the two friends, to the point where B tells A,

Only one thing, as a friend, 'tis proper I should tell you. Whatever you may fancy of your proofs and demonstrations, I'm not to be so readily refuted, as you think. You imagined, I dare say, I should have surrender'd by this time; have acknowledged my errors; have recognized your wisdom; have acted with due decorum *the under hero of a modern dialogue*, that thing of wood, set up for nothing else, than for another to shew his skill, by tipping of him down. But this, you may be satisfied, will never happen on my part.   (p. 41)

The character who should be converted to the views of the hero denies his role. Between the philosopher who will have no truck with humanity (ideas without character) and the man of the world who has run off in search of better distractions (character without ideas), commerce has ceased.

In metaphysical dialogue the fulfillment of the plot (closure, consensus) comes at the expense of character; in the comic novel (for example, *Tristram Shandy*), the investigation of character supersedes the plot. Between these extremes exists a group of philosophical dialogues (the focus of attention in this chapter) that are consciously elevating particularized characters at the expense of philosophical content; or, more precisely, the investigation of character *just is* their philosophical content. The philosophical quest shifts from the attempt to locate a standard of taste or beauty or judgment validating ethical and epistemological determinations to the problem of how one should judge oneself and other characters in the absence of any transcendental standard. The conclusion Berkeley arrived at reluctantly is asserted as a matter of principle within the anti-Platonic dialogues of Mandeville and Ramsay: "If we would know the World, we must look into it," says Mandeville's Cleomenes. "You take no Delight in the Occurrences of low Life; but if we always remain among Persons of Quality, and extend our Enquiries no farther, the Transactions will not furnish us with a sufficient Knowledge of every thing that belongs to our Nature."[21]

Mandeville and Ramsay provide a blueprint for a set of transformations characteristic of the developing novel. Each writes within the recognizable parameters of philosophical dialogue; yet for each, dialogue has become hopeless in its metaphysical aspirations, while strangely effective in directing the reader's attention to idiosyncrasies of character, conduct, and circumstance. It is this double movement – the rejection of metaphysics and an idealized conception of mimesis coupled with the affirmation of a mundane ethics focused upon realistic depictions of character and circumstance – that becomes definitive of the body of moral-didactic prose fictions we now group under the term "the novel."

---

[21] Mandeville, *Fable of the Bees, Part II*, p. 110.

8

Dead conversations: Richard Hurd's late poetics of dialogue

there was something . . . in the character of the writer imitated [Plato], of a very ticklish and dangerous nature; and of which our tribe of imitators were not sufficiently aware. A very exact critic of antiquity hath told us what it was. It lay in Plato's bringing the tumour of poetic composition into discourses of philosophy . . . And though the experiment, for the most part, succeeded not amiss (as what contradiction is there that superior genius cannot reconcile?) yet it sometimes failed even in his hands.[1]

Richard Hurd looks back in 1776 upon the works that have made up this history and sees nothing but disaster. The question no longer is whether one might imitate the best examples of the genre. Even the great Plato could not always succeed, and if he faltered, it is no wonder that moderns have failed outright. Hurd advises serious writers of philosophy (by which he also means theologians) to eradicate the tumor of poetic composition, just as he warns authors of drama to avoid serious philosophy, "lest a studied declamatory moral, affectedly introduced, or indulged to excess, should prejudice the natural exhibition of the characters, and so convert the image of human life into an unaffecting philosophical dialogue."[2]

Hurd has no interest in specifying just what it is about "poetic composition" that has proven toxic to philosophy. For such an analysis would also require him to explain why philosophy was not healthy enough to survive its amalgamation with poetry (by which he means mimetic representation). He leaves us to recall something about the eternal strife between philosophy and rhetoric, and to draw the right conclusion: for brief moments in Plato, and then less and less frequently as one nears Hurd's own day, poetry and philosophy merged. That merging, accurately described by Nietzsche in *The Birth of Tragedy*, involved the marriage of transcendental dialectic and rhetoric. But Hurd no longer believes in the comedic potential of dialogue.

---

[1] Hurd, *Epistolae ad Pisones, et Augustum*, I, 252. Other references to Hurd (apart from the "Preface" to *Moral and Political Dialogues*) refer to this text and will be given by volume number and page in footnotes.

[2] Hurd, *ibid.*, I, p. 260.

The purpose of Hurd's own intervention into the history of eighteenth-century dialogue is to set forth a "poetics" of the genre, rules to govern its correct conception and proper management. In his "Preface, On the Manner of Writing Dialogue," added to the fourth edition of *Moral and Political Dialogues* (1764), Hurd provides the most extensive critical analysis of the genre found during the eighteenth century. In Shaftesbury, discussions of dialogue were dispersed within letters, essays, and dialogues devoted to larger questions of moral philosophy, and this intertextuality supported Shaftesbury's view that dialogue was appropriate to a wide range of subject matter, including controversial religious questions. In Hurd, however, the analysis of dialogue occupies an independent preface, and the deployment of critical commentary devoted exclusively to dialogue accompanies the assertion that writers should restrict the scope of topics and the specificity with which they represent character. The appeal of dialogue – its conversational openness and familiarity, its engendering of a rhetorical community, its rendering dry lessons more palatable – cannot be indulged without restricting other aspects of the form that had been paramount during the first half of the eighteenth century: its survey of multiple viewpoints on serious religious and philosophical questions, its questioning of the motives behind abstract intellectual positions, its development of character even at the expense of argument. Ironically, an independent poetics of dialogue only emerges in unison with the claim that it has become necessary to restrict the conception and composition of the genre.

Genre and decorum: dialogue as polite conversation

Hurd begins his "Preface" with many of the commonplaces by now familiar to discussions of dialogue during the eighteenth century. It is strange, notes Hurd, that in an age teeming with writers, the form of dialogue has been "hitherto neglected" (p. viii); this fact is especially odd in light of the prestige the dialogue enjoyed among the ancients (pp. viii–xi). Then again, one is not so surprised by this neglect, given the tendency of modern writers to "reverence" themselves and their causes. For them the "direct way of Dissertation" (p. xi) remains the most suitable conduit for their inspired access to truth. It is, Hurd continues, nevertheless the case that although moderns have been sparing in dialogues, in actuality "we have what are called Dialogues in abundance" (pp. xx). These, however, are of an inferior stripe, since their characters are little more than puppets (p. xxiv).

It does not take long, however, for Hurd to come to the point. "I have thought fit," he writes,

to shew of what kind the subjects are which may be allowed to enter into modern Dialogue. They are only such, as are either, in the strict sense of the word, *not* important, and yet afford an ingenuous pleasure in the discussion of them; or not so important as to exclude the sceptical and inconclusive air, which the decorum of polite dialogue necessarily demands.   (p. xvi)

Hume's Pamphilus, we remember, had established dialogue's scope in a different way. Dialogue was appropriate to topics obvious and important, "where the vivacity of conversation may enforce the precept," and to topics "so *obscure* and *uncertain*, that human reason can reach no fixed determination with regard to [them]." Between the extremes of obviousness and obscurity, discussion of almost every topic might take place. Hurd, by contrast, confines dialogue to topics "either not important. . . or not so important" that the skeptical element within dialogue would threaten sacred truths.[3] The purpose of this delimitation of topic is clearly to exclude theology and metaphysics from discussion: "We should forbear to dispute some things because they are such as both for their sacredness, and certainty, no man in his senses affects to disbelieve" (p. xv).

Hurd restricts content not by fiat, but by the stratagem of linking an enigmatic form to the decorum of another genre deemed more stable. Whereas Shaftesbury vacillated between heroic drama and the miscellaneous essay as the form most relevant to the decorum of dialogue, Hurd has no doubt about the standard: polite conversation. At this point, a few words about the relation between genre and decorum are in order. Throughout the history of literary criticism, the concept of decorum has been used to establish distinctions among genres. Horace writes in *The Art of Poetry*, "The changing parts and tone of each kind of poetry have had their limits set ... A theme that belongs to comedy will not be set forth in the verses of tragedy. So too the supper of Thyestes disdains to be told in strains of common life which suit well enough the comic stock."[4] As a yardstick for literary performance, the statement imposes several requirements. It begins with the assumption that poetry should be evaluated in terms of the kinds of poems that have been written. At the same time, Horace acknowledges that the parts and styles of genres change. How then is it possible to evaluate a new work in terms of its genre, since every work is different in its parts? At first one suspects that limits are conventions assigned to genres by critics. The rule about not mixing tragedy and comedy would then derive from a conventional code of proper behavior assigned to each form by critics who seek to limit formal variety and

[3] An overview of the topics raised in Hurd's own dialogues conveys a sense of this middle range: his characters discuss sincerity versus accommodation as a principle for human conduct, the advantages and disadvantages of solitary retirement, whether life was better during the reign of Queen Elizabeth or in the present, the Constitution of English Government, and the advantages and disadvantages of foreign travel. These are the topics we were left with at the end of Hume's *Dialogues concerning Natural Religion* when Philo permitted rational dialogue "so long as we confine our speculations to trade, or morals, or politics, or criticism."

[4] Horace, *The Art of Poetry*, trans. E. C. Wickham, in *Critical Theory Since Plato*, ed. Hazard Adams (New York: Harcourt Brace Jovanovich, Inc., 1971), p. 69.

unpredictability. But then, with the vivid example of father Thyestes supping on his own sons, a stronger basis for limits becomes apparent. Not convention but an inherent law of propriety makes it wrong to describe that grisly scene in comic strains. Our very bodies revolt at such a possibility, just as Thyestes himself vomits upon learning that an invitation to dine has become something else. Thus, the genre distinction between tragedy and comedy must be nature's own. In this way, Horace grounds convention in nature. Decorum thus shifts our attention from the "changing parts and tone" of each genre, its specifically historical character, to the natural limits of form, a confirmation of inherent literary and social boundaries.

Critics have traditionally reinforced distinctions such as these through reference to Aristotle's *Poetics*. Aristotle also thought of poetry in terms of kinds, and throughout *Poetics* he gives rules for how kinds, especially tragedy, should be managed. In Aristotle, however, the relation between genre and decorum is complicated by two recognitions: first, that genres develop over time (they have histories); and second, that in the course of these histories, genres tend to accumulate artistic elements until the "natural" fulfillment of the genre is thought to be reached.[5] Taken together, these points minimize the applicability of decorum to genre. If decorum specifies proper distinctions among genres, how relevant will it be for works made up of many different genres? Do genres then have more than one decorum? If genres develop over time, frequently evolving from low, fragmentary, popular forms into highly complex, polite literary works, then the notion of decorum cannot designate a genre's nature, but instead only an interpretation of some stage in the genre's history (deemed its "completion" or final evolution).[6]

The difficulty of linking genre to a set decorum might lead one to question whether the relation between these is not in fact antithetical: to the degree that a genre appears to *resist* limits – to the extent it seems unruly, ill-mannered, unformed, subject to contradictory uses – the search for the genre's proper decorum will be all the more pronounced.[7] Hurd would not be so insistent upon establishing the decorum of philosophical dialogue, if the history of writers from Shaftesbury and Mandeville through Berkeley, Hume, and the "tribe" of Platonic imitators had not demonstrated the dangers of the

---

[5] For an illuminating discussion of the historicist elements in the *Poetics*, see Paul A. Cantor, "Aristotle and the History of Tragedy," in *Theoretical Issues in Literary History*, ed. David Perkins (Cambridge, MA: Harvard University Press, 1991), pp. 60–84.

[6] This discussion is based in part upon directions suggested in Rosalie Colie's *The Resources of Kind: Genre Theory in the Renaissance* (Berkeley: University of California Press, 1973). In that formative study, Colie evaluates the tradition of the *ars poeticae* from Aristotle through the Renaissance, not in order to identify the timeless properties of the genres ranked within them, but in order to assess how changes in the organization and description of generic hierarchies relate to cultural transformations: she has advanced what might be called a politics of poetics.

[7] Here again I would argue that the insistent Neoclassicism of much eighteenth-century criticism is not a sign of the prestige of ancient models, but just its opposite, an indication of the loss of classical authority in the early modern period.

form. In other words, although Hurd elaborates a natural connection between dialogue and polite conversation, it is only because he senses the relevance of other discursive models – farce, comic drama, academic debate, the encyclopedia, the novel – that he constructs a restrictive poetics of dialogue.

When Hurd attempts to understand why dialogue became such a dangerous form in the hands of its imitators (and even in the hands of Plato), he does not invoke the concept of decorum. Rather, he notes the presence of potentially irreconcilable elements (philosophy and poetic composition) bound up in a single genre, even at its very origin. Turning to Aristotle's *Poetics*, he would not have found any clearer guideline as to the decorum of dialogue; for here, too, the genre seems divided and ambiguous from the start:

There is further an art which imitates by language alone, and one which imitates by metres, either one or a plurality of metres. These forms of imitation are still nameless today. We have no common name for a mime of Sophron or Xenarchus and a Socratic Conversation.[8]

Having decided to classify genres according to mimesis, Aristotle is committed to grouping together in a nameless class the lowest expressions of parodic mimicry, popular entertainment, farce, phallic improvisation, and the highest expressions of Greek philosophy. In all probability, however, more than mimesis leads Aristotle to lump mime and dialogue together. As Bakhtin has argued, the origins of high genres are frequently to be found in low, popular forms. Hints of this same recognition filter throughout *Poetics*, especially when Aristotle describes the historical stages through which unformed comic modes (farce, invective, ridicule) passed before becoming "serious comedy," a genre with a legitimate history (1449a–b).

Hurd's fears about the "tumour of poetic composition" suggest that he thinks dialogue never outgrew its questionable origin. A vehicle for the most elevated philosophical inquiry, dialogue always risks infection from the low world of farce, mimicry, and the comic representation of idiosyncratic characters. So long as dialogue was simply described as a mode of imitation, it would be unclear whether the mirror referred to were the magical one Shaftesbury described (the one that transformed ugliness into beauty), or the more realistic one Mandeville and the skeptics turned back upon the Platonists, taking in more varied phenomena than could possibly be beautified. Unwilling to renounce dialogue completely, Hurd establishes its proper decorum by tying its imitative scope to the norms of polite conversation.

In support of the view that the genre's content and form must be restricted, Hurd narrates a brief history of dialogue. From the ideal truth-seeking of Plato, to the aimless skepticism of Cicero and the Academics, to the "frontless

---

[8] Aristotle, *The Complete Works of Aristotle*, II, p. 2316 (I, 1447a 28–31).

buffoonery" of Lucian, Hurd traces a history of decline. In Plato's dialogues, despite the skeptical tone, the purpose remained one of "exposing Falsehood and discovering Truth" (p. xiii). With Cicero dialogue fell into the hands of the "Academic Sect," which aimed merely "to shew the writer's dexterity in disputing for, or against any opinion, without referring his disputation to any certain use or conclusion at all" (p. xiv). These Academics "brought on the disgrace of the Socratic Dialogue itself" (p. xxxiii). From a vehicle for the discovery of truth, dialogue was "outraged into absolute skepticism" (p. xiv). With Lucian's dialogues of the dead, the comic elements have overwhelmed philosophy. While Socrates used irony only "to discredit those mortal foes of reason, the SOPHISTS" (p. xxx), Lucian's "frontless buffoonery" aimed at "mere wantonness." His dialogues are too much like comic drama and not enough like serious metaphysics: they have "usually, for their subject, not, a QUESTION DEBATED; but a TENET RIDICULED, or a CHARACTER EXPOSED" (p. xxxvii). In comparison with the serious dialogue, which is "absolute in itself, and fully obtains its purpose," the Lucianic model is "at best a faint copy of a higher species, the Comic Drama" (p. xxxix).

Lucian attempted to yoke together serious philosophical dialogue and comic ridicule, but, as we have seen, Hurd makes it his business to separate these:

the two excellencies cannot, in a supreme degree of each, subsist together. The one must be sacrificed to the other. Either the philosophic part must give place to the dramatic; or the dramatic must withdraw, or restrain itself at least, to give room for a just display of the philosophic.   (p. xxxvii)

The attempt to unite the excellencies of drama and philosophy had animated the discussion of dialogue from Plato through the middle of the eighteenth century. But Hurd has given up on the project. Dialogue can only be "complete in itself," unified as an artistic whole, if writers solve the tension between philosophy and drama, doctrine and play, by restraining both. Dramatic elements will either spoil serious philosophy (as in Lucian) or transmit heterodox ideas with too much force (as in *Alciphron*). Serious philosophy will either render the drama pedantic and artificial (as in the mid-century Platonists) or transform the drama into a wholly different kind of work, a philosophical fiction (as in the novels of Sterne and Diderot). Oddly enough, when Hurd offers advice to the would-be dramatist, he still allows the two excellencies to be combined. In the ideal drama, the artist unites "1. A careful study of the Socratic, that is, moral wisdom: and, 2. A thorough acquaintance with human nature, *that great exemplar of manners* ... or, in other words, a wide, extensive view of real, practical life."[9] He is less concerned about attempts to combine these elements on the stage. But prose dialogue is a different matter. In all likelihood, Hurd's real concern is with a growing

[9] Hurd, *Epistolae ad Pisones, et Augustum*, 1, pp. 24–25.

body of works that were combining serious ideas with dramatic (fictional) representations in prose. Hurd's greatest animus is reserved for novels, which he calls "hasty, imperfect, and abortive poems; whether spawned from the dramatic, or narrative species, it may be hard to say."[10]

The narrative moving from Plato to Cicero to the deviant Lucian, like the reference to a cancer arising from within, suggests that dialogue's demise belongs to its antithetical form. Thus, for Hurd any continuation of the genre will require a fundamental redefinition of its nature. He effects this redefinition by linking dialogue to the decorum of polite conversation. Throughout the eighteenth century, the primary difficulty confronting moral philosophers and theologians who composed dialogues was how to represent a credible transition from divided opinion to consensus by means of rational debate. When Hurd makes polite conversation the dominant mode establishing the decorum of dialogue, he finesses this problem entirely. First, topics creating violent disagreement among adversaries will be avoided; second, disagreement about the rules of rational debate will be similarly obviated, since the polite rhetorical community shares a complex network of directives governing conversational exchange. "As to the language of conversation," writes Hurd, "it is so much the same between persons of education and politeness, that, whether the subject be interesting, or otherwise, all that you can expect is that *the general cast of expression* will be somewhat tinctured by the manners, which shine through it; but by no means that the smaller differences, the nicer peculiarities of style, will be shewn" (p. xlviii).

The conservative force of "conversation" could not be clearer. Whereas earlier in the period Shaftesbury and Berkeley use dialogue to correct the aimlessness of fashionable conversation, now Hurd uses conversation to restrict the seriousness of philosophical dialogue. Instead of signaling a liberation from the artificiality of dialogue, as Lennard Davis has argued, conversation functions to exclude skepticism, heterogeneous characters, and indeterminacy.[11] The word "tinctured" implies that individual mannerisms function as a sort of dye that contributes to without altering the preestablished design of the whole. One need only reverse the logic of this passage to grasp its political import: instead of holding that the general "cast"

---

[10] Hurd, *ibid.*, II, p. 153.

[11] See "Conversation and Dialogue," in *The Age of Johnson: a Scholarly Annual*, ed. Paul J. Korshin (New York: AMS Press, Inc., 1987), I, pp. 347–373. While Davis is certainly correct to argue that eighteenth-century novelistic dialogue does not illustrate the heteroglossia that Bakhtin identified with the democratizing, pluralistic novel, he misstates the case by going on to link this ideal democratic function to conversation. "Natural conversation is social, interactive, and communal by nature – whereas dialogue in novels is not. It is monolithic, non-negotiable, and in that sense not egalitarian and democratic, since it proceeds from the absolute authority and unity of the novelist" (p. 358). Only by ignoring discussions of conversation and the entire tradition of written dialogues during the period is Davis able to argue that "[d]ialogues in novels are controlled, manageable units, lacking the wild-card nature of conversations, in which there is no overall plan or design" (p. 361).

of a rhetorical community causes "the nicer peculiarities of [a character's] style to be disregarded," one might say instead that it is only by disregarding such "peculiarities" that one can posit something like a rhetorical community. Hurd notes with approval the fact that in Terence the characters "all express themselves with equal elegance: even his slaves are made to speak as good Latin, as their masters" (p. li). He does not, however, advise the writer of dialogue to bring together characters of such different social ranks. Although conversation "thrives best amidst the equality of conditions in republican and popular states" (p. lix), where social inequalities remain (as remain they must), "the proper remedy ... is, to bring such men only together in Dialogue as are of the same rank" (p. lviii–lix).

Using polite conversation to restrict dialogue was by no means an unusual procedure during the period. John Constable's *The Conversation of Gentlemen Considered In Most of the Ways that Make their Mutual Company Agreeable, or Disagreeable. In Six Dialogues* (1738) conveys guidelines for the conduct of conversation within dialogues that dramatize the rules. About one acquaintance, the gentleman-narrator observes, "one might pardon him several of his other very troublesome Methods, if a habit of disputing, and Eagerness for Reputation of Wit and Scholarship, had not almost ruined in him the Hereditary Good-breeding which has long been remarkable in his Family."[12] Here the verbal and intellectual dexterity that marks Shaftesbury's Philocles and Hume's Philo is redescribed as bad manners. Differences of opinion and the liberty to declare them are permissible only to the extent they enliven and improve conversation. "Yet," adds Constable, "Opposition of Sentiment is so nice a thing, that it must be softened with all imaginable Lenitives of Civility."[13]

In Fielding's "Essay on Conversation," the first requirement of conversation, especially in mixed company, is that the participants endeavor to set each other at ease: "the art of pleasing or doing good to one another is therefore the art of conversation."[14] This art begins with the expression of "good breeding," especially the observance by the host of established social hierarchy in the greeting and seating of the guests. Because society is not ranked by degrees of understanding but by "other methods," vastly different intellects find themselves "jumbled together," which fact Fielding calls "an unavoidable imperfection in society itself." His solution, like that of Hurd, is to restrict the topics permissible in mixed company: loftier intellects must lower themselves in the presence of smaller understandings; company must find mutual subjects and lower the general tone of discourse.[15] Fielding faults

---

[12] John Constable, *The Conversation of Gentlemen Considered* (London: J. Hoyles, 1738), pp. 33–34.
[13] *Ibid.*, p. 34.
[14] Fielding, "An Essay on Conversation," in *The Complete Works of Henry Fielding, Esq.*, 16 vols. (New York: Barnes and Noble, Inc., 1967), *Miscellaneous Writings* I, p. 248.
[15] *Ibid.*, pp. 267–268.

the speaker who advances learned subjects in common conversation or who "discourses on the mysteries of a particular profession." Serious disputes on controversial topics might be permissible, but only when none but men of learning are present.

From the death of dialogue to dialogues of the dead

Hurd adds to these restrictions upon topic a lengthy discussion of the proper way to represent character. According to Hurd, every modern writer of dialogue has gotten character wrong:

An essential defect runs through them all. They have taken for their speakers, not real, but fictitious characters; contrary to the practice of the old writers; and to the infinite disadvantage of this mode of writing in every respect. Hence, the probabilities, or, what is called the decorum. We ask, 'Who the persons are, that are going to converse before us?' 'where and when the conversation passed' and 'by what means the company came together?' If we are let into none of these particulars ... we take no interest in what remains; and give the speakers, who in this case are but a sort of Puppets, no more credit, than the opinion we chance to entertain of their Prompter, demands from us.   (pp. xxii, xxiv)

Hurd apparently shares Shaftesbury's view that characters must be represented with enough realistic detail to show the reader "the bottom" or motive from which characters speak. But, as one might suspect, Hurd is not interested in making differentiation of character a primary consideration in the reader's interpretation of dialogue. When he speaks of "real" characters, he means characters who have actually lived, who are known to modern readers, and who have come to represent idealized values in the popular imagination. In the second dialogue of his collection, Hurd constructs an exchange between two opposing modes of human conduct, an ideal of detachment from life and a pragmatic principle of accommodation to circumstances. He peoples his dialogue with two figures who typify each manner of comportment – Henry More, whose *Divine Dialogues* (1668) and association with the Cambridge Platonists had identified him with the former path, and the poet Edmund Waller, whose vacillations during the Civil War and Restoration offered the popular imagination a proper name as emblem for the latter.[16]

What Hurd means, then, by "real" is actually the opposite of what Shaftesbury meant. While for Shaftesbury the insistence upon depth of characterization accompanied an attack on allegorized characters who functioned merely as puppets, Hurd wants to replace puppets with real characters who nevertheless come to perform an essentially allegorical

[16] The figure of Waller in this dialogue refers to his own choice between sincerity and accommodation as a decision to be made between Cato and Cicero. Hurd's use of historical type figures is similar to that of Johnson in "The Vanity of Human Wishes."

function. More and Waller might as well be named Sincerity and Artifice, their proper names standing for known moral and intellectual dispositions in the popular imagination. The names, writes Hurd, evoke "a thousand fine and delicate allusions to the principles, sentiments, and history of the Dialogists [and thus] keep their characters perpetually in view" (p. xli). "Real" characters who function as allegorical types allow Hurd to satisfy both senses of imitation – realistic and idealizing. He portrays actual figures, but constantly mitigates the complexity of these characters by reducing them to known moral types. It is in this way that Hurd attempts to distance himself from the concept of character at work in many novels. He begins to write a prosopopoeia, only now, instead of a stage peopled by allegorical types, we find conversations among the great dead men of the past: dialogues of the dead.

If this theory of characterization seems rather tortured, it was no less puzzling to Edward Wynne, whose "Essay on Dialogue" (1774) prefacing his own *Eunomous, or Dialogues concerning the Law and Constitution of England*, responds to Hurd and offers a defense of dialogue as a means of transmitting the history of law. Hurd's view of character is, he says, "the principal thing about which we differ."[17] "The disadvantage in general," he writes, "of introducing characters known in history, is the difficulty of supporting them ... In copying a real character ... if the lines of the portrait do not convey a striking likeness it will be little better than sign-post painting."[18] Just because a writer has selected a real historical figure does not mean, Wynne points out, that he has escaped the charge of drawing "puppets." Wynne wonders how much descriptive detail would be enough to support a character about whom much is known. If real figures are to be copied, "is the model to be adopted by halves, the character to be closely copied, and the known peculiar style of the speaker at the same time to be neglected, or at least 'infinitely restrained?' "[19]

Wynne does not evaluate the rationale behind Hurd's restrictions, though he inadvertently comes close to supplying it. He observes that in Berkeley's *Minute Philosopher* it would not have been right to affix a real name to either of the atheists: "If the person was dead, what was advanced as his notion might possibly have been a misrepresentation; if he was then living, it might have been a libel" (pp. 26–27). By implication, however, if real characters are represented in dialogue, the writer must take care to avoid controversial religious topics, which might open him to charges of misrepresentation and libel. As we have seen, this was just what Hurd wanted; thus, his statements about characterization support the restrictions he places upon content.

Hurd anticipates Wynne's objection when he acknowledges a difficulty

[17] Wynne, *Eunomous. or Dialogues concerning the Law and Constitution of England. With an Essay on Dialogue*, 5th edn. (London: S. Sweet, 1822), p. 25. Subsequent references to this work will be given by page number in my text.
[18] *Ibid.*, p. 26.   [19] *Ibid.*, p. 28.

with his own argument: "as it appeared that the speaker's *proper manners* are to be given ... it may be thought ... that the speaker's *proper style or expression* should be given too (p. xliii). But he responds: "here the subject begins to be a little nice; and we must distinguish between the *general cast* of expression and its *smaller and more peculiar features*." Hurd must distinguish between these in order to keep his poetics of dialogue from becoming a theory of the novel, for much of what distinguishes Walter Shandy from Philonous, Lovelace from Lysicles, Clarissa from Aspasia, is the degree to which the "speaker's proper style or expression" and the concrete circumstances calling these forth achieve fictional representation. The decorum of conversation seems to invite exploration of these idiosyncracies, but for Hurd conversation is used to foreclose excessive fidelity in the representation of social differences and so must not then be turned to justify an equally dangerous proliferation of fictional detail in the representation of character. The specific manners "tincture" the general cast of expression, but they do not stain the transmission of doctrine. These qualifications lead Hurd to his most far-reaching – and most contorted – declaration about character: "in Dialogue, we must have real persons, and those only: for character here is but a secondary consideration" (p. xxvii).

Having piled restriction atop restriction, Hurd places himself in the odd position of defending an interpretation of dialogue that looks very much like Lucian's reviled dialogues of the dead! He responds to the threat presented by skeptical dialogue by linking dialogue to the decorum of an ideal conversation, set in the historical past among great dead gentlemen. In this way, he writes,

We may fancy of the dead, what we cannot so readily believe of the living. And thus, by endeavouring a little to deceive ourselves, we may come to think that natural, which is not wholly incredible; and may admit the writer's invention for a picture, though a studied and flattering one, it may be, of real life.   (p. lxv)

If, as Shaftesbury suspected and the history of eighteenth-century dialogue in part proves, philosophical dialogue no longer offers a picture of real life; if dialogue – especially metaphysical dialogue – is a dead genre; then perhaps it might turn this defeat to advantage by bringing the dead to life as a utopian image of what existence might really be like, could we rid ourselves of distractions, private interests, and our bodies. A dialogue of the dead would then imitate conversation just enough to seem like real life without allowing the peculiarities of actual conversation to distract attention from the moral. The noble dead would comport themselves as perfect gentlemen, united in the search for truth.

After all, there is nothing like being dead to smooth out idiosyncracies of character, and Hell has the additional boon of providing no temporizing sanctuary for lies. "For the Dead, not wanting Sense," Fontenelle writes, punning on exactly what they *do* want, "must presently see to the End of things."[20] And he continues:

The Dead are People of deep Reflection, as well from their Experience as from their Leisure; and it ought to be believ'd for their Honour, that they think somewhat more than is usual in Life. They reason on Things above, better than we, because they regard 'em with much more Indifference and Tranquility ... I found no difficulty likewise to imagine, that they might be enlighten'd enough to agree upon every thing with one another, and consequently not to wrangle, or but very rarely. I fancy Disputing belongs only to us Ignorants, who do not discover the Truth.[21]

While this work appeared several decades before Hurd's "Preface," the statement makes clear why dialogues of the dead would continue to appeal to moralists after the middle of the century. All of the difficulties I previously associated with the "death" of dialogue – the inability to portray a credible progress from divided opinion to consensus, the aimless and distracted quality of modern conversation, the loss of any transcendental judge or principle capable of reconciling competing viewpoints – all of these limitations seem to be answered by the dialogue of the dead. Dialogue is no longer artificial because those who have passed into the next life "think somewhat more than is usual in life" (the dead are natural born philosophers). The discovery of truth is no longer doubtful because death has removed all passion, interest, and partiality from the exchange of ideas, rendering character transparent. And the third term, which had been dragged into the mud of contingency by Mandeville, Hume, Ramsay, Sterne and their comic ilk, has now reascended the throne in the figure of Hades, the shades, the nether regions, where the *memento mori* reminds one of a final tribunal that cannot be changed like trump in a game of cards.

Although several critics have noted the popularity of the dialogue of the dead between 1760 and 1780, none has offered an adequate explanation for why this variety of dialogue would become so popular for a brief period towards the end of the eighteenth century.[22] Frederick Keener, whose book on the dialogues of the dead remains the fullest treatment of the subject, is not primarily concerned with the reasons why the form underwent this short-lived revival. Explanations for the popularity of Lucian are generally offered

---

[20] *Fontenelle's Dialogues of the Dead in Three Parts ... Translated from the French by the Late John Hughes*, 2nd edn. (London: J. Tonson, 1730), p. lxiii.

[21] *Ibid.*, pp. lxii–lxiii.

[22] The exact number of dialogues of the dead written during the second half of the eighteenth century is difficult to ascertain, but according to my research and Keener's "Check List of Original Dialogues of the Dead in English, 1641–1907," the number increased sharply after 1760 (the publication date of Lyttelton's *Dialogues of the Dead*) and dwindled towards the end of the century. There were more dialogues of the dead written in England between 1760 and 1780 than there had been during the hundred years prior to 1760. Keener, *English Dialogues of the Dead: a Critical History, An Anthology, and A Check List* (New York: Columbia University Press, 1973). See also Benjamin Boyce, "News from Hell," *PMLA* 58 (1943) 402–437; and Nicolas H. Nelson, "Dramatic Texture and Philosophical Debate in Prior's *Dialogues of the Dead*," *SEL* 28 (1988) 428–441.

in passing and are not always helpful because Keener discusses the sub-genre, for the most part, in isolation from other varieties of dialogue. He implies that several factors might have contributed to its revival: an interest in travel accounts, a general air of superstition, a tendency to look towards history as a basis for moral instruction, the popularity of biography and "parallel lives," and an effort to popularize the ethical attitude of Pope's *An Essay on Man*.[23]

While a detailed discussion of the dialogues of the dead stands outside the scope of this book, we are in a position to note an odd fact: Richard Hurd, who has nothing good to say about Lucian, chooses to write dialogues of the dead.[24] One could, of course, accept his explanation: "the authority of Lucian is so great, and the manner itself so taking, that for these reasons, but chiefly for the sake of variety, the FIRST of the following Dialogues (and in part too, the SECOND) pretends to be of this class" (p. xxxix). But this would be to ignore the fact that Hurd has just finished arguing himself into writing dialogues of the dead in the course of attacking Lucian and restricting Plato. That is, while praising Platonic dialogue as an ideal mode of truth-seeking, he understands truth as that which he already knows. Thus, he needs a cap upon skepticism, and this is provided by linking dialogue to polite conversation. And since polite conversation of a realistic sort might be thought to depart from the serious lessons he means to enforce, he needs a cap on realism, and this is provided by setting dialogue in the shades, where character is re-allegorized according to dominant moral typologies. Keener notes that "many of the dialogues of the dead written in English are comparatively serious in subject and tone, less satires than dramatic meditations on history and ethics."[25]

The dialogue of the dead permitted Hurd to reconcile the two contradictory conceptions of mimesis running throughout the Neoclassical Enlightenment in Britain. That which makes fidelity to observed reality its test and that which makes fidelity to "general truths and maxims" its test stand united in a genre wherein characters debate the truth of propositions in prospect of an absolute tribunal. Viewed in this way, eighteenth-century dialogues of the dead belong to a family of genres that includes gothic romance, Spenserian allegory, Platonic imitations, Christianized satire (as in "The Vanity of Human Wishes") and (as I shall argue in the next chapter) varieties of prose fiction such as Johnson's *The History of Rasselas, Prince of Abyssinia*. These works attempt to preserve an allegorical interpretation of phenomena while granting the Enlightenment critique of both special providence (miracles) and

---

[23] Keener, *English Dialogues of the Dead*, especially pp. 4, 6–8, 10, 20, 89.

[24] Fontenelle also distances himself from Lucian, claiming that unlike Lucian, who invented some of his material, he draws entirely from fact: "I thought I had no Occasion for this Privilege [of inventing]; History furnish'd me with real Persons, and real Adventures enough, to excuse me from borrowing any Supplies from Fiction" (p. lxv). Except the small one of dead folks speaking.

[25] Keener, *English Dialogues of the Dead*, p. 14.

general providence (design in nature). The antithetical end required a
mixture of seemingly antithetical genres. Walpole's *The Castle of Otranto*
begins, for instance, with the author's apology, carried out over two prefaces,
for the "attempt to blend the two kinds of romance, the ancient and the
modern. In the former, all was imagination and improbability: in the latter,
nature is always intended to be, and sometimes has been, copied with
success."[26] My claim here and throughout this book is that writers of dialogue
often attempt the same reconciliation, only they do so *philosophically*, which is
to say, on a theoretical level. A "theory" of the rise of the novel therefore
exists in the ongoing critical discussion of dialogue; and where criticism aims
to limit dialogue to idealized representations, such a "poetics" of dialogue
takes the form of a theory of the novel in relief.

The novel in relief

I have called the "Preface on the Manner of Writing Dialogue" a theory of
the novel in relief because Hurd wages a critical campaign against the very
combination of serious topic and entertaining fiction that defines the
conversational novels of Burney, Austen, and Wollstonecraft. Hurd finds that
characters within serious dialogue are becoming too vivid; therefore he
invents a critical rationale for reintroducing types who are nevertheless real.
Hurd dislikes the combination of serious (metaphysical) topics and accurate
representations; therefore he ties dialogue to the decorum of polite
conversation wherein topic, tone, and idiom are all constrained by propriety.
And, just in case these stipulations don't succeed in killing off the patient he
claims to treat, he suggests that dialogues be set in the realm of the dead,
peopled by figures who stand for abstract moral propensities, presided over
by the sternest tribunal of all. The steps Hurd takes to transform
philosophical dialogue into an allegorized drama present us with the negative
image of the process of generic transformation he is attempting to resist, the
"fall" of philosophical dialogue into prose fiction.

Burney and Austen follow Hurd in restricting dialogue to a middle range
of topics; they share his view that characters should be "real," though not
marked by celebrated proper names (which makes them types). Their works
often set dialogues within the confines of polite conversation. But here the
similarities end. Although all consider themselves moralists, Austen and
Burney use fiction to thematize the loss of intellectual assumptions that stand
behind Hurd's stalwart defense of Plato. They conceive of moral philosophy
as an inquiry into the emplacement of beings in time. And because there can
be no appeal beyond time, characters find themselves in a world of details,
the long-feared labyrinth, with no trusty guide, no disembodied authority to

[26] Horace Walpole, *The Castle of Otranto: A Gothic Story*, ed. W. S. Lewis (London: Oxford University
Press, 1964), p. 7.

assign inevitability to choice. Characters, especially young female characters, must make their own way, and that talent, the negotiation of complex social predicaments, becomes the hermeneutic facility the conversational novel hopes to teach.

We have not thought of the novel as a kind of philosophy in part because Hurd, among others, was successful in driving a wedge between philosophy and "poetic composition," thus creating disciplinary divisions that have shaped our understanding of the eighteenth century. The divisions correspond in time with the failure of Christian Neoplatonism to realize itself *textually* within genres such as philosophical dialogue. When Hurd declared dialogue dead, what he really meant was that the project of representing human experience as if it conformed to the elevating plot of transcendental dialectic had failed. That does not mean that transcendental dialectic withers up and blows away, any more than fictional representations become aimless once their plots are no longer modeled on a dialectical ascent from matter to spirit. But it does mean that Kant, continuing the transcendental project, will have disparaging things to say about "mere examples," and novelists as different as Sterne and Austen will ridicule disembodied metaphysics.

Here is what Kant has to say about examples in the *Critique of Pure Reason*:

Examples and illustrations seemed always to be necessary, and so took their place, as required, in my first draft. But I very soon became aware of the magnitude of my task and of the multiplicity of matters with which I should have to deal; and as I perceived that even if treated in dry, purely *scholastic* fashion, the outcome would by itself be already quite sufficiently large in bulk, I found it inadvisable to enlarge it yet further through examples and illustrations. These are necessary only from a *popular* point of view; and this work can never be made suitable for popular consumption.[27]

He repeats the point even more insistently in the *Groundwork of the Metaphysic of Morals*:

It is utterly senseless to aim at popularity in our first inquiry, upon which the whole correctness of our principles depends. It is not merely that such a procedure can never lay claim to the extremely rare merit of a truly *philosophical popularity*, since we require no skill to make ourselves intelligible to the multitude once we renounce all profundity of thought: what it [such writing] turns out is a disgusting hotch-potch of second-hand observations and semi-rational principles on which the empty-headed regale themselves, because this is something that can be used in the chit-chat of daily life.[28]

Novels might be defined as works that aim at popularity in their first inquiry. What Hurd and Kant deny is that they also aim at profundity, as regards ethics. Hurd attributes the popular success of novels to the "gratification they

---

[27] Kant, *The Critique of Pure Reason*, trans. Norman Kemp Smith (London: Macmillan and Co., 1953), pp 12–13.
[28] Kant, *Groundwork of the Metaphysic of Morals*, p. 77.

afford to a vitiated, palled, and sickly imagination – that last disease of learned minds, and sure prognostic of expiring Letters."[29] Here, despite himself, Hurd comes full circle, linking the genre he would save, philosophical dialogue, with the genre he would destroy. Both suffer the "disease" of too much fictional vitality; both appear to prognosticate "expiring Letters." The great illness in each case is the admixture of generic elements that should remain distinct. Although Hurd acknowledges that genres are "arbitrary things as we account them (for I neither forget nor dispute what our best philosophy teaches concerning *kinds* and *sorts*)," he still insists that "kinds have yet so far their foundation in nature and the reason of things."[30] The mixtures found in many dialogues and all novels evince "a sort of literary luxury, which would engross all pleasures at once, even such as are contradictory to each other ... But true taste requires chaste, severe, and simple pleasures; and true genius will only be concerned in administering such."[31]

Hurd hoped to cure dialogue by distinguishing it from the novel. But when he tried to define a species of dialogue that was neither novelistic nor philosophical, he ended up defending the realism of dialogues of the dead, spawned neither from dramatic nor from narrative elements, but from the after-image of each. He embraced a dead end. What Sterne and Austen knew, on the other hand, was that "the chit-chat of daily life," the "farrago of the clack of nurses, and of the nonsense of old women (of both sexes) throughout the kingdom," could become the stuff of the most elevated philosophical fictions. Although the strict division established at just this point in time between philosophy and literature makes it difficult to see, novelists such as Johnson, Burney, and Austen follow directly in the line of eighteenth-century moral philosophers who chose to grapple with the inevitable contamination of universals by historical and psychological circumstances. They do not so much degrade as save moral philosophy. In the following chapter I discuss the relevance of eighteenth-century dialogue to the development of the novel, with specific reference to Johnson's *Rasselas* and Austen's *Sense and Sensibility*.

---

[29] The reference to expiring letters does not appear in the edition of 1776. These lines are taken from *The Works of Richard Hurd*, 8 vols. (London: T. Cadell and W. Davies, 1811; rprt. New York: AMS Press, Inc., 1967), II, 20.

[30] *Ibid.*, p. 20.   [31] *Ibid.*, pp. 20–21.

9

Utopia or conversation: transforming dialogue in Johnson and Austen

Johnson's *The History of Rasselas, Prince of Abyssinia*: accidents in the orient

Critics have never been sure what to call *Rasselas*. Elizabeth Merrill labels the book an "expository dialogue." B. H. Bronson calls it basically "a philosophical dialogue." Gwin Kolb, disagreeing with those who refer to *Rasselas* as an oriental tale, novel, or comedy, employs the term "apologue."[1] Kolb prefers this term because *Rasselas* seems to place the lesson of "The Vanity of Human Wishes" in the form of a moral tale: "Briefly stated, the 'lesson' of the book runs something like this: Man's nature, the insatiable 'hunger' of his 'imagination' – and the nature of the world produce at best only a scanty amount of happiness, which is often accidental, never lasting, and insignificant when balanced against the predominant bleakness of life. Mindful of his own limitations, the wise person will thus recognize the futility of searches for permanent felicity (although such searches are almost inevitable to man as man), ask no more of life than virtuous conduct can provide, and look to eternity and to God's mercy for the pure bliss that is unattainable on earth."[2]

Few would deny that such is Johnson's moral. Yet confusion about the work's kind may be indicative of tensions within *Rasselas* that cannot be so easily subsumed in summary. Critics are right to describe the work as an assembly of many different genres. A mythic rehearsal of a willing fall from paradise gives way to a series of philosophical dialogues framed by an oriental tale of adventure and suffering. The last scenes of the work even introduce elements of the dialogue of the dead, as the young people congregate in the catacombs of the Egyptians to ponder the meaning of life in prospect of eternity. The philosophical dialogue in quest of earthly happiness does indeed seem to produce a yearning for a return to utopia, if not in this life, then in the next.

[1] Merrill, *The Dialogue in English Literature*, p. 82; B. H. Bronson, ed. *Rasselas* (New York: Rinehart, 1958), p. xvi; Gwin J. Kolb, "The Structure of Rasselas," *PMLA* 66 (1951) 698–717; also Kolb, ed. *Rasselas* (Arlington Heights, IL: AHM Publishing Corp., 1962), p. vi.

[2] Kolb, *Rasselas*, pp. vi–vii.

While it is not advisable to judge *Rasselas* as if it were a philosophical dialogue or a novel, it is important to ask why Johnson has assimilated so many different forms into the same work. They do not fit together smoothly. The recognition Kolb chooses to place in parenthesis "(such searches are almost inevitable to man as man)" after declaring Johnson's moral to be "the wise person will thus recognize the futility of searches for permanent felicity" captures something of the difficulty. If the lesson of *Rasselas* is indeed that the search for happiness in this life is futile, the moral has been enclosed within a work that dramatizes both the restlessness of human nature (the rejection of utopia) and the importance of dialogue as a means of educating young minds. Many of the formal elements in *Rasselas* contradict its ostensible theme.

The opposition of divergent forms in *Rasselas* manifests a more fundamental incongruity in the way Johnson's philosopher, Imlac, views experience and representation. We have seen the same opposition between kinds and degrees of imitation throughout the history of eighteenth-century dialogue. In the happy valley, Imlac delivers his famous sermon on the education of the poet.

"The business of the poet," said Imlac, "is to examine, not the individual, but the species; to remark general properties and large appearances: he does not number the streaks of the tulip or describe the different shades in the verdure of the forest. He is to exhibit in his portraits of nature such prominent and striking features as recal the original to every mind; and must neglect the minuter discriminations, which one may have remarked, and another have neglected, for those characteristicks which are alike obvious to vigilance and carelessness."[3]

To the extent Johnson follows Imlac's lead, one is not surprised to find elements in *Rasselas* that assure the predominance of the general over the particular, the species over the individual, prominent and striking features over shades of difference and minute discriminations. Framing the work first as a mythic fall from paradise and then as an oriental tale peopled by a highborn prince and princess whose experiences provide immediate material for profound moral reflections, Johnson was himself in no danger of numbering the streaks of the tulip.

Yet the prince's response to Imlac's sermon – "Enough! Thou hast convinced me that no human being can ever be a poet. Proceed with thy narration" – may be provoked by more than the difficulty of the poet's training. Rasselas finds himself at the beginning of the work a prisoner of utopia, where all his needs are met, where no shade of difference threatens to unsettle the state of indolent bliss. For a young man whose "chief amusement was to picture himself . . . entangled in imaginary difficulties" (iv, pp. 17–18),

---

[3] *The Yale Edition of the Works of Samuel Johnson*, ed. Gwin J. Kolb, 16 vols. (New Haven and London: Yale University Press, 1990), *Rasselas and Other Tales*, xvi, x, pp. 43–44). References to *Rasselas* refer to the Yale edition and will be given in my text by chapter and page number.

Imlac's description of the poet as one who already knows the true "original" behind particular experience may hold little appeal. Yes, the poet as writer has *first* experienced a great deal, has encountered nature in all its complexity, and only afterward has discovered the original Platonic form. Yet the poet as moralist places the ideal first: it frames his theory of representation. Fed up with the ideal, Rasselas loses patience with Imlac's description of the poet.

Rasselas craves experience, and experience of the most diverse and detailed kinds. When the old teacher in the happy valley overhears Rasselas bemoaning his boredom, he advises him, "if you had seen the miseries of the world, you would know how to value your present state" (iii, p. 16). The conclusion, not so different from what the travelers finally learn at the end of their "experiment," cannot come first. Even in paradise, Rasselas has a will to misunderstand: " 'Now,' said the prince, 'you have given me something to desire; I shall long to see the miseries of the world, since the sight of them is necessary to happiness.' " The old man goes away "sufficiently discontented to find that his reasonings had produced the only conclusion which they were intended to prevent" (iv, p. 17).

This failed dialogue sets a precedent for a series of ultimately unresolved dialogues marking the pilgrims' search for "the choice of life." In the world outside utopia, dialogue becomes the means of educating young minds. Only here, the young people must learn a new way of interpreting complex phenomena. Even Imlac's strictures about the poet's way of reading nature are of limited use. What the young people need to learn, first and foremost, is the art of interpreting ideas and people in the absence of an ideal norm.

While in utopia, Rasselas does not mind having the results of dialogue narrated to him by Imlac: " 'You know,' said the prince, 'how little my life has made me acquainted with diversity of opinions: it will be too long to hear the arguments on both sides; you that have considered them, tell me the result' " (xi, p. 47). Outside utopia, however, Rasselas goes eagerly to the assembly of learned men "who met at times to unbend their minds and compare their opinions" (xxii, p. 84). After he learns from the Rousseau-like sage that "deviation from nature is deviation from happiness," Rasselas asks the next question: "Sir . . . I doubt not the truth of a position which a man so learned has so confidently advanced. Let me know only what it is to live according to nature" (xxii, p. 87). The philosopher responds at length: "To live according to nature is to act always with due regard to the fitness arising from the relations and qualities of causes and effects . . ." (xxii, p. 88). But this is gibberish to Rasselas, and he leaves convinced that "this was one of the sages whom he should understand less as he heard him longer." Rasselas has become a skeptical young man, traveling from assembly to assembly, judging the relative value of what he hears in public. The more he listens and observes, the more adept he becomes at participating in public conferences. Practice and participation excite his interest and make him want to spend his entire life inquiring and deliberating. Yet Rasselas is also easily disappointed, easily convinced by Imlac that the failure of the one is the failure of the many, – that dour morality of the abstractionist, the creator of types. Is it any wonder that Rasselas comes to form a prejudice against learning?

Even when Rasselas feels enlightened after his discourse with the stoic philosopher, Imlac warns him to suspect the fraud. " 'I have found,' said the prince at his return to Imlac, 'a man who can teach all that is necessary to be known ... This man shall be my future guide: I will learn his doctrines and imitate his life.' 'Be not too hasty,' said Imlac, 'to trust, or to admire, the teachers of morality: they discourse like angels, but they live like men' " (xviii, p. 74). Sure enough, as the narrative proceeds, Rasselas returns to find the stoic in abject grief over the death of his only daughter. In an exchange straight out of Fielding, Rasselas learns to gauge the distance between word and deed (the true Ridiculous):

"Sir," said the prince, "mortality is an event by which a wise man can never be surprised: we know that death is always near, and it should always be expected." "Young man," answered the philosopher, "you speak like one that has never felt the pangs of separation." "Have you then forgot the precepts," said Rasselas, "which you so powerfully enforced?"   (xviii, pp. 74–75)

The philosopher, caught in the act, belies his own teaching, negating stoicism and driving another nail in the coffin of arrogant human reason.

The sequence of unresolved dialogues outside utopia points in two different directions, only one of which Johnson finally embraces. First, it suggests that when the travelers trade utopia for the world, they enter upon a lifetime of ceaseless questioning, inexact deliberations, and imperfect resolutions. Dialogue becomes what it will be in the novels of Jane Austen, an imperfect instrument (but the best we have) for navigating one's way through a world without utopian or transcendental reference points. Second, the disappointments occasioned by human dialogues direct the travelers back to where they began, to the conclusion offered at the beginning that "if you had seen the miseries of the world, you would know how to value your present state." As we have seen throughout this study, these two alternatives seemed to follow equally from the failure of the genre: a Tory polemicist such as Roger L'Estrange could exaggerate the inability of rational subjects to mediate opposition through dialogue, thus affirming the need for absolute submission to sovereign authority; a radical deist such as Tindal could multiply viewpoints in dialogue in order to dramatize the absence of any arbitrating authority higher than the light of human reason alone. Johnson leaves little doubt which of these implications of failed dialogue he endorses. The addition of the oriental frame suppresses any positive potential dialogue might hold as a form of education in the world.[4]

---

[4] This despite the role of female conversation in saving the astronomer from madness. For a

While in utopia Imlac had explained that the poet's view of nature is shaped by a deep experience of the order of things, a knowledge – whether intuited beforehand or gained through experience need not be debated – of how nature *wants* to be known, once particulars free themselves of accidents and accidents of contingencies and contingencies of circumstances and circumstances of chance. The type, though different from what is immediately observable, expresses the greater truth. Imlac restates a fundamentally Neoplatonic and Christian view of representation. Dialogue in utopia always ascends from the complex effect to the simple cause, act to idea.

In the world, however, Imlac is forced to give a different account. He wants the young people to remain skeptical, ever vigilant against the imposter, attentive to every detail that presents itself, and aware that even the detail might mean different things. He does not want them to resign themselves, as he did, to a complacent life forming absolutes in an ideal kingdom. So he teaches them:

"The causes of good and evil are so various and uncertain, so often entangled with each other, so diversified by various relations, and so much subject to accidents which cannot be foreseen, that he who would fix his condition on incontestable reasons of preference must live and die inquiring and deliberating."   (xvi, p. 67)

The wisdom Imlac imparts in the world requires a different approach to dialogue. Good and evil are "entangled"; the young travelers must therefore embrace a paradox: if they would fix ethical choice upon "incontestable reasons of preference" they must "live and die inquiring and deliberating." To realize certainty they must embrace change! They *must* number the streaks of the tulip; they must *not* neglect the minuter discriminations. The position that Fielding parodied when placed in the mouths of the rule of right men – that "there was nothing absolutely good or evil in and of itself; that Actions were denominated good or bad by the Circumstances of the Agent" – seems now perilously close to the condition Imlac attributes to life itself outside utopia.

Johnson, like most of the writers discussed in this history, uses philosophical dialogue in combination with other generic elements (myth, oriental tale) in order to bring together seemingly incommensurable views of experience and representation. He allows his own preference for the general over the particular, for the Platonic ideal over the Lockean detail, to be associated with an existential condition that the young people *reject*. He therefore instigates an "experiment." How, through a mundane series of dialogues, might the young people arrive at the wisdom the old teacher offers from the start? How, in other words, might the education of a moral philosopher and

discussion of the pedagogical potential of dialogue in *Rasselas*, see my "Literacy and Genre," *College English* 51 (1989) 737–739.

the vision of a Neoplatonic poet be combined? Such is the "inquiry" that explains the combination of generic features in *Rasselas*.

Imlac's observations about mixed values, diversified relations, and unforeseen accidents introduce into *Rasselas* the elements that critics have associated with the developing novel. Young characters find themselves adrift in an alien world, suffering metaphysical homelessness, unable to "fix" their ethical deliberations on a transcendental reference point. Beginning as *tabula rasa* in the Lockean world of experience, Rasselas and company must accumulate knowledge of diverse, sometimes inconsistent effects. It is a frightening prospect. As she leaves the happy valley, the princess says, "I am almost afraid ... to begin a journey of which I cannot perceive an end, and to venture into the immense plain, where I may be approached on every side by men whom I never saw" (xv, p. 61). Rasselas echoes her anxiety near the end of the book: "What then is to be done? ... The more we inquire, the less we can resolve. Surely he is most likely to please himself that has no other inclination to regard" (xxvi, p. 99).

The prospect may have worried the author of *Rasselas* as well. Surely, Imlac's advice to the young travelers about good and evil being "entangled" with each other runs counter to the advice Johnson gives writers of the new prose fiction in *Rambler no. 4*. In that essay Johnson insists that however much values and characters may be mixed in reality, they must not be represented as such in fictions intended for young and impressionable minds. "That the highest degree of reverence should be paid to youth, and that nothing indecent should be suffered to approach their eyes or ears; are precepts extorted by sense and virtue from an ancient writer by no means eminent for chastity of thought" (III, p. 21). "Indecency" covers a lot of territory in *Rambler no. 4*. Most relevant, however, is Johnson's insistence that mixed characters not be represented.

The best examples only should be exhibited ... [and] it is necessary to distinguish those parts of nature which are most proper for imitation ... If the world be promiscuously described, I cannot see of what use it would be to read the account; or why it may not be as safe to turn the eye immediately upon mankind, as upon a mirror that shows all that presents itself without discrimination. It is therefore not a sufficient vindication of a character, that it is drawn as it appears, for many characters ought never to be drawn. (III, p. 22)

Johnson reserves particular disdain for those writers who "for the sake of following nature, so mingle good and bad qualities in their principal personages, that they are both equally conspicuous; and ... we lose the abhorrence of their faults" (III, p. 23). Johnson fears that mixed representations of character will lead the reader to draw a larger conclusion about the nature of human nature. Yet it is the same moral Imlac draws outside utopia: "that certain virtues have their correspondent faults, and that therefore to exhibit either apart is to deviate from probability" (III, p. 23).

For Johnson, the moralist, fiction must represent a standard of perfect-
ibility. There must be a heroic type; otherwise, readers, who are self-evidently
mixed in their common lives, will have no other model to live up to when
they entertain themselves with books. "It is of the utmost importance to
mankind that positions of this tendency should be laid open and confuted,"
writes Johnson of the mixed character. "To this fatal error all those will
contribute who confound the colors of right and wrong, and instead of
helping to settle their boundaries, mix them with so much art that no
common mind is able to disunite them" (p. 178). Yet Imlac's worldly sociology
is at odds with his utopian poetics; and Johnson, like most of the moral
philosophers who experimented with literary form during the eighteenth
century, shares the condition. The odd assemblage of generic components in
Rasselas constitutes his literary solution to the dilemmas of the late Platonist
writing in the British Enlightenment. Johnson's most important addition is
the oriental tale.

Lucianic without humor, the framework of the oriental tale transforms
each dialogue into a static portrait of the insufficiency of reason, much like
the portraits found in the "Vanity of Human Wishes." In addition, orientalist
motifs act as a *memento mori*, always confronting the young reasoners with
Limit, a dystopia whose threats produce nostalgia for the lost ideal.
Abductions, rapes, floods, madmen, and mummified remains remind them of
the vanity of human dialogues. The combination of elements rescues *Rasselas*
from becoming the kind of work Johnson attacked in *Rambler no. 4*.

While dialogue in *Tristram Shandy* occurs between beginnings and ends (but
can encompass neither), dialogue within the framework of the oriental tale
takes place increasingly within the prospect of eternity (or its negative image).
"The evil of any pleasure that Nekayah can image," says Imlac, "is not in the
act itself but in its consequences. Pleasure, in itself harmless, may become
mischievous by endearing to us a state which we know to be transient and
probatory, and withdrawing our thoughts from that which every hour brings
us nearer to the beginning, and of which no length of time will bring us to the
end" (xlvii, pp. 166–167). Imlac's sermon as much as announces the plot
Rasselas will subserve: although the educational dialogues take place in time,
no accumulation of them will bring the travelers to their end. Each dialogue
is about insufficiency, most often of reason, but also of stamina to remain
within the quotidian. The setting takes its toll. Imlac convinces the young
people they are tired of experience, with help at the end from a trip to the
crypt.

Bored and disillusioned by earthly entertainments, the entourage decides
to visit the catacombs of the embalmed Egyptians. Once below, conversation
naturally turns to the nature of the soul. The travelers wonder what sort of
people could have spent so much time and money preserving those whose
essence had fled. When one of the company offers that for the Egyptians soul

and body were thought to be combined, Imlac snaps: "Some . . . have indeed said that the soul is material, but I can scarcely believe that any man has thought it, who knew how to think" (xlviii, p. 170). When the astronomer gingerly suggests that "matter may have qualities with which we are unacquainted," Imlac waves him off. "He who will determine . . . against that which he knows because there may be something which he knows not; he that can set hypothetical possibility against acknowledged certainty, is not to be admitted among rational beings." Indeed, it becomes clear that the purpose of the discussion is not to engage the young people in a dialogue about religion but to acquaint them with a reference point that makes light of all dialogue, all reasoning, all pretentious attempts to understand. Imlac's assertion that "an ideal form is no less real than material bulk" receives silent approbation, as does his conclusion that complex effects are governed by an ultimate "power that thinks; a power impassive and indiscerpible" (xlviii, p. 173). The young people soon enough follow Imlac's trajectory, forgetting their earlier dissatisfaction with utopia. "How gloomy would be these mansions of the dead to him who did not know he shall never die," observes Rasselas (xlviii, p. 174). And Nekayah has the last word, " 'To me,' said the princess, 'the choice of life is become less important; I hope hereafter to think only on the choice of eternity' " (p. 175). Between utopian origin and eschatological end, the human character fades into insignificance. The young people become types of themselves. Plan has followed plan, none has totally succeeded; none has pleased for long. There can be only one conclusion: "Of these wishes that they formed they well knew that none could be obtained. They deliberated a while what was to be done, and resolved, when the inundation should cease, to return to Abyssinia" (xlix, p. 176).

Rasselas, then, is a strange kind of work. To say that its theme strains against its form is too easy. For there is more than one theme, and more than one form. Fundamental oppositions are situated not so much between characters as between narrative frames: novel material in an oriental tale! The orient, as secular myth, revives a lost utopia in the quotidian. In the last half of the book, what the orient impinges upon the lives of the characters – abduction by Arabs, mourning a friend's violent end, a madman who has never known the company of women, the catacombs of the Egyptians – reminds them of the direction towards which all tends. If it is not a happy recollection, it is at least welcome, after the trials and tribulations of life in the a/occident.

I have argued that a dialogue of genres occurs in *Rasselas*. It corresponds with the divided teaching of a poet/philosopher who tells us both that complex phenomena contain simple essences (general properties derived from particulars), and that "the causes of good and evil are . . . often entangled with each other." Imlac never acknowledges any conflict between these views in his teaching. But that is not so surprising. He also has remarkably *little* to say about his reasons for first entering utopia ("wearied at last with solicitation and repulses"), then leaving, and then returning again.

When the travelers reject utopia and encounter one unresolved dialogue after another in their search for happiness, they seem to have embarked upon a permanent dialectic, rising only to further contradiction. In such a condition, they *need* the kind of advice that the writer of *Rambler no. 4* seems unwilling to give. Denying that prose fiction could represent mixed characters and complex relations *while* remaining moral, Johnson closes his "apologue" off from the challenge that novelists such as Jane Austen will embrace. Johnson's princess, on leaving utopia, fears "to venture into the immense plain, where I may be approached on every side by men whom I never saw." Her condition, unrelieved by biblical myth or oriental romance, becomes the topic of *Sense and Sensibility*.

Austen's *Sense and Sensibility*: dialogue and irony

Johnson takes the failure of philosophical dialogue as a pretext for the turn back to utopia. There was, however, another conclusion to be drawn from the failure of philosophical dialogue – namely, that agents might still fix their preferences through a wholly mundane process of conversational exchange. Philosophical dialogue would be preserved in its conceptual structure – as a way of introducing fundamental oppositions of value into prose fiction – but altered in its form – divested of its mere mouthpieces for ideas, its higher criterion, its insubstantial settings, bookish speeches, and dialectical plots. One might refer to these developments in terms of an incorporation of stage comedy into prose fiction; and it is true that Austen borrows heavily from the conventions of drama. But her philosophical novels remain connected with the tradition of dialogue because their concern, from first to last, is the assertion of a viable ethics in and through fictions of characters engaged in serious moral conversation. Austen continues the project of eighteenth-century philosophical dialogue (and of moral philosophy in general) in her novels.[5]

"I will not raise objections against any one's conduct on so illiberal a foundation, as a difference from myself, or a deviation from what I consider right and consistent," says Elinor in a conversation with her mother about Willoughby and his designs upon Marianne.[6] The statement serves to

---

[5] In describing Austen as an important moral philosopher, I am seconding the line of argument Alastair McIntyre sets forth in *After Virtue: a Study in Moral Theory* (Notre Dame: University of Notre Dame Press, 1981), see especially pp. 181–187, 239–243.

[6] *The Novels of Jane Austen*, ed. R.W. Chapman, 3rd edn., 5 vols. (London: Oxford University Press, 1933), *Sense and Sensibility*, I, xv, p. 81. Subsequent references to Austen's novels are to the Chapman edition and will be given by volume, number, chapter, and page.

characterize Elinor as a serious and fair-minded individual, but it also articulates what I take to be the fundamental problem for moral philosophy after the Enlightenment: in the absence of an intersubjective standard for passing judgments, in the presence of a wholesale subjectification of ethics within the romantic cult of taste and sensibility, Austen must establish a "liberal" foundation for asserting ethical valuations. The self-consciousness with which Austen addresses this problem in all of her works places her in the great line of eighteenth-century moral philosophers; the thoroughness with which she submerges the philosophical question (and technical vocabulary) in favor of precise depictions of characters and circumstances separates her from that tradition. "It is a truth universally acknowledged, that a single man in possession of a good fortune, must be in want of a wife." That single sentence opening *Pride and Prejudice* establishes the context for moral philosophy in the late eighteenth century: the universal is asserted, but cloaked in irony; the universal is also a species of hearsay.

From first to last, ethical deliberation is Austen's primary topic. She does not follow Johnson's turn back towards utopia but instead attempts to enlarge the reader's comprehension of Imlac's quandary – that the attempt to fix an incontestable ground for preference commits one to endless inquiring and deliberating. Moral knowledge, then, is bound up in the experience of a paradox: characters have no other reference point than experience for norms that ought to direct experience. For Austen, prose fiction provides a means to sustain and complicate the reader's engagement with this paradox. And Austen's celebrated irony, more than just a tone of voice or mood of genius, is a *philosophical stance* that holds partial ideas, values, and principles in suspension, without thereby losing the will to identify the best choice in given circumstances.

Austen's pedagogical concern was shared by other novelists of her day, especially women writers who view the loss of a transcendental ground for ethics in sexual and political terms. For them it is not utopian authority in the abstract that comes into question, but male patriarchal authority.[7] And it is not a mundane ethics in general that must be portrayed, but the precarious position of female heroines who must navigate their way through complex social situations in the absence of a dependable guide. Thus, we find novelists otherwise as different as Burney, Austen, and Wollstonecraft all depicting the same moral and epistemological problem.

In Fanny Burney's novel *Evelina, Or the History of a Young Lady's Entrance into the World* (1778), a seemingly offhand remark alerts us to the fact that the heroine no longer finds herself in a world where a moral guide such as Socrates leads her Aspasia-like from error to truth. Speaking to Lord Orville, she admits:

---

[7] The third term for them is explicitly gendered in the form of a social power structure that disinherits and victimizes daughters.

"I am new to the world, and unused to acting for myself, – my intentions are never wilfully blameable, yet I err perpetually! – I have, hitherto, been blest with the most affectionate of friends, and, indeed, the ablest of men, to guide and instruct me upon every occasion; – but he is too distant, now, to be applied to at the moment I want his aid; – and *here*, – there is not a human being whose counsel I can ask!"[8]

While Evelina wishes her Socrates were more proximate, Burney's insight into the challenge facing moral philosophy in a secular age was that individuals have been left alone, with no infallible guide to direct them. The young woman, alone and beset by unfamiliar circumstances, becomes the representative figure in such an age. Because her experiences under these conditions are the issue, she cannot transmogrify into a type figure for the divine; her beginning cannot be her end. It is the very absence of a metaphysical standard for her actions that shifts emphasis from a dialectical quest for the absolute to a mundane series of encounters acclimating her to the perils of social existence.

Similarly, Mary Wollstonecraft, towards the close of her second novel, *The Wrongs of Woman: or Maria* (unfinished at the author's death in 1797), introduces a trial presided over by a judge. Here we find the structure of rational deliberation, as Hobbes described it, the same structure whose inviolability secured the success of religious dialogues in the Christian Neoplatonic tradition. In Wollstonecraft, however, the judge has become a ruthless embodiment of injustice. The heroine has sued for divorce from a sadistic and mercenary husband:

The judge in summing up the evidence, alluded to "the fallacy of letting women plead their feelings, as an excuse for the violation of the marriage-vow. For his part, he had always determined to oppose all innovation, and the new-fangled notions which encroached on the good old rules of conduct ... What virtuous woman thought of her feelings? It was her duty to love and obey the man chosen by her parents and relations, who were qualified by their experience to judge better for her, than she could for herself."[9]

With characteristic discernment Wollstonecraft mocks the comedic structure of works such as *Pilgrim's Progress*, *Hylas and Philonous*, and *Rasselas* by placing a false authority at just the point in the narrative where convention would have dictated the reader's transcendental homecoming. In place of the celestial city or the fountain of dialectic or Abyssinia, we find only a figure for naked, unjust power.

In *Sense and Sensibility* Austen also creates a world without dependable authority figures. Fathers are dead, absent, bored, or otherwise ineffectual.

---

[8] Fanny Burney, *Evelina, Or the History of a Young Lady's Entrance into the World*, eds. Edward A. Bloom and Lillian D. Bloom (Oxford and New York: Oxford University Press, 1968), p. 306.

[9] *Mary, a Fiction and The Wrongs of Woman* ed. Gary Kelly (Oxford: Oxford University Press, 1976), pp. 198–199.

Most of the other males are dangerous or unhelpful. Colonel Brandon may or may not be an exception.[10] Even Elinor's favorite, Edward Ferrars, deceives her by not confessing his prior attachment to Lucy Steele. It is not by accident that the play the company is rehearsing when Willoughby dumps Marianne is *Hamlet*. Although Austen makes the point in a more moderate way than had Wollstonecraft, the opening scenes of *Sense and Sensibility* dramatize a male-centered world disinheriting its daughters with equal ruthlessness.

In *Rasselas*, as has been seen, Johnson acknowledges the dangers of a complex nature where characters are mixed and causes entangled. The sequence of dialogues helps save the young people from disaster not because of any special interpretative facility they learn through discourse, but because one disappointment after another convinces them to retreat to utopia. For Austen's female characters, a similar option exists, at least in its secular version. It is defined by the general term "sensibility." Marianne asks Edward, " 'How can you think of dirt, with such beautiful objects before you?' 'Because,' replied he smiling, 'amongst the rest of the objects before me, I see a very dirty lane.' 'How strange!' said Marianne to herself as she walked on" (I, xvi, p. 88). Aesthetic sensibility gives Marianne the pretext for looking away from the dirt, for inhabiting a utopia of her own feelings. Marianne has imbibed the new religion of taste and so has become her own arbiter of truth. When Elinor reminds her that "the pleasantness of an employment does not always evince its propriety," Marianne retorts, "On the contrary, nothing can be stronger proof of it ... for if there had been any real impropriety in what I did, I should have been sensible of it at the time, for we always know when we are acting wrong, and with such a conviction I should have had no pleasure" (I, xiii, p. 68). Like the author of *Alciphron*, Austen dramatizes what happens when high-level philosophical ideas, such as Shaftesbury's notion of the moral sense (descending to the late-eighteenth century through Hutcheson and Smith) or the aesthetics of sublimity become objects for popular consumption.[11] Seizing upon the aesthetic solution, the young heroine finds it less and less necessary (and less and less pleasurable) to set her inner voice in the crucible of public dialogue. After she is disappointed by Willoughby, Marianne retires into solitude. A life-threatening illness predictably follows.

At its best (and one often sees it at its best in Marianne), sensibility reveals to the reader an imagination resistant to social conventions, impervious to the

---

[10] Brandon's advantage, after all, is in catching a weakened Marianne on rebound from Willoughby, and he seems strangely reluctant to raise suspicions about Willoughby's character until (conveniently) the rake's near destruction of Marianne and his seduction of the second Eliza (whom Brandon is trying to protect) come to light at the same time. Upon learning of Willoughby's involvement with his charge, Brandon challenges him to a duel, which, luckily for both parties, has no result.

[11] In *Northanger Abbey* Austen's target was also an aesthetics of sublimity, delivered to the general public through the craze for gothic romances.

small opinions of others, and alert to the restorative powers of nature. But Austen and her heroine Elinor find too much dirt in a young woman's way to adopt any framework that will blind her to it. Interpretation of mixed characters and complex relations is too difficult a matter, takes too long an apprenticeship, and is too decisive an ingredient in one's future happiness to imagine that there could be a short-cut, a shorter circuit, exempting one from the trial. The fundamental opposition in *Sense and Sensibility*, then, is between two ways of interpreting complex phenomena: Marianne's secular utopianism and Elinor's more cautious art of deliberation.[12]

For Austen aesthetics constitute a false solution to the problem of ethical deliberation in a secular age. It collapses the *time frame* of ethical choice into the blink of an eye or the pulse of the heart, and it makes the subject resistant to the circumstantial details that mitigate and sometimes correct powerful impressions. It makes young women vulnerable to men who have less to lose by feeling more. Austen, like some of the moral philosophers who wrote dialogues before her, is interested in teaching not so much a body of doctrine as a process of deliberation, a way for young readers to make the right conjectures about complex social events. She opposes the aesthetic solution because it offers the wrong kind of apprenticeship for young women.

Against the aesthetic experience, which concentrates time into an instantaneous response followed (perhaps) by reflection on our capacity to be so moved, Austen sets the marriage question, which establishes a longer time frame for choice. Within the courtship novel, reflection must precede the event, and the event itself is always anti-climactic. Austen's emphasis upon marriage is as much a matter of shrewd social observation as of philosophical intervention: in the absence of a teleological framework, Austen establishes an arena wholly within the human dimension, wherein ethical decisions remain momentous and (potentially) correctable.[13] Whereas Johnson uses the catacombs of the Egyptians to focus the young travelers' attention on what is *really* important, Austen uses another life-and-death situation, courtship in a cynical market economy, to establish the framework for inquiry.

For Austen, time provides the important distinction between the aesthetic outlook of Marianne and the empirical outlook of Elinor. Marianne takes

---

[12] For another argument emphasizing the problem of judgment in the novel, see Claudia Johnson, "The Twilight of Probability: Uncertainty and Hope in *Sense and Sensibility*," *Philological Quarterly* 62 (1983) 171–186. "*Sense and Sensibility* has as its starting point, then, epistemological problems – problems of knowing and assent – that baffle Marianne and Elinor alike" (171). See also Johnson's essay on *Sense and Sensibility* in *Jane Austen: Women, Politics, and the Novel* (Chicago and London: University of Chicago Press, 1988).

[13] The point is McIntyre's: "Jane Austen ... identifies that social sphere within which the practice of the virtues is able to continue ... Her heroines seek the good through seeking their own good in marriage. The restricted households of Highbury and Mansfield Park have to serve as surrogates for the Greek city-state and medieval kingdom" (*After Virtue*, pp. 239–240).

pride in the swiftness of her judgment. It is a sign of genius. "I have not known him long," says Marianne of Willoughby, "but I am much better acquainted with him than I am with any other creature in the world, except yourself and mama. It is not time or opportunity that is to determine intimacy: it is disposition alone" (I, xii, pp. 58–59). Elinor, on the other hand, urges caution. She does not resent the witticism that she might think it probable a couple were to be married if she saw them standing at the altar. Austen's sympathy clearly lies with Elinor. But here an interesting situation develops that bears directly on the literary structure of *Sense and Sensibility*. Although the work appears to be structured almost like a conduct manual, setting forth good and bad positions associated with characters serving as types (Elinor = sense; Marianne = sensibility); and although the sequence of actions leads to the inescapable conclusion that Elinor is right and Marianne wrong; Elinor and Austen's entire pedagogy is premised upon the difficulty of forming judgments without extensive observation, apt comparison, and careful inference. A dogmatic conduct manual assigning truth to one typed character and falsehood to another would not have activated the interpretative facility Austen hopes to instill in her readers. It is in this context that Austen's pervasive irony intervenes: though the choice between Elinor and Marianne appears simple, the narrator lets us know in any number of ways that the judgment between characters may in fact be difficult; indeed, one may wish to resist altogether the dichotomy between reason and feeling, suspicion and sympathy.

Several factors complicate the reader's interpretation of *Sense and Sensibility*. Most prominent is an irony that works to settle and unsettle the reader's judgment simultaneously. The whole time Elinor warns Marianne against hasty attachments, she is guilty of having formed one herself with Edward, who has been engaged to Lucy Steele for four years at the time he and Elinor fall in love. Although Elinor tries to teach Marianne the difficult art of probabilistic inference (gathering evidence through observation, testing the data in light of fluctuating circumstances, forming tentative conclusions through reasoned conjecture), she sometimes exempts herself from its practice. When Marianne notices Edward's ring and the lock of hair it contains, she assumes it must belong to Fanny. "Yes, it is my sister's hair," Edward lies. Marianne may or may not accept the improbable explanation, but Elinor forms an even more wild surmise. Edward must have spread the glittering forfex wide when modest Elinor herself wasn't looking, procuring a lock of her own hair "by some theft or contrivance unknown" (I, xviii, pp. 18–19). She does not ask herself whether such a theft would be consistent with what she knows of Edward's character. Her desire to believe well of Edward leads her to a mild form of hypocrisy, which the narrator describes in these terms: "she was very well disposed on the whole to regard his actions with all the candid allowances and generous qualifications, which had been rather

more painfully extorted from her, for Willoughby's service, by her mother"
(I, xix, p. 101).

How does irony affect interpretation? For one, it transforms a linear
sequence of action into something more like a tableau of moral possibilities,
all of which one would want to consider before passing judgment on Elinor
for not living up to her convictions. Elinor's instinctive suspicion of
Willoughby may not have reflected extensive gathering of data leading to a
rational calculation of probable nature, but it was accurate. By the same
acumen, she has made a decision in favor of Edward, and she will indeed be
shocked to learn she could be so deceived. So although (or perhaps *because*)
inconsistent in her principles, she is right to make the allowance for Edward
(even though Edward is lying to her face) and would be wrong if she made
the same allowance for Willoughby. Irony transforms types into fallible
characters, leading the reader to work out the "allowances and qualifications"
necessary to distinguish Elinor from Marianne and Edward from Willoughby,
though all commit similar faults.

The incident with Edward's ring is not the only time our exemplar is cast
ironically in a negative light. Elinor and Marianne are in London, and
Marianne is waiting hopelessly for word from Willoughby:

"You are expecting a letter then?" said Elinor, unable to be longer silent.

"Yes! a little – not much."

After a short pause, "You have no confidence in me, Marianne."

"Nay, Elinor, this reproach from *you*! – you who have confidence in no one!"

"Me!" returned Elinor in some confusion; "indeed, Marianne, I have nothing to
  tell."

"Nor I," answered Marianne with energy; "our situations are then alike. We have
  neither of us anything to tell; you, because you communicate, and I, because I
  conceal nothing."   (II, v, pp. 169–170)

Elinor has been "exerting" herself to deceive others about the state of her
heart after learning of Edward's prior attachment. But in her concern for
Marianne, she forgets that she has been playing a role, even to her own sister.
Marianne lets her know she knows: the one who plays no role and has
nothing to say ends up sounding a lot like the one who plays a role and will
say nothing. As things turn out, Elinor's very good reasons for concealing
information from her sister have provided Marianne with a pretext for doing
the same, perversely, when she is most in need of a confidante. Her
incommunication has something suicidal about it, Elinor's something heroic.
Again, the effect of Austen's irony is to drive attention away from the
extremes, beginnings and ends, absolute causes, static ideas, and into the
middle where causes are mixed and relations complex. When Marianne tells

Elinor "our situations are alike," she is simultaneously right and wrong –
right because they have reached an impasse, wrong because their ways to
that impasse have been completely different. The same effect is produced by
different causes.

Later, the narrator adds that the same cause may have very different
effects. Late in the book, we learn that Edward "has been entirely cast off for
persevering in his engagement with a very deserving young woman" (III, iii,
p. 282). Yet what appears an injustice turns out to be a happy turn in the
plot. When primogeniture falls to his brother Robert, and Lucy follows suit,
Robert is freed to propose to Elinor. The narrator observes, "What Edward
had done to forfeit the right of eldest son, might have puzzled many people to
find out; and what Robert had done to succeed to it, might have puzzled
them still more. It was an arrangement, however, justified in its effects, if not
in its cause" (III, xiv, p. 377). Chase after causes, the narrator implies, and you
soon arrive at an ignorant old lady dispensing fortunes at whim. Follow the
effects, however, and one is left to consider what qualities enabled these
particular characters to overcome adversity. The same point holds true for
the plot itself. Follow the linear sequence of actions and one inhabits the
world of romance, where virtuous characters realize happy fates, and vicious
characters suffer. Attend to the pervasive irony and one encounters a different
kind of work altogether, the novel of moral conversation, in which the
arbitrariness of happy endings directs attention back to the effects themselves
and the education necessary to make sense of them.

Under these conditions, "dialogue" in *Sense and Sensibility* has little in
common with the abstract metaphysical disquisitions one finds in Shaftesbury,
Berkeley, and Hume. Although dialogues on set topics abound, they are
rarely sustained or resolved. Austen holds on to the thematic importance of
serious conversation; characters appear admirable or the reverse to the extent
they are capable of sustaining intelligent conversation. Yet dialogue almost
always tells us more about the characters who hold specific ideas than about
ideas themselves. An exchange between Elinor and Willoughby early in the
novel is representative. They are debating the merits of Colonel Brandon:

"That he is patronized by *you* [Elinor]," replied Willoughby, "is certainly in his
favour; but as for the esteem of others, it is a reproach in itself. Who would submit to
the indignity of being approved by such women as Lady Middleton and Mrs.
Jennings, that could command the indifference of anybody else?"

"But perhaps the abuse of such people as yourself and Marianne will make amends
for the regard of Lady Middleton and her mother. If their praise is censure, your
censure may be praise."   (I, x, p. 50)

The abstract ethical question, "what things are worth praising and what
censoring," has been replaced in Austen's moral philosophy by the question,

"*whose* praise is censure, and *whose* censure praise?" Ethics is referred wholly to character. The exchange can only be determined in the context of a narrative that reveals behavior over time. Dialogue must be situated in a narrative; it must become "novelistic."

Set philosophical dialogues do occur at times in Austen's fictions, but like the exchange cited above, they are always turned to the investigation of character. Consider the dialogue on female accomplishments in *Pride and Prejudice*. Miss Bingley begins by praising Miss Darcy's special talents: "such a countenance, such manners! and so extremely accomplished for her age!" (I, viii, pp. 38–39). Bingley, in no humor to add praise to his sister's encomium, trivializes the point by feigning amazement that "young ladies can have patience to be so very accomplished, as they all are." Darcy attempts to turn Bingley's banter back towards more solid footing, claiming that the number of accomplished women he knows is no more than half a dozen. When Elizabeth asks him to define his terms, the conversation turns towards serious (and orderly) debate, but just as Elizabeth begins to protest that Darcy's ideal is unrealistic, the group is hushed up and ushered back to cards. Such an encounter is typical. The issue of accomplishments arises in the course of the plot and is subordinate to the distinct motivations of the characters. Caroline Bingley wishes to praise Darcy's sister at Elizabeth's expense, and Bingley by deflating the topic hopes to undermine her. The endpoint of philosophical dialogue has become the starting point of Austen's moral conversations: intellectual positions display manners and maneuvers.

Another example of a disrupted dialogue occurs shortly after this scene when Bingley and Darcy argue in Elizabeth's presence over the merits of impulsiveness. Bingley boasts that, in contrast with Darcy's slow, methodical manner of writing, his ideas "flow so rapidly that he has not time to express them" (I, x, p. 48). Darcy answers not with a defense of method, but with a reminder of his friend's earlier claim that he would quit Netherfield on a moment's notice if the spirit moved him. Bingley tries to stave off debate: "Nay, this is too much, to remember at night all the foolish things that were said in the morning" (I, x, p. 49), but Elizabeth warms to the subject and defends Bingley. The argument hinges upon the difference between action based upon unexamined feeling and action based upon rational conviction, a topic central to all of Austen's novels. As the dialogue moves towards a more formal exposition of positions, Darcy feels in his element. "Will it not be advisable," he asks, "before we proceed on this subject, to arrange with rather more precision the degree of importance which is to appertain ... " (I, x, p. 50). But this conventional arrangement of the topic is too much for Bingley. "Let us hear," he ironically adds, "all the particulars, not forgetting their comparative height and size; for that will have more weight in the argument, Miss Bennet, than you may be aware of." He proceeds to turn the dialogue into an *ad hominem* attack against Darcy, punning on his friend's greater physical bulk. Though good humored, his comments silence discussion, and the topic is not renewed once Bingley leaves.

Again, we find that serious philosophical dialogue has been disrupted and integrated into a larger narrative exploring the motives of character. The rules of debate would seem to make Darcy the winner, but the reader is unlikely to draw this conclusion. The exchange confirms our image of Darcy as proud and overly discriminating. Bingley remains a model of affability. The argument may boil down to little more than Darcy's attempt to impress Elizabeth, and Bingley's desire to leave them both alone. Does this mean that the serious philosophical question has been completely deflated in favor of the light turns of a drawing-room comedy? No. But the moral resolution of this dialogue only occurs later in the narrative. Within the dialogue Darcy raises the hypothetical case of a man who has decided on impulse to leave his home but is suddenly told by a friend to stay. His point is that someone who steps in one direction by whim will be directed as easily in the other by chance. Bingley dismisses it all as nonsense: "arguments are too much like disputes" (I, x, p. 51). But later events prove the hypothetical situation to be prophetic. A word from Darcy divides Bingley from Jane and nearly ruins their chance for happiness together. Future events uphold the value Darcy places upon prudence and methodical habit, even if the messenger of that position lacks moral authority in certain respects.

In *Sense and Sensibility* something like a set topic is announced at the beginning, and though it is interrupted by gossip and augmented by "evidence" from many other sources, the topic continues throughout the book. In chapter eleven of *Sense and Sensibility*, Elinor and Brandon turn to the problem of whether Marianne should change. Elinor hopes out loud, "A few years will settle her opinions on the reasonable basis of common sense and observation." Brandon replies, "This will probably be the case ... and yet there is something so amiable in the prejudices of a young mind, that one is sorry to see them give way to the reception of more general opinions." Elinor objects, "I cannot agree with you there ... There are inconveniences attending such feelings as Marianne's, which all the charms of enthusiasm and ignorance of the world cannot atone for. Her systems have all the unfortunate tendency of setting propriety at nought; and a better acquaintance with the world is what I look forward to as her greatest possible advantage" (I, xi, pp. 56–57). Clearly, Elinor is right and Brandon is wrong, but the kind of interpretation that decides easily between right and wrong is not what Austen is trying to teach. The question that exceeds this particular dialogue but remains alive throughout the rest of the book is whether Marianne can change *without* giving way to the receipt of general opinions, and whether Elinor's defense of female education can avoid becoming an apology for convention. When, several chapters later, Elinor admits that "I have frequently detected myself ... in a total misapprehension of character

... Sometimes one is guided by what they say of themselves, and very frequently by what other people say of them, without giving oneself time to deliberate and judge" (I, xvii, p. 93), Marianne senses an opportunity to fight back: "But I thought it was right, Elinor, to be guided wholly by the opinion of other people. I thought our judgments were given us merely to be subservient to those of our neighbors. This has always been your doctrine, I am sure" (I, xvii, pp. 93–94). Elinor, alarmed by the attack, responds, "No, Marianne, never. My doctrine has never aimed at the subjection of the understanding."

Once again, Elinor is no doubt right; yet by referring to her own position as a "doctrine," she also confirms Marianne's point. She does have a doctrine, sense, and adherence to it threatens to reduce her to a type character. In other words, the opposition between sisters retains the trappings of a formal debate (i.e. between reason and feeling); yet Austen embeds serious dialogue within a moral universe wherein, as the narrator explains, "Every qualification is raised at times, by the circumstances of the moment, to more than its real value; and she [Elinor] was sometimes weighed down by officious condolence to rate good-breeding as more indispensable to comfort than good-nature" (II, x, p. 215). Circumstances may lead Elinor to overestimate the importance of convention; circumstances already have led Marianne to exaggerate the importance of sentiments. The one threatens to become first the moralist and then a statue; the other threatens to become first the sensualist and then "dead leaves." Austen's solution is by no means a dialectical synthesis of opposition into a higher unity. Her pervasive irony leaves us with a concept of character seen not in terms of self-identity (unity of consciousness) but in terms of a restless mixture of skepticism and credulity, cynicism and faith, calculation and intuition.

In this respect, the purpose of serious dialogue in Austen's novels is the opposite of what it had been in *Rasselas*. The culmination of a series of conversations is not abdication from but engagement in the world through steady improvement in the art of rational deliberation.[14] As a mode of education, conversation in *Sense and Sensibility* subverts the work's apparent dependency upon romance conventions. The very happy and moderately happy marriages of Elinor and Marianne are almost beside the point. Here again, Austen's irony deprives the reader of an easy solution to the epistemological problems raised by courtship. Although the stock convention of poetic justice rewarding the virtuous with good marriages and the reverse with the reverse seems to be invoked, a heavy ironic overlay removes even

---

[14] In *Probability and Literary Form*, Patey observes, "Austen not only conducts her novels in the Augustan vocabulary of probable inference, of sagacity in reading signs and circumstances; she builds them as didactic structures of conjecture and expectation, as judged by the event" (p. 218).

this handhold for interpretation. After letting us know through the silent thoughts of Elinor that justice has been visited on Willoughby ("Each faulty proposition, in leading him to evil, had led him likewise to punishment" [III, viii, p. 331]), the narrator adds that *his* experience of this punishment may be limited to a "pang" of conscience, and the narrator continues, "that he was forever inconsolable, that he fled from society, or contracted an habitual gloom of temper, or died of a broken heart, must not be depended on – for he did neither. He lived to exert, and frequently to enjoy himself" (III, xiv, p. 379). Similarly, when the narrator describes Lucy Steele's fate, a note of cheerful cynicism prevails: "The whole of Lucy's behaviour in the affair, and the prosperity which crowned it, therefore, may be held forth as a most encouraging instance of what an earnest, an unceasing attention to self-interest, however its progress may apparently be obstructed, will do in securing every advantage of fortune, with no other sacrifice than that of time and conscience" (III, xiv, p. 376).

Good causes produce bad effects; bad causes produce good effects. Embracing Imlac's paradox, Austen builds the moral universe of her prose fictions on the remains of a philosophical enterprise that valued ratiocination *only* to the extent that it identified simple causes for complex effects, abstracting life from life. She accepts Hume's view that we have no means of establishing *necessary connections* between effects and causes. All we have are effects, and in this realm, judgment must be based on informed conjecture, strengthened by close observation and experience. The standard of judgment must be sought in the realm of contingency. No philosophical "as if" can dissolve the existential paradox. Lucy and Willoughby experience little more than the occasional "pang" of conscience because they lose, over time, the habit of reading the flux of occurrences (both within and without) as anything more than occasions for self-gratification.

Austen uses the conventions of the courtship novel as a cover for her more pointed polemic, a call for the education of young women. Her argument is that moral conscience may not develop unless empirical conditions favor it. Deprive daughters and sons of education, remove them from the habit of connecting before and after, act and implication, and character falls prey to the calculus of the marketplace, where the only principle is greed. Austen's pervasive irony directs us back, in other words, from the comedic conclusion of romance to the educational process young characters undergo and fail to undergo in time. The culmination of *Sense and Sensibility*, then, is not the pairing off of couples but the two conversations that occur at the end, in which Elinor teaches Marianne how to read people like Willoughby, and where Edward, confessing his moral failure to Elinor, identifies those existential conditions that kept him from developing his reason.

In the closing moments of the novel, Elinor and Marianne are able to sit together and calmly dissect Willoughby's character. Their ruminations range from conjectures about the past ("*One* observation may, I think, be fairly drawn from the whole of the story – that all of Willoughby's difficulties have arisen from the first offense against virtue, in his behaviour to Eliza Williams"), to the present ("Selfish? ... do you really think him selfish?" "The whole of his behaviour, from the beginning to the end of the affair, has been grounded on selfishness"), to the future ("Had you married, you would always have been poor ... [he would] soon have learnt to rank the innumerable comforts of a clear estate and good income as of far more importance, even to domestic happiness, than the mere temper of a wife") [III, xi, pp. 351–352]. In drawing these inferences, Elinor depends upon a fundamentally Hobbesian view of human nature. "Oh Elinor," her mother exclaims earlier in the book, "how incomprehensible are your feelings! You would rather take evil upon credit than good" (I, xv, p. 78). Yet the scene of education between sisters, and, indeed, Austen's entire emphasis upon serious moral conversations to educate young women, suggests a Shaftesburean confidence in an inborn rational conscience, which is sympathetic and selfless. Elinor says of Edward's sense and goodness, "no one can, I think, be in doubt, who has seen him often enough to engage him in unreserved conversation" (I, iv, p. 20).

To realize a balance between extremes requires experience. Another character appears at the end to remind the reader of the same point.[15] In his confession to Elinor, Edward explains why he was an easy mark for Lucy Steele:

"It was foolish, idle inclination on my side," said he, "the consequence of ignorance of the world – and want of employment. Had my mother given me some active profession when I was removed at eighteen from the care of Mr. Pratt, I think – nay, I am sure, it would never have happened ... had I then had any pursuit, any object to engage my time ... I should very soon have outgrown the fancied attachment, especially by mixing more with the world ... But instead of having anything to do, instead of having any profession chosen for me, or being allowed to chuse any myself, I returned home to be completely idle; and for the first twelvemonth afterwards I had not even the nominal employment, which belonging to the university would have given me, for I was not entered at Oxford till I was nineteen. I had therefore nothing in the world to do but to fancy myself in love ... I had seen so little of other women that I could make no comparisons. (III, xiii, p. 362)

Though Austen might be accused of portraying a world where female aspiration is limited to the right choice of mate in a domestic comedy, her ironic juxtapositions leave us with the argument, the same as Wollstonecraft's

---

[15] In philosophical dialogues, arguments sometimes pass out of one mouth and into another, especially when the author fears "persecution" for the opinion. Where Austen would otherwise be most exposed, in advancing the cause of women's emancipation through education, she allows an idle son, deprived of employment and profession, to have the last word. See Leo Strauss, *Persecution and the Art of Writing* (Chicago: University of Chicago Press, 1988).

in *A Vindication of the Rights of Woman*, that aesthetic sensibility underlies a false education and that only by equalizing opportunity for sons and daughters in the public arena will the moral condition of humankind improve. The fundamental change of horizons Edward imagines possible for himself is the hope Austen would realize for all young women: mixing in the world, bringing, as Hume might have put it (in "Of Essay Writing") the conversable world of the parlor to the scholarly world of the university; just as Austen, rare genius, has brought the scholarly world of eighteenth-century moral philosophy into the familiar conversations of the novel.

Austen takes the metaphysical either/ors that have for the most part been the subject of this book, and transforms them into ironic both/ands. Not Pyrrho or Plato, not Hume or Berkeley, skepticism or credence, but the one *and* the other, as circumstances demand. The ironic juxtaposition of views previously thought incompatible distinguishes Austen's moral philosophy. Austen betrays a fundamentally pessimistic view of human nature; yet she upholds faith in a rational conscience that guides her heroines to happy destinies. Austen's characters live in a world of surfaces, diminished prospects, broken dialogues, noise; yet the astute ones are able to piece the parts together into intelligible wholes and gain some measure of security. Increasingly, her novels leave behind the dichotomies that split the female figure in Shaftesbury's frontispiece and divided characters in philosophical dialogue. For Austen, the press of actual social and economic dangers (the "market" for marriage) is too great to allow female heroines the illusion that their "virtue" lies in deciding between false extremes or in adopting a way of interpreting complex phenomena less complex than the phenomena themselves. Austen's irony is a philosophical practice, a moral regimen, a way of holding antitheses in suspension without thereby losing the will to act. In the terms I have been developing throughout this study, irony is Austen's third term, in place of myth, in place of Berkeley's fountain of dialectic, in place of the aesthetic. Marianne must learn to become more like Elinor, and Elinor must learn to become more like Marianne. Neither loses her self when she bends towards the other. For Austen to retain the seriousness of moral philosophy while embracing what Irvin Ehrenpreis called "the heroism of the quotidian," suggests, I think, that she entered upon the writing of novels with an awareness of what eighteenth-century philosophers had been trying to do with dialogues.[16]

---

[16] Irvin Ehrenpreis, *Acts of Implication: Suggestion and Covert Meaning in the Works of Dryden, Swift, Pope, and Austen* (Berkeley: University of California Press, 1980), chapter 4.

Epilogue

Some dialectics of Enlightenment: a critique of dialectical historiography

In 1991, the Polish Academy of Arts and Sciences changed the name of its journal from *Dialectics and Humanism: a Philosophical Quarterly* to *Dialogue and Humanism: a Universalist Quarterly*. "The exceptional current events which affect above all Poland," the editors wrote in explanation, "inclined us to summarize our 17 years of activity and, in the course of the expansion of its programme, to modify the title of the journal."[1] Why did "exceptional current events" suggest the replacement of "dialectics" by "dialogue"? Turning to the editors' new introduction to *Dialogue and Humanism*, one finds little explanation for the change. Indeed, the editors do everything in their circumlocutory power to deny any fundamental change has taken place: because one of the original aims of *Dialectics and Humanism* had been to promote an encounter between Marxism (dialectics) and Christianity (humanism), dialogue can be said to have defined their purpose all along. The editors praise the role of their own journal in fostering democratic reform. What they avoid mentioning is the discrepancy between the social transformations the dialogue between Marxists and humanists helped create and the historical destiny predicted by Marxist dialectics.

Eighteen years earlier, in the inaugural number of *Dialectics and Humanism*, the editors had written, "It is our ambition to contribute to the development of Marxist philosophy in its contemporary Leninist form, for this orientation – of that we are convinced – will be winning more and more adherents among scholars and thinkers."[2] Exceptional events, history as it unfolded, proved the prediction wrong, no doubt prompting a re-evaluation of the title. Yet events seem not to have occasioned a reconsideration of the relationship between dialogue and dialectics. In 1991, as in 1973, the direction a dialogue takes is still thought to be controlled by the teleological movement of dialectics: "We wrote in the past that 'dialogue is the younger brother of dialectics.' Now we would like to express a conviction, which probably will not be shared by many other adherents of universalism, that dialectics can become a vastly useful instrument for the examination and co-creation of a wider and truly great structure of knowledge, which in the near future will

---

[1] *Dialogue and Humanism: The Universalist Quarterly* 1 (1991), ii.
[2] *Dialectics and Humanism: The Polish Philosophical Quarterly* 1 (1973), 3–4.

take on the form of a metaphilosophy. Gurvitch wrote that the façade of the future Palace of the Humanities will bear the motto 'Nul n'être ici, s'il n'est dialecticien,' patterned after the famous inscription about mathematics on the Platonian Academy" (p. v).

The editors do hint at some necessary modifications in the original claim. They distinguish between a good kind of dialectics, the tradition of "Heraclitus, Plato, Aristotle, Hegel, Marx and Sartre," and a bad kind of dialectics, "the intellectual and pseudo-scientific abuses which were committed in its name." They do not explain the difference between good and bad dialectics; nor do they indicate how a good theory produced bad practice. Although they are confronted by history in the most immediate way any materialist could desire, the theoretical questions the recent fall of Communism poses to dialectical materialism stand beyond their concern even at the moment when they reaffirm the value of dialectics for the next installment.

If in 1991 the failure of a Marxist–Leninist dialectics leads to a recognition, however reluctant, of the disparity between dialogue and dialectics, the history I have described in this book presents the opposite end of that historical development, a time when the failure of dialogue as a mode of religious, philosophical, and political discourse led in part to the subordination of dialogue within dialectic and to the apotheosis of dialectic into the scheme governing historical destiny. I say "led in part" because one of the primary purposes of this book has been to describe the strains within Enlightenment thought and textual practices, not a synthesis of contradictions. In this respect one of the most notable aspects of the intellectual and literary history of the Enlightenment is the *struggle* to control the meaning of dialectic itself. During the Enlightenment, as we have seen, writers deploy rival conceptions of dialectic within specific *kinds* of writing that are directed against other texts. As a result, the metaphysical interpretation of dialectic central to Christian Neoplatonism and its eighteenth-century continuations (metaphysical dialogues, physico-theology, versions of the design argument) deteriorates under the pressure of another sense of dialectic, equally ancient, deriving from Zeno, the skeptical (de-Platonized) Socrates, Pyrrho, and their eighteenth-century manifestations (radical empiricism, Humean skepticism, anti-metaphysical dialogues). One response to the declining efficacy of transcendental dialectic as embodied *in texts*, a response I would associate with the beginning of a counter-Enlightenment, was the transformation of the contested category (dialectic) into an incontestable description of the way ideas, genres, and institutions emerge, cohere, and change over time (dialectical historiography). Dialectic becomes a concept controlling the interpretation of diverse texts. The rational scheme capable of consolidating mixed phenomena will no longer be sought in divinity or in phenomena, but will be found instead in a process internal to history itself, the self-motion of the Concept unfolding over time.

In this book I have described the literary and intellectual history of the Enlightenment in terms of a struggle to determine the nature of both dialogue and dialectic during the eighteenth century. This struggle contributed not only to the apotheosis of transcendental dialectic in Hegelian historiography, but also to the emergence of philosophical aesthetics and the development of complex prose fictions. I have emphasized the interrelation of these developments, even though the tendency of aesthetics is to separate literary from religious and intellectual history, and the practice of dialectical historiography is to subordinate all cultural inventions to its governing logic. In these concluding comments, I wish to return to the question I raised in the introduction, namely, why I have chosen to write a generic history of dialogue and dialectic rather than a dialectical history of genre and Enlightenment.

Horkheimer and Adorno in *The Dialectic of Enlightenment* and Michael McKeon in *The Origins of the English Novel* both employ dialectic to frame their views of historical transformation; and other histories, such as Cassirer's *Philosophy of the Enlightenment*, do the same thing in effect through methodological proximity with Hegel.[3] Despite obvious differences, the concepts of dialectic at work in these studies share several important assumptions about the writing of history. First, in each case dialectic defines not an entity that *has* a history (for example, as a mode of argument or a pedagogical practice or a metaphysical assertion) but a concept corresponding with the transformational pattern of history itself. Consequently, though dialectic frames readings of the Enlightenment, no mention is made of the struggle to define dialectic during the Enlightenment. Finally, and following from the first two, these modern studies continue one of the important projects undertaken at the end of the Enlightenment, namely the transformation of dialectic from a vehicle of transcendence within Christian Neoplatonism (metaphysics), into the principle of coherence within the autonomous aesthetic object (matched by a faculty of aesthetic judgment in the mind), and finally into a transcendental scheme for reading all history *as if* it were an aesthetic object immediate to mind.

In Horkheimer and Adorno's *Dialectic of Enlightenment*, the concept of dialectic has been freed from any textual referent. Their dialectic, like the transcendental interpretation devolving from Platonism, describes inevitability, only now instead of a teleological progress towards greater illumination we find an inevitable fall into darkness, archaic violence, the return of repressed mythic forces. Specific texts and the concepts they

---

[3] I have in mind Cassirer's statement at the beginning of *The Philosophy of the Enlightenment* that the Enlightenment had to be "approached in its characteristic depth rather than in its breadth, and to be presented in the light of the unity of its conceptual origin and of its underlying principle rather than of the totality of its historical manifestations and results ... The tensions and solutions, the doubts and decisions, the skepticism and unshakable conviction of this philosophy must be seen and interpreted from one central position if its real historical meaning is to be made clear" (p. v).

develop are incidental to this reversal: "The concept, which some would see as the sign-unit for whatever is comprised under it, has from the beginning been instead the product of dialectical thinking in which everything is always that which it is, only because it becomes that which it is not."[4] Specific works become incidental because locked in a fatal necessity whereby their core concepts are undergoing reversal. The source of this fatalism is never described, any more than the vehicle of transition from sense to intellect, part to whole, was made explicit in the positive version of the same logic, Platonic metaphysics. Nor is the inevitability open to question. Because texts have been abstracted into concepts and concepts have been referred to a larger narrative controlling the formation and deformation of values, the complex mixtures of values, temporalities, and discourses present *within* specific works, as within every moment in history, have become irrelevant.

According to the dour logic of this inverted Platonic dialectic, the positive values of Enlightenment – impartial inquiry, the teaching of secular history, skeptical questioning, freedom of thought and expression, emancipation, justice – are doomed to undergo a reversal whereby instrumental reason, prejudice, totalitarianism, anarchy become their inevitable completion. "We are wholly convinced," Horkheimer and Adorno write in their "Introduction," "that social freedom is inseparable from enlightened thought. Nevertheless, we believe that we have just as clearly recognized that the notion of this very way of thinking, no less than the actual historic forms – the social institutions – with which it is interwoven, already contains the seed of the reversal universally apparent today" (p. xiii). The "reversal" occurs once "dissolvent rationality" trains its destructive critique even upon its own ideals: Enlightenment brings fascism; critical reason brings barbarism; science brings genocide. Enlightenment becomes a self-abusing robot, at once sensualized as a carnal appetite wasting itself and its progeny, and depersonalized as a machine unable to direct its own energies. "Enlightenment," wrote Hegel, "still bears within itself the blemish of an unsatisfied yearning."[5]

Two notions of historical recovery are at odds here. The claim that social freedom is inseparable from enlightened thought posits a recuperable element of Enlightenment, despite the subsequent perversion of it. But with the word "reversal" a different way of reading the past enters. The liberating aspects of Enlightenment are set within a more encompassing dialectical framework, one which telescopes historical process to the point where subsequent developments are backread as intended – or at least inevitable – consequences of the prior, such that one can write sentences like, "Enlightenment is totalitarian" and "The organization of the Hitler Youth is not a return to barbarism but the triumph of repressive equality." These are

[4] Horkheimer and Adorno, *The Dialectic of Enlightenment*, p. 15.
[5] Hegel, *Phenomenology of Spirit*, trans. A. V. Miller (Oxford: Oxford University Press), p. 349.

serious charges, if one believes at the same time that "social freedom is
inseparable from enlightened thought." Is social freedom then totalitarian? Is
equality the prelude to fascism? How, then, would it ever be possible to
recuperate positive lessons from the past, if these contain the seed (and just
what *is* a seed?) of their own reversal?

By reading the entire period in terms of a single conception of dialectic,
Horkheimer and Adorno avoid the problem that has been at the heart of this
study: why did philosophical, theological, and political antagonists all claim
the right to define dialogue and to deploy dialectic as a means of representing
temporal succession and the inevitable movement of disinterested thought?
Were all writers equally in the process of becoming reactionaries? Had their
agency as thinkers and writers already been signed over to an inescapable
fate? Were they puppets in a preassigned plot? Questions of this sort call
upon the historian to pursue a detailed study of many different kinds of
writing, major and minor, high and low, systematic and heterogeneous; they
cannot be answered by selecting out the interpretation of dialectic that
proved victorious and then using it to backread a period during which any
claim about the transhistorical nature of dialectic was highly tendentious.
What remains alive in the century prior to Hegel is the question of the nature
of dialectic, its methodology as a mode of inquiry, its validity within
theological debate, and its dangers as a prescription for social order.

Two aspects of Habermas' critique of *The Dialectic of Enlightenment* are
worth noting here. First, Habermas points out, rightly, I think, that
Horkheimer and Adorno's condemnation of Enlightenment depends upon
critical practices derived from Enlightenment reason. Habermas calls this
"the performative contradiction inherent in totalized critique."[6] If critical
reason is doomed to become instrumental reason, a tool of bourgeois
ideology, then even radical critique loses its force, for it cannot possibly
exempt itself from the inevitability. The "description of the self-destruction of
the critical capacity is paradoxical," writes Habermas, "because in the
moment of description it still has to make use of the critique that has been
declared dead."[7]

A second and equally damaging criticism involves Habermas' sense that
The Dialectic of Enlightenment succumbs to a "purist intent." By this phrase
Habermas means that Horkheimer and Adorno are not interested in the
complex processes whereby good values and practices are appropriated,
changed, subverted in history. Their reading of Enlightenment derives from
categories (myth versus reason; ideology versus critique) whose binarism
betrays a "purist," which is to say, metaphysical outlook. By contrast,

---

[6] "The Entwinement of Myth and Enlightenment," in *The Philosophical Discourse of Modernity*, trans.
Frederick Lawrence (Cambridge, MA: MIT Press, 1987), p. 119.
[7] *Ibid.*, p. 119.

Habermas stresses the entwinement of myth and Enlightenment, critique and
ideology, within concrete textual and communicative practices.

This "purist intent" comes as a result of extracting a transcendental
conception of dialectic from its historical grounding in specific kinds of
writing. Within texts, dialectic is always one feature among others. We do not
read a dialectic. We read a history, or a theological treatise, or a school
primer, or a dialogue, in which dialectic comes under discussion, or provides
a logic, or promotes skeptical questioning. Grounded in textual practices,
opposed by other texts, often opposed even by oppositional elements within
the selfsame text, dialectic has no pure form, describes no inevitable destiny,
except as a matter of interpretation. In Shaftesbury's *The Moralists*, for
instance, dialogue structures an opposition between two conceptions of
dialectic, voiced by two distinct characters, holding different political,
religious, and philosophical convictions.

Another example of the transition of dialectic from a concrete (and
contested) historical category to an overarching template for historical
narration can be found in Michael McKeon's *Origins of the English Novel*.
McKeon begins with the wise observation that "What is required is a theory
not just of the rise of the novel but of how categories, whether 'literary' or
'social,' exist in history: how they first coalesce by being understood in terms
of – as transformations of – other forms that have thus far been taken to
define the field of possibility."[8] But this exemplary inquiry into the historicity
of literary and social categories immediately wraps itself in the mantle of
Hegelian dialectics. The equation of genre and dialectic begins on the first
page: "genre theory cannot be divorced from the history of genres, from the
understanding of genres in history. Another way of saying this is that the
theory of genre must be a dialectical theory of genre."[9]

One of the purposes of this book has been to make just the opposite claim,
that the understanding of genres in history must *not* be a dialectical theory of
genre. If, on the one hand, genres are read against the backdrop of a
dialectical plot, then they lose their historical character and become reified
types, possessing inherent ideologies and epistemologies. If, on the other
hand, literary historians return to the question of genre and history, as Ralph
Cohen has suggested, then they will recognize that dialectic cannot serve as
the overriding paradigm for this or any period. In short, a dialectical theory
of historical development is out of keeping with a period defined in large part
by a struggle to determine the meaning of dialectic itself.

A historical conception of dialectic does figure in the early stages of
McKeon's account. "What is peculiar to the early modern period," he writes,
"is neither an apprehension of the problem of mediation nor a confidence of
its solution, but an unprecedented intensification of both. The tacit dialectic

---

[8] McKeon, *Origins of the English Novel*, p. 4.   [9] *Ibid.*, p. 1.

of matter and spirit is opened out, with a greater or lesser degree of skepticism, into an explicit and strenuously argued dualism."[10] McKeon refers here to two phenomena: first, the "tacit dialectic of matter and spirit" is tacit because it stands for a permanent structural contradiction within metaphysics. That contradiction derives from the fact that within the Christian Neoplatonic tradition passage is to be made from nature to the supernatural, phenomena to noumena. The contra-diction is, then, an opposition of symbolic regions, one pertaining to the realm of the directly legible, the other to what can only be grasped in translation. Dialectic provides the mode of translation. Secondly, dialectic "opens out" because scientists and religious skeptics are causing this metaphysical conception to lose its power to mediate oppositions. With this, mechanists and materialists begin to separate the material realm from the expectation that it would offer assurance of a beyond. This moment in history – the late seventeenth and early eighteenth centuries – is interesting to McKeon and to many others because the potential loss of a metaphysical dialectic leads moral philosophers to seek out new modes of cultural mediation – genres that continue and/or transform the earlier project of legitimating socio-political norms through a marriage of science and faith. One such form is the novel.

Because the survival of Christian Neoplatonism depended upon securing an avenue of transcendence from earthly sign to divine signification, one would not expect the metaphysical conception of dialectic to be abandoned without a fight. Within the British Enlightenment, a vital debate takes place about the nature of dialectic itself. In direct discussions of dialectic and inductive method, in the revival of interest in Plato and Plotinus, in the ongoing confrontation with Pyrrhonism, and in the contest to establish the true definition and proper management of philosophical dialogue, moral philosophers affirmed and challenged the "tacit dialectic of matter and spirit," which, of course, made it no longer tacit. Why does this aspect of eighteenth-century literary history remain peripheral to McKeon's study? Dialectic, which at first names an endangered mechanism within metaphysics, quickly and quietly passes into the narrative principle of his own historiography.

The strength of Hegel's philosophical account of world history was that it transferred the endangered dialectic within Christian metaphysics into the principle of historical process itself, culminating in the realization of spirit in history. This was an understandable response to secularization, one which transformed Christianity from a limited religious system into a blueprint for the destiny of mankind. Minus the eschatological vocabulary, McKeon's procedures are strikingly similar: he too transforms an historical crisis into an assurance of mediation on a higher plane.

[10] *Ibid.*, p. 74.

Consider, for instance, the terms through which McKeon describes the process whereby "culture institutionalizes itself, making tractable and even serviceable the sheer fluidity of historical process":

What they [confrontations of value] yield is a simplified model of conflict from which the contingencies of indefinite potentiality have been extracted. In effect, such a model brings into being the field of available options by schematizing them, by delimiting the alternative postures that are accessible to participants in that culture. In the present case, the conflict that begins now to emerge from public controversy is first intelligible in sequential terms. The empiricism of "true history" opposes the discredited idealism of romance, which in turn discredits true history as a species of naive empiricism or "new romance." Once in motion, however, the sequence of action and reaction becomes a cycle: the existence of each opposed stance becomes essential for the ongoing, negative definition of its antithesis.   (p. 88)

The phrasing of this passage makes it unclear whether the dialectical scheme "brought into being" to mediate mid-eighteenth-century cultural differences has its being *in* history and is therefore itself one of several interpretations of historical process at work at the time, or whether it derives from the transhistorical grasp of the historian, whose method claims an identity with the way history would describe itself if it could. At crucial points in the passage where we might expect some clarification of this question, the careful deployment of passive and intransitive verb forms obscures any precise claim. What, exactly, are we meant to make of the claim that conflicting values "yield" a simplified model? What is the force of "yield"?[11] And in the passive structure "have been extracted," who or what does the extracting? What is it that acts upon indefinite potentiality to produce a simplified model of conflict somehow identical with the Hegelian scheme? History itself? McKeon makes just this claim when he responds to the complaint that dialectical historiography makes the past look "rather 'too' dialectical."[12] He replies: "the problem lies not with the method but with the subject matter to whose features it seeks to be adequate. It is first of all not method but history that is dialectical ... anyone who would seek to disclose the dialectical process of historical experience must be in some committed (if skeptical) way an empiricist."[13]

To the extent dialectic still has any connection with skepticism, this does not seem to be an example of dialectical thinking. It is, however, pretty much

[11] The verb "yield" (as in "confrontations yield a simplified model") is precisely ambiguous. *The Oxford English Dictionary* observes, "this verb has had a remarkable sense-development in English owing to its having been used as an equivalent of L. *reddere* and F. *rendre* or their compounds." *Reddere* in Latin means to give back or restore something previously given or taken; *rendre* in French can mean the same thing, but it also conveys the sense of involuntarily rendering forth, producing, even vomiting. The verb refers simultaneously to something an object actively does, as when we say the vanquished knight yielded his sword, and to something an object cannot help but do, as when we say one moment yields to the next.
[12] McKeon, *Origins of the English Novel*, p. 420.   [13] *Ibid.*, p. 420.

the same response that Philosophy gives to Boethius, when the student questions his teacher's method: "It is the nature of the divine essence, neither to pass to things outside itself nor to take any external thing to itself ... You ought not to be surprised that I have sought no outside proofs, but have used only those within the scope of our subject, since you learned, on Plato's authority, that the language we use ought to be related to the subject of discourse."[14] One could imagine being a committed empiricist without being a thoroughgoing dialectician: Hume fits this bill. And one could also imagine dialecticians who, in order to secure the primacy of their conception of dialectic, felt it necessary to belittle or ignore rival meanings of the term, as Kant does when he distinguishes his own sense of dialectic from "a *natural dialectic* – that is, a disposition to quibble with these strict laws of duty, to throw doubt on their validity or at least on their purity and strictness, and to make them, where possible, more adapted to our wishes and inclinations; that is, to pervert their very foundations and destroy their whole dignity."[15] If history presents us with multiple interpretations of dialectic, what then could it mean for history to speak itself *in* dialectic?

My point is not just that writing dialectical historiography is inadequate to history in general. It is especially inadequate to a period in which the practice of writing dialectical historiography received explicit formulation in highly charged political contexts. Once the metaphysical interpretation of dialogue *failed*, once the representation of social differences *exceeded* the reductive capacity of transcendental dialectic to render an image of the same, writers separated dialectic entirely from texts and assigned it a higher position schematizing and delimiting "the alternative postures that are accessible to participants in that culture." McKeon's method therefore replicates one of the events occurring in its field of study: an earlier conception of dialectic – the mechanism of metaphysical teleology – passes into a narrative principle controlling the explanation of generic, epistemological, and ideological change. But why should it be the case that a *failed* mechanism of mediation *within* metaphysics takes over as the agent determining the progress of history? Even if it can be shown, that something like this transformation takes place during the eighteenth century (as when Whig historiography adopts the dialectical logic of Christian Neoplatonism as the basis for its account of historical progress), why should the modern-day historian base his narrative upon the same conceptual scheme?

While dialectical historiography appears a purely neutral (or in McKeon's terms "empirical") means of schematizing the past, there is nothing neutral about the way Thomas Pownall, writing in 1752, conflates dialogue, dialectic, and the inevitable *telos* of historical development. His *Principles of Polity*,

---

[14] Boethius, *The Consolation of Philosophy*, p. 73.
[15] Kant, *Groundwork of the Metaphysic of Morals*, p. 73.

written in dialogue form, begins with an essay called "Of the Use of Dialogue." In it, Pownall characterizes his age as a time when "the Ideas and Propositions that relate to any general Theorem have been so intangled amongst themselves, and so involved with Matter foreign to them, as to render such Theorem a Subject of Controversy; its Parts and Members will be disunited and dissipated, their Proportions and Relations destroy'd, and even the less general or subordinate Truths be found on different Sides of the Question, as the foreign Matter they are engaged with seems to incline them."[16] Matter is becoming unruly: the theorem, whose ultimate purpose is to contain "Parts and Members," expunge foreign agents, and return us to simplicity, drifts towards the chaos of undecidability and fragmentation. It is at just such a time that dialogue and its mechanism of metaphysical dialectic are most needed. Pownall explains:

The Method therefore of Reasoning, that this state of the Case seems to require, is, first, to inquire in what Particulars the even contrary Sides of the Question may agree, that so we may unite coinciding Truths. Next by Composition, to compare and sort amongst each other those less general and subordinate Truths that have been dissipated, so that they may again rank in their natural Order; and lastly, to oppose one another those mixt Propositions, whose Contrariety ariseth only from the foreign Matter annex'd to them, so that, such contradictory Matter mutually destroying itself, the precise Relation and Agreements of those Truths that remain unmixt, may appear, and by opposing, and reciprocally reducing to Absurdity, those Propositions that are entirely false, they may be reciprocally and entirely destroyed: So that the whole Truth, and nothing but the Truth, will remain.[17]

The passage makes clear why dialectic became a point of such intense contestation during the eighteenth century. Not only does Pownall frame his interpretation of history in terms of a dialectical scheme, but that dialectic also restates the stages of Cartesian method. Why refer dialectic and scientific method to dialogue? Pownall grounds dialectic in dialogue because the claims he makes under the guise of a return to the true Theorem have a social and not simply geometric implication. Dialogue is useful because it represents a process whereby characters, interests, recalcitrant materiality bring themselves to obey some hidden edict reducing the many to the one. More than just providing a literary analogue for the stages of Cartesian method, the fiction of dialogue allows Pownall to finesse the problematic turn within Cartesian method from the division of complex entities into their component parts to the synthesis of parts back into coherent wholes. Descartes could do no better than to advise his scientist to treat "as though ordered materials which were not necessarily so."[18] Kant would replace the "as though" with an "as if." But Pownall, through the fiction of

---

[16] Pownall, *Principles of Polity, Being the Grounds and Reasons of Civil Empire* (London: Edward Owen, 1752), p. v.

[17] *Ibid.*, p. v.   [18] Descartes, *Discourse on Method*, p. 15.

dialogue, has found a better solution: a genre partially contaminated by difference yet fundamentally conducive to order transforms the weak "as though" into a strong representation. The reader becomes witness to an exemplary scene in which things again assume their *natural* rank and order: contradictory matter reciprocally and entirely *destroys itself*, willing its own subordination to a higher truth.

We find here a beautiful formula, much like one already cited, for the way confrontations of value yield a simplified model over time. The blueprint supplies not only an ostensibly non-coercive remedy for excessive cultural variety, but also a plot for history. No longer able to establish temporal (or political) succession through direct appeal to a divine force, Pownall transforms nature and history into artifacts of some inner dialectical necessity, assuring a return to the pure Theorem. Since he has already admitted that nature and history as *immediately* perceived seem "intangled," "involved with Matter foreign," the true interpretation of nature and history will need to be mediated through a special kind of mirror, the one Shaftesbury used to describe metaphysical dialogue:

In the same Manner therefore that, in the Science of Optics, a Picture that has been deform'd, does necessarily, by the known Method that deform'd it, and the Rules that are to rectify it, correspond to that one specific Mirrour that will reflect it in its due Proportions, in the same Manner naturally does this State of a Theorem, and the Manner of treating it in Dialogue, seem to correspond. To this the Method of Dialogue, used by Socrates, and followed by Plato and Cicero in their Writings, seems best adapted.   (p. v)

Through a remarkable series of correspondences, Pownall unabashedly describes the process by which mind makes itself consubstantial with nature and the flow of time. Because it is never possible to apprehend directly the unity of all things, mind must engage itself with history in its vicissitudes, the theorem in its moment of dissipation. But because mind's goal remains a total apprehension, the truth and nothing but the truth, a mediation must occur, such that infinite potentiality yields a simplified model over time. Two figures for mediation enter at this point, dialogue, a literary and philosophical genre, and a special mirror, akin to the anamorphic glass of Renaissance art.[19] Each represents a distorted image of the truth; yet each, through a perceptual or cognitive adjustment, restores the image to its true form. If the nature of these double-reflecting instruments is ultimately to take in duplicity and render unity to the reader or viewer, then (by a strange but decisive logic) nature itself must in some way be a reflection of the "known Methods" by which these forms of human artifice are made. In this way nature's own

[19] For discussions of anamorphosis, see Jurgis Baltrusaitis, *Anamorphosis*, trans. W. J. Strachan (New York: Harry N. Adams, 1977) and Ernst B. Gilman, *The Curious Perspective: Literary and Pictorial Wit in the Seventeenth Century* (New Haven and London: Yale University Press, 1978).

pattern becomes knowable to mind as if it were an outside fact entering in, rather than an inside egoism imposing its consuming method upon the outside, and calling it nature's own. Just as two eyes become one at some distance beyond the nose, so dialogue passes into and out of history on the way to becoming "dialectics."

In Edward Wynne's *Eunomous, or Dialogues Concerning the Law and Constitution of England* (1774), these connections are, if anything, even more explicitly asserted. Wynne posits an exact correlation between the way English legal history developed over hundreds of years and the way a philosophical dialogue develops during a single reading:

To see it [our own government] after so many shocks, advancing each century still nearer to perfection, by the concurrence of a thousand events which time alone could disclose. To see it, at length, arrived to that just equality in the distribution and exercise of power, that for so many ages it was an entire stranger to; that at present other nations can only envy; and that we who enjoy it, can only wish may be fixed and permanent.

All this would recommend the design of that dialogue, if the execution could but in any degree be answerable to the design.[20]

As in Thomas Pownall's *Principles of Polity*, we see the "tacit dialectic" of Christian Neoplatonism being transformed into a transcendental template for the narration of history. Just as dialogue flirts with potentially infinite refractions of subjective viewpoints, so English history flirted with civil anarchy; and just as, by some unannounced genius of the form, dialogue bends these fractures back into a coherent spectrum, so, by some inhering principle of freedom, time has brought English government to "its full strength and maturity" (p. 42). Law and dialogue are bound together by argument, explains Wynne, "by which I mean the exercise of a natural rather than an artificial kind of logic" (pp. 34–35). The isomorphism between his chosen genre and a natural logic (dialectic) will "inculcate a reverence to it [English law] in others; and ... describe the structure and excellence of the machine" (p. i). It is much the same "logic" for which the editors of *Dialectics and Humanism* find themselves apologizing two centuries later.

During the eighteenth century the long tradition of metaphysical dialogue – or the formal embodiment of transcendental dialectic in philosophical fictions – comes to an end. Its end marks a failure within Christian Neoplatonism, an inability to represent the process of dialectical sublation in "comedic" terms, as a happy synthesis of characters freely acquiescing in their self-sublimation to the ideal. One might have thought that the failure of dialectic to represent itself convincingly through fictions of characters acquiescing in their own

---

[20] Wynne, *Eunomus, or Dialogues Concerning the Law and Constitution of England, With an Essay on Dialogue*, pp. 42–43.

Aufhebungen would lead to doubts about the efficacy of dialectic itself. But dialectic was too important a means of validating the suppression of difference to be abandoned just because its *dramatic* enactment in philosophical dialogues put a face on the many and showed them insubordinate to the one.

For this reason, a history of philosophical dialogue during the eighteenth century must include the efforts introduced to save transcendental dialectic from history. I have argued that one way philosophical Christians attempted to save the logic of transcendental dialectic was to initiate a philosophical discussion of beauty in the fine arts. For here, in the beautiful art object, as in the mind capable of appreciating it, the dialectical sublation of part to whole central to the design argument received a new impetus. Philosophical aesthetics resituates dialectic first in certain exemplary objects whose beauty *just is* their dialectical reduction of the manifold into unity, and later, in the mental operations of genius itself, which, for Kant, allows us to "feel our freedom from the law of association (which attaches to the empirical employment of imagination), so that the material supplied to us by nature in accordance with this law can be worked up into something different which surpasses nature."[21]

Once dialectic floats free of its historical grounding in specific kinds of writing, it becomes available as a concept. The concept has special affiliations with antitheses in history, but has the advantage that it describes the final synthesis of historical contradictions, the passage of dialogue into dialectic. From that lofty vantage point, history itself can be viewed as an aesthetic totality, all of its temporal strains immediate to the mind as a purposeful unity. As Reinhart Koselleck observes in *Futures Past*, "The aesthetic components of [idealist] historicism forestalled motivational remainder and chance far beyond their once-theological bases."[22] According to Francis Hutcheson, reading history in this way affords a most decided pleasure. We love to read histories in which "we find the secret Causes of a great Diversity of seemingly inconsistent Actions; or an Interest of State laid open, or an artful View nicely unfolded ... [because] this reduces the whole to an Unity of Design at least: and this may be observed in the very Fables which entertain Children, otherwise we cannot make them relish them."[23] This observation appears in Hutcheson's *Inquiry into the Original of Our Ideas of Beauty and Virtue* as part of an argument about the universal pleasure we take in apprehending beauty. When the historian reduces seemingly inconsistent historical phenomena to "an Unity of Design," historical narrative takes on an aesthetic coherence. Dialectical historiography thus redescribes history as

---

[21] Kant, *Critique of Judgment*, p. 157.
[22] Koselleck, *Futures Past: On the Semantics of Historical Time*, trans. Keith Tribe (Cambridge: MIT Press, 1985), p. 129; see also p. 117.
[23] Hutcheson, *Inquiry*, p. 80.

an aesthetic object, immediately present to mind *as if* its disparate elements were part of a single grand scheme. In the process, competing interpretations of forms (such as dialogue) and concepts (such as dialectic) vanish.[24]

In the *Reason in History*, Hegel bypasses the intermediary stages between rational Christianity (design) and dialectical historiography, which is to say, he bypasses the British Enlightenment. "It was for a while the fashion to admire God's wisdom in animals, plants, and individual lives," he writes. "If it is conceded that Providence manifests itself in such objects and materials, why not also in world history?"[25] More to the point, if Hume destroyed the argument from design by subverting the logic of dialectical induction, might it not be recovered in history? "We must not deem God too weak to exercise his wisdom on a grand scale. Our intellectual striving aims at recognizing that what eternal wisdom *intended* it has actually *accomplished*, dynamically active in the world, both in the realm of nature and that of spirit. In this respect our method is a theodicy, a justification of God. Thus the evil in the world was to be comprehended and the thinking mind reconciled with it. Nowhere, actually, exists a larger challenge to such a reconciliation than in world history. This reconciliation can only be attained through the recognition of the positive elements in which that negative element disappears as something subordinate and vanquished."[26]

Hegel speaks of history as the unfolding of what has been known all along, the revenge of eschatology against temporality. In effect, he places dialectic itself where Boethius had placed myth, in the seat of the transcendental third, overcoming all prior thirds by repeating in itself the dialectical movement it is meant to supervise. Vertical ascent has become a linear progress, but in each case oppositional elements in the system, divergences, differences, other destinies, are viewed as epiphenomenal impediments to the fulfillment of history's own design. The many ways of interpreting experience are swallowed up in the vortex of Method. Writes Hegel:

The perspective adopted by the philosophical history of the world ... is the sum total of all possible perspectives. It ... deals not with individual situations but with a universal thought which runs throughout the whole. This universal element is not to be found in the world of contingent phenomena; it is the unity behind the multitude

24 In *Signs Taken for Wonders*, Franco Moretti describes this erasure as a "universalizing immodesty, which follows literary historiography about like a shadow." He attributes the immodesty to "Hegel's marriage of philosophy of history with idealist aesthetics. In the *Aesthetics*, every historical epoch has in essence *one* ideal content to 'express,' and gives 'sensible manifestation' to it through one artistic form. It was practically inevitable that – following the argument in reverse – once one had defined a rhetorical form one felt authorized to link it to *the* idea – single, solitary, resplendent – in which a whole epoch is supposedly summed up" (p. 25).

25 Hegel, *Reason in History: A General Introduction to the Philosophy of History*, trans. Robert S. Hartman, ed. Oskar Piest (New York: The Liberal Arts Press, 1953), p. 18.

26 *Ibid.*, p. 18.

of particulars ... The spirit is eternally present to itself; it has no past, and remains forever the same in all its vigour and strength.[27]

That which falls outside this digestive logic becomes either evil or accidental, a stage to be overcome as spirit unfolds itself over time. With the book of Revelation reverberating in our ear, Hegel concludes:

that development of the thinking spirit which the Christian revelation of God initiated must eventually produce a situation where all that was at first present only to the emotional and representational faculties can also be comprehended by thought ... Now the distinctive feature of Christianity is that, with its advent, this time has indeed come. Its significance for the history of the world is therefore absolutely epoch-making, for the nature of God has at last been made manifest ... Christianity is the religion which has revealed the nature and being of God to man ... It is one of the central doctrines of Christianity that providence has ruled and continues to rule the world, and that everything which happens in the world is determined by and commensurate with the divine government. This doctrine is opposed to the idea of chance and to that of limited ends (such as the preservation of the Jewish people).[28]

Inevitability stands at the heart of the metaphysical interpretation of dialectic, and of those historical accounts based upon it. While dialectic (retaining a rumor of its other definition) seems to invite an encounter with "difference," that which resists being swallowed into sameness presents only a temporary impediment to a fulfillment all the more dramatically realized through an initial play of resistance. Placed in parentheses, the Jewish people, who stand here for the "negative element" in the formula but might as well be any interdicted group, are graphically removed from the final scene of humanity. They have been yoked together in an odd but telling syntactic snarl with chance, with the accidental, with limited ends, which will be *aufgehoben*, erased, destroyed, when God manifests his ultimate purpose through the realization of Spirit in the German Volk and Nation.

It was no doubt in response to claims such as these that Bakhtin penned his angry recipe for how to derive dialectics from dialogue: "Dialogue and dialectics. Take a dialogue and remove the voices ... remove the intonations ... carve out abstract concepts and judgments from living words and responses, cram everything into one abstract consciousness – and that's how you get dialectics."[29] And it was also in response to what he took to be the historical consequences of Hegel's blueprint that Martin Buber, speaking in Germany in 1953, set forth a different conception of dialectic:

---

[27] Hegel, *Lectures on the Philosophy of World History*, trans. H. B. Nisbet (Cambridge: Cambridge University Press, 1975), pp. 30–31.

[28] *Ibid.*, pp. 40–41.

[29] Bakhtin, *Problems in Dostoevsky's Poetics*, p. xxxii.

From my youth on I have taken the real existence of peoples most seriously. But I have never in the face of any historical moment, past or present, allowed the concrete multiplicity existing at that moment within a people – the concrete inner dialectic, rising to contradiction – to be obscured by the leveling concept of a totality constituted and acting in just such a way and no other.[30]

There is no room in Hegel's system for a "concrete inner dialectic, rising to contradiction." For the system is premised upon the obliteration of skeptical dialectic by its transcendental big brother. Consciousness itself, in its healthy state, cannot reside in contradiction. The concept of a dialectic rising to nothing better than contradiction, or a dialogue producing nothing better than more dialogue, or a difference that cannot be either rendered the same or destroyed, is for Hegel the sign of a decadent culture. As he writes in the *Phenomenology of Spirit*, "The Unhappy Consciousness itself *is* the gazing of one self-consciousness into another, and itself *is* both, and the unity of both is also its essential nature. But it is not as yet explicitly aware that this is its essential nature, or that it is the unity of both."[31] Spoken by one who cannot really reside in history, there being stronger directives pointing away, the verbiage can only color in a vague philosophical taint what Buber means by a permanent dialectic rising to contradiction. Buber's words are neither empty nor the sign of a "merely contradictory being." On the contrary, the permanent dialectic rising to contradiction may be the philosophical stance of one who has taken up residence in time and space – one who, despite the press of circumstances, resists the impulse to demonize and destroy the other. The dialectic is permanent because dialogue is ongoing; it rises to contradiction because the human need to finalize (in order to stave off finitude) deserves to be treated ironically, as a story among stories, a plot intersecting other plots, a destiny among destinies, and so, even when it concludes, resisting conclusion.

[30] Martin Buber, "Genuine Dialogue and the Possibility of Peace," in *Pointing the Way: Collected Essays*, ed. Maurice Friedman (New York: Harper and Brothers, 1957), pp. 222–223.
[31] Hegel, *Phenomenology of Spirit*, p. 126.

Select bibliography

Primary sources

Aristotle, *The Complete Works of Aristotle*, ed. Jonathan Barnes, 2 vols. (Princeton: Princeton University Press, 1984).

Augustine, *The Soliloquies of Saint Augustine*, trans. Thomas F. Gilligan (New York: Cosmopolitan Science and Art Service, 1943).

Austen, Jane, *The Novels of Jane Austen*, ed. R. W. Chapman, 5 vols., 3rd edn. (London: Oxford University Press, 1933).

Bacon, Francis, *The Great Instauration*, in *Francis Bacon, A Selection of his Works*, ed. Sidney Warhaft (New York: Macmillan, 1982).

Berkeley, George, *A Discourse Addressed to Magistrates and Men in Authority Occasioned by the enormous Licence, and Irreligion of the Times* (Dublin: George Faulkener, 1738).

The Works of George Berkeley, Bishop of Cloyne, eds. A. A. Luce and T. E. Jessop, 9 vols. (London: Thomas Nelson and Sons Ltd., 1949).

The Works of George Berkeley, ed. Alexander Campbell Fraser, 4 vols. (Oxford: Clarendon Press, 1901).

Boethius, *The Consolation of Philosophy*, trans. Richard Green (Indianapolis: The Library of Liberal Arts, 1962).

Brown, John, *Essays on the Characteristics of the Earl of Shaftesbury* (London: C. Davis, 1751; rprt. Hildesheim and New York: Georg Olms Verlag, 1969).

Buckler, Benjamin, "*A Philosophical Dialogue concerning Decency*" (London: James Fletcher, 1751).

Bunyan, John, *The Pilgrim's Progress, from this World to That which is to come*, ed. James Blanton Wharey 2nd edn. (Oxford: Clarendon Press, 1960).

Burnet, James, Lord Monboddo, *Of the Origin and Progress of Language*, 2nd edn. 6 vols. (Edinburgh: J. Balfour and London: T. Cadell, 1774).

Burney, Fanny, *Evelina, Or the History of a Young Lady's Entrance into the World*, eds. Edward A. Bloom and Lillian D. Bloom (Oxford and New York: Oxford University Press, 1968).

Bushe, Amyas, *Socrates, a Dramatic Poem* (Glasgow: R. and A. Foulis, 1762).

Campbell, George, *The Philosophy of Rhetoric*, ed. Lloyd Bitzer (Carbondale and Edwardsville: Southern Illinois University Press, 1963).

Cicero, M. Tullius, *De Inventione, De Optimo Genere, Oratorum Topica*, trans. H. M. Hubbell (Cambridge, MA: Harvard University Press, 1976).

Of the Nature of the Gods in Three Books, trans. Thomas Francklin (London: T. Davies, 1775).

The Morals of Cicero, containing I. His Conferences De Finibus II. His Academics, Conferences concering the Criterion of Truth, and the Fallibility of Human Judgment, trans. William Guthrie (London: T. Waller, 1744).

Tully's Five Books De Finibus; or Concerning the Last Object of Desire and Aversion ... With an Apology for the Philosophical Writings of Cicero, in a Letter to the Translator, by Henry Dodwell (London: J. Tonson and R. Gibson, 1702).

Constable, John, *The Conversation of Gentlemen Considered In Most of the Ways that Make their Mutual Company Agreeable or Disagreeable. In Six Dialogues* (London: J. Hoyles, 1738).

Cooper, John Gilbert, *The Life of Socrates, Collected from the Memorabilia of Xenophon and the Dialogues of Plato* (London: R. Dodsley, 1749).

Cosens, John, *The Economy of Beauty; in a Series of Fables Addressed to the Ladies* (London: J. Wilkie, 1772).

Descartes, René, *Discourse on Method and Meditations*, trans. Laurence J. Lafleur (Indianapolis: Bobbs-Merrill, Co., 1960).

Dryden, John, *The Works of John Dryden*, ed. H. T. Swedenberg, Jr., 20 vols. (Berkeley: University of California Press, 1966).

Fielding, Henry, "An Essay on Conversation," in *The Complete Works of Henry Fielding, Esq.*, 16 vols. (New York: Barnes and Noble, Inc., 1967).

Joseph Andrews, ed. Martin C. Battestin (Middletown, Connecticut: Wesleyan University Press, 1967).

Fontenelle, M. De (Bernard Le Bovier), *Fontenelle's Dialogues of the Dead in Three Parts ... Translated from the French by the Late John Hughes*, 2nd edn. (London: J. Tonson, 1730).

Harris, James, *Upon the Rise and Progress of Criticism* (New York: Garland Publishing Inc., 1971).

Hayter, Thomas, *A Short View of Some of the General Arts of Controversy Made Use of by the Advocates of Infidelity* (London: S. Buckley, 1732).

Hegel, George Wilhelm Friedrich, *Reason in History*, trans. Robert S. Hartman, ed. Oskar Piest (New York: The Liberal Arts Press, 1953).

Lectures on the Philosophy of World History, trans. H. B. Nisbet (Cambridge: Cambridge University Press, 1975).

Phenomenology of Spirit, trans. A. V. Miller (Oxford: Oxford University Press, 1977).

Hervey, John Lord, *Some Remarks On the "Minute Philosopher,"* 2nd edn. (London: J. Robinson, 1752).

Hobbes, Thomas, *Leviathan*, ed. C .B. Macpherson (Hamondsworth: Penguin, 1968).

Horace, *The Art of Poetry*, trans. E. C. Wickham, in *Critical Theory Since Plato*, ed. Hazard Adams (New York: Harcourt Brace Jovanovich, Inc., 1971).

Huber, Marie, *The World Unmask'd: or the Philosopher the Greatest Cheat; in twenty-four dialogues ... To which is added, The State of Souls separated from their Bodies: being an epistolary treatise* (London: A. Millar, 1736).

Hume, David, *Dialogues concerning Natural Religion*, ed. Norman Kemp Smith (Indianapolis: Bobbs-Merrill Co., 1981).

Essays and Treatises on Several Subjects: Containing Essays, Moral, Political, and Literary, 2 vols. (London: T. Cadell, C. Elliot, T. Kay, and Co., 1788).

An Inquiry concerning Human Understanding, ed. Charles W. Hendel (Indianapolis: The Bobbs-Merrill Co. Inc., 1955).

Of the Standard of Taste and Other Essays, ed. John W. Lenz (Indianapolis: Bobbs-Merrill Co., 1981).

Hurd, Richard, trans. and ed., *Epistolae ad Pisones, et Augustum: With an English Commentary and Notes ... by the Reverend Mr. [Richard] Hurd*, 5th edn., 3 vols. (London: Printed for W. Bowyer and J. Nichols for T. Cadell and J. Woodyear, 1776).

Moral and Political Dialogues with Letters on Chivalry and Romance, 5th edn. 3 vols., with a "Preface, on the Manner of Writing Dialogue" (London: T. Cadell, 1776).

Hutcheson, Francis, *An Inquiry into the Original of our Ideas of Beauty and Virtue; in Two Treatises*, 2nd edn. (London, 1726; reprt., New York: Garland, 1971).

Johnson, Samuel, *The Yale Edition of the Works of Samuel Johnson*, ed. Gwin J. Kolb, 16 vols. (New Haven and London: Yale University Press, 1990).

Kant, Immanuel, *Critique of Judgment*, trans. J. H. Bernard, (New York: Hafner Press, 1951).

The Critique of Pure Reason, trans. Norman Kemp Smith (London: Macmillan and Co., 1953).

Groundwork of the Metaphysic of Morals, trans. H. J. Paton (New York: Harper and Row, 1964).

Lancaster, Nathanial, *A Plan for an Essay upon Delicacy, With a Specimen of the Work in Two Dialogues* (London: R. Dodsley, 1748).

Locke, John, *An Essay Concerning Human Understanding*, ed. Peter H. Nidditch (Oxford: Clarendon Press, 1975).

Some Thoughts Concerning Education (Cambridge: Cambridge University Press, 1913).

Macfait, Ebenezer, Remarks on the Life and Writings of Plato. With Answers to the Principal Objections Against Him; and a General Review of His Dialogues (Edinburgh: A. Kinkaid and J. Bells, 1760).

Mandeville, Bernard, *Fable of the Bees: Or, Private Vices, Publick Benefits*, ed. F. B. Kaye, 2 vols. (Oxford: Clarendon Press, 1924).

A Letter to Dion occasion'd by his book called Alciphron, or the Minute Philosopher (London: J. Roberts, 1732); rprt., *Augustan Reprint Society* 41 (Los Angeles: William Andrews Clark Memorial Library, 1953).

Nichols, William, *A Conference with a Theist: containing an Answer to all the most usual Objections of the Infidels Against the Christian Religion*, 3rd edn., 2 vols. (London: J. Holland and J. Bowyer, 1723).

Nietzsche, Friedrich, *The Birth of Tragedy*, in *The Birth of Tragedy and the Genealogy of Morals*, trans. Francis Golffing (Garden City, New York: Doubleday Anchor, 1956).

Daybreak: Thoughts on the Prejudices of Morality, trans. R. J. Hollingdale (Cambridge: Cambridge University Press, 1982).

Beyond Good and Evil: Prelude to a Philosophy of the Future, trans. Walter Kaufmann (New York: Vintage Books, 1966).

Plato, *The Collected Dialogues of Plato, Including the Letters*, eds. Edith Hamilton and Huntington Cairns, Bollingen Series LXXI (Princeton: Princeton University Press, 1985).

The Dialogues of Plato, trans. Floyer Sydenham, 2 vols. (London: W. Sandby, 1767).

The Greater Hippias: a Dialogue of Plato concerning the beautifull, trans. Floyer Sydenham (London: H. Woodfall, 1759).

Phedon: or a Dialogue of the Immortality of the Soul, from Plato the Divine Philosopher, with a "Discourse concerning Plato" (London: J. Davidson, 1777).

Plato his Apology of Socrates and Phaedo, or Dialogues concerning the Immortality of Mans Soul, and Manner of Socrates his Death: Carefully translated from the Greek (London: Printed by T. R. and N. T. for James Magnes and Richard Bentley, 1675).

The Republic of Plato: with a Preliminary Discourse Concerning the Philosophy of the Ancients, trans. H. Spens (Glasgow: R. and A. Foulis, 1763).

Plotinus, *Enneads*, trans. A. H. Armstrong, 6 vols. (Cambridge MA: Harvard University Press, 1966).

Pownall, Thomas, *Principles of Polity, Being the Grounds and Reasons of Civil Empire* (London: Edward Owen, 1752).

Priestly, Joseph, *Socrates and Jesus Compared* (London: T. Johnson, 1803).

Ramsay, Allan, *A Dialogue on Taste* (London, 1762).

Richardson, Samuel, *Clarissa, or the History of a Young Lady*, ed. Angus Ross (London: Penguin Books, 1985).

Shaftesbury, Anthony Ashley Cooper, the Third Earl of, *Characteristicks of Men, Manners, Opinions, Times*, 6th edn., 3 vols., corrected (London: James Purser, 1737).

Second Characters, or the Language of Forms, ed. Benjamin Rand (Cambridge: Cambridge University Press, 1914).

Skelton, Philip, *The Candid Reader: or a Modest, yet Unanswerable Apology for all BOOKS that ever Were, or possibly Can be Wrote* (Dublin, 1744; rprt. London: M. Cooper, 1744).

[Spence, Joseph], *Crito, or a Dialogue on Beauty* (London: R. Dodsley, 1752).

Stanley, Thomas, *The History of Philosophy: Containing the Lives, Opinions, Actions and Discourses of the Philosophers of Every Sect*, 3rd edn. (London: W. Battersby, 1701).

Sterne, Laurence, *The Florida Edition of the Works of Laurence Sterne*, eds. Melvyn New and Joan New, 3 vols. (Florida: University of Florida Press, 1978).

Stubbes, George, *A Dialogue on Beauty in the Manner of Plato* (London: W. Wilkins, 1731).

A Dialogue on the Superiority of the Pleasures of the Understanding to the Pleasures of the Senses (London: W. Wilkins, 1734).

Sydenham, Floyer, *A Synopsis or General View of the Works of Plato* (London: S. Richardson, 1759).

Tindal, Matthew, "Christianity as Old as the Creation," in *Deism and Natural Religion, a Source Book*, ed. E. Graham Waring (New York: Ungar, 1967).

Wishart, William (attrib.), *A Vindication of the Reverend D—— B——y, from the Scandalous Imputation of being Author of a late Book, intitled, Alciphron, or the Minute Philosopher* (London: A. Millar, 1734).

Wollstonecraft, Mary, *Mary, a Fiction and The Wrongs of Woman*, ed. Gary Kelly (Oxford: Oxford University Press, 1976).

Wynne, Edward, *Eunomous, or Dialogues concerning the Law and Constitution of England. With an Essay on Dialogue*, 5th edn. (London: S. Sweet, 1822).

Xenophon, *The Banquet of Xenophon, Done from the Greek, with an Introductory Essay to Lady Jean Douglass concerning the Doctrine, and Death of Socrates*, trans. James Welwood (London: John Barnes and Andrew Bell, 1710).

Secondary sources

Adorno, Theodor W., and Max Horkheimer, *Dialectic of Enlightenment*, trans. John Cumming (New York: Continuum, 1982).

Alderman, William, "Shaftesbury and the Doctrine of the Moral Sense in the Eighteenth Century," *PMLA* 46 (1931) 1087–1095.

Aldridge, A. O., "Lord Shaftesbury's Literary Theories," *Philological Quarterly* 24 (1945) 46–64.

Armstrong, Robert L., "Berkeley's Theory of Signification," *Journal of the History of Ideas* 7 (1969) 163–716.

Auerbach, Erich, *Mimesis: the Representation of Reality in Western Literature*, trans. Willard R. Trask (Princeton: Princeton University Press, 1953).

Bagolini, Luigi, "The Topicality of Adam Smith's Notions of Sympathy and Judicial Evaluations," in *Essays on Adam Smith*, eds. Andrew S. Skinner and Thomas Wilson (Oxford: Clarendon Press, 1975).

Bakhtin, Mikhail, *Problems of Dostoevsky's Poetics*, eds. and trans. Caryl Emerson (Minneapolis: University of Minnesota Press, 1984).

Speech Genres and Other Late Essays, trans. Vern W. McGee, ed. Caryl Emerson and Michael Holquist (Austin: University of Texas Press, 1986).

Benjamin, Walter, *The Origin of German Tragic Drama*, trans. John Osborne (London and New York: Verso, 1977).

Berland, K. J. H., "'Bringing Philosophy Down from the Heavens: Socrates and the New Science," *Journal of the History of Ideas* 47 (1986) 299–308.

Berman, David, *Alciphron in Focus* (London: Routledge, 1993).

George Berkeley: Idealism and the Man (Oxford: Oxford University Press, 1994).

"The Jacobitism of Berkeley's 'Passive Obedience'," *Journal of the History of Ideas* 47 (1986) 309–319.

Bernstein, John Andrew, "Shaftesbury's Identification of the Good with the Beautiful," *Eighteenth-Century Studies* 10 (1977) 304–325.

Blanchot, Maurice, *The Infinite Conversation*, trans. Susan Hanson (Minneapolis and London: The University of Minnesota Press, 1993).

Boyce, Benjamin, "News from Hell," *PMLA* 58 (1943) 402–437.

Bracken, Harry M., *The Early Reception of Berkeley's Immaterialism 1710–1733* (The Hague: Martinus Nijhoff, 1959).

Brett, R. L., *The Third Earl of Shaftesbury: a Study in Eighteenth-Century Literary Theory* (London: Hutchinson's University Library, 1951).

Brewer, Daniel, "The Philosophical Dialogue and the Forcing of Truth," *Modern Language Notes* 98 (1983) 1234–1247.

Bricke, John, "On the Interpretation of Hume's *Dialogues*," *Religious Studies* 11 (1975) 1–18.

Brown, Laura, "Reading Race and Gender: Jonathan Swift," *Eighteenth-Century Studies* 23 (1989) 425–443.

Buber, Martin, "Genuine Dialogue and the Possibility of Peace," in *Pointing the Way: Collected Essays*, ed. Maurice Friedman (New York: Harper and Brothers, 1957).

Cantor, Paul A., "Aristotle and the History of Tragedy," in *Theoretical Issues in Literary*

History, ed. David Perkins (Cambridge, MA: Harvard University Press, 1991), pp. 60–84.

Carnochan, W. B., "The Comic Plot of Hume's *Dialogues*," *Modern Philology* 85 (1988) 514–522.

Cassirer, Ernst, *The Philosophy of the Enlightenment*, trans. Fritz C. A. Koelln and James P. Pettegrove (Boston: Beacon Press, 1955).

de Chenu, Marie-Dominique, *Nature, Man, and Society in the Twelfth Century*, trans. Jerome Taylor and Lester K. Little (Chicago: University of Chicago Press, 1968).

Clark, Gregory, *Dialogue, Dialectic, and Conversation: a Social Perspective on the Function of Writing* (Carbondale and Edwardsville: Southern Illinois University Press, 1990).

Cohen, Ralph, "David Hume's Experimental Method and the Theory of Taste," in *Englische Literaturtheorie von Sidney bis Johnson* (Darmstadt: Wissenschaftliche Buchgesellschaft, 1984), pp. 226–245.

"History and Genre," *NLH* 17 (1986) 203–218.

Colie, Rosalie, *The Resources of Kind: Genre Theory in the Renaissance* (Berkeley: University of California Press, 1973).

Cope, Kevin, ed., *Compendious Conversations: the Method of Dialogue in the Early Enlightenment* (Frankfurt-on-Main: Peter Lang, 1992).

Cox, Virginia, *The Renaissance Dialogue: Literary Dialogue in its Social and Political Contexts, Castiglione to Galileo* (Cambridge: Cambridge University Press, 1992).

Crawford, B. V., "The Prose Dialogue of the Commonwealth and Restoration," *PMLA* 34 (1919) 601–609.

Damrosch, Leopold, *Fictions of Reality in the Age of Hume and Johnson* (Madison: University of Wisconsin Press, 1989).

Davie, Donald, "Berkeley and the Style of Dialogue," in *The English Mind: Studies in the English Moralists Presented to Basil Willey*, eds. Hugh Sykes Davies and George Watson (Cambridge: Cambridge University Press, 1964), pp. 90–106.

Dowling, William, *The Epistolary Moment: Poetics of the Eighteenth-Century Verse Epistle* (Princeton: Princeton University Press, 1991).

Dykstal, Timothy, "Conversation and Political Controversy," in *Compendious Conversations: the Method of Dialogue in the Early Enlightenment*, ed. Kevin L. Cope (Frankfurt-on-Main: Peter Lang, 1992).

Eagleton, Terry, *The Ideology of the Aesthetic* (Oxford: Basil Blackwell, 1990).

Ehrenpreis, Irvin, *Acts of Implication: Suggestion and Covert Meaning in the Works of Dryden, Swift, Pope, and Austen* (Berkeley: University of California Press, 1980).

Farooqi, Waheed Ali, "Berkeley's Ontology and Islamic Mysticism," in *New Studies in Berkeley's Philosophy*, ed. Warren E. Steinkraus (New York: Holt, Rinehart, and Winston, Inc., 1966), pp. 123–133.

Fish, Stanley E., *Surprised by Sin* (New York: St. Martin's Press, 1967).

Flew, Antony, "Was Berkeley a Precursor to Wittgenstein?" in *Hume and the Enlightenment: Essays Presented to Ernest Campbell Mossner*, ed. William B. Todd (Edinburgh: Edinburgh University Press, 1974), pp. 153–163.

Fogel, Aaron, *Coercion to Speak: Conrad's Poetics of Dialogue* (Cambridge, MA: Harvard University Press, 1985).

Force, James E., "Hume and the Relation of Science to Religion Among Certain Members of the Royal Society," *Journal of the History of Ideas* 45 (1984) 517–536.

Foucault, Michel, *The Order of Things: an Archaeology of the Human Sciences* (New York: Vintage, 1973).

Gadamer, Hans-Georg, *Dialogue and Dialectic: Eight Hermeneutical Studies on Plato*, trans. P. Christopher Smith (New Haven and London: Yale University Press, 1980).

Gould, Evlyn, *Virtual Theater from Diderot to Mallarmé* (Baltimore: The Johns Hopkins University Press, 1989).

Grean, Stanley, *Shaftesbury's Philosophy of Religion and Ethics: a Study in Enthusiasm* (Athens, Ohio: Ohio University Press, 1967).

Griswold, Charles, "Reflections on 'Dialectic' in Plato and Hegel," *International Philosophical Quarterly* 22 (1982) 115–130.

Habermas, Jürgen, "The Entwinement of Myth and Enlightenment," in *The Philosophical Discourse of Modernity*, trans. Frederick Lawrence (Cambridge, MA: MIT Press, 1987).

The Structural Transformation of the Public Sphere: an Inquiry into a Category of Bourgeois Society, trans. Thomas Burger (Cambridge, MA: MIT Press, 1989).

Halsband, Robert, *Lord Hervey: Eighteenth-Century Courtier* (Oxford: Oxford University Press, 1973).

Hershbell, Jackson P., "Berkeley and the Problem of Evil," *Journal of the History of Ideas* 31 (1970) 543–554.

Hirzel, Rudolph, *Der Dialog: ein Literarhistorischer Versuch*, 2 vols. [1895] (rprt. Hildesheim: Georg Olms Verlagsbuchhandlung, 1963).

Hollingshead, Gregory, "Pope, Berkeley, and the True Key to the *Dunciad in Four Books*," *English Studies in Canada* 10 (1984) 141–155.

Holquist, Michael, *Dialogism: Bakhtin and his World* (London and New York: Routledge, 1990).

Hooker, Michael, "Berkeley's Argument from Design," in *Berkeley: Critical and Interpretative Essays*, ed. Colin M. Turbayne (Minneapolis: University of Minnesota Press, 1982), pp. 261–270.

Horkheimer, Max and Theodor W. Adorno, *Dialectic of Enlightenment*, trans. John Cumming (New York: Continuum, 1982).

Hunter, J. Paul, *Before Novels: the Cultural Contexts of Eighteenth-Century English Fiction* (New York and London: W. W. Norton & Co., 1990).

Jauss, Hans Robert, *Question and Answer: Forms of Dialogic Understanding*, ed. and trans. Michael Hays (Minneapolis: University of Minnesota Press, 1989).

Jessop, T. E., "Berkeley as Religious Apologist," in *New Studies in Berkeley's Philosophy*, ed. Warren E. Steinkraus (New York: Holt, Rinehart, and Winston, 1966), pp. 98–109.

Johnson, Claudia, *Jane Austen: Women, Politics, and the Novel* (Chicago and London: University of Chicago Press, 1988).

"The Twilight of Probability: Uncertainty and Hope in *Sense and Sensibility*," *Philological Quarterly* 62 (1983) 171–186.

Keener, Frederick, *English Dialogues of the Dead: a Critical History, an Anthology, and a Check List* (New York: Columbia University Press, 1973).

Kennedy, George A., *Classical Rhetoric and Its Christian and Secular Tradition from Ancient to Modern Times* (Chapel Hill: The University of North Carolina Press, 1980).

Kenshur, Oscar, "Pierre Bayle and the Structures of Doubt," *Eighteenth-Century Studies* 21 (1988) 297–315.

Kernan, Alvin, *Printing Technology, Letters, and Samuel Johnson* (Princeton: Princeton University Press, 1987).

Kivy, Peter, *The Seventh Sense: a Study of Francis Hutcheson's Aesthetics and its Influence in Eighteenth-Century Britain* (New York: Burt Franklin & Co., 1976).

Klein, Lawrence, "Berkeley, Shaftesbury, and the Meaning of Politeness," *Studies in Eighteenth-Century Culture* 16 (1986) 57–58.

   Shaftesbury and the Culture of Politeness: Moral Discourse and Cultural Politics in Early Eighteenth-Century England (Cambridge: Cambridge University Press, 1994).

   "The Third Earl of Shaftesbury and the Progress of Politeness," *Eighteenth-Century Studies* 18 (1984–1985) 186–214.

Kojève, Alexandre, *Introduction to the Reading of Hegel*, ed. Allan Bloom, trans. James H. Nichols, Jr. (Ithaca and London: Cornell University Press, 1980).

Korshin, Paul J., *Typologies in England: 1650–1820* (Princeton: Princeton University Press, 1982).

Koselleck, Reinhart, *Futures Past: On the Semantics of Historical Time*, trans. Keith Tribe (Cambridge: MIT Press, 1985).

Lambert, Richard T., "The Literal Intent of Berkeley's *Dialogues*," *Philosophy and Literature* 6 (1982) 165–171.

Levi, Albert William, "Philosophy as Literature: the Dialogue," *Philosophy and Rhetoric* 9 (1976) 1–20.

Levinson, Arnold, "Popper, Hume, and the Traditional Problem of Induction," in *The Philosophy of Karl Popper: Book 1*, The Library of Living Philosophers, ed. Paul Arthur Schilpp (Le Salle, Illinois: Open Court Press, 1974).

Lovejoy, Arthur, *The Great Chain of Being* (Cambridge, MA: Harvard University Press, 1966).

Markley, Robert, "Style as Philosophical Structure: the Contexts of Shaftesbury's *Characteristicks*," in *The Philosopher as Writer: the Eighteenth Century*, ed. Robert Ginsberg (Selinsgrove: Susquehanna University Press, 1987), pp. 140–154.

Marshall, David, *The Figure of Theater: Shaftesbury, Defoe, Adam Smith, and George Eliot* (New York: Columbia University Press, 1986).

McKeon, Michael, *The Origins of the English Novel: 1600–1740* (Baltimore: Johns Hopkins University Press, 1987).

McKeon, Richard, "Dialogue and Controversy in Philosophy," in *The Interpretation of Dialogue*, ed. Tullio Maranhão (Chicago and London: The University of Chicago Press, 1990).

Merrill, Elizabeth, *The Dialogue in English Literature*, Yale Studies in English, 42 (New York: Holt and Company, 1911).

Milton, J. R., "Induction Before Hume," *The British Journal for the Philosophy of Science* 38 (1987) 49–74.

Moretti, Franco, *Signs Taken for Wonders*, trans. Susan Fischer, David Forgacs, and David Miller (London: Verso, 1983).

Muehlmann, Robert, "The Role of Perceptual Relativity in Berkeley's Philosophy," *Journal of the History of Philosophy* 29 (1991) 397–425.

Nelson, Nicolas H., "Dramatic Texture and Philosophical Debate in Prior's *Dialogues of the Dead*," *SEL* 28 (1988) 428–441.

Nuttall, A. D., *A Common Sky: Philosophy and the Literary Imagination* (Berkeley and Los Angeles: University of California Press, 1974).

O'Hear, Anthony, *Karl Popper* (London: Routledge and Kegan Paul, 1980).

Paknadel, Felix, "Shaftesbury's Illustrations of *Characteristics*," *Journal of the Warburg and Courtauld Institutes* 37 (1971) 290–312.

Patey, Douglas Lane, *Probability and Literary Form: Philosophic Theory and Literary Practice in the Augustan Age* (Cambridge: Cambridge University Press, 1984).

Popkin, Richard H., *The High Road to Pyrrhonism*, eds. Richard A. Watson and James E. Force (San Diego: Austin Hill Press, 1980).

Popper, Karl, *The Logic of Scientific Discovery* (New York: Harper and Row, 1968).

Prince, Michael, "The Eighteenth-Century Beauty Contest," *Modern Language Quarterly* 55 (1994) 251–279.

  "Hume and the End of Religious Dialogue," *Eighteenth-Century Studies* 25 (1992) 283–308.

  "Literacy and Genre," *College English* 51 (1989) 730–749.

Prostko, Jack, "Natural Conversation Set in View: Shaftesbury and Moral Speech," *Eighteenth-Century Studies* 23 (1989) 42–61.

Purpus, Eugene, "The 'Plain, Easy, and Familiar Way': the Dialogue in English Literature, 1660–1725," *ELH* 17 (1950) 47–58.

Rauter, Herbert, "The Veil of Words: Sprachauffassung und Dialogform bei George Berkeley," *Anglia* Band 79 (1962) 378–404.

Redwood, John, *Reason, Ridicule and Religion: the Age of Enlightenment in England, 1660–1750* (Cambridge, MA: Harvard University Press, 1976).

Richetti, John J., *Philosophical Writing: Locke, Berkeley, Hume* (Cambridge, MA: Harvard University Press, 1983).

Ricks, Christopher, *The Force of Poetry* (Oxford: Oxford University Press, 1987).

Riffaterre, Michael, "Prosopopoeia," *Yale French Studies* 69 (1985) 107–123.

Rivers, Isabel, ed., *Books and their Readers in Eighteenth-Century England* (Leicester: Leicester University Press, 1982).

Robbins, Caroline, *The Eighteenth-Century Commonwealthman* (Cambridge, MA: Harvard University Press, 1959).

Roelens, Maurice M., "Le Dialogue Philosophique, Genre Impossible? L'Opinion des Siècles Classiques," *Cahiers de l'Association Internationale des Etudes Françaises* 24 (1972) 43–58.

Roochnik, David, "The Impossibility of Philosophical Dialogue," *Philosophy and Rhetoric* 19 (1986) 147–165.

Ryle, Gilbert, *Plato's Progress* (Cambridge: Cambridge University Press, 1966).

Safer, Elaine B., "The Use of Contraries: Milton's Adaptation of Dialectic in *Paradise Lost*," *Ariel* 12 (April, 1981) 55–69.

Shapiro, Gary, "The Man of Letters and the Author of Nature: Hume on Philosophical Discourse," *The Eighteenth Century: Theory and Interpretation* 26 (1985) 115–137.

Shteir, Ann, "Botanical Dialogues: Maria Jackson and Women's Popular Science Writing in England," *Eighteenth-Century Studies* 23 (1990) 301–317.

Simpson, David, "Hume's Intimate Voices and the Method of Dialogue," *Texas Studies in Literature and Language* 21 (1979) 68–92.

Skinner, Quentin, "Meaning and Understanding in the History of Ideas," *History and Theory* 8 (1969) 3–53.

Silk, Edmund T., "Boethius's *Consolatio philosophiae* as a Sequel to Augustine's *Dialogues* and *Soliloquia*," *Harvard Theological Review* 32 (1939) 19–39.

Snyder, Jon, *Writing the Scene of Speaking: Theories of Dialogue in the Late Latin Renaissance* (Stanford: Stanford University Press, 1989).

Starr, G. A., *Defoe and Casuistry* (Princeton: Princeton University Press, 1971).

Stromberg, Roland N., *Religious Liberalism in Eighteenth-Century England* (Oxford: Oxford University Press, 1954).

Suber, Peter, "A Case Study in *Ad Hominem* Arguments: Fichte's Science of Knowledge," *Philosophy and Rhetoric* 23 (1990) 12–42.

Tavor, Eve, *Scepticism, Society, and the Eighteenth-Century Novel* (New York: St. Martin's Press, 1987).

Taylor, Charles, *Sources of the Self: the Making of Modern Identity* (Cambridge, MA: Harvard University Press, 1989).

Toulmin, Stephen, *Cosmopolis: the Hidden Agenda of Modernity* (Chicago: University of Chicago Press, 1990).

Trowbridge, Hoyt, *From Dryden to Jane Austen: Essays on English Critics and Writers, 1660–1818* (Albuquerque, New Mexico: University of New Mexico Press, 1977).

Tuveson, Ernst, "The Importance of Shaftesbury," *ELH* 20 (1953) 267–299.

Tweyman, Stanley, *Scepticism and Belief in Hume's Dialogues Concerning Natural Religion* (Dordrecht: Martinus Nijhoff, 1986).

Voitle, Robert, *The Third Earl of Shaftesbury, 1671–1713* (Baton Rouge: Louisiana University Press, 1984).

Walmsley, Peter, *The Rhetoric of Berkeley's Philosophy* (Cambridge: Cambridge University Press, 1990).

Walpole, Horace, *The Castle of Otranto: A Gothic Story*, ed. W. S. Lewis (London: Oxford University Press, 1964).

Wasserman, Earl, "Nature Moralized: the Divine Analogy in the Eighteenth Century," *ELH* 20 (1953) 39–73.

Wheeler, K. M., "Berkeley's Ironic Method in the *Three Dialogues*," *Philosophy and Literature* 4 (1980) 18–32.

Williams, Raymond, *The Country and the City* (New York: Oxford University Press, 1973).

Wilson, K. J., *Incomplete Fictions: the Formation of English Renaissance Dialogue* (Washington DC: The Catholic University of America Press, 1985).

Index

CAMBRIDGE STUDIES IN EIGHTEENTH-CENTURY
ENGLISH LITERATURE AND THOUGHT

General editors

Professor HOWARD ERSKINE-HILL LITT.D., FBA, *Pembroke College, Cambridge*

Professor JOHN RICHETTI, *University of Pennsylvania*